The New Africa

University Press of Florida

Gainesville / Tallahassee / Tampa / Boca Raton

Pensacola / Orlando / Miami / Jacksonville

To Marijo from her friend – Lil
2002

Robert M. Press / Photographs by Betty Press

To Marijoe, who shares a
lifelong love of Teaching and
reading with Wiz
        Robert Press
    & Betty Press

THE NEW

AFRICA

Dispatches from a Changing Continent

04 03 02 01 00 99 6 5 4 3 2 1
Library of Congress Cataloging-in-Publication Data
Press, Robert M.
The new Africa: dispatches from a changing continent / Robert
M. Press; photographs by Betty Press.
p. cm.
Includes bibliographical references and index.
ISBN 0-8130-1704-1 (cloth: alk. paper)
1. Africa, Sub-Saharan—Politics and government—1960–.
2. Africa, Sub-Saharan—Social conditions—1960–. 3. Democracy—Africa, Sub-Saharan—History—20th century. 4. Human
rights—Africa, Sub-Saharan—20th century. 5. Operation Restore Hope, 1992–1993. 6. United Nations Operation in Somalia. 7. United Nations—Armed Forces—Somalia. 8. Rwanda—
Politics and government. 9. Genocide—Rwanda. I. Title.
DT353.P74 1999
967.03'2—dc21 99-17517

The University Press of Florida is the scholarly publishing
agency for the State University System of Florida, comprising
Florida A&M University, Florida Atlantic University, Florida International University, Florida State University, University of
Central Florida, University of Florida, University of North Florida, University of South Florida, and University of West Florida.
University Press of Florida / http://www.upf.com
15 Northwest 15th Street / Gainesville, FL 32611-2079

To Betty Press, my wife and partner, who with her camera traveled the same roads I did and who loves the present good and future potential of Africa as much as I do.

To Yvonne Razafindravelontsoa, our foster daughter from Madagascar, whom we love very much.

To Africans of all walks of life whose pursuit of freedom is an example for us all.

In memory of: Maxine Press, my mother and an important source of my love of life, who gave me the freedom to go anywhere and try anything good; John Press, my father, who loved life and those around him; Lee and Chloe Maxwell, my grandparents, who always had faith in life and in me.

CONTENTS

ILLUSTRATIONS

Chapter 2

Chapter 3

COLOR ILLUSTRATIONS *following page 140*

ACKNOWLEDGMENTS

As readers and authors well know, a book may be conceived by one person, but it takes a collaborative effort to make it say something worth reading and to get it completed, published, and distributed. I am solely responsible for any errors of facts, and the interpretations of those facts, based on my firsthand observations and research, are also my own. But this book would not have been possible without the help of many people in Africa and the United States. Here are some of them.

The many Africans you will meet in these pages are the foundation of the book. Their lives and actions are the basis for the analyses included in the text. I am deeply indebted to those who took the time to talk with me and share their lives, their concerns, and their dreams. The world has much to learn from Africa and Africans.

The Christian Science Monitor, my longtime employer, sent me to Africa, trusted my judgment about news and feature topics, and published my hundreds of articles and many photos of Betty Press during our eight years there. In seeking to carry out the ideals of the newspaper's founder, Mary Baker Eddy, my editors and I tried to uphold high standards of concern, fairness, objectivity, and balance between news of disasters and more encouraging stories. Former editor Kay Fanning and her managing editor, David Anabel, sent Betty and me to Africa; we were allowed to stay on by editors Richard J. Cattani and later by David Cook, who also granted me leave to write this book. Each of my numerous regional editors over the years provided skilled and loving support for our work. Longtime *Monitor* colleagues and friends David Willis, Curtis J. Sitomer and Leon Lindsay helped shape my writing and observation skills over the years. The staff of the former Monitor Radio Service helped me bring some of Africa's news to a global listening audience.

When I took leave from the newspaper and moved to DeLand, Florida, to spend time with my mother and write this book, Stetson University in DeLand welcomed me as a visiting scholar, providing an office, telephone, fax, computer services, and full library privileges. President Doug Lee and former provost Eugene S. Lubot made the initial invitation; Paul D. Steeves and others in the history department provided the office for much longer than originally envisioned; Vice President Sharam Amiri and the dedicated team of computer specialists supplied critical assistance. Margaret L. Venzke read early drafts of two chapters and made helpful comments on them. Other members of the Stetson faculty—T. Wayne Bailey, Ann Croce, Paul Croce, Anne M. Hallum, Jeff Horn, Thomas R. Horton, Eugene E. Huskey, Neal B. Long, Elizabeth A. Magarian, Gary L. Maris, Michael W. McFarland, Leonard L. Nance, William R. Nylen, Ranjini L. Thaver, Richard H. Wood, Malcom M. Wynn, and others—offered information or encouragement, or both, at various times. Senior secretaries Robin L. Carter, Dinah W. McFarlane, Sherry Kent, and Divina Bungard were gracious and patient in helping meet office needs. Library director Sims Kline, Jane T. Bradford, M. Susan Connell, David Everett, Terry J. Grieb, Betty Johnson, Susan Ryan, Peter C. Shipman, Ruth Slavin, and the others never tired of helping me track down source materials. Campus printer Ronald E. Gosselin helped me consider book titles. Stetson seniors Barbara Berry and Steve Nicks provided valuable assistance in the early stages of the book as research assistants.

The John J. and Lucille C. Madigan Charitable Foundation, Inc., provided a grant to cover some of my research expenses. Patricia J. Drabik, secretary/treasurer of the foundation and her husband, Robert Drabik, president, offered consistent encouragement and vision to help me finish the project.

Thomas D'Evelyn, literary agent in Providence, Rhode Island, and former book editor for *The Christian Science Monitor,* provided invaluable guidance through the entire conceptualization, research, and writing of the many revisions of the book. Our long conversations about the manuscript, exchange of faxes and e-mail messages, his editing comments on early drafts, and patient answers to my many questions were crucial.

At the University Press of Florida in Gainesville, Meredith Morris-Babb, editor in chief, Susan Fernandez, senior acquisitions editor, Larry Leshan, Amy Gorelick, Tom Thomson, Judy Goffman, and others, including UPF board members, worked jointly with interest and professional skills to approve and publish the book and make it available to both nonspecialist readers and those studying Africa. They did it all with a sense of enthusiasm. UPF's two manuscript readers made very good suggestions. Copyeditor Victoria Haire did an excellent job.

My mother, Maxine Press, understood why writing this book was important and why it was worth the effort. It was a very happy day for both of us when I brought her a completed copy of the manuscript, just two months before she passed away.

More than anyone, Betty Press knows the time, energy, and inspiration needed to write a book. Many evenings over dinner, Betty and I discussed details of the chapters. With unflinching support, she shouldered extra responsibilities for keeping our home going while teaching and working as a photographer; she allowed me countless late evenings and writing weekends during the approximately two years it took to complete the manuscript. (The writing period was extended by journalism classes I was happy to teach at Stetson University as an adjunct professor and by travels Betty and I made together.) I am and shall forever be grateful for her patience, faith, understanding, and love.

SOMALIA CHRONOLOGY

July 1, 1960: United Republic of Somalia is formed after independence gained from British (in north) and Italians (in south). Colonization began in 1886.

October 21, 1969: General Mohamed Siad Barre assumes power after a military coup and gains Soviet backing.

1977–78: Somalia goes to war with Ethiopia over territory. Soviets shift backing to Ethiopia; United States shifts support to Somalia, provides military aid.

1982: Somali rebels start campaign against General Siad Barre.

1989–90: Drought, civil war, and land seizures by rebels create major food shortages in central Somalia.

January 27, 1991: Siad Barre flees Mogadishu; rebel faction names Mohamed Ali Mahdi interim president, angering his rival, General Mohamed Farah Aideed. Heavy fighting ensues between them. The increased famine attracts the help of International Committee of the Red Cross and some private relief agencies.

July–September 1992: Fifty unarmed UN monitors sent to Mogadishu. Famine intensifies; a major U.S. relief airlift begins in August. UN sends in 500 lightly armed Pakistani troops, who are forced by Somali militia to remain at the airport.

December 9, 1992: U.S. Marines land in Mogadishu to escort relief convoys to famine zones. At peak, nearly 26,000 U.S. and 11,000 UN troops of twenty-four nations take part in operation.

March 27, 1993: Fifteen faction leaders sign peace pact to set up transitional government; pact is never implemented.

May 4, 1993: United States hands over military control to UN forces.

June 5, 1993: Twenty-four Pakistani UN troops killed in Mogadishu after they inspect a weapons cache near Aideed's radio station. This begins four months of nearly daily skirmishes in capital between international forces and those of Aideed, although much of the rest of the country remains relatively quiet.

June 12, 1993: UN issues warrant for Aideed's arrest.

July 12, 1993: In an unannounced attack, U.S. troops bomb a suspected Aideed command post, killing dozens of Somali civilians. An angry Somali mob kills four international journalists who arrive to photograph the damages.

October 3, 1993: Eighteen U.S. Rangers killed in battle with Aideed's forces; four days later, President Clinton orders withdrawal of U.S. troops by March 31, 1994.

1994–95 Sporadic fighting among rival clans continues.

February 1, 1995: UN abandons main compound in Mogadishu, which is quickly looted, and begins to withdraw last 8,000 troops with help from a U.S.-led multinational force that includes 7,000 marines. Final withdrawal completed in March 1995.

1995–99: Sporadic fighting continues in the south among rival clans. Aideed seizes control of Baidoa. He is killed in 1996 by gunfire in Mogadishu; his son, Hussein Mohamed Aideed, a former U.S. Marine, pursues his father's plan to achieve dominant power in Somalia for his faction. In the north, self-declared independent "Somaliland" continues to be more peaceful than the south as commerce and reconstruction take place in many areas.

AFRICA

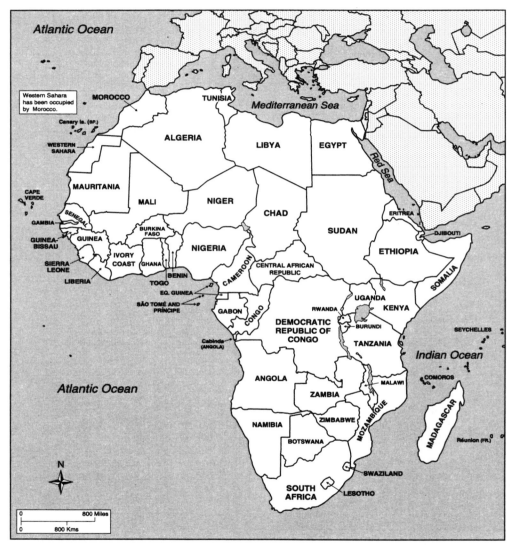

From *Maps On File.* Reprinted by permission of Facts On File, Inc. *Note:* Democratic Republic of Congo was formerly named Zaire.

SOMALIA

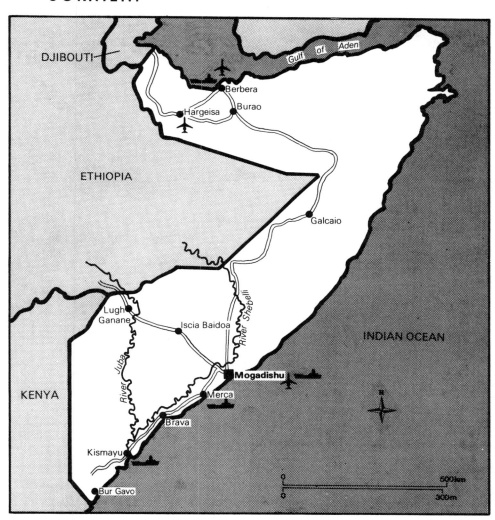

From *Maps On File*. Reprinted by permission of Facts On File, Inc.

RWANDA

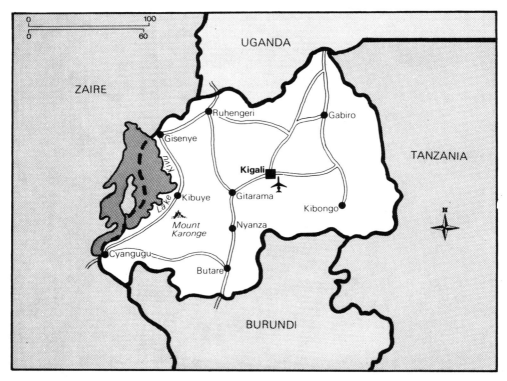

From *Maps On File.* Reprinted by permission of Facts On File, Inc. *Note:* The name Zaire was changed to Democratic Republic of Congo in 1997.

INTRODUCTION

Nasir, southern Sudan, 1993
A boy "photographs" the photographer.
Credit: UNICEF/Betty Press

THIS book is about human rights and the human spirit in Africa today.

These true stories are from Africa, but they could be from anywhere. They describe the hunger people have and the risks they sometimes take for more human rights, or freedom, and they show how sometimes those rights are trampled.

Africa headed into the twenty-first century after one of the most dramatic and contradictory decades in modern times in terms of human rights: it was both hopeful and deadly. On the whole, Africa turned more democratic after hundreds of thousands of people of all backgrounds stood up and demanded change. But there were also major abuses of human rights and failures on the part of the international community to help stop them. A civil war in Somalia showed how U.S. and UN military intervention failed when it was based on a lack of understanding of local culture and history. And the world did little more than watch as genocide engulfed Rwanda, killing up to one million people, most of them in three months.

But beyond politics and war, another, quieter change became more evident in the closing years of the century. Many people were gaining personal freedom in their own lives, including freedom from ignorance, from poverty, and from traditional social barriers such as those limiting the rights of women.

These three themes from Africa today—a resurgence of political freedom, world lessons in responding to humanitarian and political crises, and personal freedom—form the basis of this book. Many useful studies of the democratic movement in Africa have been made, and some are cited in this book. But in most of the studies the individual is missing, except perhaps for a brief mention of some. Yet individuals have played a key role in changing the face of African politics in the 1990s.

The New Africa is a combination of academic analysis, on-the-scene reporting of key events, and profiles of some of the many individuals who are part of the changes occurring in Africa today. The book examines both events and individuals in their historical and political context. It presents some of the ordinary people who took extraordinary steps to win more freedom for their country or in their own lives. The focus is mostly East and West Africa, where the author and his wife, Betty Press, whose photos accompany the text, traveled extensively from 1987 to 1995 while based in Kenya for *The Christian Science Monitor,* interviewing hundreds of government officials, including several heads of state, opposition leaders, guerrilla fighters, students, businesswomen, artists, lawyers, church leaders, doctors, children, refugees, diplomats, aid officials, and many others.

Political Freedom

A long-simmering discontent and anger with politics as usual boiled over in Africa at the end of the Cold War in 1989. Pervasive poverty and international and domestic pressures for democracy set the stage for change to some degree, but mostly it was the power of an idea, the idea of freedom, that changed the shape of African politics more than at any time since independence. Africans caught a fever of freedom which spread rapidly across the continent, prompting confrontations and other challenges to longtime authoritarian rulers. Ordinary people, not just political opposition leaders, stood up for democracy, often against great odds, sometimes against brutal force.

Chapter 1 introduces this theme. The ending of the Cold War meant the end of political chess games in Africa between the two superpowers. Suddenly autocratic leaders no longer could appeal for military or economic aid from the United States or the Soviet Union with any certainty of getting it. They were left exposed to the demands of their people for change. As the winds of freedom stirred across eastern Europe, they also began blowing across Africa. People of all backgrounds began demanding change after three decades of mostly dictatorial rule by black leaders. The release of Nelson Mandela after twenty-six years in prison in South Africa sent another pro-freedom jolt throughout Africa.

For a few years, changes came quickly. Most African states switched from a one-party to a multiparty system with competitive elections. Formerly docile parliaments became lively centers for debates on government corruption. South Africa's transformation into a democratic, majority-rule country in 1994 was one of the most hopeful changes in the decade. Success of the democratic movement varied from country to country in Africa. (In this book the term "Africa" refers to sub-Saharan Africa.) Some incumbent leaders were replaced through elections; others resisted reform and merely played the democracy "game," sometimes getting reelected. Often the opposition was poorly organized and poorly funded or was led by individuals more interested in obtaining power than creating checks on its misuse.

The pace of change slowed in the later part of the 1990s; but apart from the successes or failures of the pro-democracy movement, the ground swell of demands for more political freedom revealed to the rest of the world that Africans, like people everywhere, put great value on human rights, on individual liberties. They insisted on the right to speak one's mind, vote in fair elections, and read uncensored materials.

Chapter 1 also puts the renewed push for freedom in Africa in the context of earlier struggles in Africa and Latin America and in the 1960s by blacks in the United States. With the help of historian of ideas Isaiah Berlin, the chapter raises the question what is freedom? And with the help of Joseph Conrad, another question is probed: why is Africa's image so bad in the rest of the world? The views of several African academics who challenge the idea of winner-take-all elections and call for more inclusive, alternative approaches are also included.

Chapter 2 features individuals who have taken bold steps to gain new human rights and freedom in their countries. Students tell how they battled the police and army tanks in Mali, where democracy was restored; a student leader in Togo withstood torture by police to keep an underground opposition movement secret; in Nigeria, human rights activists risked their lives to keep the world informed of abuses under a repressive military regime. Their courage is reflected in the actions of many others in the 1990s and illustrates the dangers and difficulties of expanding human rights in Africa.

Chapter 3 shows how pro-democracy advocates can gain ground, then lose it to authoritarian governments bent on crushing reform.

With the focus on Kenya, this chapter features a daring public protest by mothers to get political prisoners released. Other Kenyans profiled include a political opposition leader, two human rights lawyers, and a young former insurance saleswoman who bravely insisted on political freedom and the rule of law as an authoritarian president tried to keep ethnic tensions hot and his opponents off guard.

Intervention

The second theme, of world lessons on intervention (or lack of it), takes a close look at two of the most important post–Cold War tragedies in Africa where human rights were trampled, Somalia and Rwanda, and shows how the two are linked.

Chapter 4 tells how the civil war in Somalia led to a famine of such massive proportions that the United States sent first a military airlift of food, then troops, to help deliver relief. It was one of the first ventures in President George Bush's "new world order." But when the U.S., European, and some African troops tried to help the United Nations bring peace to Somalia, things turned deadly. Unfamiliar with the culture of Somalia and the back streets of its capital, Mogadishu, U.S. and UN troops soon found themselves under fire from one Somali faction. When eighteen U.S. servicemen were killed in an ambush, and the body of one of them was dragged naked through the streets—a scene that flashed across television screens worldwide—President Bill Clinton called the troops home. The chapter examines why Somalia fell apart and how the United States and the United Nations were ineffective peacemakers because they did not understand the history or the culture of the people.

The title of the chapter on Somalia will remind readers of African literature of Nigerian author Chinua Achebe's acclaimed novel *Things Fall Apart* (London: Heinemann, 1958; also published in other editions). On the opening page Achebe credits W. B. Yeats's poem "The Second Coming" for that title and quotes part of the poem: "Turning and turning in the widening gyre/The falcon cannot hear the falconer;/Things fall apart; the center cannot hold;/Mere anarchy is loosed upon the world." Fortunately, anarchy in Africa today is the exception, but one of the worst exceptions in history occurred in Rwanda.

Chapter 5 tells how the United States, badly burned by Somalia, ducked the next African crisis where the ultimate human right—the right to live—was destroyed for many in a genocidal civil war. Up to one million people were slaughtered in Rwanda in 1994, most of them in just three months and often by machetes wielded by their neighbors. The killings were carefully planned and executed, the outcome of years of hate propaganda and racial tensions nurtured in part by colonialist prejudice, then by self-serving leaders in Rwanda. Could the genocide have been halted or at least slowed? Yes, according to military analysts familiar with Rwanda. So why didn't the United States or the UN try? For its part, the United States refused to send troops because of the death of their soldiers in Somalia. The United States was unwilling to risk any more lives in Africa. African troops were available to go to Rwanda, but the UN was unable to fund them without U.S. backing, which the United States withheld until the killing was over, afraid it might be dragged into the war to help the African troops. The chapter puts Rwanda's genocide in the context of other examples of mass world violence in the twentieth century, including Stalin's farm famines and the Holocaust. It probes the roots of the Rwandan genocide, showing why it occurred and how it was carried out. Chapter 6 tells the story of one family who escaped the killing.

Personal Freedom

While many Africans strove for political freedom, many more were striving for freedom as individuals. Some sought changes in social practices; others sought to expand their education and earnings to break free of ignorance and poverty. Rather than a broad, economic analysis of Africa, chapter 7 presents a number of people who have gained additional freedom of one kind or another.

A Nigerian artist breaks loose from an abusive, polygamous marriage and later establishes a tuition-free art school for low-income students, overcoming some of the social barriers women face in her culture. A Kenyan shopkeeper and a Togolese baker use small loans to expand their businesses—and profits. A Kenyan couple farming on dry land and members of a women's hand-irrigating vegetable cooperative in The Gambia tell how they made progress. The "Mercedes Benz" ladies of the West African nation of Togo talk about how they became wealthy selling cloth and developed a taste for expensive cars. Several women jurists in Mali explain how they fought to give girls the right to refuse female circumcision. Some students and teachers in two countries with civil wars—Sudan and Somalia—carry on their classes, and a model teacher in Kenya tries modern classroom techniques that her students appreciate. After a long war, female ex-soldiers in Eritrea seek greater recognition of their rights in a male-dominated society. And a young homeless man in Kenya sets out on a journey from poverty to tailoring.

★ ★ ★

As the century drew to a close, police in some countries continued to use torture, and journalists and others highlighting government corruption were being arrested. In Rwanda and Burundi, ethnic killings continued. In central Africa scores of thousands of Rwandan refugees had been slaughtered and attempts made to cover up their deaths. In parts of Somalia civilians continued to die in fighting between rival factions, though many areas were mostly peaceful. Africa today is challenged by such issues as poverty, AIDS, and numerous authoritarian governments. But the new insistence on political freedom and human rights continued in most countries, even where there was oppression. Surviving authoritarian rulers kept coming under pressure from people demanding more freedom. Individuals kept pursuing greater personal freedom.

Africa is troubled, but it is also vibrant and alive with energy and is more democratic than it has ever been. The determination of millions of Africans to make more progress will not disappear and does not depend on forms of government. Many of the changes taking place in Africa today are mental, not just governmental. Africans across the continent are expressing their long-held sense of dignity and steely insistence on human rights and freedom. This insistence provides a hopeful starting point for the twenty-first century.

★ ★ ★

Mother Teresa had a way of saying a few words directly to each person she met. When it was my privilege to meet her in Kenya, she told me, "When you write, always write something to uplift people." The examples in this book of individual sacrifice for the achievement of greater freedom, in society or personally, are uplifting. Even the harsh lessons from Somalia and Rwanda can be uplifting if taken seriously enough to learn from them.

1   AFRICAN FREEDOM
The Unfinished Journey

Sokoto, Nigeria, 1989
This Muslim girl on her way to Koranic school holds a
reusable wooden tablet with verses from the Koran.

ACROSS Africa in the 1990s, mothers, lawyers, labor leaders, students, and others took stands in favor of greater human rights against authoritarian governments. They faced riot police, staged massive demonstrations, and in some countries even fought tanks or resisted torture to gain new political freedom.

Sub-Saharan Africa,[1] the focus of this book, starting in 1989 entered a period of the most profound political change since the days of independence in the late 1950s and early 1960s. Democracy was suddenly not just a distant dream but rather a tangible goal. In 1989, the year the Berlin Wall was torn down, only five African states had what might be called democracy, with more than one political party and contested elections.[2] The rest of Africa was under authoritarian or military rule or engaged in civil war. South Africa and Namibia were still under white minority rule; Nelson Mandela was in prison.

Yet by 1995 three out of four African states had "competitive party systems."[3] Many African dictators had been ousted, replaced by men more beholden—by circumstances or desire—to the constraints of democratic rule.[4] Almost every nation had undergone major political reforms. In Namibia, white South African rule was over and the country had a freely elected black president, Samuel Daniel Nujoma. In South Africa, Nelson Mandela was president.

A powerful force had been unleashed in Africa; people were insisting on greater political and economic freedom—and getting it. As long-time Nigerian diplomat Joseph Garba said of the people's renewed taste for freedom, "The genie is out of the bottle." One academic tracker of this trend noted, "In a relatively short period the vast majority of African states moved towards an acceptance of political pluralism and a rejection of . . . single-party and military rule."[5] Despite enormous obstacles, setbacks, and deviations from the new pattern, "the markedly increased role played by democracy in African politics over the last few years is unlikely to dissipate or become atrophied in the future. Cautious optimism is justified."[6]

As the century drew to a close, however, other analysts were less optimistic. The pace of change had slowed; there were fewer demonstrations for democratic government. The rush toward democratic rule appeared to have stalled. In fact in some countries, ousted dictators returned to office, victors in the very kind of multiparty elections they had previously blocked. Even where new leaders were elected, they sometimes did little to improve the lives of the people. A few countries were bogged down with civil war; others still had military rulers or had ousted their civilian presidents in coups. One noted African writer and economist spoke of an "Africa in chaos,"[7] as he surveyed failed economic programs, and lamented the failure of most African intellectuals to grapple with the tough reform issues.

But even if the struggle for democracy was totally crushed (which is unlikely); even if it was allowed to die slowly for lack of support by people who, in the face of dire economic conditions, had to focus all their energies on survival—even then Africa and Africans would never be the same. Despite the setbacks, the hunger for freedom would continue. For the change occurring today in Africa is not just about the form of governments; it is a mental change, a renewed energizing of the human spirit.

The political chemistry has changed in Africa. People expect more freedom, more human rights, and have shown courage in demanding it, as this book reveals. Their stories are important because, in the rush to highlight the rise of the democratic movement, then in the rush to pronounce its slippage, little attention has been given to the kinds of individuals who have helped or tried to bring about change. Some excellent studies have been conducted on this renewed drive for more freedom and democracy in Africa, and in this chapter I examine some of their major conclusions. But although most of these studies are well researched and set forth intriguing theories to explain the political changes in Africa today, somehow the spirit of the Africans involved usually gets left out.

That spirit is exemplified by ordinary Kenyan mothers who defied riot police in a protest demanding release of their sons, all of whom were political prisoners. It is evident in the spontaneous decisions by students in Mali to brave not only police but tanks to try to topple a dictatorship. It is seen in the refusal of a university student in Togo— even after being tortured—to reveal the name of fellow students working against the dictatorship there.

There is strength in those actions, and others like them, a kind of gritty determination to achieve something better in life. Many of the attempts were not coordinated and were not effective in changing governments. But some were. The point is that this renewed determination to achieve more freedom, both political and personal, has come to the surface again, and it is not likely to be submerged again. This is one of the reasons for cautious optimism about the future of Africa, even as the tallying of the progress or failure of economies and governments continues. Whenever and whatever kind of long-term changes in gov-

Dakar, Senegal, 1988
Freedom from ignorance: Young Senegalese students attend an assembly program to celebrate the ideals of John F. Kennedy at their high school, named after the late U.S. president.

ernment come, this bedrock quality, this conviction that things can be better—and *should* be—is there to build on in the twenty-first century.

As dramatic as the responses of many Africans to tyranny were in the 1990s, they were not entirely new. Resistance to unjust rule goes back in African history at least to the era of slavery. African slave traders ran into resistance from the moment they entered villages to seek captives. They encountered more resistance along the long marches to the coast; non-African slave dealers met resistance from slaves on many ships and in the lands where slaves were sent to work. The same spirit was seen again during colonization: the conquest of Africa by Europe was far from peaceful. Africans waged wars of resistance, some of which lasted for years. Thousands of Africans were killed fighting the colonialists. And once the disillusionment of postindependence politics in Africa set in, when it became clear that many black African leaders were determined to use single-party rule to maintain order—and keep themselves in power, curtailing many freedoms in the process—resistance began again, at many levels, from political opposition movements to individual protest. "Although authoritarian rule was very common it had failed to extinguish the underlying belief of many Africans that a more democratic Africa was both attainable and desirable."[8] Through this postindependence period, discontent and calls for democracy continued, but without the momentum or impact seen since 1990.

Africa: Part of a World Struggle

In his second trial, in 1964, this time for treason, Nelson Mandela drew connections between the struggle for freedom in South Africa and similar struggles in other parts of the world. Under tight security, in a full courtroom which included his mother and his wife, Winnie, he gave his last public remarks before being sentenced to prison, where he would spend nearly twenty-six years of his life before his release and subsequent election as the first black president of South Africa.

"The Magna Carta, the Petition of Rights and the Bill of Rights, are documents which are held in veneration by democrats throughout the world. . . . The American Congress, the country's doctrine of separation of powers, as well as the independence of its judiciary, arouse in me similar sentiments."[9] Then he sounded a chord that vibrated across South Africa, where blacks were under the oppressive apartheid system of a white government: "The lack of human dignity experienced by Africans is the direct result of the policy of white supremacy."[10]

At the end of his lengthy statement, which took four hours to read, Mandela set his papers on the defense table, looked up directly at the white judge, and brought the courtroom to silence with his final words that day. "During my lifetime I have dedicated myself to this struggle of the African people. I have fought against white domination, and I have fought against black domination. I have cherished the ideal of a democratic and free society in which all persons live together in harmony and with equal opportunities. It is an ideal which I hope to live for and to achieve. But if needs be, it is an ideal for which I am prepared to die."[11]

Africans' current push for freedom is part of a global demand for greater freedom. Although more gains have been made in many other parts of the world, the typical forces involved—at whatever time in history—are roughly the same in all geographic locations. On one side, ordinary people call for release from tyranny; on the other, a defiant government digs in to maintain something it claims is worth even more than individual liberties: stability. Without stability, the governmental authorities argue, there would be little freedom for anyone, though this argument is often used to serve their own interests in remaining in power.

Latvian-born writer and thinker Isaiah Berlin spent years studying the meaning of freedom and its relation to values and different concepts of truth. He started by studying those who he says had the view that ultimately there is only one set of acceptable behavior: Plato, Socrates, and others. Jews, Christians, and Muslims also believe in one set of values, a divinely revealed "true answer."[12] Marx, he notes, did not seem to propose any ultimate truths. Yet even Marx, according to Berlin, believed that ultimately man would escape being victim of his own nature, that "reason would triumph; universal harmonious cooperation, true history would at last begin."[13] Machiavelli's writings challenged Berlin with the concept of choices: crudely put, the choice is between the virtues of good men and the evils of bad ones. Neither one ultimately replaces the other, according to Machiavelli. Berlin concludes, in part, there is not "one pattern" of life that reconciles all contrasting views and values. He describes the dilemma this way: "We are faced with conflicting values; the dogma that they must somehow, somewhere be reconcilable is a mere pious hope; experience shows that it is false. We must choose, and in choosing one thing lose another, irretrievably perhaps."

He continues: "If we choose individual liberty, this may entail a sacrifice of some form of organization which might have led to greater efficiency. If we choose justice, we may be forced to sacrifice mercy. If we choose knowledge we may sacrifice innocence and happiness. If we choose democracy, we may sacrifice a strength that comes from militarization or from obedient hierarchies."[14]

In Africa, as elsewhere, the argument for stability instead of democracy has its defenders, especially among the wealthy, who stand to lose more in times of upheaval. A ruler such as Marshal Josip Broz Tito in Yugoslavia argued that only he could hold his country together. One might have doubted it, but the war in Bosnia in the 1990s made Tito's argument more believable. In Somalia, Major General Mohamed Siad Barre, the army commander who took power in 1969, was popular at first; he initiated a number of reforms. When he began to lose his popularity, he started using ruthless tactics to squash dissent, claiming the measures were necessary to keep the country united. Many contend Barre merely wanted to hold on to power. But the civil war, famine, and chaos that followed his overthrow in 1991 resulted in far more deaths and destruction than anything seen during his regime, with the exception of his heavy bombing and destruction of the northern city of Hargeisa.

Freedom. How many definitions of this concept, this value, have been proposed? These definitions are often at odds with each other and thus a potential source of conflict—conflict which reduces everyone's freedom, at least temporarily. If there is a best definition of freedom, a right one, and the others are wrong, then the choice is clear. Many philosophers and religious leaders believe there is a right set of ideas or values. All we have to do is strive toward it, satisfied that we are on the right path. The struggle over a definition of freedom is one that has played out in almost every country at one time or another, including China, where Mao Tse-tung established his concept of the country's best path; the Philippines, where a peoples' revolution led to the overthrow of Ferdinand Marcos; Germany, where Adolf Hitler imposed his warped vision of freedom for the so-called Aryan race; France, which once had its revolution.

What is happening today as Africans seek expanded political rights and freedom is part of a worldwide, historic movement that once swept through colonial America and ignited a wave of civil rights protests in the United States in the 1950s and 1960s. "We shall not be moved," sang resistant blacks and their white supporters in the United States as they engaged in civil disobedience in the name of freedom. The same insistence on freedom helped shatter most Communist regimes in eastern Europe starting in the late 1980s.

Latin America made major progress in shedding dictators in the 1970s and 1980s before most African nations were taking their first steps in that direction. There are many differences between the two regions, but one common feature is their quest for democracy. Latin America's move toward democracy involved "trade unions, grass-roots movements, religious groups, intellectuals, artists, clergymen, defenders of human rights, and professional associations," a list which "could just as accurately have been written about Africa as Latin America."[15]

One group not on the list is mothers; but mothers played a role in political transformation in countries such as Argentina, Chile, and later Guatemala, protesting against authoritarian rule and human rights abuses in the 1980s and 1990s. Like their Kenyan counterparts, they demanded freedom for their sons imprisoned for political reasons. Irish mothers in the 1980s marched for peace, defying the separation "norm" of the day between Catholics and Protestants.

Africa's drive for freedom is clearly part of a universal movement. Yet often there has been a psychological barrier between Africa and the rest of the world, imposed from the outside, sealing Africa off as different, as an exception to world trends. From outside the barrier, Africa is seen mostly as a continent where a handful of egotistical rulers make most of the decisions and where the people accept this condition. The push for democracy in the 1990s showed that Africans are just as hungry for freedom as any other people.

There is also a tendency among Westerners to shrug off what happens in Africa as beyond their understanding. Africa, like anyplace else, is complex, with nuances puzzling to an outsider, but it is not beyond

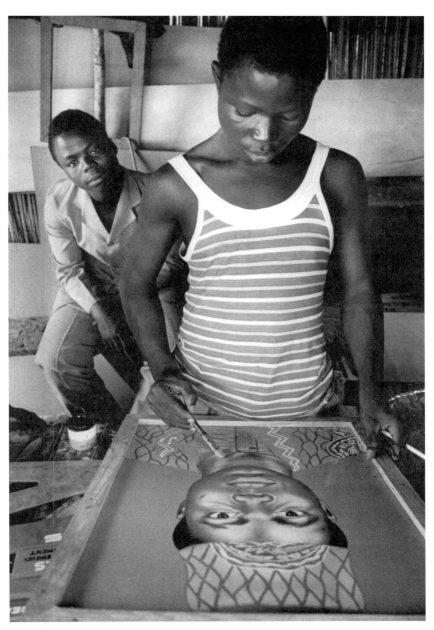

Cotonou, Benin, 1991
Freedom of expression: A. Jean Godjo Sonon paints a self-portrait in his small road-side studio.

our comprehension. People with different values are not necessarily unable to understand each other. "Members of one culture can, by the force of imaginative insight, understand . . . the values, the ideals, the forms of life of another culture or society, even those remote in time or space," writes Berlin.[16]

In 1919, when he was ten, Berlin moved from Latvia to England, where he later became a professor of social and political theory. He also became president of the British Academy and is known as a historian of ideas. He appreciated diversity among cultures but saw a certain unity among people. To mentally isolate a people or a culture in our minds as not understandable, as unknowable, is something to avoid, he argues. "We are free to criticize the values of other cultures, to condemn them, but we cannot pretend not to understand them at all, or to regard them simply as subjective, the products of creatures in different circumstances with different tastes from our own, which do not speak to us at all."[17]

Berlin saw the possibility of a "bridge" between various cultures. "Intercommunication between cultures in time and space is only possible because what makes men human is common to them, and acts as a bridge between them."[18] The universal desire for freedom is one of those "bridges," which can be seen in the lives of Africans such as Chiuri Ngugi.

★   ★   ★

Ngugi, a friend of mine, is a living "bridge" between the culture of the United States and his Kenyan culture; he is also a proponent of greater political freedom in his own country. In a letter to me in September 1996, he wrote of his letdown at returning to no job in Kenya after studying in the United States for a year and making a short visit to South Africa. "It was an ignoble homecoming." Ngugi was like many college students around the world who get a degree, perhaps travel abroad, then come home to the realities of making a living. An idealist, he discovered that during his year at law school at Columbia University in New York, little had changed in Kenya. Daniel arap Moi was still president; large-scale government corruption continued, and many Kenyans were desperate as the economy slid farther and farther downhill; and the government persisted with intimidation of its critics.

Nyahururu, Kenya, 1990
Lawyer Chiuri Ngugi with his mother.

"There is no way out of this mess," he wrote. Then he added a few lines that made me worry about him. "Some people have to suffer, sacrifice, lead the way for the realization of the beauty and dignity of the human person in a civil society under the rule of law." What did he mean by "sacrifice"? The tone made me uneasy, especially after what he had said while visiting me in Florida just before his return to Kenya: "I'd rather die guarding the right of my opponent to be heard than engage in subverting that right."[19]

We met when he was a student at the University of Nairobi. He grew up poor, like most Kenyans."The only avenue for betterment . . . and progress was through education," he said. By studying until as late as 3 A.M., he managed to finish number one or two in his primary and secondary classes. His father, a preacher, died when he was sixteen. His mother, with a warm smile and sense of humor, kept the family together with her love and down-home advice. He attended the university using a loan granted on the basis of merit, graduating with a bachelor of laws in 1987. After a year at the Kenya School of Law he was admitted to the Kenyan bar in May 1989. His choice of law as a career was based on an equation: "I equated law with justice," he said. "My dad believed in justice, being a preacher. . . . He always preached reconciliation, support for other people, harmony among people."

Ngugi said he got his sense of fair play from his mother. "She had very strong faith and she was very hardworking." He is close to his mother. "My mom has a very strong pull. . . . Everywhere I go I can still feel the hand of my mother on me, in a great way. My mom's faith, and my mom's love and commitment and sacrifice to make sure the kids are educated, is like a cry for responsibility and duty."

Just out of law school, Ngugi landed a plush job with a private company, even before he had passed his bar exam. He was given use of a company car, a good salary, and a number of other impressive perks. But there was a catch: he was soon asked to do things that legally could only be performed by a licensed lawyer; he could see his job was taking him down a path of corruption and disrespect for the laws. So he quit. His friends almost uniformly told him he was crazy to walk away from such a comfortable position. Betty and I congratulated him on his maturity and sense of ethics. He went on to start a national legal service for the poor.

Ngugi wrote in his letter of a universal goal: the rule of law. In Kenya, there was law, but it was not the rule. Laws were flouted by government officials. He enclosed a color photo of himself sitting alone on a tree stump, probably near the mud-walled home of his mother, who lives on a farm in north-central Kenya. He looked lonely, vulnerable, discouraged, except for a wisp of a smile. I had watched this young man mature from a college student to a trial court lawyer, listened to him for long stretches expounding his idealism, expressing an unbending fervor for democracy and law. He was not sure what to do now. He had to earn a living. After studying in the United States, he suddenly found himself faced with helping support the three children of his deceased sister, in addition to helping his mother. Still bothered by the corrupt politics of his country, he wanted to help improve the situation. He opened his own law practice, which allowed him to continue working for the rule of law in Kenya.

★   ★   ★

Berlin settled on the idea of a "collision of values" as the most accurate explanation of life.[20] He had long disagreed with those who saw an ultimate truth; his own ultimate truth was that there were many truths, many values, often conflicting with each other. Berlin asks, "What is to be done" in a world of conflicting and colliding values, of "mutually exclusive choices? What and how much must we sacrifice to what?"[21] He leaves the question unanswered, but he says the first obligation of a society is "to avoid extremes of suffering." To do this, Berlin says, there have to be what he calls "trade-offs—rules, values, principles must yield to each other in varying degrees in specific situations."[22] Then he challenged people like Ngugi, and all of us, to take actions in whatever country we live in and regardless of our position in life. "We can only do what we can; but that we must do against difficulties."[23]

This is what men and women at critical times throughout history have done when they fanned into flames the embers of discontent over lack of freedom, in Africa, Europe, the United States, and elsewhere. In his first trial, in 1962, Mandela made an appeal to the universality of human rights and the need for legal justice and political freedom. Facing charges of having left the country illegally and inciting a labor strike, Mandela stood before a court of the apartheid government and spoke of a conflict. "I would say that the whole life of any thinking African in this country drives him continuously to a conflict between his conscience on the one hand and the law on the other. This is not a conflict peculiar to this country. The conflict arises from men of conscience, for men who think and who feel deeply in every country."[24]

Young Africans like Ngugi may be up to the challenge. "I believe justice is the first condition of humanity," Ngugi says. "And human beings need dignity and freedom to realize their creative potentials." The state, he adds, "should be subjected to the rule of law. My highest dream is to eventually be involved in shaping the destiny of my country and Africa at large." Folding his hands, he continues, with that deadly serious look that comes over him when he discusses his core beliefs: "I'd like to see the rule of law and constitutionalism, and a veritable system of justice established throughout Africa."

So would a growing number of Africans today. And many in the 1990s took steps to try to make that happen, often with disregard to their own safety.

For most of us, standing up for a cause may mean little more than missing a day's work to join a protest march or speaking up at a public meeting. For others it involves years of working with a nonprofit organization, often for little or no pay, or financially helping support such a group. Unless you are a war veteran, freedom, including the freedom to vote, is usually something won by others. In the United States, where only about half the electorate voted in the U.S. presidential elections in 1996, freedom is underused. Freedom is also the right to criticize the head of state openly without fear of punishment and to walk down the street and not be afraid of arrest for political reasons, though in the United States minorities have complained of police harassment on the streets.[25]

For Africans in the 1990s, taking a stand for freedom meant more than inconvenience: often it meant risking injury or death. But many took the risk. This willingness to die "if needs be" for a just cause is part of the force that is pushing Africa down the road toward more freedom, as it did blacks in the United States.

Leaders of the U.S. civil rights movement faced great risks. Martin Luther King, Jr., died for the cause. In 1968, he went to Memphis, Tennessee, to help organize a sanitation workers protest and was gunned down while standing on the balcony of a motel. King once made a statement that sounded very much like Mandela's courtroom commitment to die for his cause if necessary: "If a man has not discovered something he will die for, he isn't fit to live."[26] Both King and Mandela thus pose a question many of us would like to avoid: are we prepared to die for anything?

Both men went on to win the Nobel Peace Prize, along with Mandela's counterpart in the negotiations that led to South Africa's first free elections, President F. W. de Klerk. Although few are cast into leadership roles as King, Mandela, and de Klerk were, Berlin challenges us all to "do what we can . . . against the difficulties."

Africa and the "Darkness" Label

The ongoing search for freedom in Africa is taking place against a backdrop of the world's persistent classification of Africa as mostly a negative place. Negative impressions of Africa are so strong, even among many Africans, that they tend to blot out positive accomplishments when they occur. This kind of discouraging atmosphere is not the best one in which to foster hope—and hope, as vague as that term is, is an important ingredient for future successes in Africa of whatever nature, even according to veteran African diplomats who are not at all shy about describing glaring ills of Africa.

"I chose HOPE, RESOLVE AND CHANGE, as the title of this address, since I strongly believe that all three are prerequisites for overcoming our present predicament," Nigerian diplomat Joe Garba told an audience in New York. Garba, a realist, added, lest anyone think he was talking about hope for a windfall from the West: "But such hope, resolve and change must materialize from within Africa itself. For us to believe otherwise, or for us to put our expectations elsewhere, will merely mean prolonging the lingering, malignant problems that afflict our continent."[27]

Mandela's long but eventually triumphant road from open political activist to underground opposition, to prison, and finally to the presidency of South Africa in 1994 did more than inspire people around the globe as a political event. His character offered renewed hope about the possibilities of mankind. Mandela emerged from prison with no apparent bitterness, only eagerness to get his country moving on a democratic track.

Another African who is candid about Africa's problems, Célestin Monga, writes about hope in Africa today: "If complacent optimism is unrealistic, then Afro-pessimism has no basis either." Despite many challenges, Africa is "forging new trails toward the affirmation of its dignity."[28]

Both Monga and Garba also focus on the question of leadership in Africa. The democratic process will improve when African leaders manage to stop doing so much "infighting" among themselves and concentrate on building institutions.[29] Garba pleads for African leaders who will "rise above mediocrity and also . . . show greater respect for the property of state and for human rights."[30]

* * *

Clearly wars and famines share much of the blame for Africa's negative image. But it is not just a matter of image; the issue is painfully tangible. By late 1998, for example, another famine in the war zones of southern Sudan left some 2.6 million people facing possible starvation.[31] Conflict and dying are not typical of the continent, yet journalists have often taken little time to cover positive developments. As I was reviewing some of my own articles after eight years reporting in Africa, I was surprised to find how few nonpolitical stories I had written, and how many of the stories were about conflict and dying. Part of Africa's negative image has nothing to do with modern-day journalists, however. It goes back to Joseph Conrad, who traveled to the Congo in 1890 and wrote a novel, *Heart of Darkness,* though his use of the word "dark" had more to do with the human soul than the continent of Africa. With one word Conrad, more than any other writer, fashioned an image of Africa that has stuck in the minds of many around the world. "Deepest, dark Africa"; "dark continent"—the terms conjure up images of impenetrable jungles and a sense of mystery, or foreboding, of evil or unknowable dangers.

Conrad's novel is an account of his trip up the Congo River. As his boat heads upriver, he writes, "We penetrated deeper and deeper into the heart of darkness."[32] In another passage Conrad strives to assure his readers that Africans are human—as if there was a need for such assurance: "It was unearthly, and the men were—No, they were not inhuman. Well, you know, that was the worst of it—this suspicion of their not being inhuman. It would come slowly to one. They howled, and leaped, and spun, and made horrid faces; but what thrilled you was just the thought of their humanity—like yours—the thought of your remote kinship with this wild and passionate uproar. Ugly."[33]

It was just a novel. But its impact has lasted. Conrad lures the reader into a mental trap, not by insisting that Africans are inhuman, but by encouraging the idea that they are beyond Western understanding. Saying we do not understand Africa may mean we do not want to be exposed to horrible news from a far-off place. Such news is depressing,

Efeson, Ethiopia, 1987
Freedom from hunger: These sisters lost their parents during the 1984 famine.

especially when viewed outside the context of possible solutions. People come to expect the worst from Africa.

Certainly Conrad's boat mates in the story expected the worst on their trip. His book has been cited in many other books. Journalist Blaine Harden, for example, cites Conrad's trip on the first page of his thoughtful and colorful book on Africa. Harden does go on to say that "a century of commerce on the [Congo] river has tamed much of its menace and burned off the Conradian gloom."[34] That is true. When Betty and I rode the river on a packed boat in what was then Zaire, we felt a sense of excitement rather than danger. Traders living along the shore paddled out to our boat in long wooden canoes, tied up, and floated along with us as they scrambled aboard to sell and buy everything from monkeys to household goods. As another passenger boat passed ours heading downstream, one of the passengers came to the railing wearing a cap and waving what looked like a stick. It was Mobutu Sese Seko, dictator of Zaire. In public he wore his leopard skin cap and carried a mace, his symbols of office. My biggest complaint on our ride up Conrad's Congo River was not about some mysterious cries in the jungle but the insane volume of the U.S. rock and roll hits blasting from the ship's loudspeakers.

Africa can be as frightening as a writer, or a reader, wants it to be. Even on safari, most fears prove groundless. Once on a camping trip in Kenya, I peered out of our pup tent into the darkness and saw two red eyes low to the ground coming toward us like an animal preparing to attack. I shouted to Betty and we jumped into our car. Only then did we see our predator, a civet cat, about the size of a large house cat, and not dangerous. Some safari fears are real. On a game hunting trip in Kenya, the late George Adamson was nearly killed by a lion; later the same day he was almost killed by an elephant. But he spent his last years preparing young lions to shift from captivity to freedom and especially enjoyed the birds that came to his open-air dinner table where he fed them nuts. Reading adventure tales from Africa is a vicarious thrill, a way to confront danger seated in one's living room. The notion of dangerous, unknown, "dark" Africa lives on in books and movies because we want it to live on, apart from the facts. Fear still sells.

Slavery

Africa's record does have some truly "dark" pages. The institution of slavery, for example, deprived millions of Africans of basic freedom and formed an important part of the world image of Africa for years. "The European image of Africa evolved during the era of the slave trade. Works by travelers and slave traders during this period had much to say about the cultural conditions of the 'dark continent' and, although their tone ranged from sympathetic to hostile, the overall picture was unfavorable."[35]

Slavery linked Africa and the rest of the world in a negative way: it involved Western and Arab slave traders working with African slave sellers. African slavery predated the arrival of European or Arab slave buyers. "In Africa, as in other parts of the world, warfare was a principal means of recruiting slaves."[36] And as strong centralized states were established in Africa, they often demanded that weaker states pay an annual tribute consisting of a certain number of slaves.[37] Other slaves were also accepted in compensation for such crimes as homicides or by those with food in cases of desperation from hunger. From the 1470s to 1620, the Portuguese transported slaves from other parts of Africa to Elmina on the Gold Coast, modern-day Ghana. And British ships were contracted to transport other slaves from the African state of São Tomé to Elmina during the seventeenth century.[38]

Estimating the number of slaves shipped out of Africa has been the topic of much debate. One Ghanaian scholar, using figures of Western researchers, estimates 11.7 million were shipped in the cross-Atlantic trade alone and that nearly 9.8 million landed in the New World.[39] A high proportion died between the point of capture and delivery in the Americas.

Africa is not the only continent to suffer massive trauma. The Western hemisphere "contained 80–100 million inhabitants before the Eu-

Goree Island, Senegal, 1988
From this house, now a museum, slaves were sent to the Americas.

ropean conquest of the region, with only 10 million inhabitants left after the first century of European colonization." Mexico alone had a population of 20 million in 1519, reduced to just over 1 million by 1608.[40] "If these demographic estimates are correct, the impact of European conquest and the ravages of disease upon Amerindians far exceed the worst ravages of the Atlantic slave trade upon the African peoples."[41]

Colonial Rule

Another critical page in Africa's history in terms of freedom and human rights was the period of colonial rule. Many African and other scholars write about the importance of Africans assuming the primary task of reforming their political systems; the legacy of colonialism made that task all the harder. A key element in the legacy is the way Africa was divided up by the colonial powers, with boundaries that divided some ethnic groups and put many others together against their wishes.

At a conference in Berlin in 1884 and 1885—and in diplomatic intrigues around the edge of the conference—key decisions about the future of African rule were made without the participation of Africans. When the West Africa Conference opened in Berlin on November 15, 1884, it was a snowy, blustery day. The nineteen delegates and their assistants from fourteen countries gathered around a horseshoe table to begin their work. Prince Otto von Bismarck of Germany greeted the participants, addressing them in French. "He began with a pious declaration that took them back to the '3 C's'—commerce, Christianity, civilization—and the ideals of [David] Livingstone. The aim of the conference was to promote the civilization of the African natives by opening the interior of the continent to commerce."[42] Then he reached a key point: the conference "might decide the rules for the Scramble [by Europe for African territory] but it would not debate the lines of the carve-up itself."[43] He then sat down.

The British and French had come to the conference wondering how much was at stake. Both had already laid large claims to parts of Africa and worried that the conference could threaten their claims. Now they began to relax, seeing the conference as a minor event rather than a danger.[44] The real threat to British and French designs on central

Africa was from someone not even attending the conference, King Leopold II of Belgium. He was about to cap a six-year struggle to start an empire in the Congo, playing the Great Powers off against each other. By the time the conference was over, Leopold, using various intermediaries, had secured his vast claims in Africa. "Germany and Britain had given away to Leopold most of the Congo basin, meaning most of Central Africa, a million square miles of jungle and bush. The main objective was to keep this enormous prize out of the hands of France."[45]

Although the Berlin conference did not draw up Africa's borders, it did set new rules of the game. One rule was that claims to territory had to be backed by an actual physical presence in the territory, not just verbal claims on it. "The Scramble had precipitated Berlin. The race to grab a slice of the African cake had started long before the first day of the conference."[46] The colonial powers over a period of years sliced up Africa with arbitrary boundaries, helping to set the stage for later ethnic conflicts. This also delayed attempts in many countries to fuse a national identity during the colonial era and after independence.

Most African heads of state after independence subscribed to the principle of national integrity, meaning no border changes. They had no desire to give up any of what was suddenly "their" territory. It would be some three decades after independence before this principle was overridden by wars. Two new nations would appear: Eritrea, which officially gained its independence from Ethiopia in 1993, and the Republic of Somaliland, a northern area which claimed its independence in 1991 from the rest of Somalia but failed to win international recognition.

Borders were not the only colonial legacy that would interfere with the freedom and human rights of Africans after independence. "Africa's post-colonial states are successors to profoundly anti-democratic colonial forms of governing."[47] Africa's first postindependence leaders were schooled in despotism by their colonial rulers. "Despotic forms of government were imposed upon Africans in the Belgian Congo, Portuguese Africa, and the white settler states of Kenya, Rhodesia, and South Africa."[48] Should it have been surprising that many of Africa's first heads of state after independence carried on with despotic forms of government? Should it have been shocking that Kenyan president Moi, for example, used some of the same methods of control, including certain torture techniques, as the British had used in Kenya? The inheritors of power from scheming, self-serving, and often brutal colonial rulers had, far too often, become scheming, self-serving, and often brutal leaders themselves. Many African leaders also inherited from the colonial rulers "habits of mind" and a penchant for "elitist management and personal enrichment," another word for corruption.[49]

* * *

Each colonial power had its own method of ruling. In British Africa local chiefs and others were handpicked to help run the country under the control of the Crown. This "indirect" rule was in sharp contrast to the subjugation of local leaders in French West Africa. The Portuguese used what they called a "colonial trinity" approach, consisting of three forces: a strong administration, a conservative Catholic Church, and companies that extracted mineral and other resources for use in Europe.[50]

African leaders did emerge under these systems, in different ways. Under French rule, where France's *mission civilisatrice* was the guiding principle, France groomed a relatively few cultured *évolués* for political roles within the framework of a greater France. Far less known is the "cultivation of an elite culture" of Africans in British Africa.[51] Not enough attention has been paid to the important roles these African leaders played in the pre-independence days, one scholar argues, calling them "under-appreciated African builders of durable institutions under colonialism."[52] This scholar argues that as negative as colonial rule was for Africa, it should not be used by Africans and their leaders today as an excuse to explain away current problems. Africans themselves must take responsibility for their actions today, he says. "The colonial imprint [on Africa] is indelible, but it need not be pervasive." It did have a "depressant effect" on Africa, but in time "the colonial imprint on Africa will become negligible by comparison with Africa's own imprint on world culture and politics."[53] In other words, Africa is no longer simply acted upon by the world but has become an actor, largely responsible for its own destiny.

African economist and author George B. N. A. Ayittey writes that too many power-hungry African leaders have blamed their country's problems on the legacy of colonialism, including arbitrary borders. African leaders, not the past, are the real problem, he argues. "The leadership in much of Africa has not only been a hopeless failure but also a disgrace to black people." He suggests looking forward, not backward, because "a mind deeply obsessed with the past is captured by it."[54]

Stagnation and Progress after Independence

In the late 1980s, African leaders did accept more responsibility for Africa's economic woes. They signed on almost without exception to a United Nations quid pro quo plan to generate more money for development in Africa in exchange for their admission that they were responsible for their country's economy and their promise to make certain economic reforms, some of which were politically risky. One could argue that such statements from African leaders were window dressing. When the sole bank in town offers you a loan only if you sign a statement saying you are responsible for your actions, you are likely to sign it. Until then, most African heads of state rarely admitted any responsibility for their nations' economies. They tended to blame the West, blame the former colonial rulers, blame everyone but themselves for economic and political problems during three decades of independence. Of course, pious words can be exposed as just that. Sudan's military leader, Omar Hassan al-Bashir, endorsed the rights of children at a UN summit organized by UNICEF. At almost the same hour he spoke, one of his military planes was bombing a rebel-held area in southern Sudan where a relief plane belonging to the International Committee of the Red Cross had landed to bring aid to children and others.

Since independence, Africa has made substantial progress in many areas. The percentage of students enrolled in primary schools has increased sharply, though with some leveling off in the 1990s. Africans on average are better fed, healthier, and live longer than they did at the time of independence. A vast network of roads, ports, and telecommunications facilities has been constructed, much of it with the help of foreign donors. Africans have made progress in many fields. I wrote a story on biotechnology in Africa and never had to interview anyone outside Kenya; the experts I needed were Kenyan. A number of Africans have become known in the West for their achievements, including singers such as Salif Keita of Mali, and Nigerian writers Wole Soyinka, winner of the Nobel Prize in literature, and Chinua Achebe, author of the acclaimed *Things Fall Apart.*

Food production in Africa has steadily increased since the 1980s, though gains are not enough to keep up with population growth. One of the few bright spots in population trends is in Kenya. By the mid-1980s, Kenya had the continent's fastest-growing rate of population, more than 4 percent, enough to double the population in roughly seventeen years. But between 1988 and 1993, fertility rates in Kenya dropped about 20 percent following major education efforts financed in part by the U.S. Agency for International Development. The average

Nairobi, Kenya, 1991
Many families are being educated about raising healthy children and using family planning.

number of children born to a Kenyan woman fell from 6.7 to 5.4. That meant there would be millions fewer mouths to feed in the twenty-first century than if the decline had not occurred.

"The message is, if it can happen in Kenya, it can happen anywhere," said Ayo Ajai, director of the Kenya office of the New York–based Population Council, a private research organization. Ironically, it was increased urban poverty, not economic progress, that convinced many Kenyan families to have fewer children. Poor city families living in single rooms smaller than many bedrooms in the United States realized they could not afford to raise and educate more children. Men also became more receptive to family planning measures.

But as the twentieth century drew to a close, the population of sub-Saharan Africa was still growing at roughly 2.6 percent per year, nearly twice the world average and enough to double the population of the region in twenty-seven years. "Despite notable increases in contraceptive prevalence and decreases in fertility in a few African nations, the continent as a whole is an anchor that the rest of the world is dragging on its voyage toward population stabilization."[55]

The list of other major economic and social challenges still facing Africa is a long one. AIDS, for example, has swept parts of eastern and central Africa. "Some two-thirds of AIDS cases are believed to be concentrated in sub-Saharan Africa, with HIV prevalence estimated at nearly 25 percent among adults in urban areas in the worst-hit countries, including Uganda, Zaire, and Tanzania."[56] In 1997 alone, AIDS "orphaned 1.7 million children, more than 90 percent of them in Africa south of the Sahara."[57] But AIDS awareness programs in Zaire by the early 1990s, and in a few other countries, have shown that behavior can be modified. Increased use of condoms to protect against AIDS could also slow population growth rates.

Economic growth slowed in the 1970s and 1980s in most parts of Africa. In sub-Saharan Africa the per capita GNP (gross national product for each person) in 1996 was on average only the equivalent of $510, compared to $20,240 in the more developed countries.[58] Nearly half the people were living on less than $1 a day.[59] Compared to the other developing regions (East Asia, South Asia, and Latin America), sub-Saharan Africa was doing the worst on major social indicators such as the following: life expectancy was only fifty-two years; the literacy rate was about 50 percent; just over one half of eligible school-age children were in school; just under one half were immunized for childhood diseases; Africa had the lowest daily caloric intake and the highest infant mortality rate (92 of every 1,000 children die before age five; of the seven million infant deaths in the world each year, five million occur in sub-Saharan Africa).[60]

By 1995, backed by the World Bank, more than half the nations of sub-Saharan Africa had begun major economic reforms, with some countries showing modest gains by the last half of the 1990s. Compared to a negative gross domestic product (GDP) growth rate for most of the region in the 1980s, the average GDP was up to about 5 percent in 1996. Togo, Lesotho, and Uganda averaged 10 percent growth rates between 1995 and 1997. French-speaking West African countries moved from a negative 3 percent (1991 to 1993) to a positive 6 percent growth rate (1994 to 1996). More than half of the continent's economies were growing at rates higher than the population growth rate, though "effective development" of the region would require 8 to 10 percent annual economic growth rates. Foreign investment was growing.[61]

Many Africans, however, claimed that the economic reforms were hurting the poor in the short run by forcing government layoffs and a reduction in government food subsidies, resulting in higher food prices. One of the strongest critics was Nigerian Claude Ake: "In the name of economic growth, real incomes are reduced by as much as 40 percent or more overnight. The prices of social services and staples are raised enormously, and inflation rates soar." The International Monetary Fund–World Bank reforms, he argued, do more than hurt economies. "They break down social consensus, cause violent conflict, anxiety, and deep despair, and sometimes premature death on a large scale, especially among children."[62]

Ake, like Garba and Ayittey, blamed some of the problem on African leaders. "With few exceptions, the African elites have been more interested in political survival than in development, and the conditions of their survival have usually been inimical to development."[63] He proposed a system of community-based, self-reliant development projects that put the farmer at the center of the effort. But such projects "may conflict with one another" and require arbitration by "independent third parties" based on "the rule of law," according to Kenyan political scientist Michael Chege. Now is the time to search for new solutions in Africa, Chege says. "With the Cold War over, the African intelligentsia have an unprecedented opportunity to abandon the rigid and dogmatic positions that formerly characterized debate on African politics and development. . . . Decentralized authority—even federalism—may be better attuned to African needs, given the region's ethnic diversity and political differences."[64]

Africa's Renewed Push for Freedom

Against this background, there was a renewed push for greater political freedom and democracy across the continent in the early 1990s. Two key developments in the last part of the twentieth century changed the dynamics of African politics, so that the advocates of democracy had a better chance for success.

The first development was the ending of the Cold War, which reduced international tensions in Africa between the United States and the Soviet bloc, and stripped African "client" states on each side of the ideological divide of guaranteed economic and military support. When the Berlin Wall came down in 1989, eastern Europe, for the most part, was shedding its outdated Marxist ideology and beginning to replace its Communist leaders. The visually and politically dramatic dismantling of the wall, reported throughout Africa by TV, radio, and newspapers, had an immediate effect. People began talking about the possibilities of real political change in Africa. "Events in Eastern Europe not only emboldened pro-democracy activists in Africa [they] also weakened the confidence of authoritarian leaders."[65] President Omar Bongo of Gabon said, "The winds from the East are shaking the coconut trees."[66] In Kenya, a prominent clergyman, the Reverend Timothy Njoya, suggested that the events in eastern Europe would have repercussions in Africa. His remarks were immediately denounced by the Moi government. For the next few months a strange phenomenon occurred in Kenya: almost daily, the government denounced calls for democracy as subversive, even though few except Njoya were calling for it, at least not openly. What the government knew, however, was that pressure for change was building beneath the surface; it soon would explode in the form of protest rallies, and violence in favor of multi-party elections.

The second development that boded well for democracy throughout Africa was Nelson Mandela's release from prison on February 10, 1990. Just before 4 P.M., Mandela walked through the prison's gates with his wife, Winnie. The scene, described by Mandela, was chaotic but not without humor. "[There were] . . . hundreds of photographers and television cameras and news people as well as several thousand well-wishers. I was astounded and a little bit alarmed. Within twenty feet or so of the gate, the cameras started clicking, a noise that sounded like some great herd of metallic beasts. Reporters started shouting questions; television crews began crowding in; ANC [Mandela's African National Congress] supporters were yelling and cheering. It was a happy, if slightly disorienting chaos. When a television crew thrust a long, dark furry object at me, I recoiled slightly, wondering if it were

Nairobi, Kenya, 1993
Economic freedom: Stock markets have been established in a number of African countries after years of state-dominated economies.

some newfangled weapon developed while I was in prison. Winnie informed me that it was a microphone."[67]

Some Africans told me that they thought Mandela's release had a greater impact on Africa's new drive for freedom than the fall of the Berlin Wall. Mandela's freedom sent a powerful, positive message to Africans: never give up the struggle; freedom is attainable.

As all this was happening, international lenders to Africa were insisting on economic reforms. Economic conditions had worsened in much of independent Africa. Many workers in the late 1980s were earning about what they had at the time of independence. Prices for many African export commodities were at record lows. The World Bank and the International Monetary Fund, along with most government and private lenders, began focusing more on recovery of old debts than issuing new loans; Africa had fallen far behind in debt repayments. Liberalization of the economy was seen by lenders as a way to help Africa climb out of its deepening financial hole and pay off its debts. It was not until 1996 that the Bank began a major debt relief program in Africa.[68]

Freedom: A Powerful Idea

While a few analysts argue that international pressure has been the major factor in Africa's turn toward democracy, most disagree. From what I saw during eight years covering Africa as a correspondent for *The Christian Science Monitor,* the main impetus for change has come from Africans themselves. In a few cases, such as Kenya, an international freeze on new aid just as domestic pressure was mounting brought a switch to multiparty elections. But without the local pressure, such a freeze would have had little effect. Kenya and Malawi were among the few countries where international aid was used so overtly to try to force change.

But neither pressure from abroad nor the often appalling economic conditions within a particular country seemed by themselves to tip the scales of public sentiment—and action—against authoritarian incumbents. The key, according to one exhaustive analysis of the entire sub-Saharan region, was local politics—what those dissatisfied with the government did to force change.[69] And the greatest changes came, the same analysis found, in countries where the incumbent government previously had allowed the greatest amount of political activity.[70] To put it another way: the pressure from the providers of international aid (the carrot-and-stick approach) and the poverty of the people were elements in the swift political changes that began in 1990, but the key element was the actions of Africans themselves in ending abuses of power. Their efforts met with the most success against regimes that were not so oppressive and whose political systems had already given the people some freedoms.

The people themselves had to decide enough was enough. And they did. Their long-simmering discontent, and anger, with politics as usual boiled over. In the end, it was the power of an idea, the idea of freedom, that swept across Africa like a tidal wave in the early 1990s, changing the shape of politics more than at any other time since independence.

★   ★   ★

Africa's move toward greater democracy has been led by both educated elites and ordinary people. Leaders in the movement have included academics, members of the clergy, lawyers, doctors, human rights workers, journalists, trade union organizers, students, and others. The educated middle class has supplied much of the organizing manpower and leadership of political parties and pressure groups, but at key moments, ordinary people have supplied the mass force needed to make opposition movements effective. Participation in such movements is risky at all levels. Street demonstrations sometimes end in a hail of bullets from police or the army; leaders of political movements and prominent lawyers are sometimes jailed. Historian Laurent Gbagbo ran for president in Côte d'Ivoire in 1990, lost, and was jailed for several months in 1992. Businessman Kenneth Matiba of Kenya, one of the first to call for multiparty elections, spent months in jail as a result. He later ran unsuccessfully for president in 1992 and 1997. Matiba never recovered fully from the effects of a stroke suffered during his confinement in harsh prison conditions. At one point, he had been forced to sleep on the cement floor of his cell.

Lawyers have been prominent in the struggle for democracy in many countries, such as Nigeria and Kenya, often defending each other when one of them was arrested. That one person is willing to take

up the struggle when another is forced to stop, by death or imprisonment, is an important element in Africa's political reform movement.
Often, ordinary people in large numbers have risen up in collective
anger over economic and political issues and have caught governments
off guard. In 1991, in the island state of Madagascar, off the east coast
of Africa, months of public protests against the authoritarian government of President Didier Ratsiraka brought up to 100,000 people at a
time into the streets, month after month. Sitting on a downtown street
for hours at a time, day after day, sounds uncomfortable but relatively
easy; in this case, it was also dangerous. Several opposition leaders were
murdered; and on August 10, 1991, the president's bodyguards fired
into a large crowd of demonstrators, killing some 100 and wounding
many more. The public pressure finally led to new elections in 1992,
which Ratsiraka lost by a 67 to 33 percent margin to Albert Zafy, a
medical professor and protest leader. In November 1996, Zafy and Ratsiraka ran for president again; this time Ratsiraka won.

The legal return of some of the ousted authoritarian leaders—
Mathieu Kérékou's election as president of Benin in 1996 was another
case—under the new democracy banner is one of the ironies of the
reform movement. By the mid-1990s, African and other political scientists had begun reassessing the strengths and weaknesses of the drive
for democracy in Africa, questioning, among other things, the skills of
the opposition as well as those of wily incumbents. African analysts
began questioning the nature of democracy and whether the Western
emphasis on winner-take-all elections made sense on a continent
where ethnic identities remain strong.

The mass uprising in Madagascar was not unique. "States where
mass action played a significant part [in bringing political change] include: Benin, Burkina Faso, Cameroon, Central African Republic,
Comoros, Côte d'Ivoire, Equatorial Guinea, Gabon, Guinea, Guinea-
Bissau, Kenya, Lesotho, Madagascar, Malawi, Mauritania, Niger,
Nigeria, Sierra Leone, South Africa, Swaziland, Togo, Zaire, and Zambia."[71] In Mali massive demonstrations helped topple a military regime. Africans, like American blacks when they demanded their civil
rights, were fed up with the status quo. But the freedom movements on
both continents often evoked a violent government response, even as
the leaders sought to keep the protests peaceful.

In the United States, King, following the example of Mohandas Gandhi, called on his followers to respond to violence with nonviolence as they protested the U.S. version of apartheid—laws restricting where blacks could eat, sleep, and how they could travel. King called nonviolence "the most potent weapon" available to oppressed people struggling for justice.[72] He gave these marching orders to his followers: "If he [a policeman] doesn't beat you, wonderful. But if he beats you, you develop the quiet courage of accepting blows without retaliating. If he doesn't put you in jail, wonderful. Nobody with any sense likes to go to jail. If he puts you in jail, you go into that jail and transform it from a dungeon of shame to a haven of freedom and human dignity."[73]

Gandhi developed his first notions of passive resistance in South Africa, where he lived for years before returning to lead a nationwide movement for independence in India. But in Africa, nonviolence often did not work. Mandela at first called for nonviolence; but he later helped form an armed resistance movement when he and his supporters made no progress against the apartheid government. In other parts of the continent, Africans fought back when attacked by police or the military during pro-democracy protests. African dictators had less compulsion to back off in the face of nonviolent tactics than the British ultimately did in colonial India. Many African heads of state called out their version of shock troops to bash heads, shoot, and arrest pro-democracy demonstrators. In Mali, the army used tanks against demonstrators, killing many of them before other branches of the military halted the action.

Popular Protests Help Bring Changes

As the new democracy movement in Africa began scoring victories, starting in 1989, more and more people joined it. The rush toward democracy was, indeed, contagious; each new victory encouraged more actions as the message spread across Africa that change was attainable. In many countries, people gained a greater voice in how their country was run. The gains, where they were achieved, were not uniform from country to country; nor were they always long-lasting. But the very fact that significant gains were made in numerous countries showed that people would no longer tolerate suppression; now they demanded freedom. Some examples of the changes and reverses included the following:[74]

- In Benin in 1989, massive crowds filled the streets in angry protests against longtime dictator Kérékou. At a national conference the next year he was stripped of most of his powers and, in 1991, lost his bid for reelection to Nicéphore Soglo, a former World Bank official. In 1996, Kérékou ran again, defeating Soglo. This time he was under the constraint of democratic rules, though some analysts saw signs of the old Kérékou reemerging.
- In Cameroon, President Paul Biya, facing mounting public discontent and strikes, accepted a multiparty system in 1990. He won reelection in 1992 with less than 40 percent of the vote, amid charges of fraud.
- In the tiny island state of Cape Verde, multiparty politics went into effect in 1990. The opposition won both legislative and presidential elections in 1991.
- In Central African Republic, the military agreed in 1991 to restore a multiparty system. In 1993, opposition leader Ange-Félix Patassé beat military head of state André Kolingba in the election for president.
- In Congo, opposition parties were legalized in 1990, and the government abandoned its Marxist-Leninist ideology.
- In Côte d'Ivoire, Félix Houphouët-Boigny, president since independence, agreed in 1990 to multiparty elections, which he won the same year.
- In Gabon, President Bongo agreed in 1990 to multiparty elections, which he won in 1993 amid opposition claims of fraud.
- In Mozambique, the government abandoned its Marxist-Leninist ideology in 1989 and legalized nonviolent opposition parties. Multiparty elections were held in 1994, won by the government party, FRELIMO, against the former rebel opposition, RENAMO.
- In Niger, the government accepted multiparty politics in 1991; the opposition candidate, Mahamane Ousmane, won the presidential election in 1993.

- In Tanzania, opposition parties were legalized in 1992.
- In Zambia, multiparty politics were restored in 1990; opposition leader Frederick Chiluba won a presidential election in 1991, replacing authoritarian leader Kenneth Kaunda, who had held power for twenty-seven years. But Chiluba soon began suppressing critics and the opposition, discrediting his reelection in 1996.[75]

Statistically, the gains were impressive at both the legislative and presidential level. From 1985 to 1989, only nine countries held competitive elections in which the opposition gained a presence in the national legislature. From 1990 to 1994, the number jumped to thirty-eight. The opposition's share of legislative seats in the region increased from 10 percent in 1989 to 31 percent in 1994. And in the same period, despite the long-standing pattern of presidents enjoying tenures that sometimes lasted for decades, fourteen new heads of state were elected. Still, fifteen incumbents were reelected, twelve of them in elections that "fell short of internationally accepted standards."[76]

Resistance to Reform

When Africans' pent-up frustrations with authoritarian rule erupted, beginning in 1989, changes came swiftly. But as incumbents learned to respond more cleverly to the growing discontent, playing the democracy "game" to their advantage, or using force to quell protests, the pace of change began to slow. Some gains were reversed. In Nigeria, a military government annulled presidential election results in 1993 and later jailed the winner, businessman Chief Moshood Kashimawo Olawale Abiola. In Chad, a military government, after allowing the formation of opposition parties in 1992, had instituted, by 1997, the "systematic use of torture and ill-treatment including rape in detention and summary and extrajudicial executions," primarily of suspected thieves.[77]

But sometimes even military regimes felt the pressure of the democracy movement. Nigeria faced massive labor strikes when the military annulled the 1993 presidential elections. And the uncertainty of a military regime's tenure was illustrated by events in Sierra Leone. In 1991, a new, multiparty constitution was approved in that nation; the next year, the military took over in a coup led by Valentine Strasser. When Strasser showed signs of reneging on elections, demonstrations by the public and pressure from international lenders made it clear both groups wanted an election. In January 1996, Strasser was overthrown in a coup led by General Julius Maada Bio, who went ahead with the election. The winner, Ahmed Tejan Kabbah, was overthrown in another military coup in May 1997 by Major Johnny Paul Koroma. Then Nigeria, long present in nearby Liberia as a peacekeeping force, attacked the rebel government in February 1998 and restored Kabbah to power. In areas the rebels retreated to, there were shocking reports of the murder, mutilation, and rape of hundreds of civilians, amid calls for the international community to help protect human rights in those areas.[78] In Sudan, Omar Hassan al-Bashir led a military coup in 1989 that ousted a civilian, democratically elected president. In Togo, Etienne (Gnassingbe) Eyadéma, who had seized power in a military coup in 1967, eventually allowed multiparty elections and won them in the 1990s after intimidating the opposition.

In Zaire, Mobutu, who had seized power in a military coup in 1965, restored multiparty politics in 1990 in his own way. He encouraged a proliferation of opposition parties and clandestinely started some himself to dilute his opponents' strength. By late 1996, Zaire had slipped into anarchy amid the near-total collapse of state services. In an eight-month civil war beginning in late 1996, Mobutu was overthrown by Laurent Kabila's rebel force, which included many ethnic Tutsi from eastern Zaire. Kabila took power amid accusations of wholesale massacres of tens of thousands of Hutu refugees who had fled to Zaire in fear of Tutsi revenge after Hutu carried out genocide against the Tutsi in Rwanda in 1994. Kabila's war was greatly assisted by Rwanda's Tutsi-led government, whose leaders were anxious to eliminate the possibility of refugees staging attacks against Rwanda. There was "irrefutable physical evidence of massacres of Hutu refugees by troops fighting with . . . Kabila's [forces]." Refugees found themselves attacked not only by remnants of Mobutu's army and even the former Rwandan Hutu army (when the refugees refused to support them), but by Kabila's and Rwanda's Tutsi-led army. But it was the latter two forces that engaged in wholesale killing of Hutu refugees and massive attempts to cover up the murders.[79]

Accra, Ghana, 1992
Political freedom: Multiparty elections for president were held in
1992 and 1996. Former military coup leader Jerry Rawlings won
both times. A public signboard was used to record vote totals.

how popular efforts for political reform in Africa often started with great enthusiasm but soon fizzled out."[83]

Political opponents of authoritarian regimes sometimes failed to win elections because they could not decide on a single candidate. Moi won in 1992 and 1997 in multiparty elections—each time with much less than half the vote against a divided opposition. Opposition groups often were poorly organized and poorly financed. And they tended to focus on one individual rather than on building a strong party structure.

Some of the old-guard incumbents got wise to the new democracy movement. Having seen electoral defeats of incumbents in other parts of Africa, they learned quickly how to adapt, how to make just enough political concessions to take the heat off for a while, how to tamper with the electoral machinery just enough to win again. Some heads of state used outright force or had the potential to do so, which is why there were few pro-democracy victories against military regimes. Most civilian authoritarian regimes were more subtle, calling elections quickly, before opponents could get organized, or not allowing potentially broad-based parties to run for various reasons, or passing laws designed to prevent particular strong potential candidates from running.

Many of those in the reform movement were relatively new to politics. They had not been part of the independence movement of the 1950s and 1960s, nor part of the entrenched regimes fighting democracy. These newcomers came forward at the same time as the appearance of an "authentic grass roots movement for fundamental democratic change."[84] Yet neither the new leadership in the movement for democracy nor the grassroots support for change has managed to overcome the resistance of numerous ingrained authoritarian leaders because the new popular pressure often has not "effectively and decisively challenged the autocratic basis and patterns of politics on the continent."[85] Africa, one Western scholar argued, might not have been ready socially or economically for a rapid transformation to democracy. "Everyday conditions in Africa [with exceptions] appear singularly unfavorable to democracy at present."[86] Low literacy and a poor economy were cited as unfavorable conditions. But some poor countries such as Mali, with a 30 percent literacy rate and an annual per capita GNP of only $240, made the transition to democracy, though not without difficulties. As the momentum in the democratic movement slowed by the latter half of the 1990s, some analysts were questioning basic issues, such as what kind of democracy works best in Africa.

Democracy Examined

Overall there has been progress toward greater political freedom in Africa. In 1989 in sub-Saharan Africa, only two states (Botswana and Mauritius) were "Free," according to Freedom House, an independent research institute in New York. By 1999, the number had increased to nine (Benin, Botswana, Cape Verde, Malawi, Mali, Mauritius, Namibia, São Tomé and Príncipe, South Africa). The number of "Partially Free" countries also had increased, from twelve in 1989 to twenty by 1999. The number of "Not Free" countries had declined from thirty-two in 1989 to nineteen by 1999. (The 1999 total includes two countries—Eritrea and Namibia—not included in 1989.)

The momentum toward greater freedom appeared to have slowed by about 1995: there was little change between 1995 and 1998; but neither were the gains disappearing, according to the Freedom House data. In classifying a country as "Free," Freedom House uses twenty-two criteria, including free and fair elections, a viable opposition, independent media and judiciary, freedom of assembly, and other civil liberties.

Even among many of the "Not Free" countries, something important was happening: people were becoming aware of their power to change things, or at least to try.

What were the best kinds of changes? Which ones would last? And whose concept of "democracy" and "freedom" was being used? Freedom House is not the only measuring stick for democracy in Africa. Democracy—no matter what type of democracy it might be—works best when a broad range of people are involved in it at all levels, not just at the top, according to African and Western analysts. What was lacking in Africa's new democracy movement, some of these analysts maintain, was an effective way of linking the urban and the rural populations in the political process.[87] Célestine Monga argues that it would be a mistake to say, as is commonly argued, that the pro-democracy protests were an urban creation. Urban residents may have been at the front lines of the struggle, but rural residents had long sought more political freedom.

In the rush toward freedom in the early 1990s, both incumbents and opposition groups turned to the one vehicle for change most promoted by Western governments: multiparty elections in which the winner of the presidential race takes all the executive power. Known as the winner-takes-all format, it was adopted with little question. Some African scholars and others began questioning its validity, the effect of some of the new elections, and the frequent abuse of the election process itself, mostly by incumbent regimes.

Between 1990 and early 1995, there were multiparty elections in thirty-five of sub-Saharan Africa's fifty nations.[88] But seventeen of these elections "did not bring about significant change in the direction of democracy," one scholar notes. "In seven countries (Burkina Faso, Cameroon, Ethiopia, Gabon, Guinea, Mauritania, and Togo), elections were seriously flawed; in another four (Angola, Gambia, Nigeria,

Lagos, Nigeria, 1991
Freedom of the press: After years of having mostly state-run newspapers, independent newspapers and magazines have sprung up across Africa.

and Burundi), election results were voided by subsequent nondemocratic interventions; and in six (Congo, Djibouti, Ghana, Côte d'Ivoire, Kenya, and Senegal), the elections were at best marginally free and fair. The results of this wave of elections are thus at best mixed. . . . Nevertheless, some headway has been made."[89]

★ ★ ★

Some analysts and some African leaders have blamed certain instances of ethnic strife on multiparty elections. Some contested elections intensified ethnic rivalries, according to one analyst. "Elections have increased competition for power and thus the incentive to rely on ethnic appeals to get support. . . . Ethnic conflict has intensified in Burundi, Ethiopia, Kenya, and Nigeria, all countries that held elections recently." However, the analyst notes that "democratization is rarely a painless process. . . . Thus the increase in violence cannot in itself be taken as a sign that the process of democratic transformation is seriously off track."[90]

And in some of these cases it is not clear that the elections by themselves caused an increase in ethnic conflict. In Ethiopia, after rebels won a prolonged civil war, ethnic conflict occurred in the period leading up to the nation's first contested elections, in 1992, and continued after the elections. But the scale of conflict was minuscule compared with the massive battles in Ethiopia in the later years of its decades-old civil war, which ended in 1991. In Kenya, there was ethnic conflict both before and after the elections of 1992 and 1997, as President Moi had predicted. But there is credible evidence reported by human rights organizations that in many cases the violence was organized and supported by the government.[91] This, not the elections themselves, increased ethnic tensions. The violence had the effect of pushing many potential opposition voters off their land and making the land available to supporters of the government. Friends of mine in Kenya told me their school-age children seldom talked about the ethnic identity of their classmates—until after the government-induced ethnic conflicts began prior to the 1992 election.

Nigeria actually showed how a presidential election can unite people, not increase ethnic tensions. The winner in 1993, Abiola, a southerner, drew strong support from the predominately Muslim north and from all other regions of the country. Soyinka calls this a "robust detonation" of the much-touted, much-analyzed north-south split in Nigeria. And he adds: "We cannot ignore the treason represented by the annulment of that election, for it was more than the election of an individual. It was the annulment of Nigeria's declaration that it wants to be one nation."[92]

As Africans got more chances to vote in the 1990s in multiparty elections, they often voted along ethnic lines, as in Kenya. But there were some signs, as in Nigeria, that people were breaking out of such narrow classifications when it came to voting for candidates who endorsed basic human rights and political freedom. "In addition to being Yorubas, Bamilekes, Kikuyus, or Zulus, African voters are taxpayers, employed or unemployed, Catholics or animists, inhabitants of large cities or small towns; the competition between the multiple aspects of their identity make them less likely to vote automatically with their ethnic group, which may not represent their self-interests."[93]

There are more than 2,000 ethnic groups in Africa, but ethnicity is an overused argument to explain political strife in Africa, argues Cameroon scholar Monga. The ethnic issue "has allowed African governments to deflect public opinion from the only question that really matters: their abysmal . . . record of rule."[94] Making a similar point, Nigerian analyst Ake attributes most of the so-called ethnic problems in Africa to manipulation by self-serving political leaders.

Chege suggests a way to reduce governments' opportunities for manipulating the ethnic issue. Rather than trying to "banish ethnicity from African politics," he recommends finding ways to "reconcile cultural diversity with constitutional democracy," as he says Switzerland and some large U.S. cities have done. "What are needed are formal and informal structures of power sharing to replace the winner-take-all policies" widely used in Africa.[95] South Africa's first multiracial election in 1994 followed intense negotiations between all sides and agreement on a power-sharing formula that resulted in de Klerk becoming a deputy president. The opposite approach, winner-take-all, failed to end the war in Angola in 1992 with a presidential election when rebel leader Jonas Savimbi, long backed by the United States with the help of the Central Intelligence Agency, refused to accept defeat. The war resumed.

But beyond misuse of the election machinery, and the ethnic issue, lies a larger question: what does democracy mean in Africa today? Here Ake is helpful in detailing a kind of democracy quite different from the traditional Western model. Ake suggests four characteristics of any democracy that will survive and be useful in Africa:

1. Popular power beyond just the vote. This would include, for example, a powerful central legislature sharing some of its power with local democratic organizations.
2. A social democracy that emphasizes "concrete political, social and economic rights, as opposed to . . . abstract political rights." The government would invest heavily in health and education to help people participate more effectively in running their country.
3. "As much emphasis on collective rights as . . . individual rights." This could mean a second legislative chamber known as the chamber of nationalities "in which all nationalities irrespective of their numerical strength are equal." Or elections would be held under a system of proportional representation, and parties would be required to gain a set minimum of votes over a large part of the country to win. The latter would serve to block victory by a party whose strength is primarily among one large ethnic group or groups in one part of the country.
4. Legislative membership should include representatives of nationality groups, youth, labor, women, and other mass groups.[96]

Monga steps aside from the debates over whether a Western model for democracy would work best in Africa, calling that "beside the point." What matters most, in his view, is expanded involvement by the public in the political process, something he says is often blocked by urban-based political leaders who write the rules of the game in a way that favors themselves. Popular leaders who have widespread support are considered suspect by these leaders. But ordinary Africans are wise to the political games some leaders play, and they are angry, Monga states. Their resort to violence in many countries is a "reflection of the people's desire for revenge against illegitimate governments and of the governing elite's inability to see what is really at stake. Recognizing this simple truth would be enough to move things forward, for Africa is no more cursed than any other part of the world."[97]

One way or another, Ake, Monga, Chege, and others argue for systems that allow for greater inclusion of people in the politics of Africa in the new century.

★   ★   ★

Whether they were successful or not, the new wave of competitive elections in Africa has "helped to expand the horizons of individual liberty to an extent that few could have anticipated in 1990."[98] Many individuals stood up for freedom, often putting themselves at risk. Many of them were students. Their stories and the backgrounds they are set against show some of the dangers and the difficulties in establishing greater political freedom and human rights.

2 CHALLENGING THE DICTATORS

Lomé, Togo, 1990
Mothers, students, attorneys, and many others pushed
back barriers to freedom in Africa in the 1990s.

ON the side streets of Bamako, Mali's capital, a powdery coating of fine Sahara sand pours in through any open car windows and sneaks up through cracks in the floorboards, bathing drivers and passengers. The poor foot travelers disappear in a billowing, brown wake which leaves grit between their teeth. Downtown is less dusty because most of the streets are paved. But it is a chaotic place, more like a large West African village than a city. Pedestrians are forced onto the narrow streets by sidewalk hawkers who spread their wares, selling everything from traditional medicine to the latest cassettes of Malian singers such as Salif Keita, whose music is played over scratchy speakers. Bamako is cloaked in noise. Cars and taxies blast their horns; motorbikes rev their whining engines. Under this raucous, overarching sound, loud market talk fills what's left of the ear's capacity to absorb. Keita developed his high-pitched singing voice in the Bamako markets, where his notes had to carry above the din.

Bamako is not a glitzy city, but it is too modern to give more than a hint of the antiquity of the Malian empire, whose onetime crown jewel, Timbuktu, lies far to the north, surrounded by the Sahara. There are relatively few evident signs of power or wealth in downtown Bamako, though both are present. There is a military base at the edge of the city, but soldiers are seldom seen downtown. And except for jewelry and occasional fancy cars, wealthy Malians generally do not display their affluence. They do display a taste for fashion. In contrast to the dull suits, slacks, and Western dress shirts of Kenya and many other parts of East Africa, Bamako's streets are living fashion shows. Women typically wrap themselves in large, loose cloths of rainbow colors, leaving one shoulder casually bare. Head scarfs accentuate or copy the colors of the dress but are often partially covered with a larger cloth draped over head and shoulders. Men commonly wear matching loose pants and shirts with open neck or full-length robes. In the mud mosques, robes and skullcaps are common.

A hotel, a bank, and some other offices are among the few tall buildings in Bamako. Most structures are squat, low to the ground, like a person who hunches over to become less of a target of the fine sand blowing in from the desert. Many shops are made of mud reinforced by sticks. The smoothed mud walls resemble cement. Most of the fancy homes in Bamako are not ostentatious by Western standards. There is a notable exception. Mali's powerful president, Moussa Traoré, lived in a castle of sorts, atop a steep hill at the edge of the city. He was not chosen to live up there, at least never legitimately. He simply installed himself. When Malians finally rose up and challenged him, violence engulfed the city. Part of it took place in a shopping center downtown called Sahel Verte, French for "green Sahel," that dry, vast area just south of the Sahara.

In March 1991, a crowd of Malians fled through the doors of Sahel Verte to escape policemen and soldiers rampaging on the streets in pursuit of rioters. Instead of charging in after them, police barred the doors and set fire to the place. There was no escaping.[1] It happened during Mali's three-day revolution, one of the shortest in Africa. It pit mothers, university students, and others against a dictator and his army. At first the demands were for educational and economic reforms; but the explosion of public fury at the government's crackdown on demonstrators quickly went beyond that and the people demanded Traoré's resignation. At least 100,000 people took to the streets in the second and third day of the protests.[2]

Sinaly Dembélé was studying English at the time at the National Teacher's College in Bamako. He recalled what happened the first morning of the battles. "I woke up around seven and found smoke everywhere. All the other children in my family, whether students or not, went out." What he saw was enough to intimidate all but the most determined. The military and police were chasing civilians through the streets firing tear gas; two tanks rumbled by. But instead of hiding, he joined other students on the streets. "I saw a boy fall down," he said. "We saw it was real bullets. Most of the people withdrew, but we kept throwing stones at the soldiers. One tank fired at us. We were about ten people."

Mali's battle was a contest between students, workers, opposition politicians, and others demanding political freedom and the right to be heard, on one side, and a dictator refusing to listen and intent on staying in power, on the other. It was typical of what was happening in many parts of Africa at the time; military and civilian dictators were suddenly put on the defensive by those calling for freedom and recognition of basic human rights.

As one historian notes, "The fundamental sense of freedom is freedom from chains, from imprisonment, from enslavement by others."[3] This definition is still literally relevant to some Africans in Sudan, where slavery persists, and in parts of Mauritania where slaverylike conditions continue. But millions of other Africans have felt "enslaved" by military or civilian dictatorial leaders, though a good number of them have been forced out of office since the start of the pro-democracy movement in Africa in 1989.

Mass protests against such governments grew increasingly frequent in the 1990s. Civil society—including the wide variety of nongovernmental organizations and associations—played a critical role in many of the protests. For example, in Niger, Army Chief of Staff Ali Saïbou had succeeded another military head of state, Seyni Kountché, his cousin, who died in 1987 after thirteen years in office. He endorsed the single-party system but said there could be competition within the party. In February 1990, the army intervened to stop student demonstrations at the University of Niamey on several educational issues. Several students were killed, according to official reports. In May, as student protests grew despite further security crackdowns against them, a worker's federation, the Union des Syndicats des Travailleurs du Niger (USTN), called for introduction of a multiparty system. In June the USTN organized a strike to protest the treatment of the students and a government wage freeze. In November the USTN organized a march in support of its demands for political pluralism, and an estimated 100,000 people participated in Niamey, the capital.[4]

In Nigeria, trade unionists and other groups organized mass protests after the annulment of the 1993 presidential election by the military. After General Sani Abacha assumed power several months later, the protests grew, as did the arrests by the military of opposition leaders and human rights advocates.

One thorough study of pro-democracy movements in the 1990s found that in countries where there had been numerous trade unions and other civil society organizations, including a relatively free press, there were more demonstrations. And protests came earlier than in countries with few independent associations.[5]

★   ★   ★

The rampages in Mali stemmed from deep dissatisfaction with the economy and with the lack of political freedom, especially on the part of students, who were playing an increasingly significant role in pro-democracy drives in many African countries. Mali's revolution is an example of a popular uprising that helped bring about a change of government, in this case a democratic one. Mali's experience also offers insights into the difficulties of a transition to democracy and some of the expectations people have about democracy in a very poor country.

When Mali gained its independence from the French in June 1960, it was federated to Senegal. Senegal seceded from the union two

Djenné, Mali, 1994
Markets are held weekly in front of this historic mosque. There has been a mosque on this site for centuries.

months later and the Republic of Mali was born. The first president, Modibo Keita, led the country along a socialist path and declared the nation a one-party state. In the face of internal political disputes and strong opposition to his continued rule, Keita dissolved the National Assembly in January 1968. It was both the emergence of a militant youth movement which carried out purges within Mali's sole legal political party and the arrest of several army officers that led to a successful military coup in November 1968.[6] Mali's swing to military rule was part of an African movement in that direction. In the first twenty-five years after independence, the military coup d'état became "the more recurrent instrument for changing top political leadership."[7]

A committee headed by Lieutenant (later General) Moussa Traoré as president promised to return Mali to civilian rule as soon as the country's economic problems were overcome. Had a Western military leader imposed the same condition for his departure, he might as well have declared himself president for life, which is what Hastings Banda actually did in Malawi. Traoré gradually gained most of the power, which eventually led to opposition from university students, who found they could not get the president's attention on issues important to them.

Students Lead Protests

Student activism is a feature in the politics of many countries. In France massive numbers of students clashed with riot police in 1968, demanding educational reforms. In the same period, many students and others in the United States were challenging their government's war in Vietnam. Students at all levels have played a major role in African politics, from grade school pupils striking in black townships of predemocratic South Africa, to university students who went to the bush in Ethiopia to fight a long war that led to a new government and the independence of Eritrea. University students went to the streets to protest the continued rule of the late president of Côte d'Ivoire (Ivory Coast), Félix Houphouët-Boigny, who died in 1993. Students rioted against Kenya's president Daniel arap Moi on numerous occasions and in many other African countries as democracy became more than a distant goal in Africa.

In Mali, student activism is wrapped around the political life of the country like the cords that tie heavy slabs of salt onto camels in caravans that still arrive in Timbuktu from desert salt mines. (One salt mine was used by Traoré for detention of political opponents until he shut it down in 1988, twenty years after he assumed power.) For the most part, however, Malian schoolchildren do not protest in Bamako's streets. Grade schoolers, for example, in their billowing slacks, shirts, and plastic or rubber sandals, are usually in the streets on their way to or from their mud-walled schools. If it is the first day of a new term, children carry their school desks from home. Because the desks are the children's personal property, parents fear they may be stolen if left at school during breaks. As they walk, the young pupils practically wear their wooden, homemade desks like a garment, slipping into the space between writing surface and sitting bench.

The genesis of student militancy against the Traoré government in Mali, as in many African countries, was a combination of poverty and the growing tendency of government to ignore student demands. Traoré banned political opposition parties and ran as the sole candidate in several elections. But by late 1990, "people were fed up with political dictatorship," recalled Djibril Coulibaly, a college student in Bamako at the time. During the second half of 1990, two underground opposition groups went public in Mali, the National Committee for Democratic Initiative (CNID in French) and the Alliance for Democracy in Mali (ADEMA). Both groups organized pro-democracy marches in December of that year. Djibril joined one of the marches; it attracted some 3,000 people. The march was peaceful; it drew a mix of democracy advocates: students seeking more government aid; civil servants and teachers who had not been paid for several months. Among the marchers were Montagne Tall, an opposition leader, and human rights lawyer Demba Diallo; both were later presidential candidates.

Traoré's response to the nonviolent march was violence. He reorganized his government, installing General Sékou Ly as minister of the interior. Ly cracked down on the budding democratic movement, banning marches. When opposition activists organized rallies to protest the restrictions, the government arrested some of the leaders, including Oumar Mariko, head of the Association of Pupils and Students of Mali (AEEM). The arrest of Mariko sparked more protests. In subsequent clashes with government security forces, several civilians were killed. In Bamako, Malians suddenly found themselves forced to decide whether to go home and accept further arbitrary and forceful rule by an illegitimate government, or join the swelling ranks of protestors in the streets and risk getting injured or killed. For many it was a case of spontaneous escalation: people who had not planned to challenge the legitimacy of the government began fighting back when the army shot into the crowds and arrested protest leaders. Rather than being cowed by the police, they were incensed.

Such a reaction in the face of intimidation was seen many times in the United States during civil rights demonstrations and in the willingness of many college students to continue their antiwar protests after violent clashes with police or national guards. Vietnam war opponents on the street outside the Democatic Convention in 1968 were confronted by Chicago police wielding clubs; police attacked reporters as well as demonstrators. But in Mali, the enemy would not be just police or the national guard; soon it would be the army and its tanks.

Students were in the vanguard of the protests, though they were later joined by workers, teachers, and others. Some of the initial student demands were for improved toilets and better medical services. Other demands were more costly: high school scholarships; bigger payments for boarding students at all levels. As it became clearer that Traoré was not listening to their demands, students and others raised the ante and began planning how to force him from office. "People were eager to overthrow Moussa [Traoré]," said Djibril. Outraged by government violence against them, students went on a rampage, burning some government buildings in Bamako. The police responded with more arrests, sparking yet more protests. Students began organizing underground meetings to plan further actions. The government closed down the schools. Students had set a deadline of March 21, 1991, for the government to meet their demands, but the government failed to comply. Protestors took to the streets again, and this time the army responded without restraint.

Downtown, at a bridge now known as Bridge of the Martyrs because of what happened that day, soldiers were heaving students into the river. Some drowned; others were dead before they were dropped off the bridge like trash. The military had the obvious advantage in

Bamako, Mali, 1994
Sinaly Dembélé and Djibril Coulibaly were among the
thousands of Malian students and others who fought
against police and even army tanks to help overthrow
dictator Moussa Traoré in 1991. A civilian president was
elected in 1992 in democratic, multiparty elections.

weaponry; but students and others who joined them had the advantage
of passion. Selif Keita (whose name resembles that of the famous
Malian singer) was chairman of the English Students Club at the
teacher's college. "I saw many tanks, coming from every side, shooting
people. Soldiers were shooting with rifles from the top of the tank. And
I saw some people on the ground, injured. And those who tried to bring
the injured people to the hospital were also attacked." The tanks kept
firing on the students; those not hit kept regrouping. Finally, the tanks
ran out of ammunition. It was then that a few brave students leaped up
on the tanks and threw Molotov cocktails down the turrets.

At his home, Djibril awoke the next morning, March 22, to see smoke in the direction of some government buildings. "Our group [of students] was already destroying a drugstore nearby. Soldiers came and people were scattered. The soldiers did not fire. Students ran on to a bookshop and ransacked it. When police and the gendarme arrived there, they were pelted with stones by students." By now there were thousands of people on the streets, mostly students. "We were afraid, but there were so many students; and many others joined us. We were eager to go to the market and try to destroy it," said Djibril. But the protestors were blocked by security forces. Bamako was in total chaos. Students would attack a building; government forces would arrive and attack the students; then the students would disperse, only to strike again somewhere else. The day ended with President Traoré still in power. The next day would bring more violence, however, and a turning point.

On March 23, a crowd fleeing for their lives ran for safety into the Sahel Verte shopping center. That is when security forces locked the people in and set the place ablaze, incinerating them. Such horrific violence would reappear on a massively larger scale in Rwanda in 1994, when mobs chased people into churches, then tossed in grenades, slashing to death any survivors running out. In Liberia in 1996, the capital, Monrovia, sank into temporary anarchy as rival militia forces clashed. Such scenes are what many people think of when considering Africa, though they are not typical. Most of the continent was at peace during these wars. Africa's violence, viewed from afar, is confusing. There is a tendency to lump African countries together and think of barbarity, tribal vengeance, and cycles of revenge. There were all these kinds of violence in Africa in the century's last decade—though they were the exceptions, as was the violence in the former Yugoslavia and parts of the former Soviet Union.

The day the government forces burned Sahel Verte and the people trapped inside it, mothers and students marched on the Presidential Palace. They wanted to demand an end to the fighting. "There were old women in front, because we thought they [the army] would dare not fire on them," Sinaly recalled. "But they fired on an old woman. She was seriously injured." Had the wounded person been a student or an adult male, things might have turned out differently. But firing on a woman broke one of the unwritten taboos in Mali and many other parts of the world. Such taboos are part of the glue holding societies together. Malians were stunned, then angry.

There are other examples of attacks rousing national and even world sentiment. When Chinese troops fired on civilian crowds in Tiananmen Square in China in 1989 during pro-democracy demonstrations, it brought world condemnation, though no change in the country's leadership. The massacre at Sharpeville, South Africa, in 1959 brought no immediate change either. But it had a resounding, long-range impact on the future of that country. Blacks in South Africa were angry with a government-imposed system of passes required to move from one part of the country to another. In March 1959, in Sharpeville, a small township some thirty-five miles south of Johannesburg, in a grim industrial area, several thousand people surrounded the police station. The police panicked. Nelson Mandela writes about what happened next.

"No one heard warning shots or an order to shoot, but suddenly the police opened fire on the crowd and continued to shoot as the demonstrators turned and ran in fear. When the area had cleared, sixty-nine Africans lay dead, most of them shot in the back as they were fleeing. All told, more than seven hundred shots had been fired into the crowd, wounding more than four hundred people, including dozens of women and children."[8] Messages of condemnation poured in from around the globe, including the United States. The United Nations, for the first time, urged the South African government to begin to bring about racial equality. Further black protests followed, and the government declared martial law. It would be thirty-five years before South Africans would achieve majority rule, however.

In Mali, change came much quicker. The attempted march to the president's office ended abruptly. "It was a chaotic retreat. We ran for our lives," Sinaly said, as he, Djibril, and I sat at a table at the small Hotel de la Fleuve in Bamako in 1994. Traoré offered political reforms, but he refused to step down. The next day, when a crowd gathered at a local cemetery to bury some of the victims of the previous days' violence, the military fired on the mourners. Funerals have been a rallying point for protestors in many African countries, especially in South Africa before the election of Mandela as president in 1994.

During the three days of fighting, an estimated 150 to 300 persons were killed in Bamako, according to various Malian sources; the government admitted to only about 100 deaths. Early on March 26, 1991, Lieutenant Colonel Amadou Tumani Touré, a cheerful and audacious man, led a group of officers to arrest President Traoré.

In my interview with him in the downtown office he made his own as head of state, Touré explained why he had seized power. "Faced with many young and old people and children that were dying, we felt that Mr. Moussa Traoré had not respected the oath the head of state had taken. We decided to take him out, to put in place democratic organizations." His informal style and lack of pretension, as well as the fact he had deposed an unpopular dictator, quickly made Touré, or A.T.T., as he affectionately became known by his initials, a popular man. But would he be tempted to use that popularity as an excuse to stay in power? Or might he run for president himself? "My most dear vow is that I am not a candidate, and I prefer that elections take place for a civilian as head of state," he said.

Bamako, Mali, 1992
Lieutenant Colonel Amadou Tumani Touré overthrew dictator Moussa Traoré in 1991, then stepped down about a year later after the election of a civilian president.

Military coup leaders in Africa have seldom stepped down voluntarily. Among the notable exceptions was General Olusegun Obasanjo of Nigeria, who handed over power in 1979 to an elected civilian president. He was arrested in 1995, however, by Nigerian military head of state Abacha, for allegedly plotting a coup; he was released in 1998 after Abacha died. General Obasanjo was elected president of Nigeria in February 1999. Flight Lieutenant Jerry Rawlings of Ghana was another exception. He seized power in 1979, but he stepped down a few months later after a presidential election. Then he seized power again, in 1981. In November 1992, he was elected president with 58 percent of the vote. Only 48 percent of the voters turned out. In December 1996, he won again, and 75 percent of the voters turned out in an election generally acknowledged as free and fair.[9]

In the interview, Touré spelled out three conditions he deemed necessary to avoid future military intervention in Mali: the civilian government must maintain national security for the whole country; it must "correctly run the country"; it must have "respect for the constitution." All three conditions were broad enough to leave a door open for another coup. Some eager military leader, perhaps Touré himself, might one day refer to these points as justification for intervention. Political contacts in Bamako told me that despite his popularity, Touré would not have had strong public backing had he tried to stay in office. For his popularity depended in large part on his promise to hand over power to a democratically elected president. Touré kept his promise. He first said he would step down January 20, 1992, less than a year after the coup. But the political parties were not ready for an election, so he postponed it until March.

On the Campaign Trail in Mali

Getting elected president in Mali requires a far different campaign than in Europe or the United States. TV viewing in Mali is still limited to a tiny minority, primarily in the cities, though often the owners of TVs play them in their yards or outside the gates of their property, where friends and neighbors gather to watch. There is a wide variety of newspapers, but the national literacy rate is only about 30 percent.

From the beginning, the leading candidate for president in Mali's first democratic election was Alpha Oumar Konaré, a former academician who helped organize ADEMA, the main political protest group. Konaré had earned his political credibility among opponents to Traoré when, as one of Traoré's ministers, he stood up near the head of state at a public assembly and denounced corruption in the government. His gesture was seen as a brave act, which it was under a dictator who locked up dissenters in a salt mine. In his campaign Konaré relied on the nationwide organizational presence of ADEMA and his personal appearances. I spent a day with him as he campaigned for votes in Bamako. Unlike Western candidates with their large advance teams, press following, and the rest of an entourage, Konaré traveled with only a few aides and a few reporters. His strategy was to seek out local religious and other community leaders. Through winning their support, he hoped to win over the people they represented, he confided as we approached a neighborhood gathering of notables. Presidential candidate John F. Kennedy used a similar approach in his successful 1960 race, wooing local party bosses when they still had considerable influence. He also campaigned in primary contests.

At the modest home of a Muslim leader, Konaré took off his shoes, walked in, and sat down on the mat-covered floor. Later, arriving in another neighborhood, he got out of his car and walked several hundred yards to where a group of community and religious leaders were waiting in a courtyard. Most of the men wore typical and handsome Malian robes; many also wore skullcaps. The women, sitting behind the men, wore gaily colored dresses and head scarves. Unlike some Muslim countries in the Middle East, Muslim women in Mali and most other parts of Africa do not wear veils. Konaré, in slacks and a short-sleeved shirt, plus a long green scarf, one end thrown over his shoulder, said little as he sat listening to one local leader after another greet him and tell him what to do if elected. He endured the long remarks, hunched over like a schoolboy taking instructions from a parent. Occasionally he lifted his eyebrows or wrinkled his forehead, but he maintained his silence except for brief remarks at the end.

"We're here to identify the problems," he said as he strode back to his car. But had he made any promises? I asked. "I simply said ADEMA

Bamako, Mali, 1992
Alpha Oumar Konaré campaigns in Mali's first democratic
election. He won easily and was reelected in 1997.

doesn't have money to distribute right and left. What we guarantee is good management."

Toward the end of the day, at a public rally, I saw another side of Konaré. Using a microphone to address the crowd of several hundred, he was no longer humble and quiet. His voice boomed out from the public address speakers. A young Malian in the crowd, translating Konaré's Bambara to French for me, said Konaré promised little but implied that if elected he would help find jobs for the masses. His formula for good government, Konaré told the crowd, was based on good management, honesty in accounting of public funds, a minimal state role in a free market, and a reduction of taxes to encourage expansion of business. Despite his minimal specific pledges of progress, was he still stirring up hopes that the next government could not afford to meet? And after twenty-three years of dictatorship, would the people of Mali really appreciate the importance of voting? Some Malians I interviewed the day of Konaré's rally were noncommittal, admitting they knew little about democracy and elections.

Just outside Bamako, traveling with another presidential candidate, I would find out what people in an African village expected from democracy.

Voters' Wish List

Malians, after the three-day revolution, entered a new era of expectations. People wanted more than political freedoms such as the right to free speech: Malians also wanted material progress. This ratcheting up of hopes in a democratic era, a phenomenon occurring in many parts of Africa, was happening among some of the world's poorest people. In Mali the per capita share of the gross national product, a crude measurement of individual wealth, was less than $300 a year, compared to about $500 for all of sub-Saharan Africa. Life expectancy in Mali was only forty-three years for men and forty-six years for women, much lower than in the West.[10]

Against this backdrop, another presidential candidate, attorney and human rights advocate Demba Diallo, wearing a full-length, gold-colored, Malian robe, yellow slippers, and dark sunglasses, arrived in Lassa, a small, hillside village just outside Bamako. According to the World Bank, two out of every three people in sub-Saharan Africa live in villages and other rural areas; in Mali the figure is 80 percent. Lassa is made up of several clusters of cracked mud homes, a few shops, and three schoolrooms built of solid materials with financial help from the U.S. government. The dirt road leading up a steep hill to the village is in bad condition. Built by the French when Mali was still a French colony, it has been poorly maintained. There are few cars in Lassa; many residents walk the several miles to their jobs in Bamako.

Despite its location close to the capital, residents complained that their village had been ignored by the federal government. "Our concern is that since independence we haven't benefited much," said Baba Coulibaly, a male nurse who worked in Bamako but lived in Lassa. What did the village get from the twenty-three-year dictatorship of Moussa Traoré? I asked. "Three soccer balls," said another resident. Lassa needed a maternity clinic. Some women gave birth before arriving at the hospital in Bamako. They found it hard to get a taxi to drive them to the hospital because many of the drivers were reluctant to make the steep climb up the rough road to Lassa. Coulibaly listed other needs of the village: more classrooms; a well so that women, the traditional water haulers, did not have to spend hours walking for water; and an improved health center.

Lassa was already feeling some changes by the time Diallo arrived for his campaign rally. In the months since the ouster of dictator Traoré, Nessa Kamara, a villager, had noticed something she liked: "We can freely express ourselves," she said. Had there been any tangible change? Ossman Cesse, a cook in Bamako who lived in Lassa, responded: "Things can't change all at once. The money [in the government's treasury] is zero." What did people expect from Mali as it turned democratic? I asked. Wassa Keita, a mother of three, admitted something many people probably were reluctant to say: "I don't understand what 'multiparty' and 'democracy' are." But she knew what the problems in Lassa were. "There's not enough to eat. And in the dry season there's no water. And we live in the dark—no electricity."

So I was curious to hear what Diallo would offer after Konaré promised only "good management" at his Bamako rally. The villagers were curious too. And they were as ready to fete Diallo as he was to woo them for their votes. Election banners hung from mud walls; music blared over a microphone; chairs had been set up in a small, open area surrounded by homes. Dancers entertained the crowd. From the waist up, the dancers were spirits in wooden masks trimmed with long, hairlike, frayed rope; from the waist down they were mortals in slacks and plastic shoes.

Like Konaré in Bamako, Diallo first stopped by the home of an elderly Muslim leader in the village. Mali is about 80 percent Muslim, 18 percent animist, and only 1 percent Christian. Diallo sat on a cow skin rug with the man, slipping him some money as he left. When he got to the area prepared for his speech, Diallo watched the dancing until it concluded, then he picked up two microphones. He sounded like a cheerleader, and from time to time the crowd cheered. When he finished, Diallo turned toward his car. He had to pass through a shouting gauntlet of villagers happy a candidate had come to see them, even one who had promised more than he could deliver. Another candidate, not Konaré, had stopped in Lassa and promised a road, a maternity clinic, and a health center. Diallo promised the first two, but not the health center. What U.S. presidential candidate has not promised beyond his capacity to deliver? What European candidate has not painted the choices in a race as critical and stark and told crowds he would deliver what they needed?

In Nigeria, voters are accustomed to grandiose promises, but they are not overly impressed. According to Nigerian author and satirist Uche Onyebadi, voters should keep their eye on the money—the candidates' money—and collect something from them when they come to campaign. "They know too well that the only time they shall have the opportunity to be appealed to by the politician is during electioneering campaigns. Thereafter, the politician becomes inaccessible." According to Onyebadi, a candidate may promise a road, and even assemble tractors and graders and start clearing the bush before the election. "But once the elections are over, all machines are withdrawn and the road construction abandoned . . . .until the next round of elections."[11]

A few days after accompanying Diallo to Lassa, Betty and I returned there. Coulibaly and I walked to a rise overlooking the village. There he shared his hope for the future. "Democracy should bring us something," he said. As Betty and I descended the rocky trail to Bamako, I wondered: After the people of this village had waited through twenty-three years of dictatorship for "something" and only gotten three soccer balls, would they now just sit back and wait to see what a democratic government brought them? Or would the new political climate of freedom prompt them to lobby the government or join those who took to the streets when their hopes—or demands—were not met? I came away from Lassa with a clearer notion of how democracy can be translated into a wish list, which most likely would remain unfilled for years.

Timbuktu: Blue Men, Bullets, and Ballots

Timbuktu. I grew up knowing the name only from a song. For many, the name has come to symbolize a far-off place, the end of the world. It is one of the best-known, and least-visited, towns in the world. It is also one of the oldest African cities, and the place British explorer Mungo Park never reached in the late 1700s because angry residents chased away this perceived intruder.

On January 12, 1992, the day Malians voted on their new constitution, which called for competing political parties, a step toward the country's first democratic election, Betty and I were in Timbuktu, in Mali's northern desert. There we got a sense of how a culture that had never been democratic, a culture based on kings and empires, and later ruled by dictators calling themselves presidents, would take to the concept of free elections. We also got a measure of the depth of civil strife in the area, the kind that has blocked some African countries from attaining more political freedom, and which in some cases has led to war. Timbuktu is in the region of the famed *hommes bleus,* or "blue men," nicknamed after their indigo blue turbans, whose color eventually rubs off onto their tan skin. These proud nomads of the desert

Timbuktu, Mali, 1992
Malians vote on their new constitution, which they approved. Voter turnout was low across the country.

periodically fought with the governments of Mali and neighboring Niger in their quest for greater autonomy.

In December 1991, a few months before our visit, a local government security force attacked and killed a leading Tuareg resident of Timbuktu, in reprisal for a Tuareg attack on the town. As a result, most Tuaregs fled the city. Subsequent bandit raids along the road to Timbuktu were blamed on the Tuaregs. A diplomat in Bamako claimed some Tuareg were Libyan-trained bandits who stole four-wheel-drive vehicles and killed both soldiers and civilians. Their rebellion had consequences for the rest of Mali as it moved toward elections. If the rebellion continued, warned a Malian negotiator with the Tuaregs, Colonel Brehima Sire Traoré, the election might be postponed.

After all the hype, waiting, and curiosity, our arrival in Timbuktu was a little disappointing. The roads through town are sand; the buildings are made of mud brick, usually covered by a peeling, outer coating of mud. Among the highest structures are the minarets of the mosques, pointed towers of two or three stories, with protruding sticks which allow workers to climb up the sides and reapply fresh mud from time to time, as if smearing icing on a chocolate cake. During very heavy rains, it is not unusual for the roof of a home or two to collapse. Swarms of pesky, would-be child guides, desperate for business, diminished most of the exotic excitement of the town on our walks through the back alleys. Eventually, however, all but the most persistent children gave up. On closer look you realize Timbuktu is a museum. Here and there are markers on the walls of residences of early foreign explorers. One such visitor, René Caillié, experienced the sort of up, down, then up again feeling about the town that I did.

In 1830 he wrote, "On entering this mysterious city, which is an object of curiosity and research to the civilized nations of Europe, I experienced an indescribable satisfaction." Then he took a second look around: "The city presented . . . nothing but a mass of ill-looking houses, built of earth. Nothing was to be seen in all directions but immense plains of quicksand of a yellowish white color." Then he took a third reading: "Still, though I cannot account for the impression, there was something imposing in the aspect of a great city, raised in the midst of the sands, and the difficulties surmounted by its founders cannot fail to excite admiration."[12]

At the Ahmed Baba Center, a modest collection of small, one-story buildings on a sandy street, researcher Ali Ould Sidi opened a glass case displaying books in Arabic dating back 500 and 600 years. The dry climate helps preserve them; the pages looked almost new. Timbuktu, he explained, was begun around A.D. 1080 by Tuaregs. By around 1600, it was a thriving trade and academic center, attracting many students who came from as far away as Spain to study under local tutors.

At the time of our visit, Timbuktu had a population of only about 23,000. Many Tuareg had died in the droughts of the early 1970s and mid-1980s, which also decimated their herds of camels and other livestock. A couple of miles out in the desert that surrounds Timbuktu, Betty and I found a few Tuareg families living in their traditional squat, domed huts of sticks and reed mats covered with tough fiber cloth. Near one tent, Ibrahim Malale lay on the ground, protected from the sandblast wind by only a short mat and a worn blanket. He had run away after the killing of the Tuareg in Timbuktu a few months earlier, returning only recently to discover stray donkeys had eaten the reed mat walls of his former home. Now he, his wife, and their six-year old son, Mohammed, were surviving practically in the open until he could build another home. "If there's peace, we'll stay," he said, too weak from illness to stand. He apologized for not having any tea to offer us. "The people of Timbuktu say all Tuaregs are rebels. But it's not true," said another Tuareg, sitting on a mat in the protection of his reed shelter. He gave me his name but asked me not to use it. "We're not happy they [the rebels] continue like that. People are suffering."

In Timbuktu, I climbed the steps to the small police office. Inside, a policeman sitting at a wooden table insisted that Tuaregs are "animals, murderers. The only solution is to kill them." But it turned out there was another solution: a negotiated peace. After protracted talks between the government and Tuareg rebel representatives, the two sides signed a pact in 1995 to restore civilian rule in northern contested areas. Konaré traveled to neighboring countries urging war refugees to come home. A ceremonial burning of surrendered rebels' weapons was held in Timbuktu in March 1996.

Ethnic animosity is an old issue in Africa, as in other parts of the world, though the fact that the Malian empire is centuries old has given most tribes a chance to establish patterns of coexistence. Religious animosity is another ancient fact of life. When Park made the first of two journeys to West Africa in the late 1790s, he heard the following tale of religious strains from an old "Negro" who told him of his visit to Timbuktu: an innkeeper spread a mat for him (the "Negro") on the floor and laid a rope upon it saying: "If you are a Mussulman, you are my friend, sit down; but if you are a Kaffir, you are my slave, and with this rope I will lead you to market."[13]

★ ★ ★

On Mali's constitutional referendum day, January 12, 1992, lines formed early at the schools, mosques, and other voting sites in Timbuktu. "Lines" is a generous word; crowds bunched up at the doors of polling stations, while inside, temporarily disorganized election officials shouted at each other and the voters. But the confusion soon subsided and an orderly system was established. Men and women voters filed in wearing traditional, full-length robes. Many of the men wore brown, white, or indigo turbans; others were bareheaded. All the women wore head scarves. They were handed two paper ballots (white for *oui*, or "yes," pink for *non*, or "no"). In a screened-off booth, voters put the ballot of their choice in an envelope, then slipped it into a locked wooden box.

Reverence for the ballot is widespread in Africa. In Eritrea I saw women kiss the ballot box in the referendum that officially established that country's independence from Ethiopia, in 1993, after thirty years of war. The week of the referendum, thousands of Eritreans poured into the broad, clean streets of the capital, Asmara, to march and dance until the early morning hours. War veteran amputees in fighter jackets propelled their wheelchairs down the streets or were pushed by friends. As many as 50,000 Eritreans died in the war, and nearly a third of the population fled the country. The postwar optimism was almost tangible. "People remember the odds against them [in the war]," said Tekle Fassenchatzion, an Eritrean who taught economics at Morgan State College in Baltimore, Maryland, and who had come back to vote. "They feel they can accomplish anything." There was much to accomplish: whole hillsides lay barren of trees from overcutting and lack of reforestation programs; unemployment was high even before the troops, demonstrating during their independence referendum week for higher pay, were demobilized; and women, having fought alongside men, were determined to win an equal place in political organizations and in the workplace in a peacetime economy. Democracy was not a top priority for Issaias Afewerki, who took over as head of state after leading the later war effort. He was making no promises on when multiparty elections would be held.

★ ★ ★

On election night in Timbuktu officials counted ballots by lantern light. Voter turnout was low; many people had not received their voter identification cards in time, and others stayed home to listen to a radio broadcast of an international soccer game. Just 43 percent of the voters nationwide cast a ballot. The new constitution was approved by 99.76 percent, paving the way for multiparty, democratic elections.

Municipal elections followed later in January 1992, contested by twenty-three of the country's forty-eight parties that had sprung up. This time only about 30 percent of the voters turned out. ADEMA won 214 of the 751 municipal seats. Legislative elections took place in February and March. ADEMA won 76 of the 129 seats. Only an estimated 20 percent of the voters turned out. In the presidential elections in April 1992, Konaré won with 69 percent of the vote in a two-way runoff. Again, voter turnout was a mere 20 percent.

Democratic elections had come to Mali, but given their first chance to vote in fair elections, most Malians had taken a pass. In many rural areas, voters would have had to walk miles to the nearest polling place. In Bamako, indifference played a part in the poor turnout. Some voters I spoke with were not convinced their vote would change anything. And Mali's low literacy rates probably contributed to the dismal voting pattern.

In a late evening interview, after a long day of campaigning, his voice hoarse from shouting, Konaré had expressed his concerns that if Malians supported him and his party too much, Mali would be a de facto, one-party state, something he had worked against. I can't recall any other African head of state having such preelection worries. After Konaré's ADEMA party captured an easy majority in the new Parliament in 1992, he appointed some opposition party leaders, to form a coalition government and try to ensure agreement on key policies. Some of these leaders later abandoned the coalition over political disputes.

Postelection Twists

Two years after the election, in March 1994, I returned to Mali. In January of that year, France had devalued the currency used in Mali and thirteen other former French colonies, sending an economic shock wave through French West Africa. President Konaré was installed in the same hilltop office that Traoré had used. In an interview, he was formally dressed in an elegant open collar suit. He appeared less relaxed than in previous interviews, but he still sounded candid. He acknowledged that economic tensions in the country meant there was a risk of a military coup. Diplomats and opposition leaders were also talking about the possibility of a coup. Konaré saw "a big risk of a social explosion" due to the multiple public demands on the state's meager budget. Ordinary people were grumbling about almost anything.

"There weren't traffic jams like this before," Adama, a taxi driver stalled in downtown traffic, said with obvious exaggeration. "I've tried everywhere [to find a job]," said Draman Samake, who could not afford to buy a sewing machine when his tailoring apprenticeship had ended the year before.

"In a new democracy, the road is never a royal one," Konaré said. "Democracy is a process." He insisted that even when there were serious problems, the democratic process must be allowed to correct itself and not be abandoned to military rule. It is a hope shared by millions of Africans. Konaré listened to all sides on major issues and tried to operate by consensus. Some Malians and Western diplomats in Bamako complained that he was too conciliatory, too slow making up his mind. The real problem was money. The financially strapped Malian government simply could not meet economic expectations aroused by the arrival of democracy. But a military government was unlikely to do any better, and probably would do worse, according to gross data on food production under civilian and military regimes in Africa. And while accounts of corruption in civilian regimes are "outrageous," military governments are often just as scandalous—and usually increase the size of the military beyond logical defense needs.[14]

In December 1994, I flew back to Mali once again. Prime Minister Ibrahim Boubakar Keita was using the same office the popular interim military head of state, Touré, had used. As Keita tried to speak, his private phone kept ringing; he finally asked an aide to hold his calls. He reminded me that we had met before, in a small, dusty room at ADEMA's modest headquarters where he had been working on the Konaré campaign, in charge of foreign affairs. In early 1994, students had revived their old tactics of burning public property to force the government to pay higher scholarships. But this time the government used a more subtle approach to the student riots than Traoré had applied. Prime Minister Keita did arrest student lawbreakers. He also halted financial aid to students with low grades, which gave the government extra funds to pay larger scholarships to the majority of students. It worked; the suddenly-better-paid majority of students ended their protests. "The people had become hostage of a pressure group," said Keita. "A minority cannot take the majority hostage."

In April 1997, police fired tear gas and rubber bullets to break up a banned demonstration by Malian opposition parties upset about the way legislative elections were held. People burned car tires and ran from the police. Konaré's party won the majority of seats, but the opposition claimed the elections were "tainted with irregularities." The government admitted there were organizational problems; international observers cited problems with the distribution of electoral lists, voting slips, and electors' cards but called the elections "secret and fair."[15] Nevertheless, a court annulled the results and rescheduled the elections for July 1997. Again, ADEMA won overwhelmingly.

In his reelection campaign in 1997, Konaré said he did not want to be the only candidate. Finally Mamadou Maribatrou Diaby, an opposition party leader, entered the race. Most opposition leaders boycotted the election, demanding new registration lists. In what international observers again called a fair election, Konaré won with 84 percent of the votes cast. The turnout was 28 percent of the eligible voters, up 8 percent from the 1992 election. Violent demonstrations followed the election, and a number of opposition leaders were temporarily jailed. In his new government, Prime Minister Keita appointed several opposition members. Despite the demonstrations and complaints, the government survived, amid promises by Konaré to sort out the problems.

Mali, one of Africa's poorest and least-educated countries, had turned the corner from military to democratic rule. The salt mine prisons were closed; an elected president up on the hill was listening to the people. It could end in a moment if the army or the opposition got too restless. But the people had tasted a new level of freedom, including the slow, often ponderous process of democracy, a process open to diverse views and unable to satisfy most economic wish lists. At a conference in Bamako in May 1998, President Konaré said, "The high hopes raised by democracy are far from being satisfied but oppression and poverty are not inevitable."[16]

When a Dictator Digs in His Heels

In countries with military governments, like Nigeria, pro-democracy movements were often less successful than in Mali. Nigeria is the most populous country in Africa, with an estimated 114 million people in 1999. This compares to an estimated population of 630 million in sub-Saharan Africa in 1999.[17] The military repeatedly has thwarted efforts to regain civilian rule. Because of its oil, Nigeria has the potential of being an economic engine in sub-Saharan Africa, along with South Africa. But its economy has been damaged by massive corruption, inattention to agriculture during periods of high world oil prices, and years of inefficient and at times harsh government. Most democratic rights were stripped away from the people during the 1990s by military regimes.

When Chief Moshood Abiola, a wealthy publisher, won the 1993 election for president, he received support from most parts of the country. According to initial election results released by the government for fourteen of Nigeria's thirty states, Abiola won a majority in eleven of the fourteen. Later, Campaign for Democracy, a private organization, promulgated full results, indicating Abiola won nineteen states and his opponent, Alhaji Bashir Othman Tofa, eleven.[18] His victory was based on support nationwide, not just from areas where his own Yoruba eth-

Oshogbo, Nigeria, 1992
Campaign posters for presidential primaries were put up for the
1993 election, which was won by Chief Moshood Abiola. The
results were voided by the military government.

Lagos, Nigeria, 1992
Louisa Kofo Bucknor-Akerele (*center*, holding man's hand) ran successfully for
the senate in 1991. The senate was later dissolved by the military government.

nic group was in the majority. But Nigeria's military head of state at the time, General Ibrahim Babangida, annulled the election. When General Sani Abacha assumed power a few months later, he went farther, clamping down hard on the opposition, risking provoking ethnic tensions with his use of force by police from one part of the country against people of another. He also later arrested Abiola.[19]

Yet the pressure from Nigerians for democratic change has continued, despite the risks. Nigerian attorneys Clement Nwankwo and Olisa Agbakoba, for example, started the Civil Liberties Organization in 1987, the year I arrived in Africa as a correspondent, when General Babangida was head of state. Beko Ransome-Kuti, a Nigerian medical doctor, established the Committee for the Defense of Human Rights (CDHR). All three and many others continued their advocacy for human rights even after Abacha's clampdown. While African trade unions and other organizations can wield significant clout by rallying large numbers of people for protests—such as the strike by Nigerian oil workers after the aborted election there—dedicated individuals help keep the flames of freedom burning during the long years when there are no single incidents major enough to draw masses to the streets. They often operate alone, in full view, vulnerable to repressive regimes.

On one of my numerous reporting trips to Nigeria, I met Dr. Ransome-Kuti in his medical office. He pointed up to ceiling panels damaged during one of several raids by government security agents; one of the agents carrying out his arrest had entered through the ceiling. Ransome-Kuti's soft-spoken manner contrasted with his strong conviction that Nigerians deserved a democratic government and freedom from arbitrary arrest, torture, and state murder. Such high-profile opposition can be dangerous. Ransome-Kuti, who had consistently demanded accountability from the government on controversial human rights cases, was arrested in 1994 by the military. Although he lived in the southern coastal city of Lagos, former capital of Nigeria, he was taken to a prison in the far north. In 1997 Amnesty International launched a worldwide campaign for his release. He was freed in 1998 after the death of Abacha.

Many less-known Nigerians were also subject to arrest during the time of Abacha's rule. In 1996 one human rights report stated that human rights violations by the government "do not affect only Ni-

Lagos, Nigeria, 1992
Dr. Beko Ransome-Kuti, a
leader in Nigeria's campaign
for human rights and democracy, was jailed by military head
of state Sani Abacha in June
1994, then released after
Abacha died in office in 1998.

geria's elite political classes and those involved in protests against military rule. Nigerian citizens with no political involvement are subjected
to arbitrary and brutal actions of the Nigerian government in various
forms on a daily basis. Police and soldiers are better known for extortion, torture, and summary executions than for keeping law and order."[20] Nigeria, according to the report, was in a state of permanent
transition on the road to democracy, with military rulers showing no
evidence of their commitment to basic human rights and a return to
civilian rule.

Yet some Nigerians did not give up the quest for freedom. When I
visited Nigeria again in February 1996, the secretary general of
Ransome-Kuti's CDHR, Jiti Oguyne, met with several members of our
private delegation from the United States.[21] To see us, he had to walk
past government security agents in the hotel where we were staying; the
government tolerated our meetings with such dissidents but was not
pleased about them. In a room that might easily have been bugged,
Ogunye told us: "The human rights in Nigeria are very terrible; very
bad. The regime [of Abacha] we have on hand in Nigeria is unprecedented. We've never had it worse. People are taken from their homes
and dumped in jail; the family is not told where they are. Most are kept
in solitary confinement."

Another Nigerian who met with us in Lagos was Sylvester Odion,
general secretary of Campaign for Democracy. He had been arrested
the year before and only recently released. He was visibly nervous but

just as determined to tell his story. At one point he recalled how he was held in a cell so cold the "frost was coming in. I almost froze to death. I had no clothes on. I wrote [notes] with blood from urine." He was later put in solitary. "The meals were horrible: ground leaves with oil, and too much salt. I never had contact with the outside world." His account of arrests and prison conditions concurs with those described in human rights reports.[22] Like so many Africans in his situation, despite his vulnerability to further detention, Odion had not missed the chance to speak to us—representatives of the outside world. He had no objections to our taking notes, hoping his story would somehow make a difference in world opinion about Nigeria. We would soon be on a plane home, but what about Odion and others who risked their own safety to talk to us?

On the same trip, we visited the area where the late Ken Saro-Wiwa had led a rebellion against the government over lack of economic development and environmental issues in one of Nigeria's main oil-producing zones. Saro-Wiwa was hung in 1995, convicted by a military tribunal for causing the deaths of several traditional Ogoni leaders who were said to have opposed his campaign. Human rights reports and conversations I had with his supporters indicate Saro-Wiwa was not at the scene of the murders of the Ogoni leaders; the government accused him of inciting the murders. Saro-Wiwa's campaign was not pacific, however. His movement took over a large part of the Ogoni state, chasing police away and allegedly killing some government supporters. But human rights reports make clear that when the government sent police back to the area, the police used strong-arm tactics, resulting in many more deaths and destruction of many homes. At a brief visit to the site of the murders Saro-Wiwa was convicted of, government officials made every effort to portray things as normal. They were not. There was a heavy police presence in the area. One young man, trembling, approached me, wanting to talk. Shaking with fear, he said, "I've been seen [by local government officials]." He felt in danger talking to me but was determined. He said people in the area remained afraid and that the government was not addressing the basic problem of dire poverty, which Saro-Wiwa fought against. Later that day, we met with two members of Saro-Wiwa's organization in our hotel, which undoubtedly was under surveillance. One of the two said he had to leave early because it was getting dark. I asked him if he was afraid for his life. He looked at me and said, "Anything can happen."

One Nigerian killed for his earlier outspokenness was journalist Dele Giwa, assassinated in 1986. A stubborn and fearless critic of the government in his last years as editor in chief of *Newswatch* magazine in Nigeria, Giwa came under increasing scrutiny by security agents of the head of state, General Babangida. Instead of being intimidated by interviews with the agents, Giwa often flew into a rage and told them to stop trying to harass him and his publication. Shortly before his death, he had the following exchange with Lieutenant Colonel Halilu Akilu:[23]

Akilu: "You can't just write any rubbish against the government."
Giwa: "I can write what I bloody well please. Whether or not you like it, the truth has to be told and it is not for you to tell me what to write."[24]

That was typical of Giwa. "There was something in him that ultimately rebelled, if he found it necessary to do so. . . . All through his life, at some point, he always had to preserve fiercely his individuality and independence, and in the process, dominated others."[25] After the exchange with Akilu, Giwa went back to working on a sensitive article highly critical of the government.

On October 19, 1986, at 11:40 A.M., the bell at Giwa's home rang; the guard received a parcel from two men who drove up to the house at 25 Talabi Street in Lagos in a white Peugeot 504. The large brown envelope was sealed with red wax and stamped "Confidential"; it appeared to have come from the office of the military head of state. At 11:41, Giwa sat down and opened the parcel. "A blinding flash of light, followed immediately by a deafening explosion, shattered the serenity of [the] Sunday morning. A ball of fire sprang into the ceiling. The house shook."[26] Within the hour, Giwa was dead at a hospital. Giwa's murder recalled the assassination of Eduardo Mondlane, leader of the Mozambique independence movement, by a parcel explosion in 1969.

What would Giwa have written or said about Abacha's repression of most free expression and his charade about organizing a presidential election? "The transition program [leading to a presidential election] put in place by General Abacha is a sham," said Peter Takirambudde, executive director of Human Rights Watch/Africa.[27] By 1998 most prominent opponents had been arrested, journalists writing critical

Otta, Nigeria, 1992
Olusegun Obasanjo, a former military head of state
(1976–79), gave way to an elected civilian successor.
Then, in 1999, he was elected president.

articles had been jailed, and Abacha was on his way to being chosen president in a referendum set for August. All five government-approved "opposition" parties had been told to endorse him, and had, so no election was needed. But the people protested in one of the few safe ways left to them: they boycotted the April 1998 election of a national assembly. Overall, the turnout was extremely low; many polling stations around the country reportedly had only a handful of voters. An opposition coalition of pro-democracy groups still managing to function organized the largely successful boycott. "We shall continue with discrediting this transition process and hope that we can end military rule before August," said Olisa Agbakoba, leader of the organizing group, the United Action for Democracy.[28]

Then in June 1998, Abacha died of an apparent heart attack and was replaced by Nigeria's chief of defense, Staff Major General Abdul Abubakar Salam, who quickly released many prominent political prisoners and promised to release Abiola as well. But before he did, Abiola died, apparently of natural causes, verified by an international team of physicians. He had been ill, and his family had complained he had not been getting proper medical care while a prisoner. Soon after becoming Nigeria's military head of state, Abubakar promised return to elected government. On February 27, 1999, retired General Olusegun Obasanjo was elected president of Nigeria with approximately 63 percent of the vote with some reported fraud. He took office in May.

Tortured for Freedom

Logo Dossouvi, a broad-shouldered, heavyset, friendly young man, seemed too easygoing to stand up to a dictator in the name of democracy. Yet in his finger-shaped West African nation of Togo, where the president would later use his army against critics to enforce his version of government, Logo took a stand for freedom. To win the right to express one's self freely, Logo of Togo challenged Etienne (Gnassingbe) Eyadéma, the entrenched head of state who had never faced a competitive election and who did not allow freedom of speech. Eyadéma was a member of the Kabiye ethnic group, dominant in northern Togo. In 1963 he led a revolt against President Sylvanus Olympio, who had become authoritarian. Eyadéma invited Olympio's brother-in-law, Nicolas Grunitzky, a former prime minister, to head a new government. Then in January 1967, Eyadéma, who had moved up from sergeant to army chief of staff, seized power himself.

During his long rule he had fended off numerous coup attempts. In 1985 a wave of bombings hit Lomé, the capital. Eyadéma cracked down with arrests of political dissidents. By then his lavish style of ruling was well known. David A. Korn, U.S. ambassador to Togo from 1986 to 1988, says Eyadéma ran Togo "as his own private fiefdom. . . . while most Togolese struggled in poverty, he had a luxurious palace built for himself near his hometown. He kept a fleet of airplanes for his personal use, dressed up spiffily in expensive French suits, and threw huge gala dinners at which visiting dignitaries gorged on Norwegian smoked salmon and Chateaubriand steaks flown in from Paris, all washed down with the best French wines."[29] His lavishness compared to that of Zaire's head of state, longtime dictator Mobutu Sese Seko. Not surprisingly, Togo was Mobutu's first stopover on his humiliating exodus from Zaire after he was chased out of the country by rebels in 1997.

In 1990, Logo and several other college students began distributing pamphlets challenging government statements made on the state-run radio. There was no free press, so each time Eyadéma made a major

Lomé, Togo, 1991
Human rights lawyer Djovi Gally was among the first to speak out for democracy in Togo.

Douala, Cameroon, 1991
Newspaper editor Pius Njawe, one of many brave journalists across Africa who helped establish a freer press in their countries in the 1990s.

Lomé, Togo, 1991
Logo Dossouvi stood up to dictator Etienne Eyadéma. In the background stand the ruins of a large statue of the dictator, torn down during a push for democratic elections.

announcement, Logo and his clandestine network of students wrote and photocopied counterstatements; they distributed them by motor scooter around town. It was copy machines and scooters versus a military-backed dictator. The public, used to hearing only one version of things, eagerly read the underground tracts. One night in August 1990, the police caught Logo and twelve others.

"I was at home. It was about 7 P.M. Four people came in wearing civilian clothes and handcuffed me," Logo recalled when we met the following year in Togo. "They searched my home for seven hours. They turned everything upside down. They found nothing." The police were looking for evidence to use against him in court. Logo was jailed along with the other twelve. "We were thirteen in a little cell," Logo explained. "We had made a pact not to reveal the names of those we worked with." Eleven of those arrested were soon released, but Logo and Doglo Agbelenko were held longer, in a small cell where they had to sleep on the cold, cement floor. He and his cell mate did exercises to warm up. "We prayed a lot," said Logo.

Logo was taken to a secret torture center. Such centers were once more common across Africa. (In Sudan they are called "ghost" houses). "They beat me. They tied my hands behind me. Twenty policemen beat me with sticks and kicks." In addition, police tortured Logo with electric shock during a three-day period. The police wanted him to name who had been collaborating with him to print and distribute the antigovernment leaflets. "I said nothing," Logo told me, with a steely eyed look of conviction.

On September 21, 1990, he was taken to court. Perhaps the police thought he had been subdued by the torture. If someone had beaten you up, held you for a month or so, attached electric wires to your naked body, shocking you senseless, would you stand up in a court run by the same government that tortured you and complain? Defendants knew they could be returned to their cell and tortured again for not cooperating. Logo told me his torture was frightening beyond belief—but something in him said this was the moment to stand up for freedom, regardless of the danger. So Logo stood up in court and cried foul: he described how he had been tortured. This kind of bravery is an example of the individual decisions that have complemented work by organized groups in moving the pro-democracy movement forward in

Africa. Logo's story was rapidly spread all over Lomé. And thanks in part to Togolese attorney Djovi Gally, people soon had an opportunity to use his case to express their own anger at the government.

In the late 1980s Gally had given a series of public lectures in Lome criticizing the government. But his most controversial statements came in 1989 at a lecture organized by Dudley Sims of the United States Information Service in Lomé. Most U.S. officials I met in Togo were reluctant to rock the boat and speak out against Eyadéma as he continued his almost fascist regime. Sims, looking for ways to crack the ice in Togo, organized the lecture where Gally spoke. Gally called for a multiparty government to replace Togo's one-party rule. Sims was later criticized by his superiors for organizing the lecture, but Gally credits it with helping to open the dialogue in Togo for greater political freedom. The next day, Gally was summoned to a state security office and lectured about criticizing the government.

Now, as the lawyer for Logo, Gally made a move that would turn Logo's case into a national cause leading to disruption of the country's politics. The court had disregarded Logo's statements that he had been tortured, and found him guilty. Gally got the court to delay sentencing from the day of his conviction, in late September 1990, to October 5. That gave activists enough time to organize a large antigovernment demonstration. The day of sentencing, several thousand people showed up at the courthouse, filling hallways, stairways, and the streets outside. Before that protest, "you didn't demonstrate," a Western diplomat in Lomé said, typically declining to be named. The demonstration at the courthouse in Lomé caught the police off guard. But after a brief hesitation, police charged into the crowd, bashing heads with their batons. The police won the day, but now there was momentum for change. Strikes and more confrontations with police followed. In October, Logo and his former cell mate, Agbelenko, were granted presidential pardons. By early June 1991, Eyadéma had agreed to a National Conference of government officials and dissidents to discuss Togo's political future. His agreement, however, would prove to be merely a delaying tactic in his scheme to hang on to illegitimate power.

Many dissidents in Togo were southerners. Along the West African coast there has long been a political and ethnic divide between northern and southern ethnic groups. Those in the south, where colonial governments set up their headquarters, often got more benefits—such as schools and roads—than their northern counterparts; northerners generally felt left out. Eyadéma, a northerner, was not without supporters, even in the south. One woman with high-level political connections told me at her spacious home in Lomé, between shouts to her servants, that Eyadéma had "changed the country, even if it's a one-party state. There's been improvement." She cited construction of new roads, hospitals, and schools.

I met Eyadéma in 1990 in his presidential office at a breakfast for a group of journalists traveling on a UN-organized trip to Tanzania and Togo.[30] He sat at the head of a table both long and wide, as security guards stood solemnly along the walls. "Power flows from the people," he said, presenting his case that the people of Togo still wanted him as their ruler. He showed no impatience with our many questions, including those on human rights. Eyadéma said he had sent his representatives out to sample public opinion regarding an end to the monopoly of his party, the Rally of the Togolese People.

But the debate, as Eyadéma called the series of soundings, was "a comedy," according to one Togolese intellectual too afraid to have his name used. "The government shaped the questions." A number of Togolese told me that government officials would call people together, then lecture them on what they saw as the merits of a one-party system, namely, stability. One Togolese complained that what Eyadéma had brought them was not just stability but "immobility," with no political or economic progress. His critics said that at the government hearings officials would ask the people—many of whom depended for their livelihood on government jobs—if they were happy with the president. Not surprisingly, state television announced in mid-1990 that the people had expressed a "firm and unanimous 'no' to a multiparty system." Eyadéma again insisted he was willing to step down, but that the people always insisted he stay.

In his book *How to Be a Nigerian Politician,* Onyebadi, a former Nigerian journalist, warns of African leaders who claim to have the support of "my people," as Eyadéma did. "My people is a highly amorphous term," he writes. "Nothing says my people cannot be a man's wife and their kids . . . [or] a battalion of hangers-on, jobless people, outright thugs."[31]

Eyadéma staged rallies to give the appearance on state-run television that he was popular. Astute viewers claimed they kept seeing the same people over and over again among the so-called Eyadéma supporters. I got a glimpse behind the gossamer nature of such rallies at one organized to welcome the foreign journalists on the UN tour. We were flown north to visit Eyadéma's hometown of Kara. Minibuses met us at the airstrip and took us directly to a shrinelike exhibit built as part of Eyadéma's effort to create a personality cult. The exhibit featured wreckage of a plane in which, our guides said, Eyadéma had crashed. The fact that he was not killed was supposed to be a divine signal that Eyadéma was a saintly man spared to lead Togo. Next we went to his hometown. There, in a huge open parking lot, some 800 young Togolese stood cheering the journalists. I know journalists have some popularity, but this was unreal. As the other journalists walked into a large government building for a meal, I slipped into the cheering crowd. Several participants told me it was not their choice to be standing in the hot sun; they had been ordered there by government officials.

It was just a crack in the political facade of Eyadéma's regime, but it was enough to whet my desire to find out more. My opportunity soon came and in a way I had not expected. In separate conversations and locations, which I still do not want to reveal lest I jeopardize their safety, a Togolese man and later a woman observed that I was asking questions about human rights. I was not surprised at the risk they took in talking to me. I had repeatedly seen such risks taken across Africa by people eager to get the story out about abuses by governments. As a professional journalist I often promised anonymity to my sources in such cases. In the United States, such promises, given less often, might keep an official from being fired for criticizing a superior. In Africa, revealing a name could mean the source would be arrested, jailed, tortured, even killed. The man took me aside and, in privacy, gave me a long, detailed account of some of the abuses of power taking place in the country, accounts which I was later able to corroborate from other sources, both diplomatic and Togolese. The woman asked me, in the presence of several other persons, what I was trying to learn while in Togo. I took a chance that the others were not government spies and replied that I was concerned about the well-being of all people. It was general, but it was also a clue to anyone paying attention that I was not simply writing the economic stories the UN and the government wanted us journalists to write. She gave me her card and suggested I call her. I did, and she came to meet me at my hotel, driving me to see a relative who was active in the then underground human rights struggle in Togo.

That led to another interesting appointment, with a couple who told me to sit by the large statue of Eyadéma (later torn down) near my hotel and wait for a car to come by and blink its lights. Late that evening, a car slowed down and the driver blinked the lights. I walked over to the car, got in, and was driven to the home of an educated and employed couple who had two other friends waiting. In a long interview, they detailed abuses in the country, including: arbitrary arrests and detention of suspected opponents of the regime, torture of some dissidents, and expulsion of thousands of farmers from their lands. The cleared land was slated to be a game park, but critics contended Eyadéma and other senior officials had been using the land as a private hunting ground.

Such allegations surfaced in public in August 1991 at the National Conference Eyadéma had agreed to hold, confident he would be able to control it. In a large hall in the fanciest hotel in town, delegates from dozens of political opposition groups, most of which had been operating underground, crowded in to vent their anger. Like confident peacocks, men in colorful, full-length, West African–style robes, and others in suits, stood up to speak or roamed the aisles, talking and laughing. Women delegates also were elegantly dressed. The conference had the air of a social event. A handful of senior government officials were present as well. The conference was supposed to be a dialogue on the country's future between government and its many critics, but it was almost solidly an opposition conclave. One of the first things the delegates did was to declare the conference "sovereign." Opposition delegates claimed the right to make laws and to be above all other authority in the country. It was a claim that would ring hollow before long. Delegate after delegate denounced alleged atrocities and corruption of the regime. Their remarks were greeted by roars of applause. Those few speaking on behalf of the government were sometimes drowned out by boos. The conference was exciting but surrealistic: a few blocks from a sitting dictator's office, critics were openly denouncing him.

I first met Logo at the conference. We found a relatively quiet corner at the back of the hall, and I turned on my tape recorder and listened to

Lomé, Togo, 1991
At the National Conference of opposition and government delegates, an opposition leader was elected prime minister of Togo. Togolese president Etienne Eyadéma was able to block many of the opposition's democratic reforms.

Lomé, Togo, 1991
A government-sponsored rally was staged to support dictator Etienne Eyadéma, whose photo is carried by a supporter.

his story. When he had finished, he pointed out several of the policemen in the hall who had been among his torturers. Logo said he had shaken hands with them in a gesture of reconciliation.

★   ★   ★

I left Togo just before Joseph Kokou Koffigoh, a lawyer and human rights leader, was elected interim prime minister at the conference. The delegates also passed resolutions reducing the powers of the president to symbolic ones. Koffigoh was to take up day-to-day management of the government. I took a taxi across the nearby border to Benin, which had held a successful national conference leading to elections and a new president. As I checked into a small hotel, the desk clerk asked me if I had heard the news about the borders being closed in Togo. He said tanks had surrounded the hotel where the National Conference was meeting. The government demanded the delegates come out of the hotel and go home; but they had refused. While the tanks remained parked outside, the delegates inside finished selecting interim government leaders; then they went home. Koffigoh set up his new government, even though Eyadéma said it was not constitutional. Later that year, in December 1991, Eyadéma struck back. His army, consisting primarily of his own tribesmen, surrounded the prime minister's office, firing into it with artillery. More than a dozen people were killed. Koffigoh, who hid in a protective area, pleaded for intervention of French troops. France was the last colonial power in Togo. The French had intervened before to help Eyadéma keep his dictatorial rule; now they refused to help Koffigoh establish a democracy. The French position on democracy in Africa was more one of words than of substance. Koffigoh was alive but politically dead. At one point he was escorted by the army to Eyadéma's office, where the two decided on the makeup of a new cabinet—with more Eyadéma supporters. In his well-guarded office, the following November, Koffigoh told me Eyadéma "has never wanted democracy, and he doesn't want it now."

The Togolese did get some changes. In multiparty elections for Parliament the opposition won a substantial number of seats. By 1993 there were some sixty parties. Most of the opposition lost faith in Koffigoh, considering him a "captive" of Eyadéma. Presidential elections were repeatedly postponed. When they were held, in August 1993, they were widely boycotted by opposition parties, which claimed irregularities in the election process. U.S. and German observers withdrew from election monitoring over similar complaints. Eyadéma won 96 percent of the vote, down only a few percentage points from his previous sham elections. Only 36 percent of the voters turned out. In legislative elections in February 1994, the opposition won a narrow majority.

But some things did not change. The opposition's choice of prime minister, Yao Agboyibo, was stymied when Eyadéma nominated another opposition leader, Edem Kodjo, who took office over Agboyibo's objections. In the next by-elections for the national assembly, in 1996, Eyadéma's party won and managed to sway several more members to his side, giving the party a majority. In January 1997, on the thirtieth anniversary of Eyadéma's seizing power, thousands of soldiers and civilians marched through the streets of Lomé to celebrate in another staged show of support for him by "the people." A few weeks after the celebrations, journalist Abass Dermane, editor of an opposition weekly, was detained for allegedly defaming the president in an article titled "The Horrors under Eyadéma's Regime." Abass was released a few days later, after writing an apology to the president.

But human rights had continued to deteriorate in the years since Eyadéma's questionable election in August 1993. Between the election and May 1994, Amnesty International reported, there had been dozens of extrajudicial executions by security forces, twenty-one deaths of government opponents in custody, and there were at least thirteen political prisoners, some of whom had confessed under torture. Amnesty also reported that since 1992, more than 250,000 Togolese had fled the country, fearing human rights violations.[32] (The United Nations estimated the population of Togo in 1992 was 3,763,000.)

Eyadéma stayed in contact with the leaders of the opposition, apparently not so much to comply with their demands as to keep them split. It was a pattern some other rulers were using. Eyadéma kept in touch with international lenders, as well, who continued to show their support. In May 1998, the World Bank made another loan to the government of Togo, $17 million, and with the International Monetary Fund announced plans for new loans through the year 2000.

★   ★   ★

Logo of Togo had helped pry open a Pandora's box that held changes for his tiny country—with some positive results—though the changes had not resulted in a new head of state. In Kenya, another head of state was hunkering down in the face of growing demands for more freedom, more human rights.

3 THE POLITICS OF AMBIGUITY

Nairobi, Kenya, 1992
Monica Wamwere and a group of other mothers of political prisoners
in Kenya, staged a year-long public protest to win their sons' release.

OR most tourists in the Kenyan capital of Nairobi, it was a pleasant afternoon for shopping before traveling to more game parks. Only a few of them caught a whiff of the tear gas drifting from Freedom Park.

Kenya's game parks, like those of South Africa and Tanzania, draw a steady flow of tourists from around the world. At Amboseli, on Kenya's southern border, in full view of the snowy peak of Mount Kilimanjaro, you can sit on the balcony of a luxury lodge and watch elephants browse on the grass. At dawn, you ride in a minivan onto the plains to gaze at families of elephants munching their way along a marsh. Your Kenyan driver stops the van so close you don't need a telephoto lens. Betty and I would drive down to Amboseli from Nairobi in our 1986 Toyota station wagon, a car built too low for most off-road travel but well suited for many of the maintained tracks in Kenya's parks. We adopted a strategy of continuing our game drives during the postlunch nap and tea breaks that tour drivers offer their clients. Then we could park by elephants or study a pair of lolling cheetah without other vans near us. We tried not to disturb the elephants, but sometimes they got so close we were the ones disturbed. On one occasion, as Betty held her camera out the side window, she had to change her lens from telephoto to wide angle and point her camera higher and higher as the elephants got closer and closer. A large bull suddenly stopped just behind our car. Sniffing the air, he wheeled gracefully about, facing us. Our front and rear windows were rolled down; Betty was in the backseat, on the same side of the car as the bull. Anxiously I put my hand on the key in the ignition and slipped the shift into first gear. I wasn't sure whether to start the engine and risk startling the bull or wait. I waited. After sniffing the air for a few more seconds, he turned and sauntered off noiselessly on giant padded feet.

Such are the delights of Kenya for visitors. But Kenya was not all fun, especially for Kenyans. Street crime in Nairobi, the capital, threatened Kenyans and visitors alike. The economy had deteriorated. And as in much of Africa today, Kenya's politics has all the ingredients of a classical drama: passion, suspense, cruelty, bravery, and subtle twists in the plot that leave the outcome as well as the nature of some of the characters in question.

In Freedom (*Uhuru* in Swahili) Park that afternoon, in March 1992, as most tourists went about their business of pleasure, Monica Wamwere, a short, fearless Kenyan mother with a gap between two of her front teeth, stood up in the midst of a group of mothers, many of them elderly. As Kenyan riot police began circling the mothers, she started singing a traditional song of her Kikuyu people, adding her own political words. "We are going to stay in the wilderness . . . and pray for our children to be released."

The two dozen or so mothers, many of them farmers, were on a daytime hunger strike demanding freedom for Kenya's political prisoners, including their sons, who had criticized the government. Some of the prisoners had called for free elections and an end to one-party rule. The government claimed they had tried to overthrow the regime, and, according to human rights reports and statements by some of the imprisoned, had tortured many of them to extract confessions.[1] Kenyan officials, including President Daniel arap Moi, denied charges of government torture, though they did admit that an occasional case of torture may have occurred contrary to government policy.

An open-sided canopy offered the protesting mothers protection from the sun, but they had no protection against Kenyan riot police armed with long, wooden batons and wearing face shields; some wore gas masks. The only shield the mothers had was a human one: dozens of Kenyan supporters sat in a tight circle around the canopy, arms linked, determined not to be moved.

While students in Togo, Mali, and many other African countries in the 1990s aimed at bringing about a change of government, Africans across the continent, such as the Kenyan mothers, were showing a brave determination to force governments to show greater respect for basic human rights. Such determination, carried out in protest marches and strikes, as well as the more methodical pressure of lawsuits against authoritarian governments, was having an effect in many countries, including Kenya. Even as the mothers sat there, defiantly, the politics of Kenya was changing. A year earlier, the police might simply have charged the mothers the first day of their strike and locked up their leaders. But the mothers had been striking for a number of days now, and the government seemed unsure what to do about them. This was not politics as usual. President Moi was usually much more decisive.

Kenya was still a one-party state, and Moi still ran things pretty much the way he wanted. But there had been numerous opposition rallies calling for multiparty elections; a number of African heads of state had already been forced into agreeing to such elections. In Kenya, as in most African countries, previously, police usually broke up rallies and demonstrations by political opponents of the head of state. But now pressure was being applied against leaders like Moi to open up the political system to competitive elections for the first time in decades.

Kenya, which became independent of the British in 1963, had had only one other president, Jomo Kenyatta, who had chosen Moi as his vice president in 1967. Moi was sworn in as president when Kenyatta died in 1978. Moi quickly released all political detainees. He took some popular measures, including ordering free distribution of milk to primary school children; he expanded the university admissions, doubling enrollment. The later move allowed many of his fellow Kalenjin and others to go to college, but it also played havoc with the national budget and the quality of education.

Kenyatta was a Kikuyu. He had picked Moi, a former teacher and a Tugen (part of the cluster of small tribes called the Kalenjin), to help him with political issues in which the Kalenjin were involved. Kenyatta often ignored other tribes in filling government posts, favoring the Kikuyu. Moi in turn made no effort to hide his own tribal bias, sacking many qualified senior civil servants of various tribes, especially Kikuyu, and replacing them with Kalenjin and others who often had little or no training for their new jobs. Kenyatta had stacked the civil service with members of his Kikuyu tribe and favored central Kenya—home of the Kikuyu, Embu, and Meru—in parceling out state funds. Moi shifted more economic development to other parts of the country, a move appreciated by those who benefited but resented by those who didn't, especially the Kikuyu. But many Kenyans were leery of seeing another Kikuyu elected president. They felt left out of power and deprived of many economic benefits when Kenyatta was in office. "People who lived outside the central Kenyan [predominantly Kikuyu] region . . . looked to Moi as a welcome change in the nation's ethnoregional balance of power."[2]

In June 1982, as Moi grew increasingly intolerant of criticism—a characteristic which became more evident as the years passed—Kenya, under his leadership, constitutionally became a one-party state. When Moi assumed office he adopted the slogan *Nyayo,* Swahili for "footsteps," promising to follow in Kenyatta's footsteps. But as he solidified his power, forcing out of government many of his own allies and supporters of Kenyatta, he turned the phrase into one identifying his own administration. Kenyans began talking of Moi as *Nyayo* and few dared to ask what happened to his intentions to follow Kenyatta.

In August 1982, a faction of the Kenyan air force, with some university student support, attempted a coup but failed to take control. The government eventually suspended death sentences against twelve airmen and granted amnesty to most of the other detainees. For a while, Moi continued this conciliatory pattern, including meeting with students at Nairobi University. At the same time, Moi worked to solidify his political base in the then sole party, the Kenya African National Union (KANU). And he began stacking the government with members of his own small ethnic group.

In 1986 it was revealed that a number of Kenyans had been detained under the Public Security Act and were to be charged with publishing seditious documents. The detainees were allegedly members of an underground organization named Mwakenya.[3] The coup attempt had shaken up Moi, and he was determined to root out his enemies. He began cracking down on dissidents, becoming more and more intolerant of criticism and more restrictive of people's freedoms. Moi considered the growing opposition against him as largely a Kikuyu plot. International human rights organizations contend the Mwakenya existed but never amounted to much of a threat to the stability of the country.[4] Nevertheless, many alleged Mwakenya members arrested in government sweeps were brutally tortured in 1986 and 1987.[5]

Martin Luther King, Jr., in his civil rights campaigns in the United

States in the 1960s, had promised dignity behind prison walls for those arrested during the protests. But instead of dignity, many Kenyan political prisoners found torture. "Systematic torture is carried out by the Special Branch [a government security force], who interrogate political prisoners on the 24th floor of Nyayo House [a government office directly across the road from Freedom Park]," according to a U.S.-based human rights organization.[6]

Mirugi Kariuki, a Kenyan arrested on charges of treason in 1986, suffered permanent kidney damage from Special Branch officers who assaulted him. According to documents submitted to the government by Kenyan attorney Gibson Kamau Kuria, Kariuki was "blindfolded and taken before a panel of eleven plain clothes interrogators who savagely beat him with whips, pieces of rubber tyres and timber." At later sessions, he was "sprayed with water coming out of a pipe at great pressure every day at 4 A.M., at 7 A.M., at about 1 P.M., about 7 P.M., and at midnight—that water making him feel as though he was being punched with sharp objects; being hit with two buckets of water every morning after he refused to make a confession."[7]

Another form of torture was especially hideous; it involved the use of flooded cells. The small cells were painted red or black; the door was raised a couple of feet from the ground so that the cell could hold some water. "Prisoners must either stand in the water, causing intense pain and swelling in the feet and ankles, or sit, causing damage to the buttocks and genitals as well as inducing infections in the bladder and kidneys."[8] It was not just men who were tortured. A Tanzanian woman accused of murdering her husband, a crime to which another man later "confessed" after torture, was herself the victim of police brutality. "She was stripped naked, her legs were forced open and she was tortured with pliers. Her head was covered by a tin filled with hot peppers . . . peppers were inserted into her injured genitals."[9]

Kenya had an undeserved reputation as a mecca of economic progress and political stability. This image was based on a number of factors: the presence of many European settlers; Kenyatta's charismatic and international stature; use of Nairobi as a base for many foreign journalists and development agencies; tourism; and government discouragement of probing political research by foreign scholars.[10] In reality, Kenya's economy was in serious decline by the late 1980s, a problem critics linked to massive official corruption. And as political pressure for change grew, especially from the Kikuyu, Moi showed less and less regard for human rights. If the Kenyan government had had the repressive reputation Ethiopia had under Mengistu Haile Mariam, or of the military regime that took over Sudan in 1989—countries well known for government torture—the brutality carried out at Nyayo House might have been less surprising.

★   ★   ★

It was against this background that the first of six Kenyans profiled in this chapter, constitutional and human rights lawyer Gibson Kuria, challenged the government over allegations of torture against some of the Mwakenya detainees. The other Kenyans profiled, in addition to Monica Wamwere, include: attorney Pheroze Nowrojee; a political opposition leader, Martin Shikuku; an insurance saleswoman turned political activist, Njeri Kababere; and a conservationist and political activist, Wangari Maathai.

Jailed for Telling the Truth

Gibson Kuria got in trouble doing what defense lawyers are supposed to do: defending the accused. His problem was that the accused were considered enemies of the state. It was 1987. There had been a few derailments of railroad cars, blamed on the underground movement Mwakenya, and Moi was determined to prevent another attempted coup. Word had leaked out to some Kenyan lawyers, including Kuria, that the authorities were torturing Mwakenya defendants. Sham trials were under way which lasted only a few minutes. If an accused somehow stubbornly refused to plead guilty, he was returned for more torture.[11] Three of the accused managed to get word to Kuria, asking him to represent them. He prepared a suit against the government, seeking to halt the torture and claiming damages for his clients. Before he filed the charges, he told the *Washington Post*'s Nairobi-based correspondent, Blaine Harden, that "if I am picked up, it is important that people know the reason why. I have determined that people's rights must be enforced, so I am going to press the government. I have decided I am not going to compromise on the principle even if it means being detained."[12]

Kuria is obviously a principled man. Usually looking contemplative and a bit unkempt, he works in an office that also looks unkempt: his desk and shelves are piled high with books and papers. He is most comfortable giving long, detailed talks about constitutional law; the basis of those talks is always the principle to which he is dedicated: the rule of law. He is one of the most stubborn people I have ever met when it comes to human rights, which are guaranteed under the Kenyan constitution. Kuria does what infuriates any egotistical political leader who would trample on those rights—he cites the law.

Like many African leaders, Moi was not used to that. To Moi, the law was something to be ignored when necessary. Richard Nixon tried to do that in the United States but was finally forced to resign. Coups have replaced some African leaders when the people got fed up. In the

Nairobi, Kenya, 1987
Gibson Kamau Kuria, a Kenyan human rights lawyer, was detained for alleging government torture of political prisoners, then resumed his legal work after his release.

Nairobi, Kenya, 1992
Wangari Maathai, a conservationist and political opponent of President Daniel arap Moi.

1990s, a significant number of leaders were "thrown" out by the ballot after years of disregarding the law.

On February 26, 1987, the day after Kuria filed the charges, he was detained by police, just as he had anticipated. On March 13, 1987, on page one, the *Washington Post* ran Harden's article on the alleged torture in Kenya, the day after Moi visited the White House. The headline "Police Torture is Charged in Kenya" ran under a photograph of Moi and President Ronald Reagan. Moi apparently was furious. Harden was nearly kicked out of the country; he was allowed to stay only after the U.S. Embassy pressured the government at the last minute. In one of his rare interviews, Moi told Harden, "There has never been a torture in Kenya." Then he went on to say: "If there is a minor incident, it should not be taken to mean Kenya government policy. How many people die in Michigan? Is this U.S. government policy? We are the freest country in Africa."[13] There is a scenario under which torture might have taken place without Moi's personal orders, but probably not without his knowledge. Sycophantic officials, eager to please the head of state, might have interpreted Moi's anger against the alleged Mwakenya group as a carte blanche for torture.

Shortly after I first arrived in Nairobi, in June 1987, after the *Washington Post* article, a senior Kenyan official welcomed me into his office. He did not want to be quoted by name, but he pointed out that since the president had returned from the United States there had been no more reports of torture in Kenya. It seemed to be a roundabout way of admitting there had been torture, which the official obviously realized. I felt, perhaps naively, that this particular person was offended by knowledge of the torture and glad when it stopped. Moi could hardly apologize for it or condemn it, having denied it ever happened. Systematic torture apparently did die down after the publicity on it.

Kuria was not tortured in prison, but he was subjected to tiring and humiliating physical exercises. He was released after nine months. Meanwhile, in an act that must have frustrated Moi and his team, but one which hints at the depth of resistance in Kenya and many other African countries today, Kuria's law partner, Kiraitu Murungi, filed the same papers Kuria had been trying to file. Murungi was not arrested. He later went on to win election as an opposition member of Parliament.

★   ★   ★

Another Kenyan who resisted what she saw as the arbitrary nature of the Kenyan government was conservationist Wangari Maathai, who later would be with the striking mothers the day they faced the riot police.

A Political Conservationist

President Moi had a plan to build a sixty-story building for his political party in downtown Nairobi, in Freedom Park, one of the few green spots left in the so-called Green City in the Sun. Outside the building would be a four-story statue of himself. Moi, like many political leaders, was not known for his modesty. Most Kenyan currency carried Moi's picture; a sports stadium and a main street in Nairobi, plus numerous schools around the country, also bore his name. He did not discourage visitors from bowing to him. Broadcasts on Kenya's state-owned radio and television often began with the phrase "His Excellency . . . today"—no matter what was happening elsewhere in the world. An ardent supporter of Moi might argue that all this was not ego, but nation building, an effort to instill a sense of unity. It came across as ego.

Maathai was founder of the Green Belt Movement, a private, non-profit, tree-planting, and conservation organization based in Nairobi. When she learned of the planned construction in 1989, she began a publicity campaign against it, pointing out that the land was public and needed by Kenyans. With such low salaries, many working Kenyans could not afford lunch in restaurants. Most earned the equivalent of only about a dollar a day and used any open space to eat their lunch; Freedom Park was a favorite spot. In the park, some Kenyans take naps beneath the trees; others sit on benches to chat; photographers hawk their services; ice cream vendors push carts through the crowd. Moi's planned construction would have usurped a third of the park.

Western lenders finally got involved, calling the project unsound. For one thing, there was the potential for an earthquake in the area, experts noted. Lenders also argued that it made little sense to provide development loans to Kenya if the government squandered large sums of its own money on grandiose projects such as party headquarters.[14]

President Moi was upset by Maathai's challenge on several counts. First, she was a woman; Moi rarely missed an opportunity to try to put her down her in his speeches. Second, she was a Kikuyu, which was especially irritating since he equated most Kikuyu with his opponents. Third, like most African leaders of the nondemocratic school, Moi took any criticism of his government as criticism of himself. Moi could have had the trees cut down on the intended construction site as he sought uncertain funding, but he did not. Months after donors derailed the project in 1990, Moi ordered the fencing around the site removed. Freedom Park went back to the people, with the trees. Maathai quickly dubbed the area of the intended construction "Freedom Corner."

★   ★   ★

As the pro-democracy movement was picking up speed around Africa in 1990, another Kenyan lawyer stubbornly challenged Moi's handling of an inquiry into the death of a popular critic of the government.

Accused for Insisting on Speedy Justice

The small courtroom in downtown Nairobi was packed—with lawyers. Every seat was occupied; even the aisles were full. It was an impressive moment. Many of Kenya's most respected and experienced lawyers were there, along with some new ones seeking their professional niche in a country where the law was abused by the government that was supposed to enforce it, where cases with political overtones almost always went the way the president wanted them to go because he was given the power to appoint or dismiss judges.

The accused was attorney Pheroze Nowrojee, a thin, quiet Kenyan citizen, a Parsi of Indian descent. Wearing a suit and tie, he sat at a table in the front of the courtroom. Usually the one to be presenting a case, today he was being judged. Nowrojee had dared to criticize the judicial system for delay in a sensitive case that might expose possible government involvement in the death of a popular critic of the government, Bishop Alexander Kipsang arap Muge. Muge had been killed in a car crash, August 14, 1990. The immediate question in the case: was it an accident or premeditated murder?

Just a week earlier, Labor Minister Peter Okondo had threatened that if Bishop Muge traveled to Busia, in western Kenya, he would be killed. Muge had been attacking the government on various issues, including the alleged stealing of private land by senior government officials. His attacks were especially annoying to the government because he and the president were both from the same ethnic cluster of tribes, the Kalenjin. Okondo's threat against Bishop Muge could not be ignored in a country where there had been a number of political assassinations.

As Bishop Muge was returning from Busia, having gone in spite of the minister's threat, a truck rammed into his vehicle and he was killed. The government quickly opened a case against the truck driver. The family of the bishop wanted an inquiry into the death—a broader investigation that would go beyond possible guilt of the driver to see if anyone else might be involved. The government agreed to the inquest, but only after starting the trial against the truck driver who slammed into Muge. If the driver was found guilty, the verdict would give the government a reason not to proceed with the inquest. So Nowrojee, on behalf of Bishop Muge's family, filed suit to delay the truck driver's trial to try to oblige the government to proceed with its promised inquest first. A judge heard the petition to stop the trial but delayed responding. To try to speed things up, Nowrojee told me he wrote a letter to the registrar "asking him to ask the judge what was happening, and stating that these continued delays in the judgement could be construed as being timed to have the proceedings in the truck driver's case be completed first." What Nowrojee was alleging, in so many words, was a possible government cover-up in the death of a popular dissident. The court responded quickly this time, citing Nowrojee with contempt of court. "The significance of this was not in respect of myself, but it was an attempt to intimidate the bar," said Nowrojee.[15]

Both Kuria and Nowrojee are quiet in demeanor, humble in manner. Both have a bedrock sense of justice that comes through in their carefully chosen, strong, and fearless statements insisting on the rule of law. Nowrojee is especially measured in his way of talking. When I asked him what it was that drew him to human rights cases, a dangerous choice, he responded calmly, deliberately. "I think the criteria is: is there a need? We would be glad not to be doing this, because that would mean, hopefully, that there were no cases brought arising out of violation of human rights. We would be happy to go back to contract and property transaction and bills of exchange."

That day, when he himself was judged, in December 1990, many of his fellow lawyers backed him up with their presence in the courtroom. They were, Nowrojee said, "indicating by their presence, both to the judges, and to the government—and to the public—that these charges they saw were charges against the whole profession and that they resisted that." After a long winding discourse, the judge acquitted Nowrojee, who called it "a very important victory in relation to showing the younger members of the profession that they should not be stopped in their defense of any accused person; that the clients' interests come first, and the government's efforts to intimidate the legal profession in Kenya had failed." But the government won its point, too: the promised inquest was never made.[16]

Such legal sparring with the government is not the stuff of fancy headlines. As far as I know, I was the only foreign correspondent in the courtroom the day Nowrojee was acquitted. In February 1995, at a dinner in honor of an outspoken Kenyan magazine *Law Monthly,* Now-rojee gave a stirring speech about democracy. Though ill (he ducked out and went back to bed immediately after the speech), he spoke with passion about freedom and human rights. One afternoon in his home, a few months later, Nowrojee was not hesitant to point out the kinds of tactics the Kenyan government had been using to intimidate opponents: "continuous use of the newspaper, the party newspaper, to spread a mixture of truth and lies, and to use the technique of repeating lies constantly; . . . a monopoly on radio . . . on television . . . to insure that the electoral commission is not an independent body; . . . to insure that [voter registration] is not an automatic process; . . . to block public meetings of the opposition parties."[17]

To Nowrojee, one of the most troubling legacies in his country would be the acceptance of repression. "The danger of not expressing one's political view is very, very clear. And it is the experience of the Nazi period in Germany [when] many people said that they were not political. And they thought that was the correct way to be, but all of them were subservient to the Nazi demands. If each Kenyan simply refused injustice, even to himself, oppression and this government's activities would be reduced very substantially."[18]

★　★　★

A politician with a flair for the dramatic was soon to challenge injustice in Kenya—and get away with it. His gesture would help many Kenyans overcome their fear of standing up in public for greater political freedom.

The Day Fear Broke

Sometimes a single act of bravery can nudge a people toward greater defiance of authoritarian rule. Even one day can help break peoples' fear. Such a day in Kenya was November 16, 1991, four months before the mothers began their protest in Freedom Park. The day started quietly, but it would end violently.

Tipped off by U.S. diplomats, a small group of journalists were waiting that morning outside the U.S. Embassy in downtown Nairobi. A car with tinted glass windows pulled up to the curb; a rear window was lowered, and journalists got a fresh look at the man about to defy the president of Kenya. It was Martin Shikuku, an opposition leader and former member of Parliament. He was on his way to address an illegal political rally that would denounce Moi's one-party rule. Shikuku, a man with a quick laugh, a sense of theater, and a good sense of timing, leaned toward the reporters crowding up to the window.

An outspoken opponent of the government, Shikuku was irrepressible. He had been expelled periodically from the previous Parliament for his controversial statements against the government, but it never silenced him. He once claimed in Parliament that senior Kenyan officials clandestinely were stashing away large amounts of money in Swiss bank accounts. Pro-government members of Parliament loudly challenged him to present proof. Shikuku tabled a sheaf of papers; they were not a secret list of deposits but a World Bank document on the estimated amount of money sent out of Kenya by Kenyans. It was not the smoking gun he had implied he had, but for critics of the government, it was proof enough of high-level stealing. Though not taken seriously by most Kenyans as a possible president, in part because of his lack of organizational skills and his unpredictability, Shikuku was admired for his bold candor and as someone in the forefront of the democracy movement.

Shikuku's planned opposition rally was not the first in Kenya in the post–Berlin Wall political era. In July 1990, two other opposition politicians had tried to hold one calling for multiparty elections. The two, Kenneth Matiba and Charles Rubia, were arrested and imprisoned without trial. Their rally had been scheduled for July 7. In Swahili, seven is *saba* and July is month number seven, or *saba*. So the aborted July 7 rally became known as *Saba Saba*. Police blocked the rally, triggering riots in several cities. The term *Saba Saba* became such a unifying slogan among Kenyans that Moi banned its use.

The November 16 rally Shikuku hoped to address was planned for Kamakunji, an empty field in a low-income neighborhood near downtown Nairobi. There Shikuku hoped to make his call for multiparty elections. The rally was scheduled shortly before a Paris meeting of international lenders who would decide whether or not to make new loans to Kenya. President Moi announced the rally would be illegal, which meant police and the government's paramilitary force would be

used to arrest organizers and participants. Shikuku and the other organizers had gone underground a few days before the rally to avoid arrest. That morning, only a short time before the scheduled start of the rally, was the first time reporters had seen him since he began hiding. But just as he was starting to address the journalists, he spotted a police car approaching.

"We better move," he ordered the driver. "We better move. Let's move! Let's move!" he shouted.

The police car was getting closer; the rally might never take place. But Shikuku's driver sped away, prompting a dramatic chase by police. The driver zipped down Haile Selassie Avenue and just managed to squeeze through a roadblock being set up a couple of blocks away by the paramilitary troops, who were armed with batons. A reporter for the Voice of America, Sonya Lawence, and I ran to my car and sped after him, but we were blocked by the troops. We drove in the opposite direction, then circled back on another route. On a hill a few blocks from the rally, we could see clouds of tear gas; police were chasing people away. A few reporters had gotten to the scene, where they, too, were chased and some of them clubbed by riot police. I was not eager to risk a clubbing myself; I also had an obligation to get my story out to my newspaper and its radio service instead of spending the day in a hospital or a jail. So I decided not to go to the site but stay nearby and be ready to escape from police. We began interviewing some of those who had been chased from the rally.

"They are throwing tear gas to [sic] people," said Danson, offering only his first name. Then he added, defiantly, angrily: "I'm not afraid." I asked him why he was at the rally. "Nobody wants corruption. Nobody wants to fight. They only want to talk, peacefully." Another man approached us on the hill. He, too, was angry. "As long as they [the opposition] are not going to be violent, they should be let to have a meeting, peacefully."

Nairobi, Kenya, 1992
Supporters of Kenyan presidential candidate Kenneth Matiba carry a poster of him before the country's first multiparty elections in many years. One of several candidates, he finished second behind President Daniel arap Moi and lost to him again in 1997.

From our location we could see police chasing people, and we could smell the tear gas. "Police are trying to beat people with guns," said Samuel, another young Kenyan. No one wanted his last name used. "The people are just peaceful. They want two parties. Kenya needs two parties." I turned to the crowd and asked how many were *bila kazi,* the Swahili term for "jobless." Most of them raised their hands. As we continued our interviews, we noticed a new pattern. The year before, people had run away from the aborted Saba Saba rally when police started clubbing people. This time was different. Some who had run away from the tear gas and clubbing were now heading back to the rally; they were not giving up. People were taking a stand, going defiantly back to the rally or as close as they could get to it. "We are determined to fight now," shouted another man. "It's today or never."

Just then a truckload of police stopped at the bottom of the hill. They jumped down and started jogging up toward us, carrying their batons and wearing helmets. We halted our interviews and ran to my car. I had anticipated both lanes of the divided street might be blocked—and they were—so I had parked in the median strip, facing away from the rally. We reached the car, jumped in, and drove off just as the first police got to within a few feet of the rear of the car. I gave my cassette of taped interviews to my colleague, who slid it inside her bra as a precaution in case we were stopped and searched by police. I sped down the median until we reached a section of open street. After filing my story I returned to the same hilltop for more interviews.

Shikuku had managed to reach the rally; his driver had pulled brazenly around a police car guarding the entrance to the street leading to the Kamakunji grounds. At the rally, Shikuku made a few quick remarks from the roof of a van he had switched to. Then he was driven rapidly away as police cars began chasing him. The chase proceeded along some of Nairobi's main streets to the cheers of bystanders. Sitting on the roof of the van, his legs draped over the luggage rack, Shikuku held both hands over his head, giving a *V* sign with each hand.

V in Kenya was more than a sign for victory; it was used by those calling for multiparty elections to replace Moi's one-party system. It had become such a symbol of rebellion that officials had tried to ban its use. One official even threatened to chop off the fingers of anyone caught flashing the *V;* some of Moi's aides would say anything to try to please him. But the *V* continued to be used. Even at a rally addressed by Moi, a man sitting on the ground in the front row hesitatingly flashed the *V* and even held up the headline of an opposition magazine which read "Moi Must Go." The man was partially hidden behind a police-man standing in front of him with his back to the man. Photojournalists crowded up to take what looked like a photo of the surprised police-man. But the photographers merely used the policeman's legs to help frame the smiling man flashing the *V.*

As Shikuku fled the police that day, riding exposed atop the vehicle, some Kenyans said they heard the crack of gunfire. The police finally caught and arrested him, though he was soon released. The chase was filmed by a TV crew who managed to stay near Shikuku's van. Photos of him riding victoriously through the streets were spread across local newspapers and magazines in Kenya and around the world. The rally—though largely aborted—marked a psychological turning point for many Kenyans. People had come out, refused to go home as ordered, and decided enough was enough.[19]

After the rally many Kenyans began openly expressing their disgust at being told by an authoritarian government what was best for them, at having only one party, and at having leaders they considered corrupt. People who used to tell me their political opinions only in whispers in public began airing their views without looking over their shoulder for a government intelligence agent. "The rally," said Kenyan pastor Timothy Njoya, "was a milestone. It brought together a lot of people—thousands from all directions of the city. It shows also the confidence people have with the alternative to what we are having now—autocratic and dictatorial leadership."

Another person who noted this historic moment was the U.S. am-bassador to Kenya, Smith Hempstone. One of the most conservative U.S. envoys in Africa, but also one of the most outspoken for democ-racy, Hempstone had defied President Moi's order to stay away from the rally. He and the German ambassador attempted to reach the rally but were turned away by police. Their joint appearance that day sent an unmistakable message to the government from two of Kenya's major donors: stop the intimidation; switch to democratic rule. "We would be happy to see them [the Kenyan government] clean up their act as a single party . . . but obviously we'd be most pleased if they went directly to a multiparty system," Hempstone said on the eve of the rally.

Few other American ambassadors would go on record that bluntly. I once chased the U.S. ambassador to Côte d'Ivoire up some embassy stairs trying to get a comment from him on democracy in that nation before its adoption of multiparty elections. He escaped without comment, to the amusement of some of his subordinates.

Moi Agrees to Multiparty Elections

Just days after Shikuku's ride and the police beatings at the rally, international lenders meeting with the World Bank in Paris in November 1991 agreed to freeze new aid to Kenya. Their decision was a departure from their usual wrist-slapping gestures against autocratic rulers in Africa. The Bank, the International Monetary Fund, and bilateral lenders to Kenya had been pressing Moi to make economic reforms while steering clear, at least publicly, of calls for democratization. Those at the Paris meeting decided to freeze new aid to Kenya and Malawi; the freeze was aimed at forcing economic reforms, the lenders said. Officials at the meeting took pains to avoid mentioning democracy, even though Moi and President Hastings Banda of Malawi had refused to abandon one-party rule. I called Paris, reaching an official at the meeting. My sources in Nairobi had been telling me the Bank was drawing the line in the sand for both Kenya and Malawi at least in part because of human rights abuses. Far down in my notes is confirmation by an official at the meeting that such concerns were part of the reason for the cutoff of new funds. But the public statements issued later by donor nations and the Bank focused on the need for economic reforms, in the Bank's traditional, neutral language.

The public statements might have fooled some people, but not Moi, who was already facing growing opposition at home. Within a week of the meeting Moi announced his decision to allow competitive elections in Kenya for the first time in a quarter of a century. Moi apparently believed he needed aid to keep the country going and had to make some major political gesture to obtain it. Almost the entire Kenyan development budget of the state—including construction of roads and

Nairobi, Kenya, 1992 Kenyan president Daniel arap Moi bowed to domestic and international pressure and held multiparty elections in 1992 and 1997. He won reelection both times against a divided opposition.

other public works—came from foreign aid. The potential social disruption from a halt to new projects, plus the economic penalty of no more foreign exchange for purchases abroad, might be too much for his government to sustain without provoking more riots.

Moi's decision caught some of his own supporters off guard. At the KANU party conference in December 1991, I spoke with a delegate from the northeastern part of Kenya moments before Moi made his surprise announcement to allow multiparty elections. "No," he said, Kenya did not need multiparty elections. "Yes," he said, he supported the president. "No," he could not think of any issue on which he had ever disagreed with the president. After the announcement, I spoke to the same delegate again. "Yes," he said, in an unabashed about-face, speaking just as confidently, multiparty was just what Kenya needed. If he had winked, I might have felt better. But he was just bubbling along, like most party stalwarts, parroting whatever the president said. A junior Kenyan civil servant in Nairobi gave me an honest appraisal of why government officials were afraid to speak their minds: "One mistake and you're out."

The job of low-level officials in such an atmosphere is difficult. One official in the Foreign Ministry called me and found himself in a dilemma. He complained about an article I had written about his boss, the minister, Stephen Musyoki. A few days earlier I had helped host a lunch for the minister sponsored by the Foreign Correspondents Association of East Africa. In his luncheon remarks, the minister had presented an almost paranoic view of the universe, blaming outsiders for most of Kenya's problems. The Foreign Ministry official said he found my article very "negative." I suggested he mention that to his boss, since the minister's taped remarks formed the basis for it. He said he would call me back; he never did.

★   ★   ★

A combination of stiff pressure from international lenders and strong pressure from the Kenyan public had forced a major political change. When the mothers' strike began, Moi was anxious to avoid further international repercussions over human rights, but he was also determined not to let the strike become a rallying point for the opposition.

Standing Firm for Principle

The day the mothers were confronted by the riot police in 1992, I stood among the women, not by choice or because of bravery on my part, but because I am the husband of a quietly courageous woman who is a photojournalist. Like many Kenyan and foreign journalists, I had been stopping by the mothers' strike almost every day since it began. That afternoon I received a call from a colleague; she told me that riot police were gathering at Freedom Park, and that my wife, Betty, who was taking pictures there, had given her some film. Betty wanted to ensure that some of her film got developed in case the police confiscated photographers' cameras. I quickly finished my story for that day's deadline, then drove to the protest site. Truckloads of police with batons, helmets, and face shields were milling around the area. Dozens of Kenyan supporters were sitting on the ground in a circle around the mothers; Betty was inside the circle. I made my way through the police and supporters to join her.

"Don't you think we should leave?" I asked her. "These guys [the police] are serious. They're coming in." More police had arrived and were beginning to circle the protestors and mothers. A showdown was certain. "No," Betty replied calmly. "I've been here most of the day, and I think I should stay to see what happens." She continued taking pictures. I was the frightened one, amazed at how calm the mothers—and

Betty—were when I was sure we risked getting our heads smashed. I thought of how the civil rights marchers in the southern United States must have felt as police came toward them with clubs, tear gas, rifles, and sometimes dogs at places such as Selma and Birmingham, Alabama.

★   ★   ★

One of the youngest women on the scene that day was Njeri Kababere, an insurance saleswoman who had slowly been drawn into politics. Her story is another example of how nonpolitical Africans got involved in the pro-democracy, pro-freedom, pro-human rights movement that swept much of sub-Saharan Africa in the 1990s.

An Insurance Woman Turns Activist

Njeri Kababere is a soft-spoken, modest, and attractive woman who had a small insurance business of her own. She could have stayed in that profession, but several rebellious strands in her makeup apparently came together and took her in an unanticipated direction: she was now an advocate for freedom in a land where that activity was not safe. "It is a dangerous life," she explained, as we sat on the balcony of my apartment in Nairobi on one of those frequent springlike afternoons.[20] The flowers in the garden, singing birds, and cool breeze provided a peaceful atmosphere that contrasted sharply with the harsh realities of the path Kababere had chosen for herself.

"How did you become an activist?" I asked. She recalled the 1982 attempted coup in Kenya, when some university students and lecturers she knew were arrested as subversives. "The case of David Olo Onyango particularly shocked me," she said with emotion. After the coup attempt was put down, in Nairobi, students were told to go home. Onyango took the train down toward Mombasa, on the coast. "The police usually have patrols on the train. They decided to go through the luggage. Inside his suitcase they found his university essays; one of the essays examined social and economic problems of Kenya. They just arrested him and decided the material was seditious." Onyango was tried, found guilty, and sentenced to four and a half years in prison. "I remember him asking the court, 'How do you know what is the line

Nairobi, Kenya, 1995
Njeri Kababere, a Kenyan human
rights and political activist.

between constructive criticism and sedition?'" Onyango went to prison, served his sentence, then moved to Canada. "I could immediately identify with such a person," said Kababere. "He was about my age; he was a student." She inhaled deeply, then continued. "He had a constructive mind. He was thinking about his country, about himself, about his family, and questioning many things. I would say that's how I started getting involved with politics in this country, by just seeing the injustice that I saw in courts, from 1982 onwards."

Kababere used to skip out of her insurance office and go to the courtroom to hear the Onyango proceedings. Anyone showing up at a controversial hearing was almost certain to come under scrutiny of the government's Special Branch, the intelligence service. When I first got to Kenya in 1987, several political cases were still being tried. One day as I was waiting in a courthouse hallway, an apparent member of the Special Branch began watching me. As he leaned forward, peering around several men between us, I leaned back against the wall. Then when I leaned forward to get a better look at him, he leaned back. I could never be certain whether my phone in Nairobi was tapped. One Western consultant to the government said it was unlikely, given the difficulties the government had with technical problems. Yet a journalist from the United States, Colin Clark, who was particularly aggressive in uncovering government human rights abuses, heard breathing on his line, most likely from his tappers, he said. Sometimes he greeted the apparent phone spies on the line. Clark's work permit renewal was denied, forcing him to leave Kenya. The government did not appreciate human rights observers from Kenya or abroad, especially international journalists who took an interest in the cases of political prisoners. The government seldom expelled foreign journalists, however, even though most of us regularly wrote about human rights and other topics sensitive to the government.

Many Kenyans were aware of the sham trials of students and dissidents and did nothing about them. Why was Kababere moved beyond concern to action? I asked her if she got some of her determination to be involved from her mother. Her mother was the victim of a very abusive marriage; there was a lot of violence, she explained. The family lived in a slum in Nairobi, yet Kababere's mother managed to earn enough money to send her children to some of the best schools in Kenya. "Life was very hard. And she [her mother] was very strict; very, very strict. You should never cross her path. In those days," she said passionately, her voice suddenly dropping to a whisper, "I would always think, God, you DARE not do this [cross her mother]. But now I look back and think, thank God she was that strict. My brothers, my sister, and myself take pride for her being our mother. We've seen other people being brought up in the areas we got brought up in, and they either got into drugs, a lot of drinking, or never really bothered to go to school. We used to shuttle between my mother's house and my father's house, my father's house and my mother's house." Her parents had separated. The father had been instructed by the court to pay upkeep for the children and their mother. Despite the fact that he had a good job, he did not support them, she said. Finally her mother just accepted supporting the children as her "burden" in life and set about to do it. "I don't think we ever lacked anything. Even today I wonder: I earn maybe thirty times what my mother used to earn [she laughs], so much more. And I have only one child. And sometimes I'm broke."

Kababere lived in two worlds from a very young age: the rich world of her schoolmates, from well-to-do families, and the poor one of her neighbors in a section of Nairobi known as Jerusalem. Pride played a part in her growing resolution to be actively involved in helping others. "You have to be proud of yourself. I think it's very difficult to take pride in yourself without looking at other people. If I had a good life throughout and I never cared about what other people were going through, I wouldn't feel proud of how my life is running." Another part of her activism stemmed from her school days, when she was secretary of the debating society, and both a school and dormitory captain. "I had a lot of responsibilities with the school. I remember whenever there were debates, especially political ones, I would be put up as a speaker. So even within my school days I think there was that streak—I don't know [she hesitates] whether you'd call it political or caring."

As an adult, she became an activist not just for political causes but for more mundane issues such as commuters' rights. She rides Nairobi's infamous *matatus,* privately operated minibuses which are consistently overcrowded. On those buses, the fare collectors are called "touts"; they are a special breed. Some touts are courteous; most are hardworking—even playful, executing dangerous acrobatic leaps off and on the moving *matatus* in traffic. But most touts have a reputation for being rude and pushy. Kababere, who does not like to be pushed, tried to stand her ground with touts. "How can you push us like this?" she would complain. "How can you make us sit like bags of potatoes?" A tout would reply: "Why can't you buy your own car? Why can't you take a taxi?" Kababere fired back: "No, I have a right to be in this *matatu* [she is speaking rapidly now, as if on a ride]. I have a right not to be pushed around." Sometimes she got pushed off a *matatu* at the next stop by a tout as a result of her complaints.

Kababere's efforts to stand up for human rights—big and small— included, as a student at the University of Nairobi, helping some of the political prisoners and their families. "I used to visit them in prison and also introduce myself to the families and just say, 'I'd like to help'." It was her first real involvement in Kenyan politics, a kind of backdoor approach which would lead her to broader issues. After the attempted coup of 1982, things went from "bad to worse," she said. Even before

In 1992 a group of Kenyan mothers gathered in a downtown Nairobi park to begin a year-long protest demanding the release of their sons who were political prisoners. *(Top left, counterclockwise):*
1. A protesting mother, Gladys Kariuki *(facing forward)*, wearing a Release T-shirt, is surrounded by other protesters.
2. The mothers hold the protest *(background, under canopy)* at a site called Freedom Corner in Uhuru park. Police maintained close surveillance.
3. The mothers walked to the attorney general's office to demand the release of political prisoners. *(Left to right, facing forward)*: Monica Wamwere, Njeri Kababere, and Wangari Maathai.

the coup, several university lecturers had been arrested on suspicion of trying to overthrow the government. Some were from Kenyatta University, others from the University of Nairobi. In 1986 and 1987, the pace of arrests by the government increased, as the Moi government clamped down on alleged conspirators.

In December 1990, Kababere read about Monica Wamwere's efforts in forming the organization Release Political Prisoners (RPP) to try to get her son and other sons out of prison. She went to one of their meetings—in the home of conservationist Maathai—joined, and later became their spokesperson.

★   ★   ★

One of the driving forces behind the protesting mothers was Monica Wamwere. She symbolized the courage of many ordinary Africans and their determination to win more political freedom, including the right to criticize the government.

A Mother Fights for Her Son's Freedom

Monica Wamwere became politically active after noticing that the opposition leaders preparing for the 1992 elections in Kenya did not address the issue of incarcerated prisoners. She wanted her son, Koigi Wamwere, freed. She vowed not to stop protesting until he was released.

"Why is the government so mad at Koigi?" I asked Wamwere in July 1995, three years afer the mothers' protest. "Because he speaks the truth," she said. "He likes following the truth. He doesn't like lies. And he insists on the rights of ordinary people." Koigi had been imprisoned on trumped-up charges of trying to overthrow the government with a few rifles. He had been a perennial thorn in the side of the Kenyan government due to his unwillingness to curb his tongue about the autocratic, corrupt power he saw in Kenya, especially in the office of the president. Koigi's accusations against the Moi government were similar to those from international human rights organizations, which cited political control of judges, torture by police, intimidation of journalists, destruction of a private press that printed critical publications, massive government corruption, government-inspired ethnic clashes, and the unsolved murder in February 1990 of Kenyan minister of foreign affairs Robert Ouko. Ouko's charred body was found in a field near his home just as he was preparing a report to the president on government corruption. A Scotland Yard investigator called in by Moi pointed the finger of suspicion at senior government officials before Moi called him off the case.[21]

Thunder crashed as we continued talking; it was pouring now. I had located her again for a long follow-up interview in the All Saints Cathedral in Nairobi. She explained one of her first moves to draw attention to the prisoners issue in 1991. "I started at the High Court, and I shouted at the top of my voice that people were being neglected and they were going to be killed [executed under the death penalty] without anyone knowing. When I said that, a lot of people listened to me." She found her next audience indoors, in early 1992 at a women's conference held in downtown Nairobi, in the Kenyatta International Conference Center, a tall building shaped like a giant corncob. Wamwere was asked to come to the front of the audience. Instead of talking just about her son's incarceration, she spoke of her own suffering as a result of being his mother. She said her house had been destroyed several times, apparently by government-hired thugs. The prosecution of her son had left her family destitute, she explained. "My children have never been employed. They are mostly in prison; they've not built houses," Wamwere said. The women were shocked. People did not talk about such things in public. They urged her to continue, and she did. A second mother, whose son was in prison with Koigi, was called forward to speak. She said her son and some others were about to hang for their crimes. She was not going to sit aside and let it happen quietly. "Those boys are going to hang, and we are not going to wait for them to hang."

★   ★   ★

In late February 1992, some of the mothers planned to go to the prison just outside of Nairobi where their sons were being held. They would camp there until their sons were released. This plan presented a dilemma for some in RPP, including Kababere. If the mothers went to the prison, they could easily be stopped along the road outside the city, making their protest ineffective. "So we had two choices," said Kababere. "Did we sit back and see these mothers go [to the prison] by themselves? Or did we assist them in organizing for a successful protest? We decided on the latter." Looking around for another site, the RPP chose Freedom Corner, the section of Freedom Park named by Maathai after she helped block government plans to build there. "It's right in the center of the city," Kababere explained. "It's a free park. Everybody has the freedom to sit there. And if you decided to sit there even in the night, really, it's a public park." People might just sing protest songs, she added. "People are always singing songs. And Christians are always preaching. [Lunchtime preachers attract crowds regularly in open spaces in downtown Nairobi.] And since it's a peaceful protest, this is a good place to be." There was another, more subtle advantage to holding the protest in such a public place. "It won't take the attorney general [Amos Wako] and any other person who wants to find out what is going on too long," Kababere said.

The mothers agreed to shift their protest to Freedom Corner. RPP members, including Kababere, rushed around town telling political opposition parties of the plans, mobilizing whatever support they could get in terms of funds and supplies, and began making posters for the protest. A week after the women's conference, Attorney General Wako met with some of the mothers. Wako, a lawyer who prided himself on a willingness to be reasonable, told the mothers to go home and wait for his response. But the mothers would not hear of that. They said they had been home for months waiting, to no avail. At the time, there were some fifty political prisoners, according to RPP, including eight facing death sentences. The eight had been in jail for roughly a year. "So this wasn't something you could just sit back and say, 'Yeah, I'm sure the government will do something'," Kababere recalled. "So we told Amos Wako that 'no, we were going to wait for the answer at Freedom Corner'." If Wako had really thought the women would just go home and keep quiet, he was wrong. There is a tenacity, a rocklike quality about many Kenyan and other African women. Some look strong, others don't, but it is their spiritual strength that gives them the courage to act. Wamwere and the other mothers who went on the daytime hunger strike in the park are among them. You see others in markets, on farms, in law offices—women who don't mince words, who can be pushed, but only so far.

So the protest began, across the street from the infamous Nyayo House, the government building in which a number of Kenyan political prisoners had been tortured. Across the other street from the protest was a government statue that looked like a giant black, chunky rock, topped by a rendition of Mount Kenya, a mountain sacred to the Kikuyu. A big hand protruded from the top of this rock; the hand held a mace, the same style mace Moi carried as his symbol of office. There was little mistaking the intention of the statue: Moi dominated the mountain—and the Kikuyu. It was political architecture.

There was an ethnic accent to the mother's strike. Wamwere and many of the other protesting mothers were Kikuyu, a group largely opposed to Moi. The president had been warning Kenyans they would see ethnic wars and a possible disintegration of the country if multiparty politics replaced his one-party rule.

★   ★   ★

The first day of the strike drew mostly curious onlookers. But by the second day, support for the mothers began. "A lot of people just started streaming in with glucose, water, orange squash, juices. We thought, 'Wow, we are getting somewhere'," Kababere said. At the beginning the mothers sat on the grass, leaning against trees as they welcomed family and other supporters. The mothers slept on mats under the branches of the trees. Soon someone erected an opened-sided canopy to protect the women from the weather.

Going to Freedom Corner became a kind of litmus test for the average Kenyan bent on change. It was likely that government security agents were monitoring movements at the park and could easily question visitors; the government considered the protest an illegal, unlicensed meeting. In Kenya, control of licenses, or permits, for public meetings was the method used to block many opposition rallies. Government officials argued that the only events blocked were those likely to become riots, that the licensing process was needed to keep public order. At times they appeared to be right, but no one could recall when a government rally was blocked for lack of a license. From the government's point of view, opposition leaders were not bent on reform, just on getting into power. On that point, Kababere and many other Kenyans agreed. Kenyans were deeply disappointed that leaders of the opposition had let them down, seeking to advance their own interests instead of working together to defeat Moi or bring about real reform. Most opposition leaders, for example, gave little support to proposals to change the constitution to limit the authoritarian powers of the president, apparently preferring to inherit the presidency with all its powers intact for their own use.

Since Moi had announced plans for multiparty elections, the opposition had succeeded in tearing itself apart. The original Forum for the Restoration of Democracy (FORD), of which Shikuku was a founding member, broke into two parties: Ford-Asili became primarily a Kikuyu party, and Ford-Kenya largely Luo, with nominal Kikuyu support. A third party, the Democratic Party, headed by Moi's onetime vice president Mwai Kibaki, drew both Kikuyu and Kamba support. Several smaller parties were also formed. The mother's strike offered these opposition politicians an opportunity to be seen supporting a popular cause. Yet they never fully embraced the mothers on their hunger strike. Only a few opposition figures, such as the Reverend Njoya, came almost daily to be with them.

The Attack

As the riot police began closing in that day, the mothers seemed outwardly unperturbed. Most of them were sitting; Wamwere was standing and began singing in Kikuyu. I held my microphone up to record her song; as she had done on other occasions that week, she reached out and took hold of it. The police were now walking toward us from all directions, with clubs in their hands. What followed is recorded on the tape I was making for Monitor Radio. Wamwere and some of the other mothers continue to sing. Then, shouts. Wamwere alone is singing her protest song. Next, screams.

The police waded into the ring of human protectors who sat with locked arms hoping to shield the mothers. They were armed with clubs against these unsung heroes of the day, using tear gas to force the would-be protectors to flee; many of them piled on top of the mothers in a desperate attempt to escape the police. Standing under the canopy with the mothers, I only had time to grab my microphone and tape

Nairobi, Kenya, 1992
Police with batons and shields clubbed supporters of the mothers and threw tear gas into the tent where the mothers were sitting, causing people to flee in panic.

Nairobi, Kenya, 1992
A protesting mother, Gladys Kariuki (in white T-shirt), is overcome by tear gas.

recorder and try to protect it as the first of the supporters piled onto me. I was standing next to Maathai; we were both pushed to the ground. Still more people piled on, and I feared we might be crushed or smothered. For a fleeting moment I thought calmly of death. Just then a policeman tossed a tear gas canister at us. The government later denied using tear gas against the mothers. But my head was still in the open, and I saw the canister coming toward me as if in slow motion. It slightly gashed my head, bounced off, and landed a few feet away; gas began spewing out in a cloud. It was a nasty combination: tear gas and being pinned down. With so many people on top of me, I could not escape the acrid fumes. Then the gas worked to our advantage; people on top of us began peeling off to escape the gas, dashing away in all directions.

Within a few seconds, those of us on the bottom were free to flee as well. Thinking that the police might be targeting journalists, I hugged my tape recorder to my stomach and charged at a smoky opening in the crowd. Lunging forward like a football player trying to slice between opponents, I dashed out from the canopy and toward the street in front of Nyayo House. Still leery of being chased by the police, I ran out into the intersection. It was then I realized how disoriented I was from the tear gas, which was still burning my lungs and making me cough. This was my first gassing. Ever alert to opportunity, several Kenyan pickpockets started to put their hands on me; that particular corner had quite a few. I asked them not to bother me, and they actually backed off. Then, as my head cleared, I looked around for Betty. There was no sign of her.

I walked back toward the mothers' protest site, scanning the scene until I saw her. She was still near the canopy. She had managed to duck both the fleeing crowd and the worst of the tear gas. Standing next to a canopy support pole and table, she had continued photographing. Most of the mothers had fled. Police milled around but were no longer chasing anyone; nor were they looking for journalists. Betty was able to keep taking pictures. But I wanted to get her out of there before some policeman decided to club her or grab her camera. "I need to get some more shots," Betty insisted. "No, I'm also your husband; we're going home," I insisted more strongly. Reluctantly, she followed me out of the park. We got into our car, which had not been damaged, though a large number of police had been standing by it. We drove home. One of her pictures published in *The Christian Science Monitor* showed police with clubs chasing people out of the area where the mothers had been sitting.

In a final gesture that day, several mothers stripped to the waist. "The stripping act traditionally signifies an extreme form of curse and defiance of the aggressor. In this case, the women were cursing and defying the authority of the oppressive Kenyan state."[22]

Wamwere, recalling her thoughts of that day in my 1995 interview, said that when the police broke up the protest, she was determined not to give up her efforts. "Weren't you afraid?" I asked her. "No, I wasn't afraid at all." "Even when the police came?" "Even when the police came I was not afraid. Because we were fighting for the truth. At that particular moment, we felt very bad, and very humiliated. I assured myself that even if they were to [send] us back home, I would still come back."

She was sent by police back to her home in Nakuru. She arrived there at 5:30 A.M. "By 6 A.M. I had organized myself and was on the way back [to Nairobi]."

The protest did not die with the violence of Moi's police. Instead, the mothers regrouped in the basement of the nearby All Saints Cathedral, an Anglican church. There they continued their protest, with periodic press coverage. I was a member of a community chorus that practiced and performed in the cathedral, so I frequently visited the mothers. The Reverend Njoya, a perennial thorn in the side of the government because of his outspoken criticism, continued ministering to the mothers in the church.

When I met Wamwere again in 1995 at the cathedral, we walked downstairs to the same "bunker," or basement room, where the mothers had continued their protest. The bunker is a small, fortresslike space, with two doors, one leading upstairs, and the other outside. The windows are covered with a grill mesh for security against thieves. For a year, the mothers had lived there Spartan style, sleeping on mattresses or sometimes just mats laid on the cement floor. Officially the mothers remained on a daytime hunger strike, but the issue of food became less important than their continued presence in the church as a reminder to the government that the mothers still wanted their sons released. "I went home after one year and ten days," said Wamwere, smiling, speaking loudly as always, confident she had done the right thing. She had stayed on with a group of six or seven other mothers, one of whom was eighty-two.

It was appropriate that they carried on their vigil in a church. Prayer has long been an integral part of African protests for freedom, and African church leaders often are a part of demonstrations. Individuals like Wamwere pray their way through difficult times. When I asked her how she was able to maintain her good spirits during a whole year in the bunker, she laughed. "I could remember in the Bible . . . Paul was released from jail for speaking the truth. And I had the strength of the fact that I knew Koigi had done nothing wrong, only speaking for the people. And that . . . made me happy, not sad."

During the first week the mothers were in the bunker, the police tried, halfheartedly, to dislodge them one sunny afternoon. The mothers were sitting on the lawn outside the church when a small group of riot police arrived, equipped with clubs and shields. The women ran into the bunker and locked the door behind them. Betty photographed the police as they walked around the church lawn. The leader of the police occasionally waved a menacing arm toward her. Betty and the police did a dance of sorts: the police advanced, Betty retreated; the police backed off, and Betty advanced, continuing to take pictures. A church official appeared and told the few journalists on hand that the church objected to harassment of people seeking sanctuary. Sanctuary was not always sacred in Africa. In Rwanda, during the genocide of 1994, thousands who sought to escape the killings by seeking sanctuary in churches were instead trapped in them and slaughtered.

Eventually the mothers succeeded. Twelve months after they began their protest, all but one of the approximately fifty known political prisoners had been released. (The remaining prisoner was serving a life sentence related to the attempted coup in Kenya in 1982.) Pressure on Moi to improve human rights, exerted by international lenders, may have helped convince him to release the prisoners. But international lenders had initiated the cutoff of new aid four months before the mothers' protest began and Moi had not released the prisoners then. A senior Kenyan official later told me Moi had been ready to start releasing the prisoners before the strike. But if that is true, it was a well-kept secret.

When Koigi Wamwere was released, his mother sent word for him to come to the church before going home. "I told him this is where we have been. . . . I told him I'm happy not only because of you, but for all the others who have been released." Koigi said he was glad people had come out to fight for him, especially the RPP. But once out, Koigi "assured the people that the fight is still on, because nothing had changed until then; that people had to fight on," his mother said in the 1995 interview.

A Political Spring, Then More Repression

The year the mother's strike began, 1992, was a kind of political spring for Kenya, especially for women's organizations. With multiparty elections coming in December, and already under pressure domestically and internationally to move toward democracy, the Moi government eased up on its usual pattern of repression of critics. This gave many women's groups a chance to try out their political wings. Some 2,000 women came together in February in a national convention to try to set an agenda for change. One of their priorities was to get more women to run for public office, and they succeeded. In the 1992 multiparty election, more than 250 women ran for local or national office, double the number from earlier elections. Six women were elected to Parliament, and about fifty won local government seats, the largest number ever, the result of hard campaigning and support from the various women's groups.

"Women also demonstrated a unique ability to close ranks across class, race, ethnic, religious, and other identities, and to create unity in diversity as well as a women's agenda to guide the movement in shaping democratic change."[23]

★   ★   ★

As the December 29, 1992, election for president and Parliament neared, public excitement grew. Under a constitutional amendment passed by the preelection Parliament, Moi controlled, the winner in the presidential contest had to receive at least 25 percent of the vote in at least five of Kenya's eight provinces. This meant a candidate could win only if he or she had strength across the nation, not just with one or two ethnic groups. Moi calculated this gave him an advantage over the opposition parties, whose strength was based mostly in a few provinces.

Voter turnout was the highest since 1963. There were technical delays in many polling stations over lack of supplies—proper forms, ink, and other items. It was not clear if the delays were due to poor organization or an effort to discourage voters. If the strategy was discouragement, it failed. I visited several polling stations in Nairobi. Old and young stood patiently for hours in lines snaking back in some places for blocks. Many had arrived before the polls opened. After the election there were allegations from his opponents that Moi had cheated enough to ensure his victory. But he would not have had to cheat much.

Moi was elected to another five-year term with only 36 percent of the vote against the divided opposition. If at least two of his three top opponents had backed a single candidate, they would have been able to defeat him. The opposition won 88 parliamentary seats compared to 100 for Moi's party. This produced the most notable political change: Parliament was once again a place of lively debate as opposition members raised questions about alleged corruption and challenged the government on many other issues. But despite such open talk, little was done in the way of reforms.

The public mood among those who had sought change in Kenya had reached a confident, almost cocky level before the election. After the election, many people who once had been silent grumbled out loud. Private newspapers and magazines were full of attacks on the government, despite periodic arrests of critical writers.

International lenders began relenting on their preelection aid freeze. More aid was approved in 1993; still more in 1994 and, for the first time since 1991, without any strong references to the human rights situation in Kenya.[24] Moi had played the democratic "game" and won. Now he was being rewarded with more funds and less criticism from abroad.

Nairobi, Kenya, 1992
A polling site shows crowds of people waiting to vote in 1992 in Kenya's first multiparty election in many years.

Nairobi, Kenya, 1993
Police keep crowds back as Parliament opens its
new multiparty session after the 1992 election.

Nairobi, Kenya, 1993
Parliament building.

The money began to flow again despite continued human rights abuses by the government and continued official corruption documented by human rights organizations. Moi soon reverted to many of his "old habits" of repression against critics.[25]

Moi made no movement toward accommodating the political or developmental agenda of the women's organizations. Laws and state practices discriminating against women remained unchanged. Nevertheless, some groups, such as the International Federation of Women Lawyers—Kenya Chapter, and the League of Women Voters, continued to hold political and social awareness meetings aimed at making women a more formidable political force in the future. The women's groups in Kenya had correctly linked human rights and democratic rights; their leaders, however, realized they needed better organizing, more lobbying, and more training of members on these issues to be more effective in the political arena.[26] In her study of women's issues in Kenya during this period, Maria Nzomo noted that in Kenya and many other African countries, work on women's issues was taking place "in an undemocratic context despite multi-partyism. Democratic rules of tolerance, mutual respect, accountability, and transparency, and respect for basic human rights and freedoms, have not yet been accepted by the major political players."[27]

★ ★ ★

After the 1992 election, still neglecting her insurance business, Kababere switched her focus from the mothers to efforts to get the Kenya constitution changed to limit the power of the incumbent, whoever held the post. "The Kenyan government is supposed to have three [branches]: the executive, legislative, and judiciary. But . . . the executive controls all [three branches]," she said. "The president can, and routinely does, deny permits to opposition parties to hold rallies; even weddings and funerals have to be licensed. The president also appoints government officials from top to bottom. The laws underpinning such power stem from colonial rules the British used. We want a change in the laws. We just want to live simply, and we cannot do that with the controls government puts on our lives. Kenyans have realized that what happened in 1992 hasn't changed their lives. In fact, it has plunged us into a worse situation."

A number of opposition members of Parliament were detained for short periods after the election in what critics called a pattern of harassment aimed at curbing criticism of the government. The office of *Finance* magazine, a publication critical of the government, was set ablaze and partially destroyed. A petrol bomb was thrown at the office of the Legal Advice Center, a private organization. Two security guards were shot at the LAC a month later, and another petrol bomb was used to damage the office. The government banned several other critical private publications.[28] As a result of the renewed government repression, arrests, and deteriorated economy, the public mood swung back to discouragement and a reluctance on the part of many to speak out so freely.

Ethnic violence, which began in 1991 in the period before Moi agreed to multiparty elections, subsided somewhat before the election in 1992 but then resumed after the election. Moi tried to blame the resurfacing of ethnic tensions on the switch from single-party to multiparty politics. But it became clear the government—especially key KANU politicians—was behind much of it, in part to force off their land members of ethnic groups associated with the opposition. For one thing, the uprooted were usually too afraid to return to vote near their abandoned homes, some of which were burned down. And in some abandoned areas, herdsmen of ethnic groups supporting the president, especially the Kalenjin and the Maasai, began grazing their livestock on the abandoned fields.

The government was pursuing "a calculated policy against ethnic groups associated with the political opposition. . . . Despite Moi's pronouncements, the violence has not been a spontaneous reaction to the reintroduction of multiparty politics. . . . the clashes were deliberately instigated and manipulated by KANU politicians anxious to retain their hold on power in the face of mounting internal and external pressure for change in government."[29]

The attacks were focused on the Central Province, home to many Kikuyu, among others, who were largely opposed to Moi. The attackers, often members of Moi's Kalenjin ethnic group, and often wearing similar uniforms, such as shorts and T-shirts of the same color and pattern, would attack with machetes, bows and arrows. Some 1,500 people were killed, and another 300,000 or more were driven from their

Londiani, Kenya, 1992
In the months leading up to the multiparty elections in 1992, ethnic clashes left hundreds dead and thousands (including Grace M. Kabiro and her family) homeless. There is credible evidence that the government encouraged such violence against those suspected of opposing President Daniel arap Moi's authoritarian rule.

lands.[30] The government promised to help resettle the displaced, but the program moved very slowly, despite efforts by the United Nations to help speed it up. In a few areas, members of rival ethnic groups were able to keep violence at a minimum after meeting among themselves at the local level, counteracting attempts by some of their politicians on both sides to keep things stirred up.

Another outspoken critic of the government was Robert Shaw, a businessman who had been kidnaped and locked in the trunk of his car in an apparent attempt to stop him from exposing government banking and other alleged scandals. He said that in the post-1992 election period, the government was trying "to push the clock back," reverting to its old ways. But, he contended, it would not work in the long run. "You can buy time; you can be repressive; you can put people in jail. You can ruin certain people's livelihoods; you can terrorize them. But at the end

Clockwise from left

Asmara, Eritrea, 1993
Women wind their way through the streets, celebrating their country's independence referendum.

Lomé, Togo, 1991
An elder attends a national political reform conference.

Nairobi, Kenya, 1991
The family of Pius Nyamora, former publisher of *Society*, an opposition magazine, poses in front of their home.

Lagos, Nigeria, 1989
This young man is happy with his purchase of a cassette player.

Kaduna, Nigeria, 1991 / Muslim prayers.

Above: Near Arusha, Tanzania, 1990
A woman farmer inspects her corn crop.

Below: Addis Ababa, Ethiopia, 1989
Looking for customers at the Mona Lisa beauty parlor.

Left: Nairobi, Kenya, 1990
This father and his sons stop
to pose for a picture during
their walk in Uhuru Park.

Below: Nasir, southern
Sudan, 1993
Nuer cattle camp.

Top: Abidjan, Côte d'Ivoire, 1990
Yoro Mathias plays with his niece as other family members watch television.

Above: Oshogbo, Nigeria, 1992
Nigerian artist Kings Amao is making a quilt using traditional *adire* cloth at Nike's Center for Arts and Culture.

Opposite top: Oshogbo, Nigeria, 1992
Young women, dressed in indigo-dyed robes, dance for visitors at Nike's art school.

Opposite bottom: Near Dira Dawa, Ethiopia, 1991
Young women fill plastic jugs to irrigate trees in a reclaimed oasis.

Top: Abidjan, Côte d'Ivoire, 1991
The skyline as seen from the main market.

Above: Lagos, Nigeria, 1992
A primary school.

Left: Nigerian artist Nike on a visit
to Florida, 1995.

For several months in early 1997, students protested against the government, in a campaign reminiscent of the student protests in Mali before the overthrow of its government. As the crackdown by the Kenyan government became more brutal—several students were killed—the student protests grew.[34] The root cause of the clashes was "government refusal to respect the autonomy of campuses and students' basic civil and political rights," according to one human rights report that charged the government with using "excessive force" to stop the protests.[35]

In May 1997, with another multiparty election drawing near, Moi deployed hundreds of heavily armed troops in downtown Nairobi to break up a protest rally by opposition and church leaders in Freedom Park. As he had done with regard to the 1991 rally organized by Shikuku, Moi had declared the rally illegal. One of its organizers, presidential aspirant Kenneth Matiba, went into hiding with other opposition leaders, just as Shikuku had in 1991. In what seemed almost like a rerun, though on a larger scale, of the crackdown on the mothers' strike, police and paramilitary units fired tear gas and used clubs to drive out protesters from Freedom Park.

In December 1997, Moi was elected to a fifth term, this time with 40 percent of the vote, slightly higher than his 1992 total. Once again, the opposition had failed to unite behind a single candidate. His party, KANU, won 107 seats in Parliament; the fragmented opposition won 103. Half of Moi's cabinet were defeated. A woman, Charity Kaluki Ngilu, ran for president, the first one to do so. She alleged Moi tried to bribe her with the equivalent of $320,000 not to run and to join the president's party.[36]

There were some signs that, despite the election results, the pro-democracy movement in Kenya was far from over. More Kenyans were taking an interest in the nuts and bolts of the democratic process. In 1992, some 5,000 Kenyans monitored the elections; nearly 28,000 did so in 1997. And the reelection process "reinvigorated civil society and the press—two fundamental components of any democratic system."[37]

After the 1997 elections ethnic violence increased. In April 1998, three international human rights organizations called Kenya "a powder keg waiting to explode," due to a resumption of the ethnic violence in January of that year. The violence followed the pattern of 1991–94 and appeared to have the implicit support of the government which "promoted a culture of impunity," the human rights team reported. The attacks were occurring only in areas that had supported opposition to Moi and his party in the 1997 election. In one case, Kikuyus under attack successfully fought back in an organized fashion, prompting calls from other Kikuyus to fight back more often.[38] Since 1991, "anti-Kikuyu propaganda" has been a part of some government-run broadcasts and has appeared in the ruling party's newspaper, *Kenya Times*, Kenyan scholar Michael Chege noted. He accused the government of "state-sponsored" attacks on Kikuyu as well as Luo and Luhya farmers.[39] Meanwhile, by 1997 torture had become a "standard procedure in police investigations" in Kenya, with virtual impunity for the police offenders.[40]

By late 1998 Moi had moved to defuse some of his opposition. Among other things, he appointed one of his most outspoken foes, Leakey, to run the Kenyan Wildlife Service, a post he previously held before joining the opposition. Others, however, like businessman Shaw and attorneys Nowrojee and Kuria, continued pressing for honest government and rule of law. Ngugi established a private law practice in Kenya and continued his interest in human rights. Political activist and conservationist Maathai continued challenging the government on various issues.

Moi had subverted or resisted most of the reforms Kenyans demanded in the 1990s, but no one person or system can change the human spirit, which insists on freedom. Africans in many countries had achieved new political freedoms. Where authoritarian leaders continued to block such progress, as in Kenya, the fires of political freedom were dampened. But they are still smoldering underground and will erupt again and again.

★   ★   ★

In Somalia, and later Rwanda, the issue was not one of greater political freedom but of survival. Civil war and, in Rwanda, genocide challenged the international community's ability and will to respond effectively to humanitarian and political crises abroad.

4 THINGS FELL APART
Somalia

Baidoa, Somalia, 1992
Thousands fled to emergency feeding centers such as this
one, run by Irish Concern, to escape famine and fighting.

SIXTEEN Special Forces attack helicopters carrying nearly 100 of the most elite U.S. soldiers, men of Delta Force and army Rangers, roared into the air over Mogadishu, Somalia, that bright Sunday afternoon, October 3, 1993. Their pilots had taken part in the invasion of Grenada and Panama, searched Iranian waters for patrol boats attacking oil tankers, and carried Green Berets into the Iraqi countryside hunting for SCUD missile launch sites. Usually this supersecret unit of the 160th Aviation Regiment flew only at night; their nickname was the "Night Stalkers" and their motto: "Death waits in the dark."[1]

But fresh intelligence indicated two of the top aides of Somali general Mohamed Farah Aideed were meeting in a house deep within the section of the city controlled by his militia. Maybe Aideed himself would be there. Since Aideed's forces had killed twenty-four UN soldiers from Pakistan in Mogadishu June 5, the United States and the United Nations had been trying to capture him and his senior aides.

U.S. troops had arrived in Somalia the previous December to guard shipments of relief food to starving civilian victims of a civil war among rival militia that had pushed Somali dictator Mohamed Siad Barre out of office in January 1991. Some militia were also looting relief shipments. The foreign troops had helped curb the looting. Now, in a bid to rule Somalia, Aideed and his militia were continuing the war, making it likely that another famine would occur if the U.S. and UN troops pulled out.

The UN had taken over command of the multinational force in May 1993, but U.S. forces remained and they still had the most military muscle of any foreign troops in Somalia. Now, in a dramatic effort to try to grab Aideed, or at least his top lieutenants, the United States was sending some of its crack troops and the "best of the best" of its flying units into a neighborhood that UN troops had failed to secure. It was an area where Aideed's forces, men in wraparound Somali skirts and flip-flops, were armed with machine guns, heavy caliber weapons mounted on vehicles, and rocket-propelled grenades capable of bringing down a helicopter, part of the stockpile left over from years of military aid to Somalia from the former Soviet Union and the United States.

The attack began well for the U.S. troops. Blackhawk helicopters quickly reached the targets—a house and the Olympic Hotel. Troops slid down ropes; some took control of the buildings while others took defensive positions on the surrounding streets. But Somali fire began coming at the men and planes from "windows, doorways, and rooftops."[2] Then came the rocket-propelled grenades. One of the Blackhawks was hit and crashed. Another crashed later.

Though the U.S. troops could not know it right away, a fourteen-hour battle had begun that would reveal the limitations on how much Western nations are willing or able to help African nations safeguard the most basic human right of all: the right to live.

By the end of the battle, eighteen U.S. servicemen would be dead; the body of one of them would be dragged naked through the streets of Mogadishu, the capital, a scene splashed across world newspapers and television screens. There was an immediate, angry public reaction in the United States: bring the troops home. The U.S. public decided they did not want to support casualties in a war they did not understand.

But there would be another, much greater effect from those eighteen U.S. deaths that day for Africa in the rest of the 1990s and for the new century ahead. Somalia was the first African example in the post–Cold War period (which is often counted from the symbolic fall of the Berlin Wall in late 1989) of what role outside military forces might play in times of crisis.

What happened in Somalia set the tone for what happened in several other crises in Africa, including Rwanda, where up to one million people were killed in a genocidal war in 1994. And the turmoil in several other countries, including Liberia in the early 1990s, Zaire in 1997, and Sierra Leone in 1998 showed that Somalia, though different in many ways, was not an isolated case of extreme violence.

After Somalia, the United States, and by implication most Western countries, would no longer risk sending soldiers to Africa, no matter how great the need. The fact that freed black slaves had formed the backbone of Liberia's politics since the 1800s made no difference on the U.S. decision to stay away as that country fell apart. West African peacekeeping forces did go to Liberia at the height of the war to try to stop the killings.

If there had ever been a serious notion of the United States as the world's post–Cold War "supercop," Somalia cracked that notion, at least in cases where the overriding U.S. interest was simply one of safeguarding human rights. Safeguarding U.S. troops was not a policy without exceptions, however; U.S. and European forces would go to the former Yugoslavia as things fell apart there, threatening Europe with a tidal wave of refugees.

But the United States' conclusion that it cannot help slow down killings in Africa during a crisis is flawed, in my view, based on my firsthand coverage of the war in Somalia as a journalist, interviews with scores of Somali on all sides of the conflict and with other analysts, and examination of many reports and books on the conflict. The United States could have been more effective in Somalia if U.S. military leaders—and their troops—had learned more about the Somali culture, history, and politics. Lacking that, they were bound to step into the middle of a no-win situation, which they did by lining up against one faction instead of staying neutral. I hope to show in this chapter that if the United States had a better understanding of Somalia, it might have avoided being drawn into battles there. This in turn might have led the United States and other Western nations to be more confident about sending troops to Rwanda to try to halt the genocide in that country.

There is no way to be sure what U.S. officials might have done had things turned out differently in Somalia. But there is little doubt that Somalia was decisive in keeping the United States out of Rwanda, where it might have been able to reduce the scope of the genocide. The Somalia-Rwanda connection will be examined more closely in the next chapter.

On a strictly tactical level, the battle in Mogadishu showed that a well-armed militia, even one in which the men wore wraparound skirts and flip-flops, could beat the best-equipped and best-trained Western military in urban guerrilla warfare. U.S. and UN intervention was complicated by a striking state of affairs in Somalia at the time, one that would be in evidence several times during the last decade of the century: as a result of the civil war, there was no central government; no central authority represented the country. Sierra Leone, Liberia, and Zaire also collapsed as states in the 1990s, though toward the end of the decade these countries had begun re-forming a national government.

★   ★   ★

After the battle in Mogadishu that afternoon, one American pilot, Cliff Wolcott, would be dead; a second, Michael Durant, would be a prisoner. Durant, badly injured and beaten, his face swollen and bruised, was forced by his captors to appear in a video aired on international television. But the image most viewers in the United States would later recall was that of Master Sergeant Gary Gordon, from Lincoln, Nebraska, whose naked and mutilated body was dragged through the streets by smiling Somalis, a display caught on film by Paul Watson, correspondent for the *Toronto Globe and Mail,* who risked being beaten himself by the unpredictable mob. Watson won a Pulitzer prize for the photograph.

Gordon and Sergeant First Class Randy Shughart, from Newville, Pennsylvania, both Delta Force snipers of the U.S. Special Forces, had attempted to rescue Durant after his Blackhawk crashed in the warren of narrow back streets in the midst of Aideed's territory in south Mogadishu. As the rescue helicopter neared the crash site, "Gordon grinned, raised both thumbs, and went to the back of the aircraft with Shughart to prepare for what they knew was a very dangerous mission."[3] Moments later the two men jumped about five feet to the ground and headed toward the crashed aircraft.

Downed pilot Durant had been decorated for his flying in the invasion of Panama in 1989 and in the Gulf War the following year. Now in Mogadishu, a grenade had hit his plane's tail rotor. The plane crashed upright; though several men were badly injured, his crew was still alive after the impact. Soon Shughart and Gordon were outside the cockpit trying to pull Durant from the plane. But before they could get him out they had to turn to fight approaching Somali militiamen. Intense firing broke out. Shughart was hit and fell. Gordon raced back to the helicopter to get another weapon, handing Durant Shugart's automatic M-16 rifle. "Gordon looked back at Durant with a slight smile and said,

'Time to get some more Somalis'." It was the last time Durant saw Gordon alive. A Somali mob overran the crash site. Durant threw up his hands. The mob began beating him and tearing off his clothes and equipment before some Somalis held the others back from killing the injured pilot. "They had taken my clothes and they continued to beat me," he said later. "They started parading me around in the streets naked." They beat his face and head with canes and clubs.[4]

Just four days after the battle, President Bill Clinton, facing an avalanche of public sentiment against the killings of the servicemen, announced a March 1994 pullout date for all U.S. troops from Somalia. I was in the United States on home leave from my assignment for *The Christian Science Monitor* in Africa, based in Nairobi, Kenya, from where I covered the Somali famine and civil war through frequent visits. I saw the television portrayal of Gordon's naked corpse being dragged through the streets, just a fleeting glimpse in the newscasts, but a shocking enough scene to sear itself into my mind and the minds of millions of Americans.

Several years later, while teaching an elder hostel course on Africa at Stetson University, in DeLand, Florida, I asked how many of the nearly fifty members of the class recalled seeing that image. Most of them raised their hands. Americans who saw the coverage at the time asked: Why are we in Somalia? Why are they killing our soldiers who went there to help Somalis?

What went wrong? Just ten months earlier, in December 1992, U.S. troops had landed on the beach of Mogadishu to a jubilant welcome by thousands of Somalis. They had come to stop the armed looting of relief food by militia, to get the food to displaced civilians, uprooted by the war and starving in large numbers. Now Americans were questioning even that humanitarian gesture.

Clinton had failed to explain clearly to the American public that a shift had occurred in the U.S. mission in Somalia, from providing humanitarian aid as a neutral party to using force against one militia in an attempt to bring peace. Is the United States its brother's keeper? How bad do things have to be before the United States risks military engagement to stop suffering? In order to help, is the United States or any other Western nation willing to accept the price of body bags being sent home to grieving families and an angry public? Is there such a thing as peacemaking without risk of casualties? Had the United States any business being in Somalia?

There is in most people a streak of generosity, an undeniable good. But generosity and kindness are sometimes tempered and opposed by other sentiments. In his poem "The Road Not Taken," Robert Frost wrote of two roads and his decision to take "the one less traveled by."[5] In life we travel several roads simultaneously, pulled in contrary directions along the way, battling counterimpulses of selflessness and selfishness, kindness and harshness, patience and bruskness, action and reaction, resolve and indecision, understanding and confusion. Sometimes we are sure we understand an issue, only to discover later we do not. Somalia was such a case, and for many, so was Vietnam.

★　★　★

U.S. helicopter pilot John Plummer was in Vietnam in 1972. Plummer spotted bombing targets and ordered air strikes. In June that year he ordered an attack on the village of Trang Bang. Twice he had been assured there were no civilians in the village, only soldiers.[6] The next day he saw what became a Pulitzer prize–winning photo by Nick Ut showing a group of children running from the village. One of them was a naked girl, Kim Phu, screaming in pain and confusion; napalm had burned off her clothes. Her image would haunt him for years, through three marriages and two divorces, through his bout with alcohol and through his dreams. "It took me a long time, but I came to realize I would never have any peace unless I could talk to her," said Plummer. "I had to look in her eyes and say how sorry I am."[7]

In the fall of 1996, Plummer, who had since become a minister, went to Washington, D.C., where Kim was to address veterans at the Vietnam Veterans Memorial. In her remarks, recalled Plummer, she said: "If I could talk face-to-face with the pilot who dropped the bombs, I would tell him we cannot change history but we should try to do good things for the present and for the future to promote peace." Plummer managed to get a note to her with the message that he was in the crowd, that he was the one who ordered the bombing. By the time she got the note, he was right behind her. She stopped and turned. "She just opened her arms to me. I fell into her arms sobbing," Plummer said. "All I could say is, 'I'm so sorry. I'm just so sorry'." She patted his back and said: "It's all right. I forgive, I forgive."[8]

Forgiving is a form of kindness. Both qualities are apparent in Frost's "Death of the Hired Man." Frost tell of a gruff, resentful farmer complaining to his wife that Silas, an old hired hand who had run out on him earlier, had returned. The wife tries to remind him that the old man is worn out and should be allowed to keep the dignity of being of service again. She persuades her husband to go in to comfort the dying man, which he does, only to return in a moment. "Dead" is all the farmer said.[9] When I read this story, I resented the farmer's crassness, but then I realized Frost had him going to comfort the man and that when he returned to tell his wife the news he first took her hand in his.

★   ★   ★

On one of my visits back to the United States during the Somali crisis, I was on a televised panel discussing international topics before an audience. A young boy rose and addressed a question to me: with so many needs of people in the United States, why should we help people in other countries? I paused, searching for words I had never managed to find to my satisfaction until then. First I asked if he played football. Then: if players are injured, does the medical team help just some of them, depending on what part of the field they are on? I said it was time to start thinking of the world as a giant football field, of the world's people as players united in humanity, one family, and begin seeing ourselves connected to everyone else. The world has responded to many disasters, including the famine in Ethiopia in the early 1980s. The outpouring of concern and aid that saved thousands of lives there gave birth to the popular song "We Are the World." It was frustrating when Ethiopia faced another famine in the late 1980s as its long civil war continued. Once again the world responded; relief agencies still in Ethiopia from the earlier famine acted quickly. Famine was averted, a little-told story.

The Land of *Heer*

Somalia is a long, slender stretch of land on the Indian Ocean and the Gulf of Aden. Well before Europeans divided it up, Arab families settled along the coasts in the ninth and tenth centuries, bringing with them their Islamic religion.[10] The Muslims found a society that had some similar values to theirs, including what the Somalis called *heer*, an unwritten code of conduct, widely accepted in Somalia. It emphasized "interdependence and inclusiveness and thus formed the basis for social order."[11] Rather than breaking down *heer*, Islam complemented it with its insistence on seeing fellow believers as brothers. "Traditional pastoral Somali economy therefore was community-oriented in its production and kin-relations and, later, Islamic principles defined the main frame of reference for political and cultural life."[12] Muslim traders from the Middle East established further inroads into Somalia's way of life, leading to the growth of Somali traders and export merchants.

The arrival of the Christians was far more traumatic. In the late 1800s, the area was the focus of European competition involving the Nile, territory farther west, and Somali cattle. The British, installed at Aden, across the gulf, wanted to check French influence in the area. To this end, the British cooperated with the Italians; the French cooperated with the Russians. The French, British, and Italians all signed agreements with northern Somali clans in the 1880s to purchase cattle. But all four foreign governments had their eyes on gaining control of neighboring Ethiopia, which they failed to do.[13] Somalia, at that time, was a "nation" of widely scattered clans, not a "state" with a centralized political structure. And the territory was soon divided into five sections. The British in 1886 established a "protectorate" in the north, with Hargeisa as the capital, using indirect rule; the Italians took control of the south, initially in 1889 and fully by 1927. Mogadishu was the southern capital, where the Italians used direct rule and "eventually the most brutal facets of fascism."[14] The French took control of what is now Djibouti, which has an important port for today's landlocked Ethiopia. Other Somalis came under British colonial rule in northern Kenya, and Ethiopia claimed another portion. The Somali flag's five stars represent these five sections.

The invasion of Somalia by these Christian nations, for that is what it was, provoked an unsuccessful guerrilla war led by Ogadeni religious leader Said Mohamed Abdille Hassan, from 1900 to 1920, against the Ethiopians and the British. Just as significantly, "the intrusion of the powerful forces of the international market and imperialism led to the corrosion of the old Somali moral order."[15] The moral and social rules that had worked well for an isolated, highly pastoral society were challenged as Somalia was thrust into international trade and politics.

Somalia was granted independence from both the British and the Italians in 1960, and the two independent nations joined within days of gaining their freedom. The main political leaders came from the traders, artisans, bureaucrats, and literate religious leaders, but most of them were more interested in "gaining personal advantage" than building a state.[16] Southerners took most of the positions in the new government, leading to jealousies and an abortive revolt in the north in 1961. By the 1969 elections, the number of political parties exceeded sixty, with party leaders appealing to their clans for support, fanning a sense of clan competition. The man named premier, Mohamed Haji Ibrahim Egal, a northerner, garnered much criticism for the corruption, inefficiency, and nepotism of his government. Years later he would be chosen to head a breakaway northern state, Somaliland.

On October 15, 1969, a policeman assassinated President Abdirashid Ali Shermarke. Six days later the military staged a bloodless coup, led by Barre. At first Barre was popular. He announced the goal of restoring the morals of the country; he launched literacy campaigns and extended health and veterinary services; and he plunged into a round of public works and social reforms. In 1970 he introduced "scientific socialism," setting up local community development groups using the unemployed, among others, and putting orphans and street children into Revolutionary Youth Centers where they were fed, clothed, and educated in new revolutionary ideals. He also attempted to create a personality cult: local government offices and public places featured "the new ruling trinity": Marx, Lenin, and Barre.[17]

But Barre lost much popular support in 1977 when he failed to make headway on his stated plan to gain control over Somali populations under foreign rule. Backed by generous Soviet support, he launched an attack on the Ethiopian area known as the Ogaden. The lightning attacks penetrated deep into the region. Then the Soviets, eager to curry favor with Ethiopia, a bigger plum in the Cold War than Somalia, switched sides. In 1978, with massive assistance from the Soviets, Ethiopia pushed its foe out of the country, which damaged Barre's standing among Somalis. With the Soviets now aligned with the new Ethiopian regime of Mengistu Haile Mariam, who avowed he was a Marxist, the United States sided with Somalia. Barre became an ardent, or at least vocal, anti-Communist, as U.S. funds and military aid began flowing into Somalia. But Barre was never able to get as much military support from the United States as he had from the Soviets. In the post-Barre civil war, both sides would use arms that came largely from these giant stockpiles of Soviet and U.S. military hardware, though each side also had to make new purchases.

Barre claimed he wanted to rid Somalia of clanism. Clans are the ethnic groups Somalis identify with and turn to for help in times of danger; clan awareness tends to be higher during war or drought. A clan may be spread out over a large territory, sometimes over territory that is not contiguous. Somalis have developed complex methods for settling disputes between clans. But clan consciousness can also be the target of "elite manipulation," deliberate efforts by the educated class to control clans or lead them into conflicts.[18] Barre manipulated clans to maintain his power, employing old-fashioned divide-and-rule tactics to keep his opponents off balance.[19] The corruption of the Somali clan social system by Barre is an example of a leader destroying a state to stay in power.

African leaders are not the only ones who have used ethnic politics. In a peaceful political system, ward politics in cities such as Chicago, New York, and Miami has long had an ethnic focus. Canada's wrestling with the future of Quebec is partly an ethnic issue. At the other extreme, ethnic conflict has been evident in many parts of the world and is "pervasive, persistent."[20] Africa has had numerous instances of such conflict. Togolese president Etienne (Gnassingbe) Eyadéma, for example, relied on his own northern ethnic group, the Kabiye, to fill key military posts to repress southern tribes.

As Barre continued consolidating his personal control over the government, becoming more autocratic, opposition to his regime grew. There was an abortive military coup in 1978; Barre had the leaders executed in public. He also increased the size of the military, which had been around 3,000 soon after independence, to 120,000 by 1982. The army had a horrible record of human rights abuses. "The army of liberation had been converted to a huge army of repression."[21] More and more Somalis came to despise the state and its cruelty. "Increasingly, the state was identified with concentrated power, fear and intimidation, and disregard for any form of law and due process."[22] An Africa Watch report stated, "Both the urban population and nomads living in the countryside have been subjected to summary killings, arbitrary arrest, detention in squalid conditions, torture, rape, crippling constraints on freedom of movement and expression and a pattern of psychological intimidation."[23] Land grabbing was another feature of Barre's regime. During the mid 1980s, Barre's government, which included a growing number of his family members, pillaged many rural communities near the Shabelle and Juba Rivers, prime farmland in a parched country. It had already expropriated large tracts of lands there. Barre was following a centuries-old pattern of stealing southern lands; the bulk of it had been taken by northern clans. The pattern continued in the post-Barre era.[24]

In 1981, opponents primarily of the northern Isaak clan formed the Somali National Movement (SNM). The SNM operated out of Ethiopia until Somalia and Ethiopia signed a peace pact in May 1988, requiring each country to expel rebels of the other. The following month, members of the SNM fought their way into several key northern Somali cities, including Burao and Hargeisa, killing a number of senior government officials. In reprisal, Barre sent his son-in-law, General Mohamed Siad Hersi (known as Morgan), to bomb Hargeisa without restraint. In the three-month battle of Hargeisa, an estimated 40,000 people were killed and some 400,000 people in the area fled to Ethiopia.[25] More than 70 percent of the buildings in Hargeisa were destroyed.[26] Refugees I interviewed who had fled to Ethiopia from Hargeisa told of planes intentionally bombing and shooting civilians in the streets.

The scope of the destruction was still evident when Betty and I went there in early 1993. I had never seen such devastation. We stopped in front of the ruined home of Fadua Aden, who stood outside with her daughter, Nura Awil, and her grandson, Mohamed. "It was a bomb,"

Hargeisa, northern Somalia, 1993
This school was still in use even after it sustained damage in the civil war.

she said, explaining the damage. There were gaping holes in some walls; the home had no doors or windows—and no roof; roofs were one of the items often looted after the war. Hargeisa was returning to life, however. Somalis coming back from abroad were rebuilding homes and businesses from the rubble. Typically they began by clearing a single room, squeezing in the family until they could afford to continue reconstruction. But they had to be careful. Barre's forces had planted thousands of mines, including some wickedly set inside homes to maim or kill those who returned. By the time of our visit, most of the mines had been cleared from the city, though many remained in other parts of the north. Land mines were also a problem in many other wars, including those in Angola, Sudan, and beyond Africa in countries such as Afghanistan.

In 1989, the Hawiye clan established a political-military opposition group, the United Somali Congress (USC), based in Rome. Its military wing was headed by General Mohamed Farah Aideed. In 1990, Hawiye based in Mogadishu formed a "Manifesto" group calling for the resignation of Barre. He responded by arresting many of them. During my first visit to Somalia, in December 1990, I met with representatives of

Manifesto. Despite the arrests of many of their members, they were holding meetings directly across from a police station. By then the opposition to Barre was so strong, Barre apparently lacked the will to arrest more of the Manifesto members. Strange things were happening: the wife of Ali Mahdi, a key USC financier and hotel owner turned politician, who was soon to become interim president of Somalia, was working in the security office of Barre. Mahdi's soon-to-be archrival, Aideed, later claimed Manifesto was too close to Barre.

Collapse of the State

By late 1990, the Somali state had essentially collapsed; the central government was barely functioning. Most basic services had ceased. The state was a hollow shell about to crack in pieces. It is worth pausing here to look at just what that means because the collapse of a state affects not only the human rights of its population but the way other government and relief agencies respond to the crisis. Somalia's experience offers insight into the nature of a collapsed state.

Other African states that "collapsed" in the 1990s include Liberia (in the early years of the decade) and Rwanda (in 1994). Zaire, later renamed the Democratic Republic of the Congo, had practically collapsed as a state by the time rebels seized power in 1997, and Sierra Leone essentially collapsed the same year under military leaders who conducted themselves like thugs.[27] Beyond Africa, parts of the former Soviet Union went through turmoil after the Berlin Wall fell. Azerbaijan suffered a horrible conflagration and butchering of people. Much of the former Yugoslavia fell into the abyss about the same time as Somalia, drawing greater and more rapid world response than the Somalia crisis did, which led to complaints by UN secretary general Boutros Boutros-Ghali that the world was operating on a double standard, one for whites and one for nonwhites.[28] The Russians pulled out of Afghanistan in 1988, leaving a pro-Soviet government which held on to power for three years. But after that the country had no effective government as rebel groups competed for power.

Some political scientists see patterns in the way a state collapses. The collapse is seldom a sudden thing. "The slippery slope, the descending spiral, and the downward trend are the marks of state col-

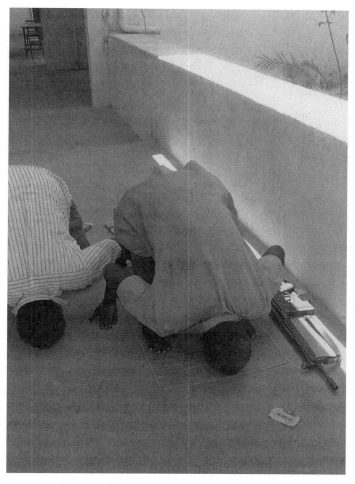

Mogadishu, Somalia, 1991
A Somali Muslim fighter lays his
gun at his side while praying.

Mogadishu, Somalia, 1991
Many buildings in the capital were
heavily damaged during the civil war.

lapse, rather than deadlines and triggers."[29] The collapse of a state is not without hope of reversal. "State collapse is a long-term degenerative disease. However, it is also one whose outcome is not inevitable: cure and remission are possible."[30]

How did Somalia collapse? Somalia, like other collapsing states, appears to have gone through several phases, including the government going on the defensive against its opponents at the cost of carrying out its normal functions. One effect of this was the absence of "a political agenda for participation and programs."[31] In Somalia, as in many countries, the agenda of the leaders became political survival. Instead of seeking to survive by meeting the demands of the citizens, Barre and his entourage concentrated almost entirely on self-enrichment and repression of real or suspected opponents. In some collapsing states, key factions that make up the central government are so busy fighting among themselves they lose control over the countryside. "Local authority is up for grabs and local power-grabbers—future warlords—grab it."[32] This happened both during Barre's decline and during Somalia's post-Barre civil war. Somali scholar Hussein M. Adam sees seven landmarks along the road to Somalia's collapse.

1. Personal rule. Barre moved through three stages of rule: an advocate of "scientific socialism" (1970–77); autocrat (1978–86); tyrant (1987–91, the year of his overthrow).
2. Military rule. Barre's major expansion of the army and his control of it ensured his power.
3. Rule by clan favoritism. Barre increasingly depended on his own Darod clan family when making appointments in the army and other key posts. There was a growing perception that Barre was favoring three divisions of the Darod clan confederacy: his own, the Marehan; his mother's, the Ogaden; and his son-in-law's (Morgan's), the Dulbahante.
4. Campaign against the elite or educated class. Barre made deliberate purges of educational institutions and other places where clan members were showing promise, shifting them to military, espionage, and other government posts. This damage to the Somali elite class speeded state collapse.

5. Poisoning of clan relations. Barre's troops armed some clans and encouraged them to fight other clans. This left long-lasting scars on Somalia's traditional system of cooperation between clans.

6. Urban state terror. As in Argentina, young people began disappearing in Somalia as a result of state repression. In one incident, in July 1989, forty-seven people were taken from their homes in the middle of the night and executed on Jasiira Beach, near the capital.

7. Neofascist campaign against the north.[33]

In practice, Barre's government was much more balanced in terms of clan representation than most people acknowledge.[34] But by January 1991 Barre's forces had lost control of most of the north to the SNM. He was overthrown on January 27, 1991, and forced to flee Mogadishu.

One of the failures of the international community in trying to help Somalia after Barre was ousted was that it acted as if there was still a state. Plans were developed that required a central government to make them work; but there was none.

A New Civil War

In late January 1991 I flew to the Somali capital of Mogadishu, just a few days after Barre had been forced to flee. The heavy cloud cover during most of the flight from the Kenyan capital of Nairobi to Mogadishu, in a small, chartered plane, allowed me to postpone concerns about the safety of going into the heart of a country without a government, to a city full of arms, where looting was rampant. For now, we journalists could sit in our comfortable cocoon and gaze out on a peaceful and numbing gray. Our only immediate worry was whether the pilot, though a veteran of bush flights, would find the airport by instruments without benefit of landmarks or help from the ground. He told us the control tower in Mogadishu was no longer operating. The ending of the government had not been peaceful. Somalia was not one of those countries that had used the ballot box to turn out an incumbent, as some African nations were beginning to do. But the battle of Mogadishu in January 1991 had brought a lasting peace, or so the winners thought at the time.

A society with deep traditional roots, where male (almost exclusively) community leaders commanded the respect of the people, where family and clan were more important than official title or rank, had risen up against a tyrant and won a war. Desert nomads, goat herders, businessmen, politicians, scholars, and many others had joined forces to chase out of power the man who had tried to unbind the very social ties that were supposed to keep the country intact. Barre had played one clan against another in a murderous scheme to hang on to power, nearly destroying traditions of interclan cooperation.

But now that he was gone—chased from the capital in a convoy of small tanks—some Somali politicians were telling visitors how the country would come together. Most other African countries were in the midst of a pro-democracy movement that had begun in 1990; people were demanding more political freedom, and in a growing number of countries were getting it. Longtime dictators were suddenly on the defensive as massive demonstrations, combined with some international pressures, forced one of them after another into agreeing to hold competitive (multiparty) elections, often for the first time in decades. Most African nations had to contend with many ethnic groups, many languages, and different religions. Somalia, on the other hand, was composed of only one ethnic group (Somali), one religion (Islam), one language (Somali). Peace and representative government would come easily, optimistic Somalis were saying. It sounded good; unfortunately it would not turn out that way. Too much damage had been done during the Barre years from 1969 to 1991 to allow a quick fix after he was gone.

★ ★ ★

The tower at the Mogadishu airport had been looted, but our pilot brought the aircraft down through the clouds with impressive precision, coming into the open directly in line with the runway. We were met by Somali men of the Hawadley clan, who put us in a four-wheel-drive vehicle with several guards with machine guns and took us on a tour. The city had suffered far less physical damage than I had imag-

Mogadishu, Somalia, 1991
Rebels celebrate the downfall of long-time Somali
dictator Mohamed Siad Barre's government.

ined, though a few areas were gutted and many buildings were pock-marked with holes from artillery or machine guns. Looting had been thorough: even electrical wiring and water supply equipment had been stolen. Telephone and telex links to the outside world had been destroyed. But on the whole, the city still stood. Some buses, often without windshields, had begun operating again; in open markets, milk, tea and a few other items were for sale. Some shops had reopened. On many corners and along the roads, rotting bodies had been covered with lime powder as a protection against disease. Our escorts stopped at one damaged building, pulled away some branches in the front yard, and exposed several corpses not covered with lime. Perhaps they had been left there to show journalists and other visitors. The street fighting in Mogadishu during the takeover had been intense. All but one or two of the foreign relief officials had fled for their lives. One who stayed was Dr. Willi Huber of SOS-Kinderdorf, an international charity helping children. Looters ravaged other relief offices, but Somali women had lined up in front of the SOS compound, which was treating sick and homeless children, to protect the place with their bodies. It worked: the looters respected the women and did not enter the compound. I later spoke with a Somali doctor who continued operating inside the SOS compound during heavy fighting. When bullets whizzed through the operating room, he ducked, waited for a lull, then stood up and finished the operation. He was the first of many dedicated Somalis I would meet who, with no political agenda, were determined to do what they could for their fellow Somalis and their country in this dire time. They showed the same spirit and hunger for freedom as those I was meeting elsewhere in Africa who were engaged in various forms of political protest; but for many in Somalia, the struggle for freedom was at a very basic level: they were fighting for the right to live, the freedom to see another day.

Many saw the overthrow of Barre's regime as a war of liberation that held the promise of real political freedom. In the middle of a main street several young Somali men holding machine guns stood proudly atop one of the tanks of the defeated Barre army. When Betty approached to take their photograph, they waved their guns jubilantly. Sitting on the turret was Abukar Ali Mohamed. "I shot a lot of people—to get democracy and make Somalia free from the dictatorship of

Barre," he said. He had accomplished half of his goal: Barre was gone. The other half—democracy—would have to wait.

We were driven up a hill to Villa Somalia. Our Somali driver attempted to drive through the gates, past some other Somali guards, but the guards were furious and started yelling. After a long argument, the guards allowed us to pass. We learned that the guards were from one clan while our driver and escorts were from another. It was our first example of the kind of post-Barre disputes over the spoils of war that would lead to the division of Mogadishu and continued fighting in parts of the country. The scene at Villa Somalia was one of calm disorder. Barre's residence, with its wide staircases, was a series of bare, looted rooms. Several men sat outside on a sofa and chairs they had hauled out of the residence.

Mohamed Egal Osman, an older Somali in the group, described Barre as a "shameful man" for having fired rockets and tanks on his own people during his final days in power. Some young rebels said they had climbed over the walls of Villa Somalia, opening fire on those still guarding it. I spoke to one of them, still strutting around the compound, armed with a machine gun. He was proud of having helped rid the capital of a dictator. Could he have had any notion of what would follow?

★   ★   ★

The swearing-in ceremony for a provisional government took place in early February 1991. One by one, as guards with machine guns stood outside the two-story building used for the event, the new ministers, representing the major clans, placed a hand on a Koran, the Islamic holy book, and took their oath. "Somalia can be united, provided they get the right government, with the right leadership," Mahdi, the now interim president, had told reporters the day before, relaxed and barefoot in his brother-in-law's modest but nicely carpeted living room. He said his aim was to "fill a gap until a broad-based government with the consultation of the opposition forces is made." I had a nagging feeling I should address him simply as "Mr.," rather than "Mr. President," because he was not elected and his control was limited primarily to the city.

Mahdi chose the majority of his cabinet from his Hawiye clan. Mahdi was a member of the Abgal subclan of the Hawiye; Aideed was also Hawiye but of the Habir Gedir subclan. Somali clans form shifting alliances with other clans when it suits their interests. Sometimes clans or even subclans fight each other, as would be the case between the Abgal and Habir Gedir. Mahdi's appointment did not sit well with the other clans, nor among other subclans of the Hawiye. As I was leaving the ceremony, a Somali businessman I knew from my previous visit beckoned to me. I followed him into a hallway one floor beneath the room where the ceremony had taken place. He laughed at me for paying so much attention to the new cabinet. Aideed, he said, was on his way to Mogadishu and angry that Mahdi claimed to be interim president. Aideed and his men bitterly resented the way in which they felt Mahdi and the Manifesto politicians had seized power while he and his guerrillas had fought to bring Barre down.

The Darod and the Isaak clans in the north were also upset with Hawiye control of Mogadishu. These two clans had been major real estate owners in the city and had now lost much of their property to the Habir Gedir. As much as 60 percent of the houses in Mogadishu probably belonged to members of the Darod and Isaak clans before 1989.[35] Most of this property was looted after Barre fled; the Hawiye took over much of it in the absence of the owners. Later Aideed established control over the southern portion of the capital, while Mahdi took over north Mogadishu.

Although the international community—and most journalists—would focus on this conflict in Mogadishu between the two rivals, other cities, including Kismayu, Baidoa, and Bardera became crucial hot spots in the struggle. And outsiders almost overlooked another war—over farmland in the south-central part of the country. Somalia was a clan struggle and a property struggle. Those who did not understand this found the war bewildering.

One civil war to oust Barre was over; another was about to begin.

Aideed bid his time against Mahdi, waiting for an opportunity to strengthen his political position in the capital. His chance came in July 1991, when Aideed was elected chairman of the USC, giving him a political power base from which he soon challenged Mahdi militarily in Mogadishu. The first fighting between the two sides came in Septem-

Mogadishu, Somalia, 1992
General Mohamed Farah Aideed, who helped overthrow dictator Mohamed Siad Barre, later became the target of an unsuccessful manhunt by U.S. and other soldiers after Aideed's militia was blamed for killing Pakistani soldiers in the UN force.

ber 1991. Hundreds were killed in just four days of fighting; thousands were wounded. In November, a general war broke out in Mogadishu between Aideed and Mahdi; the city was divided between their camps. A so-called green line between them became a dangerous no-man's-land.

Heavy artillery attacks were launched indiscriminately and with deadly frequency from both sides of the line. At least 5,000 to 30,000 were killed in the city before a cease-fire was declared in early March 1992.[36] By then both sides were showing signs of exhaustion. On a trip to Mogadishu with several other foreign correspondents during the bombing, I visited the home used as the office of Médecins Sans Frontier (Doctors Without Borders). I had just asked if there was a danger of this house being hit by a rocket and had been told no, when one whistled over the roof and landed a couple of blocks away, in the compound of a hospital. I noticed at lunch that many of the MSF foreign staff looked almost ghostlike; their faces were practically without expression, pale, showing extreme exhaustion. They worked long hours and never knew when a shell might kill them, too.

A Somali mother told me she had been preparing a spaghetti lunch for her family when two rockets hit her house, killing one of her children immediately. A second child died in the hospital. As I rode around the city with various relief officials, I tried not to think of the dangers of the random rockets being fired into the area from Mahdi's side. I was relieved when our plane, which had been late in returning, finally lifted us out of the city later that day; but I was also suddenly struck by the plight of those we were leaving behind.

War, Hunger, and Death

UNICEF studies show that in wars today, nine of ten victims are civilians. In Somalia's case, the victims were not usually killed by bullets, bombs, or mines, but by hunger. Former Tanzanian president Julius Nyerere once quoted an African proverb that when the elephants fight, the grass suffers. In Somalia, military leaders such as Barre, Aideed, and Mahdi were the elephants; the farmers were often the grass; and much of the grass died.

The south-central farmlands between the Juba and Shabelle Rivers became a prime area of conflict and starvation as clans and subclans fought each other. In the south-central triangle between Mogadishu, Kismayu, and Belet Huen (or Belet Uen), fighting broke out between rival militia of the various clans after Barre was chased out of Mogadishu. From his retreat post in the southwest, Barre sent General Mohamed Hashi Gani of his own Marehan clan to take control of the central Somali farming town of Baidoa in October 1991. Gani and his men were soon expelled by the local Rahanweyn with support from Aideed's forces.

In January 1992, Gani's group retook Baidoa. This time there were no clashes, possibly because Aideed was still engaged in a war in Mogadishu against Mahdi. Then in April 1992, Barre himself moved to Baidoa, sending Gani to fight Aideed in Mogadishu, on the assumption that by then Aideed's forces were weakened.[37] With help from the Hawadley and Murusade clans, Aideed's Habir Gedir were able to repulse Gani at Afgoi, a town less than twenty miles from Mogadishu.

All this fighting devastated the people of areas such as Baidoa. Barre and his remaining military forces had pursued a scorched earth retreat

Baidoa, Somalia, 1992
Many young children were saved from starvation at
feeding centers such as this one, run by Irish Concern.

on his way to his southwest home area of Gedo. They destroyed crops, animals, and homes of civilians as they crossed through the Rahanweyn area, including Baidoa. These communities "were devastated by looting, rape, and massacres during a period of military occupation by various factions."[38] This was part of Somalia's agricultural bread basket—and it was devastated. Barre's soldiers "looted all the sorghum stores, they looted all the livestock" in and around Baidoa, says a Somali veterinarian from Baidoa. "And that was the main cause of death in Baidoa."[39]

In a village near Baidoa, months after Barre had been chased away by Aideed's forces, the driver for the relief agency we were traveling with stopped to let Betty and me walk around. It was a scene of desperation and disorder. (At the time we did not think about mines that may have been in the area.) The thatch-roofed huts of stick and mud walls were still standing but abandoned. Personal papers, including school notebooks, had been left in a jumble on the dirt floors. Even more significant, the underground grain storage bins had been torn open and were empty.

The death rate in Baidoa as a result of the war was horrific. The U.S. Centers for Disease Control and Prevention estimated 40 percent of the population, including 70 percent of its children under five, died of hunger or disease. At the peak, up to 300 a day were dying in Baidoa, similar to death rates in other towns fought over by militia.

In Baidoa, a town of only about 50,000 to 60,000 normally, 4,500 people had died in the previous four weeks, said Mouse Adeen, a UNICEF doctor and native of the area, when I met him there in August 1992. By then some 40,000 people were in feeding programs in Baidoa, many from the surrounding area. For Somalia as a whole—particularly in the central region of the country, which includes Baidoa—the number of people who died from fighting and famine between 1991 and 1993 was estimated to be 240,000.[40] Much of the land in Somalia is primarily devoted to livestock maintained by nomads. When drought or conflict hits such an area, herdsmen usually are able to flee with their animals. But farmers are not as mobile, and they often refuse to leave their farms and homes until it is too late, until they are already dying.

In August 1992, when I first flew into Baidoa with several other reporters (we were not the first journalists to arrive) in a small plane, no one came to the airstrip to meet us. Aideed's men controlled the airport, and the town was full of armed bands driving around on their "technicals," stripped-down, four-wheel-drive vehicles with the top cut off to allow room for heavy caliber guns. The pilot landed but took off again to circle the town, as a way of letting our host, a relief agency, know we had arrived. I went with him. As we flew low in circles over the city, I was aware of two things: most of the metal sheeting roofs had been looted, leaving residents exposed to the rains; and we were within easy firing range of any trigger-happy young fighter below with a rifle, machine gun, or artillery. I suddenly felt very vulnerable. By the second time we landed, our Rahanweyn escorts had arrived. At the entrance to the bombed-out airport, some members of Aideed's militia did not let us pass until they asked our escorts a few questions. It became clear in snatched conversations with the local Rahanweyn that Baidoa was still an occupied town. Though residents apparently had suffered worse under Barre's occupation, many were not happy with Aideed's forces being in charge. "They loot us; they shoot us," one Rahanweyn, working with a private U.S. relief agency in Baidoa, whispered to me as we rode along with some of Aideed's fighters. "They have the heavy guns."

The Rahanweyn, many of them settled farmers, have never had the arms that most of the other, more nomadic clans have had. Barre forcibly recruited Rahanweyn to fight his enemies in the north. Former Baidoa resident Abdi Aziz Mohamed Ali, who moved to the United States in 1995, said the lack of arms among the Rahanweyn had a lot to do with their occupation and their attitudes toward life compared to more aggressive nomadic clans elsewhere who joined the militia. "The nomads are willing to die; the farmer is not willing to die. The farmer is not willing to kill; the nomad is going to kill. It's different psychologies."[41]

That August day in Baidoa, we drove directly to one of four feeding centers for famine victims run by the Irish charity Concern. It consisted of several small rooms for the most serious cases and a large open courtyard where hundreds of women and children sat on long, green strips of shaded plastic on the ground where they were fed. Many of the children were gaunt, with emaciated, thin legs and shrunken faces. I saw a mother there one day with a baby on either side of her; one of the babies had just died, and the other appeared to be dying. The mother was weeping, silently. Many children had open sores on their bodies. In front of the feeding center, other Somalis were digging shallow graves for those who had arrived in Baidoa too late. Harado Maalim Mohamed crouched by one of the freshly covered graves, where her granddaughter, Medina, had just been buried. "She died early this morning," the grandmother said. "She was very, very thin." Two of her other grandchildren had also died recently.

Just as wrenching as the child starvation was the adult starvation. One group of displaced Somalis who had finally left their village south of Baidoa were lying on mats and on the ground behind an abandoned building at the edge of town where a newly arrived relief agency, World Vision, was just starting to provide food for them. An exhausted nurse from the United States looked around the courtyard of the building, nearly overcome with dismay at the dying adults in front of her. She was the only trained nurse at the site but had several Somalis helping her. Many of the men and women were too weak to sit up and eat what was offered, and at first there were not enough cooked rations for everyone. I stopped my reporting and began taking water and food to the dying, trying to comfort them in any way I could. Politics that causes such misery seems stupid and cruel; rarely do the perpetrators suffer in the least. The militia leaders I had seen looked well fed.

Relief agencies in Baidoa were collecting bodies each morning by truck because most families lacked the strength and the money for a proper burial. "It's a pity it had to wait to get to this," said Anita Ennis, a nurse working for Concern. Like the Somalis, she and other foreign relief workers were dismayed at how long it had taken the world to focus on the tragedy of Somalia. "The situation is desperate," said Gregoire Tavernier, of the International Committee of the Red Cross (ICRC). As the dying continued in Somalia, relief agencies, such as Concern, the ICRC, CARE, Catholic Relief Services (CRS) and World Vision, were the main distributors of relief food. But they could not keep up with the demands. By March 1992, when Algerian Mohamed Sahnoun, the UN secretary general's first special representative to Somalia, arrived on a fact-finding mission, 500,000 Somalis had fled to neighboring countries and hundreds were dying each day.[42]

Unheralded Heroes: Somali Relief Workers

As the crisis grew, more and more international relief workers flew into Somalia, carrying out exhausting duties, living in sparse conditions, taking risks of getting shot or knifed in towns where armed militia were everywhere. For example, in Baidoa the main warehouse of the ICRC was raided; several workers were killed. There were still bloodstains in the courtyard outside the warehouse when I visited the site a few days later. In Kismayu, Sean Devereux, a cheerful, outgoing employee of UNICEF, was murdered. Devereux had begun discussing in interviews with journalists what he knew of alleged massacres by a militia leader then based in Kismayu. He also had just refused a demand by Somalis employed by UNICEF for a pay increase, a refusal which may have angered some of the Somali workers. Kurt Lustenberger, a Swiss employee of the ICRC, was shot and killed in Bardera by men demanding money.

Western relief workers got some well-deserved press coverage—never enough; Somali workers got even less, but they were just as committed and brave. For example, when a foreign employee of the ICRC was attacked by a Somali gunman in Mogadishu, a Somali relief official jumped in front of him to try to shield him. Both men were killed.

One of the most outstanding Somali relief workers I met during more than four years of reporting on the Somali war was Amina Sheik Mohamed, who worked for Concern in Baidoa. On repeated visits to Baidoa, Betty and I admired her tenacity, courage, and strength as she cared for the dying and nursed many children back to life. One day Amina was kneeling down beside a hollow-faced boy lying on a mat on the ground in the shade of a tree. Someone had brought him to Baidoa two days earlier. Amina was spooning some rehydration liquid into the boy's mouth; the boy feebly tried to take a sip. I was about to ask the child's name when Amina stopped spooning. The child had died that instant. I looked first at the body of the child, then at Amina, with tears in my eyes. I had seen death all around me—and would see much more in Somalia and later Rwanda: people dying, people dead. But until then, no one had actually died before my eyes. I continued writing down what happened next, despite the pain in my stomach, the momentary feeling of helplessness and despair.

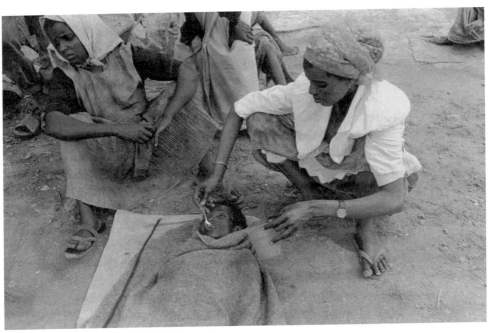

Baidoa, Somalia, 1992
A Somali relief worker, Amina Sheik Mohamed, employed by Irish
Concern, worked tirelessly to save lives and help stem the rising
death toll. For this child, help came too late; the child died.

Amina had seen death many times, but she was not calloused, not
hardened. For a moment she closed her eyes, then she slowly waved a
hand across the air in front of her, as if trying to erase the scene. She
gently pulled a gray cloth over the child's face, took a deep breath,
stood up, and continued her work. She asked an aide to carry another
child in from the courtyard to a small room where she attached an
intravenous drip to his desperately thin arm. She had many other lives
to try to save.

Many lives were saved in Somalia by such help. At the Concern
compound where Amina worked, Betty photographed a mother and
her two children in 1992; one of the children was starving. Each time
we returned to the Concern relief center in Baidoa, the child was stron-
ger. Several months after our first visit, just before the mother took her

two children home, Betty photographed the three of them one last time. Both children were chubby and healthy. *Life* magazine published Betty's "before" and "after" pictures March 23, 1993.

While many Somalis fled their country, some who had been abroad returned. Miriam Mohamed, a Somali nurse, came back from her studies in India to tend to the sick and dying in the midst of heavy fighting in Mogadishu. Betty and I met her one day at a UNICEF feeding center. I asked why she had risked returning. "These are my people," she smiled, bending down to embrace a young girl. She said there were very few trained nurses in Somalia at the time and she wanted to help. She had also helped save her husband, who had been wounded and pinned down under cross fire in one of the many interclan battles after Barre's overthrow. Miriam borrowed a vehicle, drove into the midst of the fighting, pulled her husband into the vehicle, then raced away.

Many other Somalis understandably hesitated to return to their country during the conflict. An agricultural expert who had studied in the United States told me in Nairobi he wanted to return to Somalia to farm, using modern techniques that would serve as an example for other farmers in Somalia. But he was afraid because of the lawlessness and murders still plaguing his country. Meanwhile, as the dying continued along the roads to Baidoa and in the feeding centers there and in other towns, the governments of developed countries finally began to take note of the suffering. Some private, international relief groups had been working in Somalia before the fall of Barre and were quick to return after the coup. The United Nations moved slower.

The World Begins to Respond

In January 1992, a full year after Barre was deposed, the UN undersecretary for political affairs, James Jonah, was sent to Somalia to try to help negotiate a cease-fire, which was reached in early March 1992. From the beginning Aideed was skeptical of UN involvement in Somalia. He repeatedly said in interviews that he welcomed humanitarian aid but not political interference. He did not trust the new UN secretary general, Boutros Boutros-Ghali, who he felt had been too close to Barre when serving as Egypt's foreign minister.

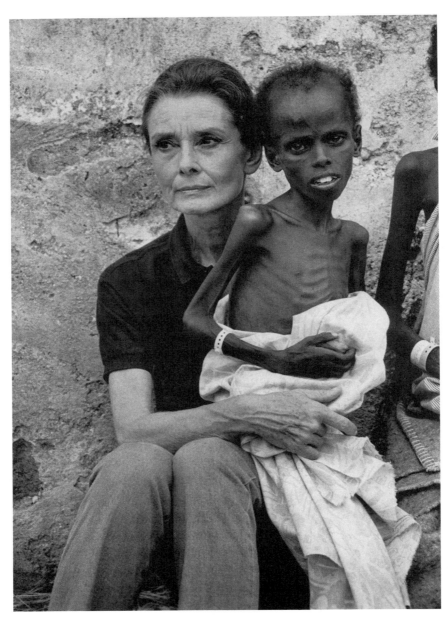

Baidoa, Somalia, 1992
UNICEF goodwill ambassador Audrey Hepburn visited Somalia to
bring world attention to the plight of Somali women and children.
Credit: UNICEF/Betty Press.

After the March 1992 cease-fire, Boutros-Ghali sent a civilian UN team to Mogadishu to lay plans for observing its implementation. Soon 50 unarmed UN monitors were sent to the city, followed by 500 lightly armed UN Pakistani guards who took control of the airport in Mogadishu to allow relief flights safe passage. Both groups proved ineffective in curbing the rising anarchy. The guards were confined by Somali militiamen to the airport, almost like prisoners. Sahnoun, the UN special representative for Somalia, was later forced out of the post by Boutros-Ghali for criticizing in public the slowness of the UN response to the Somali tragedy. Ironically, Boutros-Ghali shared the same frustration.

Meanwhile the U.S. presidential campaign was heating up. Among other issues, Democratic candidate Clinton criticized Republican president George Bush for not taking decisive action to help the starving in Somalia. Those of us foreign correspondents based in Nairobi filed many articles on the Somali crisis during 1991 and 1992. My own reports described people starving in Mogadishu. But the July 19, 1992, front-page story by *The New York Times* correspondent Jane Perlez about the dying in Baidoa brought new U.S. awareness about Somalia. The article described people so famished they were dying in feeding lines. I should have gotten to Baidoa sooner myself, though I was soon filing many articles from there.[43] My newspaper allowed me to make many trips to various parts of Somalia from 1991 until my departure from the region in 1995. I was given time to report on areas at peace as well as those at war and on efforts to rebuild Somalia as well as the destructive actions by a few groups to destroy it. Many journalists, whether owing to pressure from their editors or their own lack of interest, spent little time reporting positive developments in Somalia.

On August 14, 1992, Bush announced plans for Operation Provide Relief, a U.S. military airlift of food to Somalia. Bush said politics had nothing to do with his decision or its timing, coming less than three months before the presidential election.[44] Once delivered, much of the food was looted because the U.S. troops stayed on the ground only a few minutes after each flight. Unload and get out: those were the orders.

Many relief groups had worked out delivery systems using local guards, but much of the food was stolen anyway. The United States decided that only an international military force could safeguard the food convoys enough to stop most of the stealing. But if the marines took over deliveries of food, warned one human rights analyst, all the "delicate webs of agreements and contracts" that relief agencies had worked out to get food delivered and not looted would be destroyed.[45]

In late 1992, Bush approved a plan for a U.S. military force to go to Somalia to try to stop the looting and get food to the starving. It would prove to be a complicated mission. The United States was about to send troops to a collapsed state, whose central government had disintegrated, and which held no major political or strategic interests. Why did Bush approve the plan? "What seems clear is that it was truly his [Bush's] personal decision, based in large measure on his growing feelings of concern as the humanitarian disaster continued to unfold relentlessly despite the half-measures being undertaken by the international community. Presumably, growing criticism from the numerous involved NGOs [nongovernment organizations; that is, private charities], from the Hill [Congress], and from the Clinton camp was a contributing factor."[46]

Bush wanted it to be a short-term mission, with troop withdrawals to be under way by the time Clinton was sworn in as president in January 1993. But it would be March 1994 before the last U.S. troops left.

"I Never Saw a Landing Like This One"

Many people knew approximately when the U.S. troops were coming ashore: they arrived December 9, 1992. International TV network crews were waiting in Mogadishu, along with print journalists, photographers, and—later in the day—thousands of Somalis. Navy Seals swam ashore before dawn, emerging with night vision goggles, only to be temporarily blinded by a curtain of photographers' flashes and TV lights. It could have been a dangerous moment: battle-ready forces meeting an army of reporters crowding forward for a good shot. Fortunately, no one pulled a trigger. Later that morning, a perspiring marine, William Sears, from Coronado, California, standing on the beach in full battle gear, holding his rifle, looked around. "It's a strange sight," he said, as his gaze swept over the massive crowds of Somalis on the beach peacefully watching the landing crafts coming ashore and unloading men and vehicles. Gunnery Sergeant Franklin Reis, of Richmond, Texas, also looked around in amazement: "I've been in quite a few landings. I've never seen one like this."

The only control power the U.S. soldiers needed that morning was crowd control. One frustrated marine kept shouting to Somalis to back up so spray and sand blown by the landing craft would not hit them. He was having no luck. I asked a Somali for the words "back up" and then told the soldier. When he used them, people suddenly moved back, much to his delight. The soldiers had expected a worse reception. Somali gunmen had been attacking food convoys regularly. On November 11, gunmen had attacked trucks carrying food to Baidoa; some forty people were killed in the battle.[47]

The U.S. landing at Mogadishu was historic for three reasons: It was the first time an international military force had been deployed to Africa to deliver relief supplies to prevent starvation; it was the first such

Mogadishu, Somalia, 1992
Landing in Mogadishu, U.S. soldiers found crowds of Somalis and journalists watching them.

intervention without the consent of the country's government—there was no central government at the time of the landing; and it was the first time U.S. ground troops had been deployed in Africa since the end of World War II except for training exercises.[48] Some analysts thought that the U.S. air war against Iraq in January 1991 should provide a lesson for its intervention in Somalia. The United States had initiated this action as a result of Iraq's occupation of Kuwait. But the United States had failed to kill or dislodge President Saddam Hussein, who remained in power. "The lesson of Iraq is that we ought to think through what the root problem is so we don't have to go in again on a more costly basis," one analyst said.[49]

The root problem in Somalia was a complex one. The state had collapsed under Barre; his victors were carving up the country; the system of interclan coexistence had been severely battered. Now foreign troops had arrived. The starving would be fed; that would largely succeed. But the basic problem, the political one, would remain until the Somalis—if they could—reestablished a system of coexistence. Otherwise the country would remain fragmented, dangerous. From the start, the view among many Somalis and the few Westerners who knew much about Somalia was that a quick withdrawal of U.S. troops, as envisioned by President Bush, would accomplish little. After news that the United States was planning an intervention lasting only a few weeks leaked out from Washington, one relief official in Nairobi said U.S. officials "don't understand the realities of Somalia if that's what they are thinking."[50]

Closer to Somalia, U.S. ambassador to Kenya Smith Hempstone sent a cable to the State Department warning of the dangers of a U.S. military force in Somalia. His December 2, 1992, cable warned that U.S. troops would be vulnerable to sniper fire and mines, and he cautioned that a Western nation taking charge in a Muslim country could provoke a backlash from Muslims outside Somalia. Hempstone also wrote that the operation might "reunite the Somali nation against [the United States], the invaders, the outsiders . . . who may have fed their children but also have killed their young men."[51] He was largely ignored by the State Department and the White House, though he was right about the vulnerability of U.S. troops.

Landing day, as the airport and nearby main port in Mogadishu were filling up with U.S. soldiers, their officers began planning to send troops to interior towns such as Baidoa. Death rates in Baidoa had come down significantly but largely because many of the most vulnerable, especially young children, were already dead. "Where are all the starving people?" is the question I was most frequently asked by earnest young U.S. Marines after they landed in Somalia. They looked around at the crowds of healthy Somalis watching their arrival and wondered if what they had been told about Somalis dying was true. Knowing their sincerity and obvious desire to be of help, I could never bring myself to tell them the stark truth: "You're too late; most who were starving are already dead." The post-Barre civil war that had caused much of the starvation was far from finished, however, and the United States and other troops saved many lives by keeping survivors fed and minimizing food looting.

The issue of disarmament came up almost immediately. What should be done about all the guns Somalis had? That first day the troops arrived, I spoke with numerous Somalis, who said they hoped the United States would disarm militia and restore order to their ravaged country. They said they would help the marines locate hidden weapons. Machine guns and rifles were abundant; almost every family had a weapon for self-defense, if not for looting. But the Western troops paid little heed to arms. My Somali driver, for example, simply lay his machine gun on the floor behind his seat when we passed through checkpoints of U.S. or French Foreign Legion troops.

U.S. policy on disarmament was ambivalent. No immediate effort was made to detect or seize weapons, nor would any consistent search-and-seizure policy be carried out later. Disarmament went from a hot topic to one rarely even discussed by the U.S. military or diplomats. In the final months of the UN military presence in Mogadishu, after the United States had pulled out, "technicals," the heavily armed Somali vehicles, were once again on the streets. Major armed clashes between rival Somali clans were again the rule, not the exception.

In the first week after the arrival of the U.S. military in Mogadishu, U.S. Marine Colonel Fred Peck told reporters, "If we see weapons openly displayed in an area over which we hold control, we will consider them hostile." Robert B. Oakley, U.S. special envoy to Somalia for Presidents Bush and Clinton, said disarmament was impractical: "We can't disarm New York or Washington; how could we disarm Mogadishu?"[52]

With its overwhelming military force, the U.S. troops might have been able to round up more weapons than they did, especially large ones, including vehicle-mounted weapons. But they would have had to act quickly. Within days of their arrival, Somalis were spotted fleeing with heavy weapons toward the Kenyan and Ethiopian borders. Ethiopian president Meles Zenawi told me in an interview in 1994 that he had ordered his soldiers to stop the entry of any Somalis with such weapons. Somali sources said some weapons had been buried far from Mogadishu. Italian troops in Belet Huen, a central Somali town, did round up and destroy some heavy weapons. In Mogadishu, some heavy weapons of both Aideed and Mahdi were put in caches subject to UN inspection. It was a clash in Mogadishu, after Pakistani Muslim soldiers inspected one of Aideed's caches, that led to the unraveling of both the UN and U.S. missions in Somalia.

Well before that, however, there were signs the foreign intervention was heading into problems, especially in the coastal city of Kismayu, whose port and airport made it a prize fought over by rival militia. The lack of understanding of Somali politics by the occupying forces was becoming quite clear there. Kismayu was to become the first example in Somalia of the limited effectiveness of an international military force trying to act as a peacemaker. Kismayu "provided an early test of [U.S. and UN troops'] commitment to enforce a cease-fire and maintain the military status quo."[53] They failed the test.

"We'll Kick Ass"

When Barre fled Mogadishu in January 1991, Morgan, his son-in-law, retreated to Kismayu, where he had some ties to local ethnic clans. Morgan had been in charge of Barre's merciless bombing of the northern city Hargeisa, a deed that earned him the title "butcher of Hargeisa." But now, with Barre overthrown, Morgan joined forces with Barre's enemy, Mahdi. Morgan later lost control of Kismayu to Colonel Ahmed Omar Jess, who also had fought on Barre's side but had since become aligned with Aideed. So the Mahdi-Aideed rivalry of Mogadishu was being played out in Kismayu by proxy, with Morgan on Mahdi's side and Jess on Aideed's. Most senior U.S. and UN military officers I spoke with in Somalia appeared to know little about the country's politics, though it lay at the heart of the war the United States was trying to curb. They especially showed a "disturbing unfamiliarity with the Kismayu conflict."[54]

On January 25, 1993, six weeks after the first U.S. troops arrived in Somalia, a combined U.S.-Belgian force launched an attack that turned back a column led by Morgan, who was headed toward Kismayu to try to recapture the city. A month later, Morgan's forces changed tactics and seized much of the city despite the presence of the same international forces. This time, instead of advancing as a unit on Kismayu, where Belgian tanks and U.S. armored personnel carriers were guarding major intersections, Morgan sent his men—and women—into the city one by one or in groups of no more than two or three. They came in looking like herders, not soldiers, according to a U.S. military spokesman. Morgan got women to carry firearms under their skirts. Once in Kismayu, he routed Jess's forces out of most of the city.

The change of power in Kismayu, under the noses of U.S. and Belgian troops, was only the first of many Somali power shifts the foreigners were unable to stop. The following month, on March 17, 1993, Morgan's force took over the rest of Kismayu, clashing with Jess's forces directly in front of Belgian tanks, using women at the front of the attack. The Belgians did not shoot. "What were we supposed to do, fire on women?" one Belgian soldier asked later. Kismayu was the first clear indication that Somali soldiers could outfox the much better-equipped Western forces. Unfortunately, the lessons of Kismayu were largely ignored by the U.S. and UN bureaucracy in Mogadishu, where things would turn deadly before long.

Somalia, especially Mogadishu, was to become a textbook example of the mismatch between the kind of "overwhelming" force Colin Powell, chairman of the U.S. Joint Chiefs of Staff, had called for in the Somali operation and an effective, urban guerrilla force whose tactics resembled a pack of African hyena nipping at the heels of a large buffalo until they brought it down. In Africa, it is not always the biggest and strongest animal that survives a hunt.

Another example of the mismatch of forces came in Kismayu as the U.S. military began reducing its troops in Somalia in early 1993, as part of its go-home-early plan. A U.S. offshore, rapid deployment force was assigned to respond to emergencies in Somalia. Some 500 troops in that force sailed into Kismayu waters two days after Morgan's militia took over the city from Jess. They came aboard the USS *Wasp* under the command of Commodore Ken Pyle. If the local militia leaders were "contemplating upsetting the balance of power, the U.S. force is prepared to take action," he told me on board. He made no mention of the fact that the balance of power had just shifted and the United States, with troops in the city, had been unable to stop it. Though Morgan's forces were now in charge of Kismayu, Jess was nearby and planning revenge. The U.S. troops arriving on the *Wasp* were putting themselves in the middle of Somali politics by supporting the temporary balance of power, which now favored Morgan.

A marine commander on board the *Wasp* said the United States would "kick ass" if any militia leader tried something. How, exactly, would it do that? I asked. He said there were "crowd control" techniques that could be applied, and on a piece of paper he drew some lines I didn't understand. The marines were there to "send a message to the warlords," he added. Which warlords? I asked. He hesitated, perhaps uncertain or unaware of who the "warlords," or militia leaders, in that area were. But it was no secret which Somali forces controlled the city. And since Morgan was happy to have his force in charge of the city, any message the U.S. presence was sending about keeping the political status quo had to be addressed to Jess. I went looking for Jess the next day to see if he was getting the message.

The U.S. forces were not searching for him; they were busy doing things in town like putting up sandbags near where Belgian troops had already done so. Western relief officials watched with some amusement at the futility of the exercise, for that is what the Kismayu operation seemed to be, an observation U.S. officers, speaking privately, did not deny. Belgian intelligence officers welcomed me to their makeshift headquarters in Kismayu—a couple of military vehicles parked behind a small building. They shared their rations, much tastier than U.S. Meals Ready to Eat, or MREs. (One evening I was sitting on some boxes in a hallway near the Belgian operations center at the port in Kismayu, eating an MRE, or trying to. A Belgian soldier took pity and invited me over to enjoy the fresh-cooked meal his troops were eating nearby.)

The Belgian intelligence officers had no idea where Jess was, but they agreed to take me with them to check an area where he had been seen the previous day. We drove some distance from town in a jeep. Along the way one of the Belgian soldiers threw packets of cookies to Somalis; hungry Somalis of all ages scrambled for the packets, and the Belgian soldier seemed pleased. He took pride in his cookie marksmanship, seeing how close he could get them to the feet of people. It made me angry: it reminded me of feeding animals at a zoo. The scrambling was undignified and emphasized the helplessness of the people. I wondered why the Belgians didn't just stop and distribute food in a respectable way, though with just one box they might have been mobbed.

The Belgians were unable to find Jess, so when we passed through a village I asked them to stop. I walked over to some Somalis standing by a store and asked them if anyone could show us the way to Jess's camp—that I was a journalist and traveling with the Belgians. The men told a young boy to accompany us. He climbed onto the back of our jeep, and we continued up the road a few more miles. At a side road, the boy indicated we should turn. At the end of that dirt road was another one; it ended in a cluster of trees. I got out. After introducing myself as a journalist, and asking for an interview with Jess, I was told by a Somali man to sit down. He pointed to a log. In a few minutes, a short, solid man came out: it was Jess. He sat down on the log, and we talked as U.S. jets screamed overhead.

"What message are you getting from all this?" I asked, pointing to the planes.

"No message," he said "I want the U.S. and UN troops to go home so I can take over Kismayu."

So much for the show of force. The U.S. military presence in Somalia reminded me of someone clapping with one hand: lots of motion but not much effect.

Reporting the War in Somalia

If Somalia was confusing to the U.S. military, it was also confusing to journalists—and dangerous. A number of journalists were killed; Betty and I considered ourselves fortunate to have come out unscathed. My main task was to try to understand not only the daily events but their background. This meant building trust with Somalis of competing factions to obtain insights on their views. It took time, repeated visits, a lot of travel, and still there was so much more I always needed to learn. But at least I was able to convince many Somalis that I was listening to their views and reporting them.

The Somalia story emerged in pieces: the collapse of the state, including the decline of the central government during the time when Barre pitted clans against each other to keep them off balance and himself in power; the civil war and anarchy that followed the fall of Barre; relief efforts; and the foreign military intervention. The overall story was multilayered, yet I could penetrate some of the layers by traveling through the country, listening to a wide variety of Somalis, and cross-checking their accounts when possible. Somalis often were surprised, but usually helpful, when queried by an outsider about leaders in addition to Aideed and Mahdi, about political and military strategies, and about clan politics.

One of the features of Somali politics that makes it seem byzantine is that clan alliances are fluid. Members of a clan or subclan will change their allegiance when it serves their interest. The Hawadley are an example. The Hawadley, a major clan, supported Aideed and his Habir Gedir subclan militia when Aideed was battling Barre. The two clans continued to cooperate after Aideed occupied south Mogadishu. When Aideed and Mahdi fought and divided the city, establishing the "green line" of bombed-out, abandoned buildings downtown between territory of the two sides, the Hawadley remained aligned with Aideed. By early 1993, however, Aideed's forces began pushing southward, grabbing more farmland, including some the Hawadley had taken. Aideed's men in Mogadishu also seized some property belonging to the Hawadley. As a result, the Hawadley finally declared war against the Habir Gedir.

In August 1994, Aideed's forces attacked the Hawadley-dominated town of Belet Huen, in central Somalia near the Ethiopian border, driving the Hawadley out. Shortly after Aideed's men took charge, I flew back to the town with a private relief team assessing needs. The Hawadley, who had lived primarily on the east side of town, had fled; streets there were practically empty. On the west side, where more than a dozen non-Hawadley clans lived, life went on as normal. The unpaved side streets on the west side were full of people; outdoor market stalls were piled with goods. Interviewing people was difficult. Typical of an occupied zone, residents feared to criticize the occupiers. Nor did they want to criticize the Hawadleys in case they retook the town.[55]

Before the takeover, when the Habir Gedir forces seized control of the main road near the town, the Hawadley had forcibly expelled some 100 Habir Gedir families from Belet Huen. Aideed's forces retaliated, capturing the town, looting Hawadley properties, and forcing the Hawadley to flee. In the process, the Habir Gedir captured a contingent of Zimbabwean UN troops, later releasing them, again illustrating the relative ineffectiveness of the UN troops in controlling fights between clans.

★   ★   ★

Covering the war had light and dangerous moments. As things began to sour for the U.S. and UN troops, as Aideed's forces began fighting them in mid-1993, most journalists stayed at the Al-Sahafi Hotel in Mogadishu. It was located near an intersection leading to the airport, which was in U.S. and UN hands after December 1992. From the roof of the Al-Sahafi, where journalists gathered to relax in the early evenings after filing their day's story, one had a view of much of the city. Blocks of whitewashed homes with flat roofs hinted at peace and the Mogadishu that had been a tourist spot. But there were plenty of reminders of the war. Now and then a Somali gunman on a nearby rooftop would fire at one of the U.S. Cobra helicopter gunships sweeping over, lights out, on another mission. The gunman's tracer bullets left red trails arching skyward. Since we journalists were in plain view of pilots, we always hoped the newly arrived U.S. pilots had been briefed that our group on the hotel roof, with night vision lenses pointed at their aircraft, was friendly.

Snipers could turn our way, too, so most of the time we sat rather than stood on the roof, protected by a low wall. One night in response to Somali music blaring out from across the street, we put on Bruce Springsteen's "Born in the USA" and turned up the volume, blanketing the evening air with an acoustical protest. Rival Somali factions sometimes peppered the Al-Sahafi Hotel with automatic weapons, not as a target, but because two groups were firing at each other from opposite sides of the building. Fortunately, I was not there on those several occasions.

Some journalists bravely went wherever there was gunfire. In June 1993 Pakistani soldiers, on a rooftop in Mogadishu, fired from behind sandbags on a group of Somali protestors entering the main intersection below. The Pakistanis denied using machine guns against the crowd, but a tape recording made by journalist Paul Watson captured the sound of either a machine gun or rapid-fire automatic weapons. A television crew caught what appeared to be Pakistani troops on the roof using machine guns. The Pakistani command denied the use of such weapons. The crowd was unarmed except for a possible Somali shooter at the rear of the group, who some observers said fired into the crowd to force the demonstrators toward the Pakistani guns and provoke a showdown to create further animosity against the United Nations.

I freely admit I was not among those who rushed to battles. But I found myself impelled to go close to one the morning I was shaken awake in the hotel by aerial bombing. A U.S. spy plane with computer precision was chipping off parts of Aideed's house in a deliberate intimidation campaign. I jumped out of my bed; my roommate, a Japanese journalist, was already on his feet. We ran up to the roof and watched the attack. Soon helicopters were raking Aideed's neighborhood with fire. I wanted to see if the intense fire was killing civilians, so I went into the streets. I ran behind correspondent Watson alongside a wall. Snipers on the other side were firing into the street, so we ran close to the wall, sprinting across intersections until we got to one near the battle.

At the intersection near Aideed's house there were a number of young Somali men. The attack was by the United States, so I had planned to tell Somalis I met that I was from Canada. But when they asked my nationality, I blurted out "American." Yes, I added quickly, the pilots attacking were Americans, too, but "I'm down here with you; if you get hit, I'll get hit." They stared at me for a few long seconds. Many Somalis carry knives, and despite the presence nearby of an Italian tank crew I was nervous. I was already frightened by the whiz of snipers' bullets overhead. I kept talking, trying to assure them I just wanted their views. Finally, they began answering my questions. Several other journalists wanted to try to get closer to the area under attack, only about a block away, but the Somalis with whom I had been talking told me it was too dangerous.

The helicopters were still flying low over our heads, spewing out bullets. That morning I saw something that convinced me the battle against Aideed's forces could be a tougher one than most of us had imagined. Despite the intensity of the air attack, the Aideed fighters did not turn and run. They merely fell back, building by building, and continued firing at the helicopters from the side. It was this fearlessness that would help bring them victory. And it was Somali rage that would bring the deaths of four of my colleagues.

Four international journalists were killed at the site of the U.S. bombing of a meeting of Aideed's supporters, a meeting which included many civilians, in May 1993. I was not in Mogadishu at the time. Journalist Scott Peterson told me he arrived at the site before the other four and had been struck on the head by some angry Somalis. Yet he was fortunate; he managed to get back to the Al-Sahafi Hotel. Reuters photographers Dan Eldon, a British-American, and Kenyan Hos Maina; Anthony Macharia, a Kenyan soundman for Reuter television; and Hansi Krauss, a German photographer, were killed at the scene. They were beaten to death by Somalis enraged by the U.S. attack on civilians with no warning. Another Kenyan journalist, Mohammed Shafi, who had gone with the four was lined up against a wall to be shot, but the gun jammed. He frantically pushed his way through the mob and leaped onto a moving pickup truck whose driver threatened to take him to the local market, where he, too, would likely have been beaten to death. But he convinced the driver he was a friend of Aideed and they deposited him, badly wounded, at the Al-Sahafi.

Maina was a friend of Betty's and mine, a gentle and courageous photographer, always willing to help others, never pushy, never trying to claim extra credit for himself. During riots that accompanied an aborted coup in Kenya in 1982, Maina was one of the few photographers brave enough to go out on the street, taking his photos with a camera hidden in a basket he was carrying. Eldon was known as the "mayor of Mogadishu" among his friends for his casual, cheerful manner and appreciation of Somalis. He could talk easily with everyone and seemed at home in a city of turmoil. He cheered up fellow journalists with funny stories and even sold postcards and T-shirts of Mogadishu.

In Nairobi one evening I watched as bodies were unloaded from a small aircraft. The mothers of the two Kenyans broke into loud wailing when the body bags were brought off the plane. As I felt the pain of the families, I couldn't help wondering how the mothers of the Somalis killed by the U.S. bombs must be feeling. Could their grief be any less heart rending? I was angry at the U.S. attack on the civilian meeting. Another colleague, Keith Richburg, of the *Washington Post,* who was frequently assigned to Mogadishu during his three years in Africa, also reacted to the killing of the four journalists: "I didn't cry when my friends died; I became obsessed. . . . I talked to military officers who planned the operation, who called it 'a good hit' and the people inside 'punks' and 'gangsters.' I talked to a State Department officer who told me, 'Maybe we killed some people we wouldn't have wanted to kill, but we also got the guys we were after'."[56] Richburg saw a moral flaw in the attack. "Something had happened to the United States in this first post [Cold War] military expedition in Africa—we were behaving like they were. We had come into the jungle (or in this case, the desert) and adopted their survival-of-the-fittest rules. We had lost our moral high ground."[57]

★   ★   ★

Another's death makes one think of one's own mortality. We journalists, like relief workers, always assumed we were going to make it through the war, that somehow the bullets, bombs, and rockets would not hit us, that we could carry on with our work unharmed. One day I saw another Kenyan TV soundman, Hassan Ali, being taken to a hospital in a pickup truck. I jumped in with him and later helped carry him into the operating room. He was flown back to Kenya, where he eventually recovered. I was angry at the circumstances in which he had been

Mogadishu, Somalia, 1992
A Kenyan TV soundman,
Hasan Ali, was knifed by
angry Somalis while filming
in front of a mosque. The
author (*right back*) helped
carry him into a Somali hospital.

knifed by a Somali who robbed him and another Kenyan of their cameras. An Italian producer who had hired the Kenyans had insisted on
their filming in front of a mosque despite Somali warnings on the scene
to go away. Such warnings should have been taken seriously. The producer later bought back the stolen equipment, encouraging further
armed robberies.

Somalia the Sunbird

Occasionally a gunfight would break out within a few hundred yards of
our hotel in Mogadishu. I would creep to the doorway leading onto the
roof, trying to look out without exposing myself to fire. One day, in the
midst of such a battle I saw a bird sitting on a ledge of the roof, its
singing nearly drowned out by machine gun fire. The good qualities of
Somalis during the war were like the beautiful greenish and bronze

colors of an African sunbird, glinting momentarily in the sunlight, then disappearing in the noise and shadows of violence.[58] During four years reporting on the war, flying there from Nairobi in comfortable chartered jets of relief agencies or on dawn cargo planes, sleeping on sacks of grain, packing plastic water bottles, a bedroll, and notebooks, I saw contrasting aspects of Somalis. The killings and the massive starvation were the shadows of the country; the selfless, brave work of Somali relief workers and the tenacity and courage of the people, their endurance and will to live, were the sunbird qualities.

Sometimes the gentle qualities of a Somali made me set aside my deadline reporting. One such person was a man in a hospital in Mogadishu, a dismal facility with few amenities, few doctors, and crowded with wounded and sick. A stray bullet had hit him when he had gone out looking for bread for his children, paralyzing him. One year later I came across the same man, still lying there, still trying to be cheerful and to stay alive. I was so moved I spent hours getting a U.S. military doctor from the base at the airport to come examine him. The doctor came, but he had to be guarded by a U.S. military escort—a truck with several armed soldiers. The soldiers had not had much contact with Somalis off their base. Two of them, a man and a woman, took pictures of themselves outside the hospital with a small camera, posing with Somali children. They seemed delighted to meet some of the people they had come to help. For a fleeting moment their two worlds came together: the children offered smiles and eager handshakes, spontaneous gifts these soldiers might remember as much as, or more than, the hardships or even the dangers of Somalia; for their part, the soldiers offered their genuine affection for the children, taking a break from acting like members of the military.

The children of Somalia. I had seen so many dying, but so many more were still alive with curiosity, hope, and laughter. Later, some youth became not only mischievous but dangerous, as they stole equipment from troops—sometimes hopping moving military vehicles and grabbing anything they could pry loose. For the most part, it was not like the situation in Liberia, however, where child soldiers were among the killers.

Somalia and its children affected some of the troops who came from abroad. Canadian soldier Vincent Fowles, sitting in the back of a truck

Baidoa, Somalia, 1992
U.S. soldiers take time to meet some Somali children.

Baidoa, Somalia, 1992
Children in a Somali orphanage delight in catching raindrops.
Credit: UNICEF/Betty Press.

in Belet Huen, told me one day: "I saw kids drinking water as dirty as my laundry water. They use string to hold their sandals together. When I get home, I'll look at myself and say, 'I've got enough'." After covering Somalia for a while, I began to say the same thing. I gained a new appreciation for basic things: a meal; a place to sleep; being alive.

One group of children who got a lot of attention lived at a small, rustic orphanage in a schoolhouse at the edge of Baidoa, the epicenter of the famine. Reporters, relief officials, diplomats, soldiers—everyone went to the orphanage. I learned in interviews with some of the children that many of them were not orphans, but their parents were unable to provide for them. The orphanage offered safety and Spartan meals. The rooms, bare except for beds, opened onto a single dirt courtyard. Wooden boards with Koranic lessons written on them with erasable ink were stacked next to the trees in the courtyard. The children laughed and played in the rain one afternoon, including a little girl in Mickey Mouse slippers sent from abroad.

★   ★   ★

Historian Isaiah Berlin once wrote that "to be lonely is to be among men who do not know what you mean." His words could have applied to Americans looking at Somalis and Somalis looking at Americans. "Exile, solitude," Berlin wrote, "is to find yourself among people whose words, gestures, handwriting are alien to your own, whose behavior, reactions, feelings, instinctive responses, and thoughts and pleasures and pains, are too remote from yours, whose education and outlook, the tone and quality of whose lives and being, are not yours."[59] Lack of understanding between people of different countries naturally leads to miscalculations; Somalia was no exception. Somalia was a tragic example of how lack of understanding can lengthen the psychological distance between an African country and the West.

For many in the West, when things go wrong somewhere in Africa, they see all of Africa as a continent without hope; the country in trouble becomes the bellwether for all the other ones. "Somalia, then, became the prism through which I came to view the rest of Africa," wrote one American journalist after covering the war there. "It was to become the metaphor for my own disillusionment."[60] At a time when many Africans were seeking greater freedom in their lives and often needed Western cooperation to get it, such analysis was unfortunate. It was also inaccurate; Somalia was not typical of Africa.

As noted earlier, most of those who came to Somalia did not understand the history or the culture or the politics of the people. Somalis were "virtually unanimous that the international community failed to understand them and their country, failed to sufficiently consult with Somalis before making key decisions regarding their fate and well-being, and failed to draw sufficiently on the limited number of people familiar from previous experience with the country."[61] U.S. military personnel arrived in Somalia with a small booklet explaining some basic elements of Somali society, yet most I spoke with had little understanding of Somalia. This unfamiliarity led to an "us-versus-them" attitude toward Somalis as Aideed's side became increasingly convinced that the United States and the United Nations were in Somalia to block their goal of taking over the country.

Land of Oz: UN Headquarters in Somalia

The decisions when to fight and whom to fight were made behind the long white walls surrounding the former U.S. Embassy, which became the UN headquarters as well as the U.S. political base as the conflict heated up. I called the massive compound the Land of Oz because of its pretense at power despite its inability to change the military or political situation in Somalia. From the outside, the compound was quite impressive, but inside it seemed almost impotent.

The people inside were quite isolated from the reality of Somalia. As the streets grew more dangerous, their main contact with Somalis was limited to those working in or visiting the compound. For most personnel the wall around the compound was as much psychological as physical. Many times a reporter entering the compound was greeted with "What's it like downtown?" "Downtown" was where we journalists and, until it got too dangerous, most private aid workers lived. A siege mentality had set in among most UN and U.S. personnel, and not without cause. Once Aideed was targeted, his supporters felt free to fire on U.S. or UN personnel, which they did in ambushes. The occasional mortar fired into the compound was also enough to make life in Oz unnerving. Protective gear was issued to UN employees. One woman working in the press unit of the United Nations who wore a helmet and sometimes a flak jacket had a mortar explode next to her trailer one evening.By day the compound was full of Somali clerks, cleaning crews, construction workers, and others. Among them were almost certainly Aideed supporters. It was widely assumed that Aideed sympathizers may have given U.S. and UN military forces wrong information on the whereabouts of Aideed during the months international forces were hunting for him.

Journalists dealing frequently with U.S. and UN press officials sparred with them on numerous occasions. The officials were friendly, sometimes helpful, but often under constraints that kept them from disclosing the full truth. For example, after one battle between U.S. and Aideed forces, a U.S. military spokesman would not confirm whether any U.S. personnel had been wounded. The spokesman did say no one was missing. He was talking from the compound by radio to a group of us journalists at the Al-Sahafi Hotel; we were unable to reach the compound due to heavy fighting on the street that day. I asked the spokesman why he could not confirm if any U.S. soldiers were hurt since they had accounted for everyone. How could he be sure they were alive and not know if they were wounded? On another occasion, a UN official who had come to help reestablish a Somali police force was asked by a foreign reporter why the UN was working with a notorious thug from the Barre years on the new force. The official, apparently unaware of the record of the ex-Barre man, made a general statement about how the UN was screening applicants.

Despite the dangers of traveling outside the UN-U.S. compound, some U.S. officers relished the risk. One who worked for the U.S. Psychological Operations office gave me a ride one day in his jeep. He drove rapidly down sandy side roads to a relief agency office a few blocks away, clenching a cigar between his teeth like a smoking version of John Wayne. He could have ridden in an armored personnel carrier, but he preferred the jeep, despite the possibility of snipers. Some UN troops who got outside the compound did more harm than good. "Egyptians were selling vehicles [at the port in Mogadishu]; Nigerian forces were selling passes into the UN compound; Pakistanis were caught leaving [Somalia] with crates of 'military equipment' that turned out to be full of UN air conditioners and appliances."[62] The corruption at the port got so blatant that the UN official in charge of port security brought the matter up at a meeting with a senior UN official in Mogadishu, alleging Egyptian troops were involved. It was a delicate matter because the secretary general of the UN was Egyptian. Rather than listen and take note, according to another participant in the meeting, the senior UN official ordered the port security man not to disparage Egyptian troops. Later, the senior official did inspect the port.

In the part of the compound the United States was still using for its own operations, a newly arrived U.S. military intelligence officer spoke with me at length as we stood under a tree. He seemed eager to learn but as confused as we reporters over the shifting orders given to the military regarding the purpose of the U.S. mission in Somalia. Unlike many other officers, however, he admitted his bewilderment. The U.S. military strategy was confusing: U.S. troop strength was built up, then reduced, then built up again. The United States never established a clear policy on disarmament. The mission's purpose also kept changing, from humanitarian and noninvolvement in politics, to hunting Aideed, and later to negotiating with him, even flying him to a peace conference in a U.S. plane.

Elusive Peace

The U.S. peace strategy was also confusing. U.S. envoy Robert Oakley, as energetic and sincere as he was, fell into the trap of trying to negotiate mostly between Aideed and Mahdi and never developed the wider range of contacts the first UN special representative to Somalia, Sahnoun, did. Sahnoun contacted not only the heads of militia but traditional and other community leaders. His dismissal by Boutros-Ghali after criticizing the slow-moving UN bureaucracy left the United Nations in Somalia without the one person already well along the road to working with a wide variety of Somali authorities. That range of contacts was necessary to understand Somali political and military maneuvering.

Somalis, like any other people, see and describe events from their viewpoints. Once you appreciated clan bias or loyalty, which changes according to events, Somali politics was not impossible to fathom.

There was also a logic behind most of the fighting. Fighting was seldom random and usually in response to attacks or as part of a plan of conquest in a contested area.

Meanwhile peace was becoming an ever more distant goal.

Things might have gone better if the U.S. and the UN officials had known more about peacemaking in Somalia.[63] The United States, joined later by the UN, tried to broker peace agreements between the lead militia leaders, primarily Aideed and Mahdi. This effort usually consisted of separate negotiations with each side to seek agreement on a cease-fire in Mogadishu (several were reached, most of short duration) and on the formation of a coalition, central government. The United States and the UN often worked together on these negotiations, but the former continued to make its own direct contacts with the two sides from time to time.

Aideed was not opposed to agreements. On March 27, 1993, he signed one in Addis Ababa, Ethiopia, with other leaders of the warring factions. This agreement called for the establishment of a Transitional National Council (TNC) to run the country; it would be composed of fifty-four representatives from eighteen regions (three represenatives, including one woman, per region), five additional seats for Mogadishu, and one nominee from each of the main political factions. Each region would establish a regional countil and under it district councils. At the time, Aideed claimed control of enough regions to give him control of the TNC, but his claims proved to be an exaggeration. In any case, the establishment of regional councils was never completed. The agreement fell apart as Aideed and rival factions fell into new rounds of fighting, but many district councils were set up with the help of the United Nations.

Other peace pacts brokered by the United Nations would follow, with few lasting results. The UN-brokered conferences had time limits of several weeks, while traditional Somali peace talks took several months. The signatories to some UN-sponsored pacts signed only after the UN deadline for the peace talks expired, or more precisely, after the United Nations threatened to stop paying hotel bills for the delegates in cities such as Nairobi and Addis Ababa. There was nothing like the prospect of paying their own hotel bills to get intransigent Somali faction leaders to sign a treaty, shake hands in front of the cameras, then go home and do nothing—until they began fighting again.

There were three even more fundamental weaknesses in the peace-making process which the United States and the United Nations generally did not recognize.

1. The collapse of the Somali state left rival groups arguing about who had the power to represent whom at peace conferences. This infighting at preparatory meetings was more important to the Somalis than the actual peace negotiation because it determined how important one group was in relation to the others. Failure to recognize this important nuance "was central to nearly every failed peace conference."

2. Somali factional leaders also saw peace conferences as a place to gain prestige to enhance their position in dealing with challenges to their leadership within their own clans. Somalis I interviewed said Aideed had at least three rivals for leadership of his own Habir Gedir subclan of the Hawiye, including Osman Hassan Ali ("Ato"), a former financial backer who later fought against him. Because the focus of the UN-organized peace conferences was primarily militia leaders, with less attention paid to other community and traditional clan leaders, the conferences tended to enhance the position of people like Aideed and Mahdi within their subclans. This reduced chances for others to make serious contributions toward peace.

3. Some Somalis benefited from war. Somalis who had seized valuable real estate in Mogadishu or farmlands in the south had little interest in a peace that might require them to give these spoils of war back. In this respect, not only was peacemaking in Somalia an unpopular pursuit, it was dangerous, especially for would-be Somali peacemakers.[64]

A Somali Botanist and Peacemaker

Ahmed Warfa is a tall, slender, and roughly handsome man, slightly bald, with gray hair and a wispy gray beard. With his dignified manner when he walks, he looks royal—and he is. Bloodlines on both sides of his family trace back to the equivalent of Somali kings. Warfa became a peacemaker after civil war forced the closure of the Somali National University in Mogadishu where he was a professor of botany. (He said he identified in the harsh Somali scrubland a tough little plant that goats eat and which today bears his family name.) He needed a job so he began working for the United Nations, first translating, then helping to set up district councils under the Addis Ababa peace agreement. The militia leaders of Somalia, including Aideed, did not want the councils set up unless they controlled them. So for Warfa's tireless efforts to help establish councils, he became a marked man.

On the afternoon of February 24, 1994, Warfa was being driven home from his UN office in Mogadishu. As the car neared his house, he spotted a group of men quarreling at the metal gate. When his driver slowed to let him out, Warfa heard one of the men say, "He's here; he's here."[65] Within seconds, the men sprayed bullets toward his car. His

Nairobi, Kenya, 1995 Ahmed Warfa, a Somali botanist, was a UN employee during the UN operation in Somalia.

driver was wounded but managed to speed away with him. Warfa was hit five times and was admitted to a Pakistani-run hospital in the city.

"Some people were happy I was injured, hoped that I was killed, or handicapped," Warfa said after he had recovered and moved to Nairobi. "The warlords did not want me going around [working] at the grassroots to establish district councils. The most hated people by the warlords are the intellectuals, because they are the ones who understand [what is happening in Somalia]." He was working at the Swedish Life and Peace Institute's Nairobi office, doing what he could to reconcile rival Somali factions whose representatives were in Nairobi. There was one faction he was not eager to meet with, however—Aideed's, whose men may have been the ones who tried to kill him.

But while peace was running into obstacles in southern Somalia, there was progress in the north.

Making Peace the Somali Way

In a schoolhouse at the edge of the town of Boroma, dozens of community leaders in long robes and, many of them, turbans, gathered from different parts of northern Somalia in February 1993 for a peace conference. They came from all parts of a region that in May 1991 had declared itself independent of the rest of the country, taking the name Somaliland. Their leaders had set up a provisional government. (So far no other nation had recognized it.) Since then, rival factions had fallen into conflict, and the provisional government had become discredited amid charges of corruption. The Boroma peace conference was an attempt to bring people back together again and select new leaders—the Somali way. For one thing, that meant leisurely negotiations where all views could be aired at length, rather than the usually hurried UN conferences. The meetings ran from February to May 1993.

It was my first experience visiting a Somali peace conference. Between the initial organizing sessions, the dusty streets of the town filled up with elders, as Somali traditional leaders are called. At a crowded local restaurant I sat down with one of the oldest elders and asked him how they could control the kind of armed bandits who had menaced my wife and me—and even some of the elders—on the way to the peace conference.

"They will obey us," he said with assurance, shaking a long, bony finger to emphasize his point.

Could unarmed, elderly men like himself really curb the violence racking the new country? Elders in Somalia have always played a key role in keeping peace. Unarmed, but highly respected in traditional Somali society, they are neither elected nor selected by politicians. Their base of legitimacy comes from their role in the community as respected civil leaders. Some are known as *Ugas,* a word usually translated as "kings." But unlike despotic kings, they exercise their influence peacefully. They listen to grievances, weigh the facts, and generally try to counsel and advise in line with what appears to be the majority tendency. Sometimes, however, they call men to arms.

In the midst of the civil war, especially in Mogadishu, armed militia often disregarded the elders. But even so, elders never completely lost their influence in Somalia and continued to have the respect of most ordinary Somalis. On numerous occasions during the post-Barre years, elders used their influence to curb militia activity, sometimes as mediators. In Belet Huen, for example, one *Uga* of the Hawadley clan helped negotiate a truce with rival factions.

★   ★   ★

Betty and I arrived for what we thought were the closing days of the conference. So much for Western thinking; the conference was just starting. It was being held without UN sponsorship and without U.S. involvement. In contrast to the UN conferences, which were held at luxury hotels in large cities, delegates to the Boroma gathering met in a schoolhouse—many of them even slept on mats on the school's cement floor—in a town where camels and pedestrians far outnumbered vehicles on the dirt streets.

Overall, the conference "represented a good example of the Somali decision-making process. The long Boroma [assembly] was a marvelous opportunity to air a lot of old quarrels, bad feelings and rank stories. A lot came out into the open. People shouted at each other. Poetry was written and recited, a very essential element in public Somali life. Some other people were made fun of. Quarrels were resolved through public excuses, arranged marriages and exchanges of ceremonial gifts [related to] the compensation of honor so important in Somali culture.

Boroma, northern Somalia, 1993
A Somali elder attends a traditional and successful peace conference.

In a way, one could say that the political and cultural display of social dynamics became essential."[66]

The Boroma conference had significant results: selection of a head of state for "Somaliland" and resolution of some major ethnic disputes, though some fights continued to flare up from time to time. Former Somali prime minister Ibrahim Egal was chosen as the new president.

The man he replaced, Abdurahman Ali, nicknamed "Tur," would later side with Aideed in a power struggle against Egal. But the coming together of major ethnic groups in Somaliland as a result of the Boroma assembly gave Egal a broad base of support against such attacks. In late 1994, fighting between forces of Egal and Tur broke out in Hargeisa, forcing three-fourths of the population to flee, many to Ethiopia. By early 1995, the fighting spread to other parts of Somaliland. Egal was reelected president for another five years at a national communities conference in early 1997. Somaliland still had not received international recognition.

Aspects of the Boroma experience might have become a model for UN and U.S. peacemaking efforts. But like the unheeded military lessons from Kismayu on the limitations of a superpower dealing with a local insurgency, the peacemaking lessons from Boroma went largely unnoticed by officials of the United States and the United Nations, who were focusing on curbing Aideed in Mogadishu.

The Turning Point

On June 5, 1993, Pakistani UN troops inspected one of Aideed's arms caches located next to a radio station that his supporters used for propaganda. Aideed and Mahdi had agreed to UN inspections of their arms caches. For several days prior to the inspection, pro-Aideed announcers had broadcast invectives against the United Nations, charging that body with planning to take over the station. By the time the Pakistanis carried out their inspection, emotions among Aideed's supporters had been whipped to explosion level. According to U.S. officials, "within ninety minutes [of the inspection] angry crowds were assembling at other locations in south Mogadishu. In midmorning [Aideed's Somali National Alliance], taking cover behind stone-throwing women and children, ambushed a group of Pakistani soldiers on October 21 Road. SNA militia and civilians elsewhere in the city confronted the Pakistani patrols, which were caught by surprise."[67] Twenty-four Pakistani soldiers were killed and many more wounded in the attacks, including some who had been distributing relief food. Some of their bodies were mutilated by Somalis. In the weeks that followed, UN and other officials debated whether the attack was planned or spontaneous. One thing was clear: "few understood that the SNA had worked itself into seeing any interference with the radio station as a *casus belli*."[68] Why not?

The deputy director of the UN operation in Somalia, U.S. major general Thomas Montgomery, was commander of all U.S. forces in Somalia. (U.S. forces in Somalia worked with the UN but were never under its control.) He assigned twenty-two armored personnel carriers to the Pakistani inspection team, anticipating possible trouble. But when I spoke with the Pakistani commander, he said he was unaware of the heated propaganda Aideed's station had been broadcasting about the perceived threat to the radio station by UN inspectors. Had he known about the broadcasts, he told me, he would have sent the inspection team with additional protection. Why didn't he know? Somalis hired by the United States had been translating broadcasts at the former U.S. Embassy compound just across the street from the Pakistani headquarters. Apparently no one thought to warn the Pakistanis.

Now the UN saw itself in a bind: if it did not respond quickly and forcefully against those deemed responsible for killing the two dozen UN troops, other UN troops around the world might be seen as vulnerable. The day after the attack, the UN Security Council passed a resolution authorizing "all necessary measures" to capture and prosecute the guilty. Aideed was named in the initial draft of the resolution, but in the final version, only his SNA was cited.[69] The United States was strongly behind the efforts to go after the killers. Since the attack took place in the part of the city under Aideed's control, UN officials assumed Aideed was responsible, an accusation Aideed later denied. Whether or not Aideed was behind the attack, it almost certainly was carried out by people loyal to him. The UN resolution, passed before conclusive evidence was available back in New York, put the United

Nations and, as it turned out, the United States, squarely in opposition to Aideed and his militia. That, as poet Frost said of his choice between two roads, "made all the difference."[70]

The United States Joins the Killing

The United States had come to deliver food and then to safeguard its delivery. It was not a political strategy. But that changed. The United States stayed on after the UN forces arrived, at first just to allow time for an orderly transition. But the transition dragged on as the UN moved slowly in establishing itself. Meanwhile Aideed grew increasingly restless with the international presence, especially when the troops began trying to impose a military status quo on Somalia and to patch together a political structure in which he, Aideed, would likely not be in charge but have to share power. This was the background against which the attack on the Pakistani soldiers occurred. Still on hand and battle ready, the U.S. military took a giant turn away from its attempted positioning as a neutral force and joined the UN efforts to capture the attackers, which meant going after Aideed.

The decision to go after Aideed started the United States and the United Nations down a much different road in Somalia, a road lined with more danger and uncertainty, a road that would, in the end, pit American might against the more supple and quick-moving Somali gunmen, who would outmaneuver the Americans militarily and politically and send them packing. The startling thing is that it appears most UN and U.S. officials did not fully appreciate at the time what a difference the new road would make in the final outcome of the Somali intervention. "From conversations with both senior and mid-level officials directly involved with Somalia, it is evident that there was not real appreciation of how much of a change of policy and mission this was for UNOSOM II [the UN operation in Somalia at the time] and the United States forces associated with it. Nor was there a realistic appreciation of just how tough it would be to successfully take action called for by the Security Council against the SNA in the back alleys of South Mogadishu."[71]

There were other miscalculations, part of what Berlin said can happen between cultures whose "words and gestures" are unfamiliar to

each other. Before the first U.S. troops arrived, one of the most common assumptions among both Westerners and even some Somalis was
that the Somali militia would turn tail and run at the sight of well-
equipped and well-trained U.S. troops. I, too, believed this. What neither I nor most Americans knew was just how tenacious the militia of
Aideed would prove to be in the face of the overwhelming U.S. and
other military force.

Part of the tenacity came from the money they received from the
United Nations and from the nature of Somali militia. Nearly all of the
UN offices and residences in Somalia, before most operations were
shifted to the U.S. compound for safety, were located in the part of the
city Aideed controlled. He and his supporters had seized the property
and in turn rented some of it to the UN and other international agencies at exorbitant prices. It was a racket that provided additional money
for Aideed's militia to keep fighting. The United Nations thus helped
pay the ones who later turned on them.

Somali militiamen operate like sharks: when there is a kill, there is a
feeding frenzy. Militia leaders have to provide enough for their men to
feed on or risk losing their "loyalty." Frederic Cuny, a consultant to the
U.S. Agency for International Development (USAID) who later disappeared, and presumably was murdered in Chechnya, estimated
Aideed's militia was earning enormous sums of money from the rents
and the hiring of his gunmen to guard food convoys. In mid-July 1991,
the ICRC made a payment of "about $1 million" to Aideed's financial
supporter, Ato, in Mogadishu for security and cargo handling, according to Cuny. "Within 48 hours, an equivalent amount showed up in
Lisbon for an order of ammunition," Cuny said.[72] An ICRC official in
Nairobi said the most the ICRC paid for gunmen in a typical week was
$3,500 countrywide. A senior USAID official who served as President
Bush's relief coordinator for Somalia said the protection money relief
agencies were paying "concerns me a lot" and "to an extent" was fuel-
ing the conflict.[73]

★   ★   ★

Retired U.S. admiral Jonathan Howe, the UN special representative in
Somalia at the time, hesitated to go after Aideed, but not for long. Soon
after the attack on the Pakistanis, he issued an arrest order offering

$25,000 for Aideed's capture. The move ruptured almost all peaceful contact between the United Nations and Aideed's forces. Like a Western sheriff, Howe put out a "Wanted" poster for Aideed and some of his top assistants. Though officially he said only that Aideed was the target, it soon emerged that U.S. helicopter crews in Mogadishu had also been given photos of several Aideed aides being sought. "You know about that, too?" Howe said in one of my interviews with him, shaking his head at yet another leak to reporters.

There were "good grounds for arresting Aideed," not just for the attack on the Pakistanis but "to bring him to justice for crimes against humanity in causing the deaths of many thousands of Somali noncombatants in the period before the UN troops came on the scene."[74] Aideed's rival, Mahdi, and other Somali military leaders were also seen by one human rights leader in the United States as "culpable for such deaths"; and some UN officials were thought to be guilty of having "disregarded the need to minimize civilian casualties."[75]

As a result of the original U.S. plan to get its troops out of Somalia quickly, the United States turned over command of the international intervention force in Somalia to the United Nations in May 1993. But the United States did not withdraw from Somalia after the handoff to the United Nations; the political and military situations were too fluid to justify an immediate pullout. Even so, the U.S. handover to the United Nations was premature, according to Howe. "The United States should have comprehended that the UN was weak and should have accepted that it had a genuine need for substantial assistance." Howe blamed the U.S. eagerness to get out of Somalia and its lack of full support for the UN mission on "conflicting goals" of U.S. policy. "The United States wanted the UN to succeed, but it did not want to increase its involvement."[76]

★　★　★

On July 12, 1993, the United States officially abandoned its role as a neutral force in Somalia. The United States attacked without warning a meeting of Aideed supporters and clan elders. The United States and the UN justified the attack, approved by the White House and at UN headquarters, by describing the site as the SNA command center, where attacks on the U.S. and UN troops were planned.[77] At least

Bardera, Somalia, 1992
A U.S. soldier is on guard at sunset. This Muslim town (mosque in background) was the scene of many battles between Somali factions.

twenty civilians were killed, according to the United States. Aideed
claimed the number was much higher; the ICRC estimated the total
was close to seventy. Aideed's supporters said the gathering had been
held to assess the political situation, a plausible story since elders were
involved who might not have been present at a strictly military strategy
session. If not true earlier, it was certainly true from that moment on
that "regrettably for the operation and for Somalia, UNOSOM and
Aideed were now at war."[78] And so were the United States and Aideed.
The immediate result of the bombing was the murder of the four international journalists who arrived to report the casualties at the scene.

The whole international mission in Somalia had changed. What had
begun as a world response to starvation was now a war against one
Somali faction. The main focus of the Somalia mission had gone from
humanitarian to military.[79] In less than three months, the Somalis
would take their full revenge and beat the U.S. troops at their own
deadly game.

Death No Longer Waits in the Dark

The final U.S.-led battle against Aideed's forces, the battle that saw the two U.S. helicopters downed, eighteen U.S. soldiers killed, and a high number of casualties on the other side, had continued through the night of October 3, 1993. Now it was dawn, and the men of the Tenth Mountain Quick Reaction Force were preparing to fight their way out of their encircled position and back to the safety of a local stadium. A column of Malaysian and Pakistani armored vehicles had reached them; the body of pilot Wolcott and many wounded had been loaded on board. "As we left our perimeter the Somali fire increased just like we expected," First Sergeant David Mita later recalled.[80] The convoy crashed through the Somali positions, but in the process the armored cars sped up, exposing some forty Rangers who had been running alongside them and using the vehicles as cover. "The Rangers bringing up the rear started running harder. They fought building to building and block to block. . . . The exposed soldiers later called this run for their lives the 'Mogadishu Marathon'." The convoy broke up as the Pakistani and Malaysian drivers sped away seeking safety.

U.S. commanders in the city could see what was happening by way of videos from the navy Orio spy plane overhead. Pilots of some of the Cobra helicopters could also see and began circling and firing to protect the exposed Rangers. "Those helicopters saved us," remembered Ranger Specialist Melvin DeJesus. "The brass casings from the bullet cartridges came down around us like rain." The convoy finally reformed, and the Rangers fought their way out of the shooting gallery only to be taunted by a crowd of jeering Somali women and children. The troops continued back to the stadium without further incident.

Admiral Howe later faulted the United States for not sending the additional tanks U.S. forces in Somalia had requested, tanks he believed might have helped turn the tide in the battle.[81] But the tanks "would not have headed off the shootdown of the two helicopters and the ensuing firefight . . . [and] it is unlikely they would have been on the scene by October 3," said one former U.S. Defense Department official.[82] More important, "neither the Congress nor the public, and perhaps not the higher levels of the White House, adequately understood that the Somalia operation had been for several months a volatile and high-risk military endeavor."[83]

Many Bronze Stars, Silver Stars, and Distinguished Service Crosses were awarded to the troops for their part in the battle. Gordon and Shughart were awarded posthumous Congressional Medals of Honor. In a letter to his wife, Carmen, found among Gordon's personal effects when his mutilated body was returned to his family, he had written: "Carmen my love, you are strong and you will do well in life. I love you and my children deeply. Today and tomorrow let each day grow and grow. Keep smiling and never give up, even when things get you down. So in closing my love, tonight tuck my children in bed warmly. Tell them I love them. Then, hug them for me and give them both a kiss goodnight for daddy."

Changing the Color of the Guard

Within four days of the killings of the U.S. servicemen, President Clinton, besieged by an angry American public and a Congress just as angry, set the March 1994 pullout date for the last U.S. troops in Somalia. Clinton sent Oakley back to negotiate the release of Chief Warrant Officer Durant and that of Nigerian UN soldier Umar Shantali. Aideed's decision to release the two was "exceedingly difficult" for him because his supporters strongly opposed this action, Oakley told reporters in Mogadishu. Aideed's faction was angry over the many deaths of their people at the hands of U.S. and UN forces. But even as he set the final pullout date, Clinton sent additional troops as one more attempt to send a "big guy" message to the Somalis not to mess (further) with U.S. soldiers. The gesture proved hollow: the extra men did little more than guard themselves. This was in no way a reflection on the dedication of U.S. troops but rather a result of an ambivalent U.S. policy that had run up against the reality that the war had little public support back home. A bunker mentality long evident in UN headquarters became just as evident among U.S. troops. At the peak of the foreign intervention in Somalia, there were some 28,000 U.S. troops assigned to the operation. By February 1994, there were only about 5,000 U.S. troops left in Somalia. Once the United States announced a pullout date, other Western nations began planning their own withdrawal.

But a curious thing happened: there was not only a change of the guard in Somalia but a change in the color of the guards. As the majority white nations were leaving, majority black and brown nations dug in to stay; more would come later, paid by the United Nations for their services. Somalia became almost entirely a black/brown peacekeeping effort. The predominantly white nations had concluded it was too dangerous for them to stay; apparently it was not considered too dangerous for soldiers of color from countries such as Pakistan, India, and Botswana to stay.

"Lots of people see it as unfair," Abbas Zaidi, Pakistan's diplomatic representative to Somalia, said in an interview in Nairobi when the color change occurred. I pressed him to say what I suspected he felt—that it was cut-and-run time for the whites, but that the people of his country and others like it were expected to stay to do the dirty work. Somalia was becoming a racially segregated peace effort. Finally Zaidi got to the point. "The various commanders [of other countries with troops staying] are saying if *one* [his emphasis] white, Western nation could stay on," then it would be less unfair.[84]

It was not only an issue of fairness but also one of safety—safety for those staying on. Zaidi was pragmatic; he knew the departure of the big powers meant departure of most of their big guns and the U.S. and other Western intelligence systems, as ineffective as those had proved. The presence of the big-power nations had meant Somali militia leaders could never be sure what might happen if they resumed full-scale war. Now that threat was gone. Troops from the developing nations, Zaidi said, would have to rely more on "political and diplomatic initiatives." He said his troops would not fire "unless fired upon."

The international military effort in Somalia was effectively over.

Global Fallout from Somalia

The impact of the U.S. and UN defeat in Somalia had wide-ranging effects. The main one: the decision by the United States to do nothing to stop genocide when it broke out in Rwanda in 1994.

"After failure in Somalia, the international community would again sit by as Rwanda imploded with a minimum of a half-million persons slaughtered in an orgy of genocide."[85] (The experience in Somalia also left the United States more hesitant about its military role in Bosnia and kept U.S. troops out of Burundi, Rwanda's ethnic twin, which was experiencing genocide in stages.)[86] The defeat in Somalia "fundamentally changed the course of U.S. foreign policy," marking a turn back toward isolationism in the U.S. Congress.[87] "Whether the new isolationism proves temporary or permanent will depend on how Americans come to view their role in the post–Cold War world."[88] It also depends on what lessons Americans draw from the Somalia experience. Somalia challenged the idea of using U.S. troops to respond to humanitarian disasters in the midst of a war. U.S. troops would not have been killed in Somalia if the United States had not sent its military there in response to the famine during the civil war.

As part of the response to Somalia, the U.S. government came up with Presidential Decision Directive 25, issued in April 1994 after intense debate within the Clinton administration. It placed many new restrictions on use of U.S. forces in UN operations, "restrictions that have more to do with avoiding military casualties and embarrassing media coverage than with solving the problems of the countries concerned."[89] It came out just as Rwanda was collapsing under genocidal waves of killing. The new U.S. guidelines on use of its troops abroad provided justification for the United States to stay out of Rwanda as 800,000 to one million people were being slaughtered there. As in the biblical story of the Good Samaritan, when it came to Rwanda, the United States chose to be one of those who walked by on the other side of the road.

Chester Crocker, a former assistant secretary of state for African affairs, said "no one is especially proud of our performance in Rwanda, the first victim of the post-Somalia backlash. [The] . . . setbacks on the ground [for U.S. troops in Somalia] inevitably led to a reassessment in Washington and New York as to what peacekeeping entails, a reconsideration which has had resonance in Bosnia, Haiti, and Rwanda."[90] By pulling out of Somalia, the United States made a crucial decision; it was a turning point in the U.S. contribution to world peacekeeping efforts. The United States was sending a message to the international community: it was willing to help seek peace—but only if it was nearly risk free. By early 1997, even purely humanitarian emergencies that might involve U.S. troops were being viewed differently. In March 1997, U.S. defense secretary William Cohen said U.S. foreign policy could "no longer be swayed by humanitarian concerns."[91]

The United Nations began reassessing its own world peacekeeping efforts after Somalia. "Reeling from such peacekeeping failures as Bosnia, Somalia, and Rwanda," the UN by mid-1997 was "questioning its definition of peacekeeping, and debating its future role in policing global conflicts." A senior UN peacekeeping official said, "The building of peacekeeping may stand, but it is heavily mortgaged and its foundations are fragile."[92]

An unsavory part of the international military effort came to light after the foreign troops left. In July 1997, a Canadian commission concluded that Canadian troops had murdered a Somali civilian in March 1993 and that the senior leadership tried to conceal the incident. Two Canadian soldiers were imprisoned. And in May 1998, a Belgian soldier was sentenced to jail for six months for offering an underage Somali girl to a friend for his birthday and tying a second child to a moving vehicle in 1993.

Lessons from Somalia

At least five major lessons from the Somalia crisis can be applied to future international crises involving the United States or the United Nations.

Lesson 1. When a state falls apart, the United Nations and countries responding have to decide whether the collapsed state can be put back together or whether a fragmented state is the most that can be achieved. Somalia involved more than a war and a famine; it involved the disintegration of a state. Not only the central government but most local governments ceased to exist as anarchy spread. Police, courts, and administration no longer existed in most of the country. The United States and the United Nations focused on ways to try to resuscitate the pieces of the state and put them back together.

The idea of a united Somalia remained the centerpiece of UN plans right through the moment when the last UN troops were hunkered down in 1995 on a small strip of beach at the Mogadishu airport, wait-

Saving lives in Somalia
Baidoa, Somalia, 1992
(*Top*) *Before:* Bishaaro Macalin (*left*) with her emaciated three-year-old, Fadima, who is being fed by a relief worker with Irish Concern.
(*Bottom*) *After:* Three months later, Bishaaro is found in the feeding center with a recovered Fadima (*right*) and her one-year old daughter, Amina.

ing to be evacuated with the help of the United States. Just outside the airport perimeter, hostile militia waited, eager to take over the terrain, which they quickly did after the last troops left.

Reconstructing a collapsed state requires a difficult choice. Either you find new leaders to create power structures "from the bottom up," or you turn to the old ones with the hope that "the source of the problem must be the source of the solution (foxes will act responsible in hen coops if given responsibility)."[93] In Somalia, the United Nations and the United States turned to the militia leaders to try to reconstruct a new state. It didn't work. Some analysts suggested trying to strengthen local and regional structures without attempting to build a Western-model state, but their voices were little heeded.[94]

Lesson 2. Delayed humanitarian responses mean higher death tolls. This evident point needs to be recalled again and again. The U.S. and UN humanitarian intervention in Somalia in response to the famine probably saved thousands of lives. But many more lives were lost because help came too late. The international community need not have waited to intervene until the Somali state collapsed and famine was rampant. Earlier, effective intervention either as Barre's rule was waning or in the early months after his ouster "might have halted the descent into complete collapse and thereby limited the degree of political reconciliation and institutional reconstructions necessary."[95]

There is a danger of drawing "the wrong conclusions" from Somalia, as one analyst cautions.[96] Americans and others looking back at Somalia should remember not only the deaths of U.S. servicemen but the Somali lives saved in the earlier phase of the intervention. Americans should not recoil from the Somalia experience but use it in other crises to figure out how to provide help more quickly and effectively and how to reduce chances of conflict in the process. The Clinton administration took "half-steps, symbolic actions, and misplaced even-handedness," and failed to realize that "impartial intervention is a delusion." Military intervenors should "carve out" areas of control so humanitarian operations can take place with minimal risk. A new humanitarian unit of the United Nations, attached to the Security Council, could direct such relief.[97]

Lesson 3. Peacemaking must be based on a knowledge of the culture, history, and politics of the country at war. Most U.S. and UN efforts to negotiate peace in Somalia failed. Too much effort was focused on just two men, Aideed and Mahdi, shutting out other potential Somali peace brokers around the country. "Somalia was like a big jigsaw puzzle with 2,000 pieces," but the United Nations "tried to look at it as a puzzle with two pieces."[98] Several peace pacts organized by Somalis without the help of either the United Nations or the United States worked relatively well. Part of the problem was that few Westerners knew much about Somalia and its traditional ways of peacemaking. The United States did not understand that Somali factions leaders used peace conferences to bolster their own positions within their sub-clans. And most outsiders missed entirely the ongoing war between factions over farmland in the south. Attempting to bring peace without knowing why the sides are fighting is of little use.

The Somalia experience thus may yield valuable lessons for reconciliation initiatives in other complex emergencies.[99] Post–Cold War peacemaking requires "the highest levels of political-military skills." Despite the risks and isolationist tendencies in Congress, the United States "cannot remain neutral before disorder and suffering."[100]

The U.S. military in Somalia never moved beyond being a bully, a tough guy with a lot of weapons, to the far more subtle role of a powerful but respectful visitor, knowledgeable about local politics and traditional peacemaking. Powell, among others, had urged President Bush to use "overwhelming force" in Somalia, as the United States had in the Gulf War. Overwhelming force was seen as a quick way of intimidating would-be looters of food relief. But it did little to bring peace or help Somalia rebuild politically.

Lesson 4. Gunmen in flip-flops can beat U.S. and UN troops. The violence against the U.S. and UN troops came primarily from one Somali faction: the Habir Gedir subclan of the Hawiye, whose military leader was Aideed. The other factions generally welcomed the international presence. Once the United States and United Nations abandoned their attempted neutral role and went after Aideed, they had to relearn another lesson: it is difficult for a conventional army to fight guerrillas, in this case in urban areas. Given that the United States did not want to cause large-scale civilian casualties, even sophisticated weaponry was of little use in trying to capture Aideed in the back streets of Mogadishu.

Lesson 5. Peacekeeping is risky business. How effective can an international military intervention be if the intervenors and the public back home are not willing to accept casualties? If a nation's leader fails to explain the reasons for a war, the public is unlikely to support it once casualties start to mount. President Clinton failed to explain clearly the reason why the U.S. military was fighting in Somalia. And the public reacted vehemently when eighteen U.S. soldiers were killed in a single battle in Mogadishu.

Views on acceptable risks differed among the forces in Somalia. As the international UN peacemaking mission was ending in February 1995, with the last Pakistani soldiers preparing to leave, Pakistani brigadier general Saulat Abbas summed up his views in an interview with me. "We've been able to save a lot of people from hunger, disease. But we've not been able to contribute anything politically," he said. When I asked him whether it was worth the effort, he replied: "We lost 33 dead and 88 or 89 wounded. On the humanitarian side it was worth it. As far as casualties are concerned, that's part of military life."[101]

Unfinished Puzzle

Once the last UN troops left Somalia, in February 1995, militia continued to hold sway over much of the country. There was no national government, no state; but there was no lack of military and civilian authority at the local level. "Local communities have adapted to the prolonged collapse of the state by developing and in some cases rediscovering a variety of informal systems and mechanisms that, to varying degrees, provide minimal functions of day to day governance. [Among the various groups at the local level were] elders, faction leaders, intellectuals, clerics, district council members, businessmen, militiamen, former civil servants, women's groups."[102] In Mogadishu there were "Mafia-like" extortion rackets run by freelance groups or militia benefiting from a continuing state of conflict. Yet even leaders of some of these groups encouraged order so that business could be carried on more easily.[103] Somalia was stateless, without a central government, but it was not "anarchic. . . . Indeed, in some parts of Somalia local communities enjoy[ed] more responsive and participatory governance and a more predictable, profitable, and safer commercial climate than at any time in recent decades—all without the benefit of a central government."[104]

When Aideed died as a result of gunfire in Mogadishu in August 1996, his son, Hussein Mohamed Aideed, a former U.S. Marine and his father's chief of security, continued his father's campaign to make their subclan dominant in the broken country. There was less factional fighting in 1997 than in any year since 1991, but "scores of unarmed civilians were deliberately and arbitrarily killed by armed militia, some in artillery bombardments."[105] And as renewed fighting in Kismayu in 1998 showed, the jockeying for power among rival clan militia was far from over.

The problems Somalia faced as the century drew toward a close were immense. "It would be wrong to underplay the difficulties facing this ruptured society. Schools and hospitals have been destroyed, social services operate on a minimal level, and insecurity prevails in many areas. There is still a problem of malnutrition, while disease exacts a heavy toll," reported a European investigative team visiting Somalia in early 1997.[106]

Somalis interviewed by the team expressed "a mixture of fatalism and optimism." Few believed there was a solution to the country's problems just around the corner. Yet there was progress: most of the country was at peace, with fighting confined largely to the south and parts of Mogadishu; entrepreneurs were trading, "filling the markets with consumer goods . . . ; foreign exchange was coming in from a large livestock export business. And doctors, health workers, teachers and local administrators were back at work, often with little or no pay, trying to mend the social fabric of the nation."[107] Somalis might not be able to put the pieces of their national government back together again, but even as deadly battles for power continued in some areas, the people who had survived the wars and famine were carrying on the best they could with energy and spirit.

★   ★   ★

The loss of eighteen U.S. lives in one battle in Somalia left U.S. officials unwilling to commit troops to try to stop the genocide in Rwanda that took up to one million lives. Military experts later said that had a significant international force intervened in Rwanda, many people could have been saved.

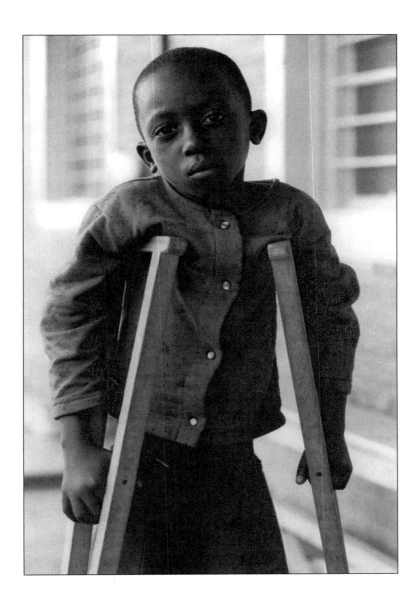

5   GENOCIDE IGNORED
Rwanda

Kigali, Rwanda, 1994
This girl on crutches lost the use of her leg in the 1994 civil war in which up to one mil-
lion people were slaughtered in a planned genocide by Hutu against the Tutsi minority.
Credit: UNICEF/Betty Press

I T was a crazy place to be reading William Shirer's *Rise and Fall of the Third Reich:* on the balcony of a luxury game park lodge in southern Kenya. But after the dawn game drive in our white Toyota station wagon and following a breakfast of fruit, omelette, tea, and toast, I sat in a large wooden chair on the stone balcony overlooking a grassy meadow where elephants often browsed. I was trying to come to terms with a question that had been nagging me since college days: how could a nation fall under the control of an Adolf Hitler?

As a college student I had walked across the University of Missouri campus to buy Shirer's book secondhand from another student. Then I set it aside with the promise to read it later. The book had been on one shelf or another in every one of my residences since then. Now, years later, on vacation between reporting assignments in East and West Africa, I was finally reading about Germany's buildup to genocide. There was no way to know that the following year I would be reporting on another of this century's genocides, that of Rwanda; it would prove to be one of the world's quickest mass killings.

Some one million people would be slaughtered, most of them in just three months, between April and July 1994, in that tiny, beautiful country, an African Switzerland in the heart of the continent, where tourists used to go to see gorillas in the mountains.

Most of the dead would be Tutsi, a minority tribe in Rwanda (14 percent); the killers were mostly of the Hutu majority (85 percent). Thousands of Hutu considered moderates or sympathizers with the Tutsi were also killed. Behind the genocide lay several centuries of complex cooperation and relationships as well as colonial preference for the Tutsi. The Tutsi were taller and had finer features than the Negroid-looking Hutu; therefore the Tutsi must be smarter—according to the European thinking at the time. Then there was the pressure of overpopulation: Rwanda was one of the most densely populated countries in the world. A series of massacres around the time of independence, which was in 1962, caused many Tutsi to flee the country and left behind a residue of mistrust between the two groups.

But in the end it was political manipulation, including hate propaganda, carefully used to fan existing fears and prejudices, that would whip the Hutu majority into a frenzy of genocidal killings that sent them out to hack their Tutsi neighbors to death with machetes. It was not just a racial conflict, as the outside world at first thought; by organizing themselves and executing a finely honed, nationwide plan, the Hutu nearly succeeded in exterminating the Tutsi.

The story of how genocide developed in Rwanda is one of the most intriguing and horrifying stories to come out of Africa in any century. This ultimate in loss of human rights, the loss of the right to live, is a story that bears telling. Refusing to read or hear about it is to say, in effect, I don't care; or to place less value on Africans' lives than the lives of victims of Hitler's much-studied genocide. Yet the Rwanda story is not well known.

There is another aspect of the story: why, for the most part, did the world watch the killings happen without trying to stop them?

After the killings, the Western world would forget Rwanda as other issues grabbed the attention of the press and political leaders. I would not have the luxury of being able to forget once my reporting work thrust me into Rwanda's tragedy. I knew I would have to make an accounting of it as a reporter and also for myself. I knew I could not witness a country's agony on such a scale and walk away without trying to understand what happened and—my question about Nazi Germany—why.

Rwanda and World Violence

The genocide in Rwanda should not be seen in isolation from other examples of genocide or mass killings. In 1915, some 350,000 to 1.5 million Armenians were massacred in Turkey. Under Hitler's genocide, nearly 6 million Jews were killed.[1] There are other cases of massive world violence in the twentieth century, including the wholesale murder of Chinese during the Japanese occupation; the collectivization and resulting famine under Stalin, which caused the deaths of an estimated 14.5 million Ukrainians, Russians, and other people of the former Soviet Union, including 3.5 million who were arrested and died later in camps;[2] and Cambodia's nightmare under the Khmer Rouge during which 1.2 to 2 million people were killed or died between 1975 and 1978 in a nation the size of Missouri. These later examples of world violence are what one analyst calls "political" genocide.[3] The same analyst adds that in the United States "the first modern genocide was that of the American Indians, and it was largely 'successful'."[4]

Each of these mass killings was horrible, but somehow the Rwanda killings come off looking particularly barbaric. Reminded of the 1994 genocide in Rwanda, a friend of mine said she had heard of the killings but had forgotten the name of the country. Then she attributed the Rwandan massacres to the acts of "savages." Was Rwanda's genocide more "savage" than the others? The slaughter of innocent Rwandan civilians, often by crude means, was savage. But how does one describe the repeated and well-documented gunning of thousands of civilian Muslims by Serbs in Bosnia? Certainly the following scene indicates savage acts. "Hundreds of dead Muslim prisoners lay in rows on the ground. Five Serb soldiers stood next to the corpses. A bulldozer was digging a mass grave."[5] And so does this one: "By now, the gym in Grbavci was packed with what looked like 1,000 to 1,500 men. A third of the men sat in other people's laps. The Muslims were ordered to take off their hats, shirts and jackets when they entered. A large pile of clothes sat at the front of the gym. Serbs searched it for valuables."[6] From the gym the prisoners were taken for a short ride by truck, lined up, shot, and buried in mass graves. The mass killings in Bosnia during the early 1990s were, in at least one important way, very similar to those in Rwanda: neighbors often killed neighbors.

Is there a word other than "savage" for the methodic gassing and cremation of German concentration camp inmates? There are many political and cultural differences in the context in which the Holocaust and the Rwandan killings occurred, but both have some facts in common: they were cases of genocide; hate propaganda was used to demonize the targeted victims; state machinery was used in carrying out the killings. The average German was not involved in the actual execution of Jews, but Hitler's attempt to annihilate Europe's Jews was a "process [that] required the cooperation of every sector of German society. The bureaucrats drew up the definitions [of who is a Jew] and decrees; the churches gave evidence of Aryan descent; the postal authorities carried the messages of definition, expropriation, denaturalization, and deportation; business corporations dismissed their Jewish employees and took over 'Aryanized' properties; the railroads carried the victims to their place of execution. . . . the operation required and received the participation of every major social, political, and religious institution of the German Reich."[7]

In Rwanda many ordinary people took part in the killings. But government officials or people with close connections to the government drew up lists of key victims and trained death squad militia; political party officials worked with these militia. "Even if the circumstances of the Jewish genocide are different in regard both to the scale of the killings and in the methods used, it, or something very like it, has happened again."[8]

The genocide of Rwanda and the Nazi Holocaust are in turn connected with some other examples of evil human behavior in both distant history and some uncomfortably recent history in the United States, according to Jewish theologian Richard L. Rubenstein. "The Holocaust was an expression of some of the most significant political, moral, religious and demographic tendencies of Western civilization in the twentieth century."[9] He goes on to cite the slave trade from Africa as an example of early negative tendencies. "North American slaves were among the first group of human beings who lacked all effective legal and political rights and who were forcibly detained in areas of concentration in a country that regarded itself as an heir of the religious and cultural traditions of the Western world."[10]

Rubenstein hastens to point out the different treatment of slaves and concentration camp inmates, but then he writes: "That, however, is not the fundamental issue. The institution of slavery in America is further evidence that the [Nazi] death camps were the end product of a very long cultural and political development involving all of the major countries of the Western world, rather than the specialized and extraordinary hatred of the Germans for the Jews. On the contrary, taken together, the record of the British, Portuguese, Dutch, French, and Spanish in Africa, Asia, and the Americas is quantitatively as bloodstained as that of the Germans. . . . For all its uniqueness, the Holocaust must be seen against the horizon of the unprecedented magnitude of violence in the twentieth century."[11]

He cites an example from World War I: ten million killed, some 6,000 a day, including, at the Battle of the Somme alone, approximately 410,000 Britons, 500,000 Germans, and 190,000 Frenchmen in fighting that advanced British lines just six miles. He mentions the Armenians; the Sino-Japanese War; the Spanish Civil War; the Stalinist purges and victims of his man-made famines; Hiroshima and Nagasaki; and the wars of Southeast Asia. We now can add the bloodstained record of the Hutu in Rwanda in carrying out their "savage" genocide against the Tutsi, not as a singular, strange event, but as one in a long chain of mass world violence.

Smaller-scale state violence includes the use of prisoners for medical experiments by the Nazis, and the fairly widespread use of medical experiments on prisoners in the United States.[12] The latter prisoners, U.S. officials have argued, normally are paid a nominal fee for "volunteering" for such experiments. But as a reporter whose assignments have included prisons, I know inmates are looking not just for a little money to buy some cigarettes, but for an entry in their record that a parole board might like. Some of the tests on U.S. prisoners have been gruesome. In the experiments on black prisoners with syphilis, decades ago, half the group was treated and half, unbeknownst to them, received placebos, to test the effectiveness of the medicine. "The organizer of the experiment had cold-bloodedly condemned the prisoners who received the placebo to the mutilating effects of disease and/or death in the name of scientific rationality." The syphilis experiments differed from those on Nazi concentration camp inmates. "The American prisoners were completely unaware of what was being done to them. Most of the Nazi victims had some idea of what was happening."[13] In May 1997, President Bill Clinton apologized on behalf of the U.S. government to the few survivors of the experiments. "I am sorry," he said at a public ceremony.

"The history of the twentieth century has taught us," observes Rubenstein, "that people who are rendered permanently superfluous are eventually condemned to segregated precincts of the living dead or are exterminated outright."[14]

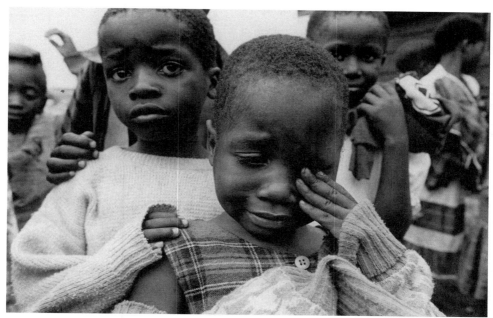

Near Goma, Zaire, 1994
As more than one million Rwandans fled to Zaire, thousands
of children, including these, were separated from their families. Relief groups set up centers to try to care for them.
Credit: UNICEF/Betty Press

It is doubtful that anyone will ever be absolutely sure how many
people were exterminated in the genocide in Rwanda. Many bodies
were simply dumped into rivers or common, unmarked graves, or left
to rot in forests. International relief organizations, the United Nations,
and other groups have tended to use estimates ranging from 500,000
or 800,000 up to one million dead, most of them in just three months.
"When it comes to numbers we are really awash in a sea of speculation.
The figure of one million dead makes sense," according to René
Lemarchand, professor emeritus of political science at the University
of Florida and author of *Rwanda and Burundi* (London: Prager and
Pall Mall, 1970). Lemarchand has visited Rwanda many times, including after the 1994 genocide, and has continued to publish analyses of
both Rwanda and Burundi.

The largest portion of his estimated one million victims included civilians killed by Hutu militia and individuals but also included: those killed in battles between the Hutu and Tutsi armies; the thousands who died of disease and starvation in the Hutu refugee camps in Zaire; and refugees killed in eastern Zaire after the war when ethnic Tutsi and other groups hunted down and massacred Hutu who had fled both Rwanda and the original refugee camps in Zaire during a rebel take-over of the Zairean government beginning in 1996.

Many Hutu members of opposition parties in Rwanda were killed by Hutu extremists in the genocide. Lemarchand, in an interview with the author in October 1998, estimated that "about 50,000 to 60,000 Hutu from the south and central parts of Rwanda were killed."

"Genocide" Defined

"Genocide" is a word to be used sparingly. On December 9, 1948, the General Assembly of the United Nations passed a resolution that made genocide an international crime. Article 2 of the resolution states:

> In the Present Convention, genocide means any of the following acts committed with intent to destroy, in whole or in part, a national, ethical, racial or religious group, such as:
>
> a. Killing members of the group;
> b. Causing serious bodily or mental harm to members of the group;
> c. Deliberately inflicting on the group conditions of life calculated to bring about its physical destruction in whole or in part;
> d. Imposing measures intended to prevent births within the group;
> e. Forcibly transferring children of the group to another group.

The UN's special rapporteur, or investigator, on Rwanda, René Degni-Ségui, said the Rwandan case qualified as "genocide" under the UN definition. About the same time, UN secretary general Boutros Boutros-Ghali, and U.S. secretary of state Warren Christopher also labeled the Rwandan Hutu killings of Tutsi as "genocide."

I find it hard to explain why I think it is so important for people to be familiar with the genocide in Rwanda, a tiny African country otherwise not of much global importance. The alternative—not knowing what happened there—seems to me tantamount to saying that it does not matter. Certainly, no one can say the murder of one million lives is not important, but anyone can pay it little heed. I have a better appreciation of the magnitude of the tragedy when I focus on the importance of each life lost in Rwanda. Each person was an individual; most had a family, with the same dreams of prosperity and healthy, educated children as any one of us. All who were killed were part of that greater family of man. Everyone who died on a hill or in the streets of Rwanda was just as important as anyone else. The genocide in Rwanda showed the worst side of human nature. By contrast it underlines the need for the opposite behavior, that of love and understanding. In the midst of the killing in Rwanda, there were many heroes, otherwise ordinary people who risked their lives to save others.

A closer look at what happened in Rwanda, and why, may also shed light on what the role of outside governments should be in cases of mayhem. Most governments avoided sending troops to Rwanda to try to stop the killings. Four years later, in 1998, U.S. president Bill Clinton would admit the United States and others had not done enough to try to stop the genocide. I believe the United States and the rest of the international community had a moral obligation—and, under the UN charter, a legal one—to try to stop the genocide.[15]

My interviews in and about Rwanda with both Hutu and Tutsi, as well as my examination of human rights investigations, books, and other materials, have helped me understand not only what happened but why it happened. I would like to share what I have learned with my readers. I begin with the story of Manuel, one of the near victims of the genocide. After an initial targeting of the few Tutsi officials in government and well-known Hutu moderates when the genocide began in April 1994, the killings spread quickly to ordinary Tutsi like Manuel, a farmer. Readers should be warned that he and others describe scenes that are upsetting. But not to know of them should be even more upsetting.

Manuel's Story Begins

An illness starting shortly before the first killings prevented me from reaching Rwanda before most of the mayhem had ended. I was still tired in June when I joined a group of UN and private relief officials on a two-day drive through southwestern Rwanda, where the French military had established a so-called safety zone. One stop was at a camp on a hillside in a rural area called Nyarushishi, near the city of Cyangugu. It was for Tutsi who somehow had survived attempts by the Rwandan majority Hutu to kill them. Now these Tutsi were living, still fearful, under the protection of the French.

I noted earlier that the world, for the most part, just watched the genocide in Rwanda. The French did more than that, sending troops to secure one corner of the country for two months, probably saving 10,000 to 13,000 lives, including some 8,000 Tutsi at the Nyarushishi camp. But such numbers pall against the total estimated killed in Rwanda. The French arrived after most of the killing was over and left before peace was restored. (I will return to their controversial intervention later in this chapter.)

The scene at the camp was deceptively serene. Rows of tunnel-shaped grass-and-stick huts, covered with neat, UN-issued white plastic, dotted the slopes. Little children played in the dirt; families or surviving lone individuals sat in the sun or prepared meals over outdoor wood fires. But Betty's camera caught children in slacks and short-sleeved shirts reaching to the bottom of a barrel used to mix food, scraping up remnants and licking them off their hands. On closer look I saw people lying in exhaustion on the grass by their huts.

Manuel, a thin, soft-spoken Tutsi, told me his story after I approached a group of young men and identified myself as a reporter. We sat together on the grass. I picked him out of the group on instinct, partly because he was not pressing his story on me but was willing to tell it. He asked me not to use his family name, fearing possible retribution by Hutu if he survived. We sat in a tight semicircle as other Tutsi pressed close to hear, nodding their agreement with Manuel's version of events, which also squared with later human rights reports. He stopped talking whenever someone he did not know walked by close enough to hear. Despite the presence of the French military, even in this camp the Tutsi did not feel safe. A few days earlier, the French had stopped a group of Hutu men—armed with axes—heading for the camp.

Some 55,000 Tutsi normally lived in Manuel's part of Rwanda, in and near the city of Cyangugu, on the border with Zaire. Now most of those known to be still alive were in this camp.[16] The French were already talking of pulling out of Rwanda; they had arrived in June and would be gone by late August. Where would Manuel and the other Tutsi hide? Where could they be safe after the French left?

Fleeing to the Woods

Before the war, Manuel led a life typical of farmers in Rwanda. Farming there has nothing to do with large fields and big, air-conditioned tractors. Most farmland is cut up into small plots generally worked by hand and animals. Farm homes are modest, usually built of stick and mud walls. When the killings began, Manuel ran into the woods with

Nyarushishi refugee camp, southwest Rwanda, 1994
This Tutsi man survived the massacres by Hutu.

his wife and two children, hoping things would get better. Hutu and Tutsi had clashed before. He had no way of knowing that this time the stakes were much higher, that this time Hutu were bent on eliminating every Tutsi they could catch. And he had no idea there were two wars under way.

One war was between the Rwandan army, composed almost entirely of Hutu, against the Tutsi-led rebel military, made up mostly of Tutsi refugees who had grown up outside Rwanda and now saw a chance to return home. This was the conventional side of the Rwandan conflict. The other war, the one Manuel was caught up in, was even worse. This war pitted neighbor against neighbor, civilian against civilian, in manhunts in which Hutu hunted Tutsi like animals, killing them in their homes, on the road, or in the woods.

Not far from Manuel's camp is a large woods. It looks inviting. But in mid-1994, thousands of Tutsi took refuge there, trying to hide, usually unsuccessfully, from Hutu mobs raping and killing. One who survived in that area, Viateur Gahongayire, accused a local mayor and two school officials of organizing manhunts of Tutsi. He named an assistant mayor as guilty of carrying out Bosnia-like exterminations. "He would come to a place and get all people killed, and then call in a caterpillar [bulldozer] to bury them all in one mass grave. . . . They would throw between seventy and one hundred people in one." Latrines were also used for dumping bodies, he said.[17] Those who fled to the forests had little food and water and often only sticks and stones to protect themselves against Hutu civilians or the gendarmes. "The gendarmes drove us into the forest and many people were killed," said another survivor, Jean François Nzeyimana. "We were about four hundred people when we entered the forest but only forty-five got out."[18]

After the French arrived, some Tutsi crept from those woods practically starving. One group hailed passing international journalists, who alerted French troops, who in turn took the Tutsi to protected camps. At his unit's encampment at an abandoned school complex on a hill near the town of Gikongoro, French navy officer Marin Gillier told me what he had seen when he first reached the woods. "We found in one valley several hundred bodies, from two months to two days old. Some had been killed with bullets, others with machetes. There was supposed to be 4,000 to 5,000 Tutsi [who had taken refuge in the woods]," he said. "We found 800 [alive]. Everywhere you walked there were bones."

Hutu and Tutsi had clashed periodically since a major conflict in 1959, which some analysts think was the irrevocable dividing point between the two groups. The genocide of 1994 would dwarf all the other conflicts combined, though from his hiding place in the woods, Manuel could not know this. He just knew the killings were continuing and that he and his family could soon be discovered.

"After two days I realized it was getting worse. I decided to leave my hill." For a Rwandan to leave his hill is like a nineteenth-century American or European leaving the town he grew up in, his security, his home base, to move on to the uncertain life of a big city. Manuel and his family fled to the one place they thought they would be safe: the cathedral in Cyangugu, the nearest city. The local priest received them as well as thousands of other desperate Tutsi.

But there would be no safe place in this war. A few days after he arrived at the cathedral, Manuel heard the mayor of Cyangugu, Joseph Bugarama, order them out. "He told us to go to the stadium" in town. "He said if we didn't go to the stadium that the *interahamwe* would destroy the cathedral." *Interahamwe* is Rwandan for "those who attack together." In this case it meant the Hutu civilian militia of the governing, Hutu-dominated political party. *Interahamwe* was a word of terror for Tutsi.

Concentration Camp in a Stadium

Some 5,000 Tutsi were crammed into the small stadium at the edge of the city on April 15, 1994.[19] The day I met Manuel, I also visited the stadium. I could envision perhaps hundreds of people crowded into the modest facility, not 5,000. Once herded inside the walls, the Tutsi prisoners—for by now the pretext that they were there for their protection had become a transparent lie—were given little food. There was only one water tap and no sanitation facilities.[20] From what followed, it soon became clear Hutu militants in control of the area were not concerned about amenities for the Tutsi. The stadium had become a concentration camp in every sense of the word, and soon the Hutu began systematically killing the "inmates."

Without accounts such as Manuel's, there is a danger the world will forget what it failed to try to stop in the first place. The world will never forget, nor should it, the Holocaust; details are passed down to each new generation through books, films, plays, poems, and, so far, by accounts of the dwindling number of survivors. But who is talking about Rwanda? Subsequent world events, including Bosnia, pushed the Rwandan issue farther back in the public's mind, if it was still there at all. Yet it would be no more accurate to call Rwanda's upheaval typical of Africa than it would be to point to the implosion of the former Yugoslavia, taking place as Rwanda fell apart, and call that typical of Europe.

Manuel continued with his story, still sitting on the hillside. "The mayor came with a list. The first time he took more than thirty Tutsi prisoners from the stadium. They were killed with machetes. One survived."

The main weapon used in Rwanda's genocide was not the gun but the machete, one of Africa's most widely used tools. Normally it is reserved for whacking back persistent undergrowth choking farm crops. One version is also used to cut the lawns of the wealthy. I used a machete once: I joined a group of farmers in the East African nation of Tanzania, adjacent to Rwanda, who were clearing a field with machetes. Each time I came to a bush, I reached down by hand and pulled the branches back to expose the stem to my machete chop. Seeing this, a man working next to me cut a notched stick to use in pulling branches back. I used it on the next bush only to find a large snake curled up beneath the branches. Had I used my hand for one more bush, I could have been bitten. I scooped the snake up on my machete and held it out, asking if there was any local taboo against killing snakes. The other men came running over, took a look, then quickly knocked the snake to the ground and slashed it to death with machetes. It wasn't until someone translated the name of the snake from Swahili to English that I realized it was the very poisonous puff adder.

I had been protected by the man who prepared the notched stick. Was this spiritual protection, or human protection, or both? My upbringing leads me to see a divine hand in such acts. But what about the act of genocide? And what about the protection Tutsi needed, probably prayed for, and didn't get? What kind of divine power would allow mass

Goma, Zaire, 1994
In a refugee camp near Goma, a Rwandan woman recovers from machete wounds. Many victims of the genocide were killed by machetes.
Credit: UNICEF/Betty Press

killing? If, as I believe, genocide could not possibly be associated with a divine power—which is the source of good, not evil—what is it associated with? Perhaps that last question is one more reason we prefer to turn our heads from genocide; it's just too big an issue to contemplate, too unsettling to our faith, too discouraging to our concept of man. Genocide stems from man's worst tendencies, as Rubenstein pointed out.

When I was a child, I saw some black-and-white snapshots my father, John Press, had brought back with him from one of the concentration camps in Germany. They showed naked, emaciated bodies stacked like piles of wood. It was so horrible it was almost unreal; or maybe I wanted to think it was unreal. My father rarely spoke about the photos. One day, years later, I found him throwing them out. I scooped them up, put them in a box, put the box in storage, and have not looked at them since. They are not forgotten, however; nor will they be in my lifetime. I no longer need the photos: the images are burned into my mind.

Another image that has stayed with me, since the afternoon working in Tanzania with the farmers, is that of the machete. I learned two things about it that day: the machete is a powerful tool; it can also be a powerful instrument of death. Using a machete, a strong-armed farmer can slice through a tough root or even a small branch with ease; the human skull is similarly vulnerable to the blade. Many of my wife's close-up photos of skulls in Rwanda show a gash, the result of someone slicing downward with a machete, or sideways if the victim was already on the ground. There are many cases of Rwandans being sliced up arm by arm, leg by leg, left to die in anguish, begging for death by a bullet.[21]

At the stadium where Manuel and his family were sent, the pace of killing by machete was picking up. "The second time they took more than forty. The third time, they chose people by just pulling them out—everyone they saw in a good shirt. They took more than fifty." In a ghastly echo of the warped logic of the Khmer Rouge in Cambodia, Hutu militia first targeted the educated and intellectuals, whom they assumed were Tutsi. Later, not even the children were spared at the stadium or elsewhere in Rwanda. Marianne, a nun and nurse, recounted her days working in the intensive care unit of one of the hospitals in Kigali, the capital, shortly after the genocide began. "I remember a three-year-old boy with a bullet in his right leg, a three-week-old baby with bullet wounds in the forehead, and a nine-year-old boy who had practically the top of his head cut off and a fractured arm. I kept asking myself: what kind of human beings can do this to children? Many had wounds that it is better not even to think about. The soldiers and *interahamwe* did not want wounded Tutsi, children or adults to be taken for medical care. Most were finished off at the first roadblock."[22]

A macabre notion on the part of the killers, according to survivors, was that baby Tutsi would grow up to be Tutsi soldiers and therefore must be killed along with the adults. Whole families were also murdered to eliminate claims on the farmland of Tutsi survivors. Thousands of Tutsi children were massacred without hesitation. Rwanda was one of the most populated countries in the world, a fact some analysts say contributed to the genocide.

Manuel tried to escape from the death camp stadium with his wife and two children. "We forced our way out. But the soldiers blocked us. We were forced to return. There were *interahamwe* along the route with machetes and grenades." According to a human rights report, "On April 29, [the] military and militia killed more than 300 of the original 5,000 hostages who had been held since April 15 at [the] stadium in Cyangugu."[23]

Across the country, rape was another hallmark of Rwanda's orgy of violence. In one of many accounts of survivors told to human rights investigators, Maria Goretti told how Hutu raped her and her daughter, along with a large number of other women. "My daughter, my sister-in-law and I were not only raped, we were raped and beaten every day for a month. They put about thirty women and girls in a house. They beat up the other women so badly that they all died. . . . What they did to the women they killed is just too terrible. They were literally beaten to death with sticks. . . . They stripped them down to their underwear before they killed them. Some were left completely naked and then paraded. Some were forced to walk several kilometers while naked on their way to being raped or killed or both."[24]

There is no way of knowing how many women were raped or held in sexual slavery. But "systematic rape was one of the instruments of genocide."[25] The raping was not an attempt by the Hutu to try to impregnate Tutsi women as a kind of cultural domination; many of the women raped were then killed. About a third of those who lived did become pregnant, according to a survey of 304 rape victims by the Tutsi government after the war. Some 2,000 to 5,000 unwanted children were born in Rwanda to mothers raped during the civil war.[26] Because of the stigma attached to rape victims in the society, many of the mothers ended up impoverished and unable to find a new husband. Many contracted AIDS and other sexually transmitted diseases from the rapists.[27]

Beginning on May 11, 1994, the surviving stadium residents were moved to the camp where I met Manuel, a few miles out of the city. Perhaps the move was an attempt to hide the atrocities from outsiders, such as international relief workers; or it may have been a gesture by the less militant Hutu, who hoped moving the Tutsi out of town would give

Musambira, Rwanda, 1994
This Hutu woman saved these Tutsi children from
being killed and cared for them after the civil war.
Credit: UNICEF/Betty Press

them a better chance of surviving, away from the crowds of Hutu in the
city. The Hutu military transported stadium survivors to the camp on
buses. But along the few miles of road, many Tutsi were pulled off the
buses and killed by Hutu mobs. And the Hutu menaced the Tutsi after
they arrived at the camp. In late June, the day before the arrival of the
French, Hutu militia circled the camp "with the intention of killing us,"
Manuel said. "They had guns, grenades, and machetes." But the Tutsi
were spared. "Colonel Innocent Bawgamenshi, a Hutu, sent gendarmes to protect us," said Manuel.

Some Hutu Saved Tutsi

The Hutu extremists' goal of total annihilation of the Tutsi was not
realized. The Tutsi rebel army entered Rwanda from Uganda and by
July 1994 had forced the Hutu army and militia to flee to the French-
patrolled zone or to a neighboring country. The Tutsi army had won the

war. Despite the extreme risks, many Hutu helped Tutsi survive during the genocide, working upstream against a dangerous flood of hysteria and cold scheming by Hutu hard-liners. Some Hutu police, presidential guards, even members of death squads, helped save Tutsi.

In Kigali, shortly after the Tutsi army had won the war, I visited a slum neighborhood where streets are dirt alleys between one- or two-room mud homes. As I sat with Ladislas Mugarura, a Tutsi, in his tiny, lantern-lit living room, he told me of "good Hutu," even including some who were involved in the killings. He described another aspect of the killings: Hutu who did not want to kill Tutsi often were threatened with death by other Hutu. "Those [Hutu] who didn't want to kill someone were killed unless they managed to escape," he said. Mugarura said he has compassion for his former Hutu neighbors who fled, even those who were part of the death squads, knowing they may have been coerced. According to one human rights report: "Using propaganda, bullying, the promise of looting and outright force, many ordinary people were made into members of the *interahamwe,* and were compelled to kill. But many others killed for greed—stealing money or taking over land in a country where land was scarce. The killing had a momentum that built quickly, changing the norms of society. . . . the extremists nearly succeeded in making mass murder a socially-normal activity."[28]

The kill-or-be-killed phenomenon also showed up in the opening trial of the UN tribunal, in The Hague, on crimes against humanity committed in the former Yugoslavia. In June 1996, Drazen Erdemovic, a low-level, Bosnian Croat soldier fighting with the Bosnian Serbs, broke down in court and sobbed as he admitted taking part in a summary execution of hundreds of Muslim men. "If I had refused, I would have been killed together with the victims. When I refused they told me, 'If you are sorry for them, line up with them and we will kill you, too'," Erdemovic told the court. He said in his defense that he had a wife and a baby son. He pled guilty to crimes against humanity.[29]

Erdemovic said his victims were killed in groups of ten, shot in the back by himself and fellow soldiers of the Bosnian Serb army's Tenth Sabotage Detachment. He admitted killing seventy men, whose bodies were plowed into a mass grave. Thousands were killed in a similar manner in Bosnia. Among those on the court's wanted list for organizing mass killings were Serb leaders General Ratko Mladic and Radovan Karadzic, who continued to evade arrest as Erdemovic entered his guilty plea.

★   ★   ★

In the Rwandan war, Mugarura had avoided being killed by Hutu extremists with the help of a Hutu. For more than two months, he had hid in this tiny home I was now visiting—a one-bedroom, whitewashed, mud-brick home off an alley in the Kamicanga neighborhood.

The living room where we sat was furnished with only a few chairs and a trunk covered with a small piece of tapestry. On one wall hung a map of Africa, another of Rwanda, and a mat inscribed "We pray to God, who is our light." Mugarura's protector was a Hutu shopkeeper, Emanuel Sebahire, who had risked his own life bringing him food each day before dawn. From a corner of the living room, Jean-Claude Kwizera, a young Tutsi whose parents were murdered, said even some *interahamwe* protected Tutsi at the roadblocks put up by Hutu to catch Tutsi.

There are many other examples of Tutsi being helped by Hutu, including the following:

- Marie Claire Kayigabwa, a twenty-two-year-old Tutsi student in the city of Gitarama, fled a Hutu mob and took shelter in the home of a Hutu friend, Françoise Rwimabera, who hid her for two weeks. She survived.
- In Kigali, Thérèse Mukarusagara's husband and two teenage sons were killed and her house burned. She escaped with an uncle and two of her children. They were hidden by a Hutu shopkeeper in the ceiling of a house he was building. He brought the Tutsi family food twice a day. They emerged safely when Tutsi rebels seized the city in July.[30]

Roots of the Genocide

While some Hutu were trying secretly to help Tutsi, many more were trying openly to kill them. Genocide is egoism carried to an extreme; the perpetrator believes that "I am important, but 'they' are not." Yet it is more than that. It is the loss of sensitivity to what it means to be a human being. To take someone's life in the horrible manner in which many Hutu killed Tutsi in Rwanda and many Serbs killed Muslims in Bosnia is to deny the humanity of the victim. As Rubenstein warned, once a group of people are stripped of their identity as people, it is easier to limit their freedom and eventually eliminate them altogether. Many American soldiers in Vietnam, for example, called the enemy "gooks," not North Vietnamese or Vietcong. Killing a "gook" is easier than killing a person. A "gook" is not a person, not someone with a family.

In Rwanda, the Hutu had a dehumanizing name for the Tutsi: *inyenzi,* or "cockroach." The name first was applied to Tutsi commandos in the 1960–63 raids on Hutu in Rwanda, "partly in spite and partly because, like the cockroaches, they [the Tutsi fighters] tended to move at night."[31] Hutu extremists began using the name again in 1992 to describe the fighters of the Rwandese Patriotic Front (RPF), the Tutsi-led rebel force based in neighboring Uganda.

The killing of the "cockroaches" was done openly and methodically, often led by local Hutu officials. Manuel and other Tutsi I spoke with at the camp insisted that the mayor of Cyangugu and a local business-man, Edward Bandestsa, organized many of the killings at the stadium. Tutsi have named many such alleged ringleaders, who made no attempt to hide their acts, apparently because they assumed there would be no survivors.

In the hills, often it was not a stranger killing a stranger. Frequently in rural areas it was Hutu killing people they had grown up next to. In the densely populated countryside, overpopulation and land scarcity were two of the underlying embers of discontent fanned by Hutu extremists into flames of genocide against the Tutsi. Rwanda's pregeno-cide, mid-1993 population was 7.4 million, with a projected population of 16.7 million by 2025. Rwanda is small—only 10,169 square miles (26,338 square kilometers), about the size of Vermont. The average prewar population density was more than 700 per square mile. A visitor to Nebraska or many other midwestern farm states finds a square mile easy to spot: it is the area bounded by four roads and including fields and several farm houses. It is difficult to imagine 700 people living within such a confined space.

But population and land pressures alone were not enough to bring the Hutu to the point of trying to exterminate the Tutsi. Both groups had adapted to overcrowding and land shortages over the years, living in relative peace with each other at least until 1959. The high population in such a small nation, however, led Rwandans to develop a highly centralized society, with tight social controls.[32] This would later work against the Tutsi when the Hutu used these social networks to mobilize killers from all levels of society.

To understand how relations between Hutu and Tutsi deteriorated, one has to look at the history of Rwanda, as well as the political manipulations and careful preparations for genocide in the year or two leading up to 1994. At the root of the conflict is the question who is a Hutu and who is a Tutsi, which has been much debated over the years. According to one European historian, they are two separate races: Hutu are Bantu, and Tutsi are part of an exodus probably from southern Ethiopia.[33] Others contend the two are one people, sharing one language and culture. The RPF took the position that distinctions between Tutsi and Hutu are "social" and not a question of distinct ethnic groups.[34]

In the precolonial years, the Tutsi had economic and social advantages over the Hutu: Tutsi generally were wealthier, the main cattle owners, while Hutu became known as farmers and generally owned fewer cattle. Distinctions between Hutu and Tutsi were somewhat fluid, with some Hutu achieving the status of Tutsi. Intermarriage between Tutsi and Hutu partially obscured the stereotypical physical image associated with Tutsi (taller, thinner) and Hutu (shorter, heavier). When the first European explorers arrived in the area, they found Tutsi kingdoms. "The Tutsi dynasty had made significant conquests in the interior since the end of the seventeenth century, eliminating the Hutu kings and chiefs one by one and no doubt thereby stirring-up tensions between castes."[35]

Historical fact and myth combined in Rwanda to create an image of Tutsi superiority, which in turn played an important role in Hutu-Tutsi relations. "Rwanda, a very small, compact and historically well-defined nation, was built in the late nineteenth and early twentieth century into a complex, unique and quasi-mythological land. With time this cultural mythology *became* reality, i.e., the social and political actors moved by degrees from their real world into the mythological script which had been written for them (in a way, with their complicity)."[36]

Europeans concluded, after seeing the institution of the Tutsi monarchy and noting the fine physical features of the Tutsi, that the Tutsi were superior to the Negroes (Hutu). It was a racist assumption that would haunt the country in years to come. One of the Europeans who reached that conclusion was John Hanning Speke, the famous Nile explorer. He took the fact of Tutsi kingdoms and added the theory that their ancestors were of "a superior civilization."[37] Later-arriving Europeans accepted this concept of Tutsi superiority as fact, sometimes creating their own myth about the origins of the Tutsi and their abilities. Colonial administrators pushed the myth to their own advantage, using the Tutsi minority to help them govern a country 85 percent Hutu. The colonial rulers also gave the Tutsi special advantages in training and formal education, stressing the differences between Hutu and Tutsi for purposes of control. The Germans, in the early part of the century, favored the Tutsi as the superior race and gave them military assistance to help their conquest of Hutu chiefs. After World War I, the Belgians continued this same, one-sided policy. "Thus in short, if the categories of Hutu and Tutsi were not actually invented by the colonizers, the policies practiced by the Germans and Belgians only served to exacerbate them."[38]

Just as important was the impact all this had on the Tutsi themselves. "The result of this heavy bombardment with highly value-laden stereotypes for some sixty years ended by inflating the Tutsi ego inordinately and crushing Hutu feelings until they coalesced into an aggressively resentful inferiority complex."[39] This attitude and the increasingly authoritative Tutsi monarchy, which was expanding its control over more Hutu lands, caused growing resentment among the Hutu. "Deprived of all political power and materially exploited by both the whites and the Tutsi, [the Hutu] were told by everyone that they were inferiors who deserved their fate and also came to believe it. As a consequence, they began to hate all Tutsi. . . . The time bomb had been set and it was now only a question of when it would go off."[40]

One scholar on Rwanda and Burundi argues that relations between Tutsi and Hutu were complex and that often they were much more interdependent than is generally recognized. He contends that in Burundi, which has the same ethnic mix as Rwanda but a different political history, it is a "myth" that ethnic conflicts are due to historical antagonisms.[41]

Ethnic pride also grew among missionary-educated Hutu and was increasingly articulated during the late 1950s, in the years just prior to independence. Hutu intellectuals began characterizing the Tutsi as "Ethiopian" invaders and began verbally attacking their predominant role in society. In 1959, ethnic tensions turned to violence. Activists of a pro-Tutsi political party attacked a Hutu subchief who was a key figure in an all-Hutu political party. Hutu groups responded by killing some Tutsi officials. Tutsi officials answered with reprisals against the Hutu. Several hundred people of both groups died. The events of 1959 did not change the way Hutu looked at the Tutsi, but it boosted the Hutu's self-image.[42]

As African nationalism spread rapidly across the continent, the Belgians did a flip-flop, shifting their support from the Tutsi minority to the increasingly vocal and powerful Hutu majority. The Belgians named more Hutu chiefs and subchiefs; until then, almost all such posts had been filled by Tutsi. The Hutu won local elections in 1960, and by 1961 had declared an end to the Tutsi monarchy. In 1961, some Tutsi who had fled Rwanda began making raids from neighboring countries. Following one such Tutsi attack, Hutu killed an estimated 10,000 Tutsi. In July 1962 the Belgians granted independence to Rwanda. Tens of thousands of Tutsi were driven off their land by Hutu shortly after independence; many fled into exile. By 1964, following more clashes, some 150,000 Tutsi had escaped the country.[43]

Tensions between the Tutsi and Hutu flared again in 1972. In 1973, Major General Juvenal Habyarimana, who was then minister of defense and head of the national guard, led a bloodless coup against President Gregoire Kayibanda, a Hutu and the country's first president. Habyarimana, president until he was killed in 1994, favored not only the Hutu majority but those Hutu from his own part of the country, thus incurring the wrath of Hutu from other areas in Rwanda as well as that of Tutsi at home and abroad.

In 1989, the year after Habyarimana was again reelected president—with 99.98 percent of the vote, in an election with no other candidates—crop disease, soil degradation, and population pressures re-sulted in several hundred deaths by starvation.

Rwanda's coffee income was hurt by low world prices.[44] In May 1990, a Rwandan government commission recommended a more lib-eral policy toward Tutsi refugees who wanted to return home. But Ha-byarimana, instead of adopting the recommendations, called for fur-ther study, in effect saying no to the return of the Tutsi. This was a touchstone issue for the RPF. In October 1990, the RPF invaded north-ern Rwanda from their bases in Uganda.

Ugandan president Yoweri Museveni officially looked the other way. He claimed no part in the RPF invasion or even knowledge of its prepa-rations, although many RPF officers had served in Uganda's army. There is little chance Museveni's intelligence system did not alert him to a military buildup under his nose. Museveni also consistently en-dorsed the aims of the RPF and criticized the Rwandan government.

Habyarimana responded to the 1990 invasion by the RPF with large-scale arrests in and around Kigali, mostly of Tutsi. Fighting had not reached Kigali, but Habyarimana used the occasion as an excuse to crack down on suspected Tutsi allies of the RPF. Belgian and French paratroopers were dispatched to Kigali at the Rwandan government's request in response to the RPF attack. Sporadic RPF incursions into Rwanda continued until a cease-fire was signed in July 1992. Whatever trust and cooperation might still have existed between Hutu and Tutsi in Rwanda before the Tutsi invaded in 1990 evaporated after the attack. The subsequent buildup of Hutu militia, with government support, only added to a feeling of pending doom among many Rwandans.

Even a war might not have led to genocide, however. Political ma-nipulation by Hutu extremists in government, it later became clear, managed to turn existing Hutu fears and hatred of Tutsi into the com-bustible mix that became genocide. Calls by some Hutu and Tutsi for reconciliation and political power sharing were drowned out, especially in the northern part of Rwanda, Habyarimana's stronghold. Only un-der international pressure, and probably to buy time to strengthen his own position and that of the Hutu militia, did Habyarimana begin negotiations with the RPF. Hard-liners dominated the government during the rule of Habyarimana and were against sharing power with the Tutsi. Moderates favoring cooperation with the Tutsi tried to build up opposition parties after the president conceded to their legality under international pressure in the early 1990s.

More fighting occurred early in 1993 when negotiations for a coalition government broke down. By late February, another cease-fire had been signed. In October 1993, the UN Security Council adopted Resolution 872, authorizing a UN cease-fire monitoring team of 2,500 personnel for Rwanda. In late December 1993, a contingent of 600 armed RPF soldiers was escorted to Kigali by UN troops as part of the peace agreements reached at Arusha, Tanzania, between the RPF and the government of Rwanda. The agreements called for a coalition government and a merged military and police force. Hard-liners in the government were strongly opposed to the accords. There are indications Habyarimana had no intention of fully implementing them; he continued to arm and train Hutu militia against the Tutsi.

Signs of Approaching Genocide

After the RPF attack in 1990, the Rwandan government began creating a "self-defense" program. Guns were distributed to supporters of Habyarimana, especially to members of his party, the Mouvement Républican National pour la Démocratie et le Développement (MRNDD), or National Republican Movement for Democracy and Development. Another organization allied to the MRNDD was the Coalition pour la Défense de la République (CDR), or Coalition for the Defense of the Republic. Both the CDR and the MRNDD formed civilian Hutu militia, which were in the vanguard of the killings of Tutsi from at least 1993 onward and "killed far more people than . . . uniformed members of the Armed forces."[45]

An ad hoc international commission determined that President Habyarimana and his government "tolerated and encouraged the activities of armed militia attached to the political parties, in clear violation of Rwandan law."[46] In effect, these militia did much of the dirty work for the government in carrying out a gradual campaign of political terrorism against Tutsi. "The militia of the MRNDD and the CDR are the most aggressive of the armed [civilian] groups, and the Tutsi and members of other parties represent by far the largest number of

Kigali, Rwanda, 1993
Hutu political demonstrations like this one took place prior to the genocide.

victims," according to a human rights report in June 1993, ten months before the genocide erupted.[47]

But the arming and training of militia was only one sign of a buildup to genocide. Another was the arrest of 8,000 to 10,000 people, some 75 percent of whom were Tutsi, including priests, intellectuals, and businessmen, after the October 1, 1990, invasion by the RPF.[48] Their treatment was one more indication of the pending explosion. Many of the detainees were severely beaten or tortured. Some were not fed for up to eight days. At one detention center, in Gikondo, "a man . . . was tied to a tree like a goat and shot. He finally died two days later after suffering horribly," according to a woman detainee in the detention center. "We heard his cries," she said.[49]

There was still another harbinger of disaster: a series of massacres of Tutsi. After the RPF attack in 1990, local authorities incited Hutu living in Kibirira, a rural area near the city of Gisenyi, in the northwest, to attack their Tutsi neighbors. More than 300 Tutsi were killed. In January 1991, when the RPF struck again, they captured the northern city of Ruhengeri for a day, releasing hundreds of prisoners. More than 300 Bagogwe, a subgroup of Tutsi, were killed in the following weeks in northwestern Rwanda by police, military, civilian officials, and ordinary people. Increasingly, ordinary Hutu took part in the killings of Tutsi. The attackers generally lacked guns, using instead machetes and sticks, just as they would in 1994. In one such case, mobs attacked Tutsi on the night of November 7–8, 1991, in Murambi.

It was not always the number of victims that provided a clue to the coming genocide; sometimes it was the viciousness of the attacks. Hutu violence against Tutsi in late 1991 included the following cases:

- An eighty-five-year-old woman chased from her home by a mob was stabbed to death with a spear while trying to hide behind some corn stalks by her fence.
- Men raping a girl of eighteen rushed off to join in the pillaging of the home of the girl's grandmother, but not before lodging a spear in her foot to keep her pinned down so they could continue raping her later.
- A Tutsi woman eight months pregnant received eight blows from a machete to various parts of her body.[50]

The pattern of neighbor killing neighbor was becoming clearer. The government of Rwanda blamed these incidents on opposition parties and took no action to punish the perpetrators, some of whom were known and accused by Tutsi survivors.

"Planned, Systematic" Genocide

Habyarimana was returning from another peace negotiating session with the RPF in Arusha, April 6, 1994, when his plane was shot down over Kigali. His death in the plane crash sparked, but did not cause, the ensuing genocide. Exactly who shot down the plane was not clear. Some blamed Hutu hard-liners; others intimated that elements of the French government may have had a hand in the affair. But regardless of who did it, there is clear evidence that the "genocide" that followed was, as UN investigator Degni-Ségui reported in June of that year, "planned, systematic and atrocious."[51]

Degni-Ségui, dean of the faculty of law at Abidjan University, in the West African state of Côte d'Ivoire (Ivory Coast), presented evidence exposing the meticulous planning behind the killings and the way they were encouraged and carried out by the Hutu.

1. A campaign of incitement to ethnic hatred and violence orchestrated by the media belonging to the government, or close to it, such as Radio Rwanda, and above all Radio Television Libre de Mille Collines (RTLMC), or, in English, Free Radio/Television of One Thousand Hills.
2. Distribution of arms to civilian militia after the RPF attack on Rwanda in 1990, and the training of militia at military installations from November 1993 to March 1994.
3. The "exceptional speed" with which the massacres began after Habyarimana's plane was shot down. A provisional government was formed within a few hours. Crude barricades were set up across most roads in Kigali "between 30 and 45 minutes after the crash of the aircraft, and even before the news of it had been announced on the national radio."
4. "The existence of lists [before the plane crash] giving the names of persons to be executed."[52]

Among the first victims were prime minister Agatha Uwilingiyimana, one of the few Tutsi in the government; Joseph Kavaruganda, president of the Supreme Court; and several other key members of the government. Ten Belgian members of the UN observer force were

Kigali, Rwanda, 1993
Among the first victims killed was Tutsi prime minister Agatha Uwilingiyimana.

killed that first night trying to protect the prime minister; some of their bodies were mutilated. The first wave of killings included more Hutu than Tutsi victims, as hit squads hunted down prominent Hutu moderates.[53] But the focus of the Hutu killers quickly turned to Tutsi, urged on by hate propaganda from the government radio.

In a country where television is practically nonexistent for the average Rwandan, radio is the way most people get their information. By early 1993, the radio in Rwanda was being used to incite Hutu against the Tutsi. In its report in March 1993, an ad hoc international commission composed of several key human rights organizations documented the role of the RTLMC, the national radio, in "heightening tensions between groups and political parties."[54] RTLMC was a private broadcasting station which began operating in September 1993; the owners were directly tied to high government officials. The president of the board of directors was Félician Kabuga, a wealthy businessman whose son married Rwandan president Habyarimana's daughter. Technical assistance came from George Ruggiu, an Italian by birth who later became a Belgian citizen. The RTLMC editorial position was totally against the Arusha peace accords Habyarimana had signed.

After the second attack by the RPF in 1993, the radio put out a false report that the RPF had massacred 500 civilians in a camp for displaced persons.[55] As the massacres by Hutu of Tutsi progressed in April 1994, the RTLMC got even more vitriolic, with broadcasts such as this one: "Fight the *inyenzi*, pound them. Stand up. Keep away from lies and rumors. If they pound you with heavy artillery, bombs, go into bunkers. Then after that you take your spears, clubs, guns, swords, stones, everything, sharpen them, hack those enemies, those cockroaches, those enemies of democracy, show that you can defend yourselves—support your soldiers."[56]

The RTLMC repeatedly broadcast statements aimed at stirring up frenzied hatred against the Tutsi, and secondarily against Hutu moderates seen as accomplices to the Tutsi. Degni-Ségui quoted Reporters Without Borders as stating that the RTLMC broadcast that "by 5 May [1994], the cleansing of the Tutsi must be completed," and that "the grave is still only half full: who will help us fill it [with dead Tutsi]?" He also reported the comment of a senior UN official that in Rwanda, with

Benaco Refugee Camp, Tanzania, 1994
Rwandan refugees stand on the highest point in their camp to get better radio reception for war news.

an illiteracy rate of about 55 percent among those fifteen and older, such inflammatory remarks on the national radio had a dangerous effect.[57] "They hold their radio sets in one hand and their machetes in the other, ready to go into action."[58]

The day the president's plane was shot down, RTLMC told its listeners, "The Tutsi need to be killed." The station called on Hutu to "hunt out the Tutsi," claiming "the RPF is coming to kill people; so defend yourselves."[59] One can imagine the fear such broadcasts must have caused. There was an element of truth in the warnings: the RPF had attacked several times, and the rebels were determined to return to Rwanda. In Hutu homes, stories of fighting the Tutsi dated back to 1959, but stories of resentment of the Tutsi and domination by them dated back centuries.

Journey into Rwanda's Killing Fields

My encounter with Manuel and other survivors of the stadium concentration camp took place in June 1994 during the first of numerous trips back to Rwanda. I had been to the country only once before, in 1993, and had failed to detect the genocidal explosion building up. Most reporters and diplomats also missed the pending catastrophe, though a few human rights groups in 1993 were noting a worsening pattern of abuses, primarily by Hutu.

Covering the genocide was dangerous for reporters, and it deeply affected some of them. A colleague sat in my living room in Nairobi one day while I was still recovering, explaining how he felt to have been in a land of such death. Though he had not personally witnessed killings, as some reporters had, he was there when many homes in Kigali were still crammed with human bodies. The images were fresh in his mind, and he had a hard time describing what he had seen. When I arrived in Rwanda, I could still smell the stench of decomposing corpses on some streets in Kigali and along country roadsides. Many bodies had been left unburied.

I visited a house near Kigali several months after the Tutsi captured Rwanda. A UNICEF employee had received word that her relatives' bodies were lying untended in the ruins. We turned off the highway onto a secondary, unpaved road, then drove up a narrow dirt track. Back roads were sometimes still mined, a risk no one wanted to discuss. When we reached the home, we saw that the windows and doors had been smashed out. Inside two back rooms, partly destroyed by a grenade or other explosion, lay a horrible jumble of skeletal remains, apparently including members of the woman's family. Bits of clothing remained on the bones; a metal spring bed lay twisted in the debris. A local resident, still terrified, said the victims had been told by local Hutu officials to stay in the house; then they were murdered by the officials. The UNICEF employee wept silently. Just moving around the building was risky because of the possibility of mines. Several piles of dirt looked suspicious. I prayed as I walked around looking for other bodies. Rwandans discovering their family in such conditions had begun planning burial ceremonies as a final tribute to the departed, and as a way to try to close a chapter they hoped would never be reopened.

★ ★ ★

Fighting was still going on when I arrived in Rwanda in June 1994. Tutsi rebels were close to claiming victory; the Hutu army had mostly fled to Zaire and other countries. But Tutsi were still being slaughtered in areas the RPF had not reached. The biggest area was the so-called safety zone that the French had set up in southwestern Rwanda.

The French record in Rwanda is mixed. France had helped arm and train the Rwandan army in recent years. A diplomat in Kigali alleged that the French even took part in some battles against the RPF. The French were far from being a disinterested party: they ignored the government's "massive violations of human rights" and publicly backed peace talks with the Tutsi while "arming and training [Hutu] death squads and militia."[60] But as the genocide in Rwanda continued, only the French had decided to intervene, though not until late June. By then the Hutu government was on the run. It appeared the French

Rusumo, Rwanda, 1994
Soldiers of the Rwandese Patriotic Front (RPF), a mostly Tutsi force, forced the Hutu government to flee the country after three months of heavy fighting.

intervened to protect the falling regime they had backed. French forces drew an invisible line around a huge section of southwestern Rwanda, declaring it to be off limits to the RPF, and dubbed their intervention Operation Turquoise. The French zone became a safe haven—until months after the war—for far more Hutu than Tutsi. All of the one-million-plus Hutu who fled to the zone were not killers, but there were undoubtedly many killers among them. Creation of the French zone "certainly protected some escaped Tutsi, but [also] permitted the organizers of genocide to get out of Rwanda via Zaire or other routes."[61]

Tutsi like Manuel almost certainly would have been killed if the French had not gone into Rwanda when they did. But the French arrived much too late to save most Tutsi in the area. The French presence was sparse, despite the fact that killings of Tutsi were still taking place. Many Tutsi were still hiding from the Hutu while others waited nervously in French-guarded camps like the one where I met Manuel and Antoine.

No Sanctuary

Antoine was sitting in the same close circle with Manuel, there on the hillside. He, too, asked that his last name not be used. He explained that he had taken refuge along with nearly 5,000 Tutsi in a church in Shangi, a village a few miles from the camp where we now sat. As the genocidal killings spread, it was natural for Antoine and many other Tutsi to flee to churches. They thought they would find sanctuary.

In the original film version of Victor Hugo's *The Hunchback of Notre Dame* there is a moving scene where the hunchback swings down from the cathedral on a rope, just as the woman who had befriended him is about to be hung. He sweeps her off the gallows and swings back to the church. Lifting her overhead as he stands triumphantly near the top of a bell tower, he shouts to the crowd below, "Sanctuary. Sanctuary." By the custom of the day, she was safe as long as she stayed in the church, though a mob later stormed the cathedral. In Rwanda there was no safety for those who sought sanctuary in the churches. The churches became hunting grounds.

The Hutu *interahamwe* (militia) and soldiers came to the church in Shangi April 29 armed with grenades, guns, machetes, and spears,

Antoine recounted in vivid detail. The killers were led, he and others in the group insisted, by Cyangugu mayor Bugarama. Not content with having flushed out most of his town's Tutsi into a death camp stadium, Bugarama now went after other surviving Tutsi hiding in the church. The same thing was happening across the country. There were massive casualties in churches during the genocide in Rwanda:

- 2,800 were slaughtered in four hours in a church in Kibungo by Hutu militia using grenades, machine guns, machetes, and R4 rockets; only about 40 people survived;
- 6,000 were attacked in a church in Cyahinda; only about 200 lived;
- 4,000 perished in a church in Kibeho;
- 500 were murdered in a parish in Rukara.[62]

Even orphanages were not spared. Twenty-one Tutsi children in an orphanage in Butare were killed along with thirteen Rwandan Red Cross volunteers trying to protect them.

Human Rights Watch estimates 4,000 people were killed in the Shangi church where Antoine took refuge. The attacks were heinous and effective. "First they threw in grenades," Antoine said. Then, after firing through various openings in the parish church walls, "they broke down the door." The pattern of first tossing in grenades, then attacking those fleeing the church was repeated in many parts of the country. Those who managed to dash out of such death traps were met by others armed with machetes and clubs with nails sticking out the end, another popular Hutu weapon against Tutsi. Jonathan Randal of the *Washington Post* visited the church in Shangi and noted "a pattern of bloody hand prints visible from floor to ceiling—a virtual diagram of how desperate Tutsi stood on each other's shoulders in a vain effort to reach the ceiling crawl spaces and roof to hide from their Hutu killers." One is reminded of the Jews in World War II and their desperate struggle to escape the gas chambers.

"What's terrible is they buried them in a common grave," said Antoine, speaking of the Tutsi bodies. As in Bosnia, mass graves were dug for some of the victims. One of Betty's photos shows the remains of some 600 people massacred in the Ntarama church near the town of Nyamata. As a tribute to the victims, local residents had decided to leave the church as it was found. There are several gaping holes in the

Muyumbu, Rwanda, 1994
UNICEF staff member Anne-Marie Kabatende (*center, wearing head scarf*) and others stand in front of her destroyed home where her family was massacred by Hutu.
Credit: UNICEF/Betty Press

Nyamata, Rwanda, 1994
Skulls of victims of a massacre in Ntarama church near Nyamata. The photograph was found at the site and is probably of some of the victims. Many of the skulls show machete blows.
Credit: UNICEF/Betty Press

brick walls. The floor is piled with human debris and remnants of clothing. Outside the church dozens of human skulls, many smashed open or bearing machete slice marks, are laid out in a silent, sightless testimony from the victims. In front of the skulls, someone had laid a photograph of four schoolgirls probably killed in the church. They appear to be primary school students in a classroom. As with my father's photos from World War II, I look away from the photograph of the skulls after a few seconds, then back again. The skulls have nothing to do with humans, I want to convince myself; these are not remnants of lives. Then I glance at the photo within the photo, of the four girls, and I cannot avoid making the connection: yes, these were people.

Can surviving Tutsi from such villages ever accept back Hutu who might have done some of the killing there? Perhaps. Shortly after the war, UNICEF and other organizations helped reunite many displaced children with surviving family members. Often the social workers were Tutsi and the children Hutu.

Barricades of Death

Despite the scattered presence of French troops in the "safety zone," almost all the roads we drove along in the southwest in June 1994 were blocked with the same kinds of barricades that had been set up in Kigali and most other cities. Such barricades became death traps for the fleeing Tutsi. Many were simply a pole across the road, supported by rocks, benches, chairs, or posts. Crowds of men armed with machetes waited at each barricade to demand a person's national identity card, which stated if the individual was Hutu, Tutsi, or Twa, the 1 percent of the population also known as pygmies. Having a Tutsi or no identification card meant almost certain death, unless the intended victims could bribe their way through.

I entered Rwanda from Burundi, which was having its own ethnic slaughters, a kind of genocide by installments that led to a Tutsi military coup in August 1996.[63] I was traveling in a two-vehicle convoy with Betty, another journalist, a U.S. diplomat, several UN relief specialists, and some representatives of private relief agencies. On the first day, we passed through about forty barricades, each one a moment of frightening uncertainty. A few hundred yards inside Rwanda, on a narrow, paved road, we had to stop at one of the last immigration posts still run by the collapsing Hutu government. Several members of our group did not have Rwandan visas; I had obtained one in Nairobi. We were all allowed to continue. By this time Tutsi rebels had methodically advanced on Kigali from their northern strongholds and had taken the capital, and now they were dug in around the edges of the French zone, not eager to take on the French military. The RPF was also busy securing other parts of the country.

For a while that morning we were forced by the narrow road and many curves to follow a large transport truck belonging to the International Committee of the Red Cross, which was feeding Tutsi and Hutu alike. I wondered if the truck would be blocked by Hutu extremists anxious to starve out the remaining Tutsi in the zone. Now we were into the backwoods country of Hutu death squads. At the first village we saw a group of men in civilian clothes trotting quickly in formation and carrying sticks. It appeared to be a training exercise of a local militia. It was unnerving. In striking contrast, the sound of hymn-singing wafted out of a nearby church.

One day, after the war, in a massive Hutu refugee camp in what was then Zaire, I saw hundreds of Hutu jogging in a long snaking column through the camp. It looked medieval and terrifying. Militants among the refugees threatened other refugees who wanted to return to Rwanda, telling them they had to stay and form an army to fight the Tutsi. This pressure was enough to keep most of the refugees from going back to Rwanda, as many wanted to do and later would when they got a chance.

As we drove on that morning just inside Rwanda, we came to several barricades in the first border village. At each one, unfriendly looking men with machetes scrutinized us. At one barrier a man asked to see our passports. Would they use the lack of visas as an excuse to send us back? Our driver held out a passport with a visa, and the barrier was removed. No one in our group spoke of what might happen if we were not allowed through. The presence of several diplomats and a couple of journalists seemed to be of no consequence to these men. We all felt extremely vulnerable as we penetrated deeper and deeper into this last big bastion of Hutu strength.

The next day, in a village beyond the area the French protected, men attending the barrier raised it for the first of our two cars to pass through, then began lowering it as the second car, in which I was riding, approached. Our driver paid no heed and rushed through before they could drop the pole back down. Another journalist, who traveled along the Rwandan-Burundi border not long after us, stopped on the Burundi side and peered across. He saw bodies, apparently Tutsi, sprawled out along the road. I once visited a border crossing point between East and West Berlin, before the wall came down. Fleeing East Germans must have felt like fleeing Tutsi trying to escape, only to be killed a few yards from freedom.

There were many reports of bodies strewn around barricades in Kigali and other parts of the country as the genocide continued. To avoid barricades, thousands of Tutsi in the area we were now passing through had fled into the wooded hills where they had become targets of manhunts. As we traveled on, I kept wondering, Where are the French troops? They were, we learned, mostly in the main towns in the zone.

On a paved road outside the city of Gikongoro, we stopped in the dense forest. A group of fleeing Rwandans, including Tutsi, had stopped their trucks and cars, which were crammed with personal goods. Fearful of going forward, they were also frightened of returning to Gikongoro, a stronghold for Hutu militants. They were trying to make it to Zaire, but to get there they had to pass through numerous Hutu-manned barricades with no French troops to protect them. As we talked with them, a stink beside the road proved to be a rotting human body. A woman traveling with us recognized a woman in the fleeing group who, nearly hysterical, begged us to go get French troops to escort them to a camp ahead. We promised to relay their request to the French. When we met the French forces, a few miles farther, they said they had another priority—guarding a small road that might be used as a Tutsi rebel infiltration route. They said they could not escort the convoy; but we later heard they did, taking the group to a French-guarded camp closer to Zaire.

When we arrived in Gikongoro, it was flooded with displaced Hutu fleeing nearby RPF advances. Some terrified Tutsi in town were trying to pass as Hutu. The main intersection in town, where a two-lane, paved road crosses a dirt one, was a human sea of people standing around with little to do and nowhere to go, especially if they lacked the money to travel onward into Zaire.

I tried to find a Rwandan who had called me in Nairobi, Faustin Hitiyise, and who might be there en route to Zaire. I found someone who had seen him a few days earlier. All I knew was that he was fairly young, thin, and wore glasses. I stood for forty-five minutes on a spot overlooking the main intersection, scanning for someone with glasses, but few people were wearing them and no one fit his description. Although the town appeared calm, this was deceptive. "You see that man over there," a frightened Tutsi college student said to me in a low voice as we walked along a side road. "He's checking ID cards." Those with Tutsi cards would be killed, regardless of the presence of French troops in the town, the student said. This student was hoping to be evacuated on one of the French helicopters. I later met him in Nairobi, where he was on his way back to college studies in Italy. What terrible stories he would have for his classmates.

Leaving Gikongoro the next morning, we soon passed beyond the French-patrolled area. Heading south toward Burundi, we found ourselves driving "upstream" against a human tide of Hutu flowing out from Butare, one of the main cities in Rwanda, which had just been captured by Tutsi fighters. Hutu militants had killed many Tutsi there. Women, men, and children carried their most important survival items, often on their heads: sleeping mats, bags of grain, extra clothing for the cold nights outdoors. The procession flooded the dirt road and spilled over onto the shoulders, parting just enough for our vehicles to pass slowly through. Village after village was jammed. Cooking fires were burning everywhere, enveloping the air with a fog of smoke. Villages consisted of stick and mud homes and sometimes a primary school made of the same materials.

The fleeing Hutu were pouring along this back road to avoid an attack by Tutsi on the main road. Many intended to go all the way to Zaire to escape the Tutsi. We also wanted to avoid a battle, so we veered off our intended route and toward what villagers said was another border crossing back into Burundi. Tensions were high in the area. As we drove through a tiny village, a crowd of men and women were huddled together. Our car windows were tinted, so it was difficult for anyone to see in. But as we made a sharp curve I rolled my window down partway and stuck my hand out and waved. The effect was like magic. Almost simultaneously, most of the crowd raised their arms and cheered, despite the fact that we did not stop. I can only guess they were relieved to see they had not been abandoned by the outside world. They may have thought we were a French military reconnaissance or a medical team.

We reached the border just before sunset, but the gate was locked and had been for months. The key supposedly was with an official back in Gikongoro. We had little choice but to stay the night at the border and try to figure out our next move in the morning. As we sat in our cars, unsure of where to sleep or how safe this area was, night fell. A group of men appeared and slowly walked around our cars; some of them pressed their noses and hands to the windows. We were far from French protection, but not wanting to stay cooped up all night, we got out of our cars and began greeting people. There was little response. Language was not a real barrier, since we and some of them spoke French. There seemed to be a coldness in the air that had little to do with the temperature. As I looked closer at the men I saw they were poor, probably farmers. Most of them were barefoot. They were not carrying weapons, not even machetes; they seemed merely curious.

That evening our group pooled sandwiches and snacks and laid them on a cloth on the ground. We ate our meal by headlights. I later asked a border official if we could bed down in the small office complex where he and his colleagues worked. He immediately agreed, giving us use of two cement-floor, bare rooms. In the morning we simply drove around the barrier, squeezing between two border post buildings. A Hutu immigration official helped push our vehicles through the muddy passage.

We were not sure if there were mines in the road ahead, but we drove on across the small no-man's-land between the border posts without a problem. On the other side, one of the relief workers with us hopped out at the barrier, bowed, and explained to the Burundi immigration officials what they already knew about our presence. They lifted the pole, our last barricade of the trip, and I felt a surge of relief as we left behind the land of mass killings, even though we were returning to another one.

When French troops pulled out of Rwanda, in August 1994, soon after the RPF took power, United Nations troops replaced them. Later, an impatient RPF-led government took over the towns of the former French zone. Many Hutu who panicked and ran were shot and killed by RPF soldiers. The RPF was finally in control of all its territory.

Abuses by Tutsi Rebels

Authorities of the deposed Hutu government started organizing small armed attacks on Rwanda from refugee camps in Zaire. They also alleged that Tutsi were carrying out "systematic massacres," Degni-Ségui noted in his UN report on Rwanda. But, he added, "there is no eyewitness evidence to confirm this information."[64] There were, however, reported instances of killings by the RPF during—and after—their takeover of Rwanda in the wake of the genocide against their people. But the scale of such abuses in no way compares to the tidal wave of killings by the Hutu against Tutsi and moderate Hutu, according to Degni-Ségui. In his report he wrote there is little doubt that the Tutsi-led RPF "has been guilty of summary executions." He cited a case in which the RPF, on June 9, 1994, "killed a number of members of the clergy, including two bishops and the Archbishop of Kigali." But reports of large-scale massacres by the RPF are "rather rare, indeed virtually nonexistent, perhaps because little is known about them," the UN special rapporteur wrote.[65]

A U.S.-based human rights organization, writing in May 1994, while the killing was still under way, refuted charges of systematic killings by the RPF.[66] But in a report in October 1994, Amnesty International cited eyewitnesses and other reports suggesting that "hundreds—possibly thousands—of unarmed civilians and captured armed opponents of the RPF have been summarily executed . . . [many] in a series of arbitrary reprisals."[67]

Some Rwandan clergy blamed the RPF for killing hundreds of civilians. But the reliability of the Rwandan Hutu clergy is suspect. For example, several prominent Hutu church leaders supporting the Habyarimana regime met with reporters in Nairobi in mid-1994, after most of the genocide was over. They denied seeing any atrocities carried out by the Hutu. They cited only allegations of killings by the RPF, a completely biased account. Several reporters who had been on the scene many times during the killings were so angry at the clergy's one-sidedness that they nearly walked out of the press conference. The Hutu clergy seemed entirely unwilling to present anything resembling a balanced picture of events. Some of their reluctance may reflect independently documented RPF atrocities against the clergy.

The RPF itself admitted to killing some civilians, blaming indiscipline among their troops. There were other reports of civilians killed either by Tutsi civilians, or the RPF, or both, after being tied up. Some senior RPF soldiers were involved in the deaths of numerous Hutu living in camps for the displaced in the former French zone. There was no indication these officers were punished for their actions. Privately, some Tutsi officials in the new government told me and other reporters it would require almost superhuman discipline for a soldier to return home and not want revenge after finding his family had been massacred by Hutu. Lack of a judicial system after the war left many Tutsi convinced that personal retribution was the only way to respond to their personal losses.

The World Watched It Happen Again

Except for the late, and controversial, entry into the fray by French troops, the rest of the world largely watched genocide happen in Rwanda and did little to try to stop it. "At the time of the genocide in Rwanda, the international community stood by while more than half a million people were slaughtered."[68] Speaking of the growing ethnic conflict in neighboring Burundi, Tanzania's former president Julius Nyerere said in June 1996, "If there is an eruption of killings there, the international community must not sit again with its hands folded, as we did in Rwanda."[69]

After the French pulled out, a French military officer told me he thought French troops, had they been deployed quickly, could have stopped or at least slowed the killing in Rwanda. The French had men, arms, and vehicles in Kigali when the massacres began and could have beefed up their presence quickly, the officer continued. "What did they [the killers] have?" he asked rhetorically. "Clubs and machetes."

Four years after the tragedy, in 1998, there was a public round of finger-pointing mixed with some apologies, starting with an emotional statement by General Romeo Dallaire, the French-speaking Canadian officer in charge of the UN troops in Rwanda when the massacres began. He said the Hutu extremists, even relying mostly on crude weapons, could "kill 1,000 people in 20 minutes." He also told the UN's International Criminal Tribunal for Rwanda in February 1998, with his voice cracking and tears running down his cheeks, that given rein-forcements, his UN troops could have prevented the genocide: "Many people had been pressured into [participating in the killings]; they were acting out of fear. If we had had a force that could have convinced them that it was riskier to go to the barricades than stay at home, we could have stopped it."[70] But at the time of the outbreak of the killings, the UN had fewer than 3,000 troops in the country. And shortly after ten Belgian peacekeepers were killed, the UN ordered the withdrawal of all but a few hundred troops, leaving the UN forces incapable of doing anything more than securing a few key locations to which hunted Rwandans could flee.

The French troops in Kigali when the massacres broke out were there to monitor the earlier peace accord; they were not assigned to try to stem violence or go on the offensive. Instead, the French troops, like the Belgian troops in Rwanda when the mass killing began, concen-trated on getting their own citizens out. CNN showed troops escorting Westerners out of Kigali in early April 1994. "The international relief [at the rescue of Westerners and departure of most UN personnel] was both legitimate in respect of those non-Rwandan lives saved but shameful in view of the vast numbers of Rwandans left to their fate."[71]

★ ★ ★

The UN knew in advance that a genocide might be in the making, and took no steps to prevent it. Dallaire added in his testimony that he had faxed a memo January 11, 1994, to UN headquarters saying what a former member of the security staff of Rwandan president Habyari-mana had told him: that arms were being distributed among the Hutu majority and lists of targeted Tutsi and moderate Hutu were being drawn up. The informant offered to help the UN raid the Hutu arms caches, which Dallaire notified the UN he intended to do.

The Dallaire fax to the UN became public in 1995; the UN response, from the office of Kofi Annan, who later became secretary general, was revealed in an article in the *New Yorker* magazine May 11, 1998.[72] The reply Dallaire got back from UN headquarters said that under the current mandate of the UN in Rwanda, such offensive actions were not allowed. Instead of changing the mandate to allow offensive operations, the UN told Dallaire to take no action; it was suggested he share the informant's information with the government and insist that the plan be stopped. The response was sent under the name of Annan but signed by his deputy, Iqbal Riza, who later became Annan's chief of staff when Annan became secretary general. "I was responsible," Riza said, adding, "this is not to say that Mr. Annan was oblivious to what was going on." He added that the UN secretary general's office would have gotten copies of the Dallaire fax. He said the Dallaire fax was properly handled: "We get hyperbole in many reports."

A week after the *New Yorker* article was published, a former top French general told a French parliamentary commission looking into the Rwanda genocide that "the international community could have halted the massacres if it had been less cowardly." Then, his own voice cracking with emotion, he blamed Canadian general Dallaire directly. "I may shock you but the honor of a soldier is to know how to disobey. He might have been sacked later but my feeling is that with those 2,500 men he could have halted the massacres which were then limited to Kigali."[73]

Annan, who at the time of the genocide was in charge of the UN's peacekeeping operations, defended himself before the Rwandan Parliament on a brief visit there in May 1998. In hindsight, he said, "we see the signs which then were not recognized. Now we know what we did was not nearly enough . . . to save Rwanda from itself, not enough to honor the ideals for which the United Nations exists. We will not deny that in their greatest hour of need the world failed the people of Rwanda." He also said "the world must deeply repent" its failure to stop the genocide.[74]

Rwandan officials were furious with Annan for having failed to take actions that might have avoided the genocide, and they let him know that. He was met at the airport by only one senior official, without ceremony. The president, vice president, and prime minister boycotted a dinner in Annan's honor. And Foreign Minister Anastase Gasana blasted Annan and the UN in a speech before Parliament, with Annan sitting beside him. A few days earlier, a spokesman for Annan had tried to share the blame with the international community. "The fundamental failure was the lack of political will, not the lack of information. . . . No one can deny that the world failed the people of Rwanda. We should be asking how we can ensure that such a tragedy can never happen again, and how the international community can best assist the people and government of Rwanda."[75]

Why the United States Stayed out of the Conflict

The U.S. decision to stay out of Rwanda was critical and set the tone for the international response. It must be seen in a post-Somalia context. In March 1998, during the most extensive Africa trip of any U.S. president, Bill Clinton, speaking at the airport in Kigali, called the genocide in Rwanda the most rapid "slaughter" of the century. He said the "international community" must share the blame. Then, after hearing from some of the survivors, he admitted: "We did not act quickly enough after the killing began. We did not immediately call these crimes by their rightful name: genocide. All over the world, there were people like me sitting in offices, day after day after day, who did not fully appreciate the depth and the speed with which you were being engulfed by this unimaginable terror."[76]

If true, his admission is an example of the failure of the U.S. government to keep its president informed of key world events. If true, it is also an example of how a president can fail to keep himself informed of something widely reported on television and in the newspapers. "The information was there," about the nature and extent of the killings, said Janet Fleischman, Washington-based Africa specialist with Human Rights Watch.[77]

I believe Clinton knew what was happening in Rwanda. The killing started suddenly, but it lasted three months. It began just as South Africa was inaugurating Nelson Mandela as its first black president, and there were many other world and domestic events vying for his attention. But Clinton was a detail president. And even though until

1998 he had never been to Africa, he was president during most of the Somalia episode involving U.S. troops.

That episode was the real reason the United States did not send troops to Rwanda—why, in fact, the United States attempted to delay an international military response to try to stop the killing. U.S. troops entered Somalia in December 1992 with a mission from the outgoing president, George Bush, to help deliver food to the starving. Anarchy in the wake of the overthrow of Somali president Mohamed Siad Barre in January 1991 had led to civil war between rival Somali factions, which in turn had caused massive famine in contested areas. Much relief food had been looted in the lawlessness engulfing central Somalia. The U.S. intervention in Somalia, though late, initially was a success: troops helped get more relief food delivered. But after U.S. and other international troops in Somalia stayed on to try to end the civil war, they became targets of one Somali clan, or faction, led by Mohamed Farah Aideed.

It was a single battle in October 1993 that made the difference. Eighteen U.S. Rangers were killed; the naked body of one Ranger was dragged through the streets of the Somali capital, Mogadishu, a scene millions of Americans saw on television. Within days, and acting under intense pressure from the public and Congress, Clinton set a departure date for U.S. troops from Somalia. His deadline, March 1994, turned out to be just one month before Rwanda exploded.

This was a turning point in U.S. foreign policy: the United States, at least under Clinton, would no longer send its troops on peacekeeping missions that did not directly affect its national security—regardless of the humanitarian needs. The intervention of U.S. troops in Bosnia in late 1995 would be presented by President Clinton as in the U.S. interest. But a Somalia, Liberia, or Rwanda would be allowed to fester on its own, except for provision of humanitarian aid or a possible "surgical" military intervention to provide logistical aid or rescue Americans. During the 1992 presidential campaign, Clinton had described his vision of an international, United Nations–led army "standing at the borders of countries threatened by aggression, preventing mass violence against civilian populations, providing humanitarian relief and combating terrorism."[78] The episode in Somalia changed all that.

In 1995, reflecting on the deaths of the U.S. soldiers, General John

Shalikashvili, chairman of the Joint Chiefs of Staff, said: "Something has broken down in the debate about the use of force. Eighteen people died so thousands and thousands could live. To me that's glory." Anthony Lake, Clinton's national security adviser, who was standing next to Shalikashvili, nodded.[79]

In fact, both men were wrong about the positive impact of the eighteen deaths in Somalia. Their deaths did not mean thousands could live. The earlier mission to deliver food helped keep people alive. But the shift of gears to a peacemaking mission based on ignorance of the culture and the politics of Somalia did little to help keep people alive— Somalis or Americans.

As the killing proceeded in Rwanda, one U.S. official I spoke with, who had been in contact with senior officials from the National Security Council and State Department, said the United States was determined not to get into another Somalia-type situation. And facing a strengthening Republican opposition, soon to take over both the Senate and House leadership, Clinton did not want to lose another foreign policy round over such a far-off place as Rwanda.

On May 3, 1994, as genocide in Rwanda was expanding rapidly, and exactly seven months after the deaths of the eighteen U.S. servicemen in Somalia, Clinton signed Presidential Decision Directive 25. It put strict conditions on U.S. military participation in international peacekeeping operations. According to one newspaper account at the time, PDD 25 "reflects concerns after ill-fated peacekeeping operations in Somalia and Haiti and comes after more than a year of fierce interagency feuding."[80] The new directive effectively put a brake on any U.S. military involvement in a peacekeeping operation in Rwanda. "The initially negative U.S. reaction to a proposed UN peacekeeping force for Rwanda was widely seen as due to the operation's not meeting PDD 25 requirements."[81] Madeleine K. Albright, U.S. permanent representative to the United Nations, said the United States would insist on answers to key questions before deciding whether to commit U.S. troops to any UN peacekeeping operation: "Will the UN involvement advance U.S. interests?; is there a real threat to international peace and security?; [are there] clear objectives[?]"; and is there a clear "end point" or exit plan?[82]

Not only did PDD 25 block U.S. military intervention in Rwanda, it left the United Nations floundering there. "The PDD clearly signified an abrupt end to any new initiatives [for the UN] on Rwanda, which would be impossible to implement now without American agreement."[83] The United States was "absolutely paralyzed by Somalia," a senior UN official said in 1998, when the international leadership was wringing its hands and casting blame in connection with Rwanda's genocide. A European diplomat put it this way: "The Security Council was traumatized by what had happened, but Washington was more traumatized than the others." Then-UN secretary general Boutros-Ghali repeatedly asked the Security Council to send a bigger force to Rwanda. But when the council agreed to send a force of 5,500, the

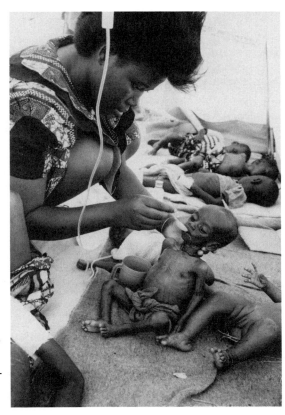

Katale Refugee Camp, near Goma, Zaire, 1994
A relief worker cares for babies during an epidemic.
Credit: UNICEF/Betty Press

United States forced a delay until there were moves to end the violence.[84]

Eventually, after most of the genocide was over, the United States
did send some 2,300 troops to help with logistics and relief efforts
aimed, primarily, at the more than one million refugees, predominantly
Hutu, who had fled to neighboring Zaire. It was ironic that the United
States had not responded when the Tutsi were being slaughtered, but
rushed to help members of the ethnic group responsible for most of the
slaughter, the Hutu, when they were dying in refugee camps. The needs
of the Hutu refugees were staggering, everyone agreed. And among
them were undoubtedly many innocent people as well as killers. A frustrated Western relief worker in Rwanda said she was glad to see the
world responding to the needs of the Hutu refugees, but, she asked,
where was the world when the Tutsi were being slaughtered?

The United States "Dithered" as Genocide Continued

As the killing spread in April 1994, Salim Salim, Tanzanian secretary
general of the Organization of African Unity (OAU), told UN secretary
general Boutros-Ghali he had collected commitment pledges from
African nations to send 5,000 troops to Rwanda. The UN's role would
be to equip and transport the troops and provide logistical support
once they arrived. Boutros-Ghali asked the UN Security Council to
approve payment for this.

According to former U.S. assistant secretary of state for Africa,
Herman J. Cohen, the quick dispatch to Rwanda of an African peacekeeping force could have brought the killings to a halt. But the United
States, among other nations, balked, arguing there was no detailed plan
for the operation of the African troops in Rwanda or their exit. Behind
the United States' "dithering," which went on for about two months—
while genocide took its toll, and nearly took the life of Tutsi like Manuel
and Antoine—was a deeper issue, said Cohen, who was assistant secretary from 1989 to 1993. "I had heard back here [in Washington] there
was a feeling in D.O.D. [Department of Defense] that African troops
would get into difficulty and it would require U.S. troops to come in
and rescue them in a 'slippery slope' syndrome." That scenario would
have had U.S. troops returning to Africa soon after the U.S. military

pullout from Somalia. The feeling among U.S. officials was strong that the United States must "not get burned twice," Cohen added. The African troops finally arrived in November 1994, well after the genocide had ended. Cohen gave two reasons for his belief that these troops could have stopped it completely had they been deployed earlier. First, "most of the killing was being done by ordinary civilians frightened into a state of hysteria by the extremists. They were telling Hutu to kill every Tutsi before the Tutsi killed them. The presence of foreign troops on the ground, being brought in by American aircraft, would have had a calming effect." Second, Hutu extremists would not have had such a free hand to organize killings in the presence of African troops. The United States could have airlifted up to 1,000 African troops into Rwanda within days, Cohen contended, recalling how it airlifted Moroccan troops into southern Zaire within seventy-two hours to quell a rebellion there in the 1980s.[85] On the other hand, West African peacekeeping troops stationed in the Liberian capital of Monrovia failed to prevent ethnic-based militia in the city from engaging in all-out fighting in 1996.[86]

Without reinforcements, the several hundred UN personnel still in Rwanda could do little to stop the killings. They were, however, able to rescue many Tutsi and others trapped in various parts of Kigali and to protect them. Most of the UN personnel in Rwanda were not what one would call "front line" troops. The majority were doing administrative work. The small number of UN troops still going out on the street were soon engulfed by the artillery battles that broke out between the RPF and the Hutu army. As the battles grew more intense, the mass killings, as discussed earlier, were mostly being carried out by people armed with machetes and clubs. UN artillery and heavy weapons would probably have proved as useless in stopping these killings as the big weapons of the United States and other nations had been in stopping guerrilla warfare in Mogadishu.

Kigali's main streets are easily navigable by military or any other vehicles. But the back alleys, where much of the poor population lives and where much of the killing took place, are a labyrinth, as I found out when another journalist and I accompanied Mugarura to his home. (Mugarura was the Tutsi who had hidden in his home during the killing.) By the time we got near his dwelling, it was night; none of us carried a flashlight. We walked uncertainly, feeling our way with our feet and hands along narrow mud alleys crisscrossed with ruts, ditches, and sewage canals. The heart of the slum had some larger passageways, but any military vehicle would have become stuck on turns, making it an easy target. In the initial days of the killings, the Hutu militia spread out in such neighborhoods. Anything short of a block-by-block occupation or destruction of the entire neighborhoods might not have stopped the murders once started.

While more foreign troops probably couldn't have stopped the killing, they might have contained it. They might have kept genocide from engulfing towns such as Butare, which remained calm for ten days after the outbursts began in Kigali. Butare was the most important southern city in Rwanda, an intellectual center with a university, and a hotbed for opposition to the hard-line Hutu government. International troops stationed in Butare might have prevented the interim Rwandan president, Théodore Sindikubwabo, from coming there and making an inflammatory, anti-Tutsi speech which sparked the Butare massacres.

★   ★   ★

Apparently missing from most of the official discussions in Washington about the United States and Rwanda was a strong moral argument that people were dying as a result of genocide, and perhaps the United States should help. It is often said in the United States that we should first take care of our problems at home before taking on those of the world. But there are times when the suffering of others is so great that nations capable of responding should do so. For the United States, the price of going into Rwanda might have been the loss of more soldiers. But the price, in terms of human suffering, of staying out and encouraging others to do the same was staggering. After years of hearing the message from the Holocaust to stay vigilant, to keep those events fresh in mind so that it would never happen again, the United States and Europe (except France, which had helped arm the Hutu forces) stood by when they might have made a difference in Rwanda. The world had let genocide happen again.

Justice and Reconciliation?

As genocide was spreading across Rwanda, some UN and other officials were already talking about the need to bring the perpetrators to justice. If they were not, these officials argued, the world would be sending a message to future mass killers: you can get away with it. The officials called for an international tribunal to try the guilty, as the Allies had done after World War II. The world had to know that it was not just a few ringleaders behind all the murder, said one non-Rwandan analyst. "The society is guilty." A UN official who had traveled in most parts of Rwanda said he hoped the world's attention to the needs of Hutu refugees didn't shift attention away from the need to prosecute the killers.

In 1996, a UN tribunal finally began for crimes against humanity in the former Yugoslavia. An independent tribunal had begun in Ethiopia in December 1994 for those accused of crimes during the days of Red Terror in the 1970s under ousted head of state Mengistu Haile Mariam.

A UN tribunal on Rwanda eventually began, in Arusha, Tanzania, but proceedings crawled along for months in preparatory work. The first accused, the former mayor of Gitarama, Jean-Paul Akayesu, went on trial in September 1996.[87] The tribunal moved so slowly that most Tutsi had little faith that justice would be served by it. In May 1998, Jean Kambanda, who was prime minister of Rwanda at the time his government led the genocidal attacks, pled guilty at the tribunal and promised to testify against other ringleaders. In September 1998, both men were found guilty. In Akayesu's case, the judges ruled that rape and other forms of sexual violence in Rwanda in 1994 constituted genocide as well as the killings. Legal experts said the inclusion of rape under the UN definition of "genocide" set a precedent.[88] In Rwanda, some 120,000 prisoners awaited judgment on charges of crimes against humanity in the genocide.[89]

★ ★ ★

During the massacres of Tutsi, few Hutu would talk about them, especially in public. One who did was Jean Damisen Uzabakiliho, in Gikongoro, while the town was still under French protection. On a street crowded with Hutu, he said Hutu killers were acting under a kind of

"mass psychology." (Cohen's word, "hysteria," may be a more accurate one.) "No one could control it, and we deplore it [the killings]," said Uzabakiliho.

A second Hutu in the town, Jean Marie, who asked me not to use his family name, said of the slaughter by Hutu, "I can't understand it." Then we walked together up a rocky street leading to an open field overlooking part of the town. There, out of earshot of anyone including his friends, Jean Marie had something else to say. "We need goodwill and moderation on the two sides [Hutu and Tutsi]."

In an interview in a hotel he was using as a temporary office in Kigali, just after the war, Rwanda's prime minister, Faustin Twagira-mungu, a Hutu, told me: "If there is no reconciliation, we can't have a nation. If the Tutsi say, 'We'll rule the Hutu with overwhelming power,' it [Rwanda] explodes."

Reports of returning Tutsi soldiers killing some civilians overshad-owed hopes for early reconciliation. There were some counterattacks by remnants of the Hutu army. In 1997, for example, between January and August, some 6,000 people were reportedly killed, according to Amnesty International. "The specter of genocide still hovers over Rwanda," the report stated.[90] In northern Rwanda, hate propaganda against the Tutsi reemerged in 1997 in areas infiltrated by Hutu extrem-ists.

Rwandans who dared criticize the human rights abuses by the new Tutsi-dominated government risked death. One of the last indepen-dent journalists in Kigali, Appollos Hakzimana, was shot to death after criticizing the government's counterinsurgency policy. Previously he had been arrested and beaten, but despite threats to his life he had continued his work. Innocent Murengezi disappeared in Kigali. He had been one of the few lawyers in Rwanda willing to defend Hutu accused of genocide.[91]

Many ordinary Hutu found themselves caught in cross fire between the Tutsi-led army and Hutu rebels still fighting the government. News of such violence convinced most Hutu refugees it was dangerous to

Kigali, Rwanda, 1994
Hutu suspected of participating in the genocide were crowded into Kigali Central Prison to await trial by the new Tutsi-led government.
Credit: UNICEF/Betty Press

Near Goma, Zaire, 1994
An impromptu Rwandan refugee camp formed as up to a million refugees fled
to Zaire. These soon became death camps as thousands died from disease.
Credit: UNICEF/Betty Press

return. Nearly one million Hutu had fled to camps set up near the Zaire
border town of Goma, and hundreds of thousands of others escaped to
Tanzania and Burundi or other camps in Zaire. In the camps, hard-
liners began arming and training a Hutu army to return to Rwanda.
They vowed to return much sooner than the thirty-five years it had
taken the Tutsi exiles of 1959 to fight their way home.

There was little spirit of reconciliation within the camps. Militants
feared certain arrest if they went home and feared being abandoned by
the masses of poor Hutu who might consider returning. So they
whipped up the fears that anyone going back would be subject to death
or imprisonment. But it was worse than that: some Hutu refugees attempting to return were killed by Hutu extremists. Most of the refugees
were caught between fear of staying in squalid camp conditions and
fear of going home.

At the height of an early epidemic in the camps near Goma, some 2,000 people were dying daily. I drove with UNICEF Rwanda director Nigel Fisher along a road leading out of Goma toward the sprawling camps of tents and plastic shelters set up on unforgiving lava fields. With no sources of clean water, the death rate had soared. And at first there was not enough food for the mushrooming number of refugees. For several miles, bodies lined the roadside. Many were wrapped in sleeping mats, one of the few possessions of the refugees; one mat was tied with a red bow, a final sign of love for the departed. But many bodies were simply left by the roadside, their limbs frozen in contorted positions, only partly clothed, abandoned by relatives too weak to care for themselves, much less for the dead.

Conditions in the camps gradually improved due to the heroic work of relief officials from around the world, backed by an international outpouring of food and materials. Weeks later, I met an old man lying ill in front of his tiny hut of plastic and sticks. I asked him why he hadn't gone home. Until then, the first reason refugees had been giving was fear of retaliation by the Tutsi. But the old man, lifting his upper body on one elbow to speak, said transportation and lack of money were his main reasons. Fear of being killed came last on his list.

★   ★   ★

Many refugees also faced the prospect of arrest on genocide charges. In Kigali, shortly after the fighting ended, I visited the small federal prison. In the United States, prison officials generally accompany a visiting reporter, but at the front gate to the Kigali prison, I was let in by myself. Inside I was anything but alone. The courtyard was awash in people, mostly standing. Some wore the pink shirts of the prison, but those uniforms had quickly run out. The old prison, a series of rooms with bunks, built around a courtyard, was designed for about 800. Incredibly, there were then about 5,000 detainees in the prison, and the number was rising daily as Tutsi soldiers driving pickup trucks delivered new Hutu suspects.

For lack of space, many men had to take turns sleeping on an open-sided, raised cement platform covered by a tin roof in the center of the courtyard. When it rained and everyone tried to crowd under the roof, even sitting space was at a premium. The men had to sit with legs spread and with the man in front of them crammed up between their legs. Standing up meant losing their place to sit down; then they had to stand in the rain because the cells already were overflowing. The cells reminded me of drawings I have seen of slave ships. The tiers of bunks were divided into small cubicles, with up to six men sleeping in each one, tight against each other. In a separate room were more than a dozen children, watched over by an adult prisoner. (Nationwide some 2,000 children were in detention.) Several dozen women, some with babies, were squeezed into a separate, narrow wing. Some, perhaps many, of the prisoners had been involved in the massacres. But some Hutu told a story of Tutsi army personnel, or other Tutsi with connections to the new government, occupying houses of those arrested. There was no way to sort out who might have been locked up because they had decent houses.

Only a few people were working in the prosecutor's office, just outside the prison gate. A dozen detainees sat on the porch, waiting for action on their cases. Sometimes a few were released. Inside the office officials worked without the help of a computer to keep track of the thousands of cases. A computer was later donated. An anguished UN official told me a clear case could be made for the UN to supply tents and fencing for temporary prisons to relieve the overcrowding that was taking lives each day. But, the official asked privately, what would it look like to the world community if the UN started building prisons? The UN, the official said, could not afford politically to get into the prison business. And no one else wanted to either, so the overcrowding and dying in prisons continued.

In August 1994, with many Hutu militants still holding out in the French-protected zone, I met in Kigali with Patrick Mazimhaka, vice president of the RPF, which had just won the war. We sat at a table in the Hotel des Diplomats, whose dining hall was back in operation, along with the tennis courts. The building had been spared destruction because it had been used for talks between the now-ousted Hutu government and the Tutsi forces. Mazimhaka took a napkin and began writing down figures with a pen when I asked him how many Hutu should be prosecuted for genocide. Until then, as far as I knew, no one in the RPF had publicly estimated the number. The killings, he said, were well orchestrated and involved essentially most of the Hutu army

(20,000), the civilian militia set up by the government party (30,000), and organizers at the regional and local level (50,000). This total of around 100,000 Hutu "are responsible for one million deaths," he insisted. "They must all be tried and punished."[92] An even greater number of Hutu participated in the killings but did not lead them, including men and "women and kids who cut up their neighbors," said Mazimhaka. They, too, must be tried, but they could be pardoned on the basis of being "temporarily insane," he said.[93]

His point was clear: the RPF wanted justice. But the country also needed reconciliation to rebuild a nation, Prime Minister Twagiramungu had said. Hutu were the nation's main farmers, the main food producers. They were also heavily involved in commerce and trade. Without them, the prime minister warned, there would be no Rwanda as a functioning state. Tutsi returning from Uganda and other countries, however, were happy to be home at last and not worried about who would occupy empty lands and houses.

Another senior RPF official told me reconciliation was the key issue for postwar Rwanda. He asked how a Hutu and Tutsi child could grow up together after what had happened. Some form of punishment had to be meted out on the killers. But for the mass of villagers who might have taken part in the killings, he suggested not prison but some kind of community service after their admission of complicity. His suggestions were an attempt to come up with a middle ground solution, between prosecuting scores of thousands of Rwandans and doing little to restore a sense of justice among the Tutsi survivors.

In January 1998, the man who really ran Rwanda, Vice President Paul Kagame, said the solution was to put the masterminds of the genocide on trial, then execute them in public; those who carried out the genocide should be put to forced labor; those who were incited to join the killing should be handed over to traditional courts.[94] The first public executions were held later that year in Rwanda in the face of strong criticism from international human rights organizations, which claimed the trials were unfair because the accused received inadequate defense. Rwanda's new regime had nailed two messages to their door, both addressed to the Hutu refugees: come home, we need you; and those among you who killed someone will be punished. Once again, history had reversed the roles of the two main ethnic groups in

Rwanda. Once dominant, the Tutsi, who had fled the country to build up an army and wait for a chance to come home, were now back and in charge.

Sorting out who did what during the genocide would take a long time. Among the many postwar accusations was one from the Tutsi that some Catholic clergymen had participated in the killings. About half of Rwanda's prewar population was Catholic. In March 1996, Pope John Paul II released a statement saying that the Roman Catholic Church could not be held responsible for the genocide in Rwanda, though individual members may have sinned. "All members of the Church who sinned during the genocide must have the courage to bear the consequences of the acts they committed against God and their fellow man," the pope said.[95] In a prewar book, *Fire in the Hills: The Revival which Spread from Rwanda*, H. H. Osborn, a retired missionary who had worked in Rwanda, writes about the years of successful church work there.[96] But neither Catholic nor Protestant churches were able to stem the tide of killings in Rwanda. A Rwandan clergyman who blamed the Rwandan churches said "we stayed silent" when earlier, smaller massacres were happening in Rwanda.

On a street corner outside the temporary office of UNICEF in Kigali, after the Tutsi had declared victory in July 1994, I asked a Rwandan UNICEF employee to tell me his story. That is all you had to say at that time for someone to pour out their personal tale of grief. He told his story quietly, and briefly. He said he had lost about thirty members of his family, including his wife, who was mutilated before she was killed by Hutu extremists.

"You must be very angry," I said. "You must want revenge."

"No," he corrected me. He said he was beyond anger. He said Hutu and Tutsi had to reconcile now "or it will happen all over again. We must get along."

Later I learned that he had important political connections to leaders in the RPF. Was he saying what he believed, or was he saying what he assumed I and most Westerners wanted to hear—that Rwandans must have reconciliation? I wondered how I would feel if my family had been killed the way his was. Reintegration, "if it is to succeed in Rwanda, must be a mental and emotional journey, as well as a physical

UNICEF and Save the Children set up a program in Kigali, Rwanda, in 1994 to reunite children with their families after a civil war.
Credit: UNICEF/Betty Press

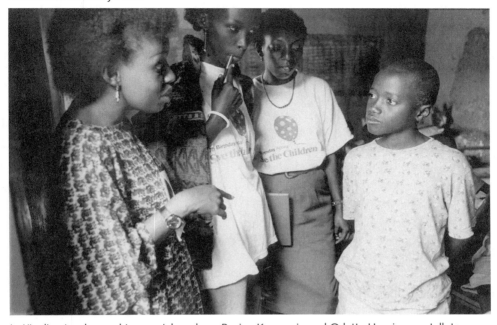

In Kigali, a teacher and two social workers, Rosine Kamagaju and Odette Uzayisenga, talk to Egide, fourteen, before taking him back to his family.

Egide and his eight-year-old brother, Mbonigaba, are reunited with their mother in Rwamagana, Rwanda. Their father was killed during the conflict.

Egide's mother thanks the social workers for returning her children.

return."[97] However reconciliation takes place, Rwanda deserves the help of the world community that ignored the genocide in the first place.

Genocide by Installment in Burundi

As the world puzzled over how genocide had happened in Rwanda, and lamented world inaction, it was taking place more slowly in Rwanda's ethnic twin neighbor, Burundi. And once again, the world largely watched. Since a military coup in 1993, some 150,000 people had been killed in ethnic clashes by mid-1996.[98]

Both Rwanda and Burundi had the same ethnic proportions. But unlike Rwanda, in Burundi the Tutsi minority had been in power since independence. And they controlled the military. In 1993, Melchior Ndadaye was elected as Burundi's first Hutu president in the nation's first free election. Incumbent military leader Pierre Buyoya, a Tutsi, had counted on his popularity to win the race. Buyoya did capture a portion of the Hutu vote.[99] After the election, the Tutsi kept control of the military, rendering the presidency practically a captive office.

In mid-1993, I was one of the few foreign journalists to interview President Ndadaye before he was assassinated by elements of the Tutsi military just three months after taking office. In the interview, I noted he had spoken earlier in the day on the need for reconciliation. I asked him if he considered it conciliatory to purge Tutsi from most senior government posts, as he had been doing. I heard his response, but my wife's camera caught something more. In the silence of her prints I later saw a man who had been relaxed gradually lean forward and clench his fists. He looked angry, and in the photos he looked as if he were shouting, though he wasn't. "The minority [Tutsi] has to share power with the 85 percent of the people who were previously excluded from power. The population wants native people whom they know," he said, referring to the Hutu who wanted Hutu to take the posts Tutsi had held, for the most part, since independence, three decades earlier. Burundi's Tutsi resented the purges, but Hutu extremists were pushing for even greater ones; they resented the president's appointment of a Tutsi prime minister, Sylvia Kinigi. "We're on a tightrope without a net," said government spokesman Jean-Marie Ngendahayo, who later fled to South Africa after ethnic killing increased in Burundi.

During the brief presidency of Ndadaye, a Western diplomat told me the purges "could lead to a dangerous situation if they go too far." The purges, a diplomat from another country said, risked causing a military coup. Or they might be giving the Tutsi-dominated military an excuse to do what they wanted to do, and might do anyway: reassert their power. A leading Burundi journalist, Innocente Muhozi, said the purges could reignite tensions between the Hutu and Tutsi. "If they [the new Hutu government] continue to play the ethnic game, the massacres could recur."

They did, in 1993, starting with the assassination of Ndadaye.

Ndadaye's successor, Cyprien Ntaryamira, a Hutu, became president in February 1994, after much wrangling between Hutu and Tutsi in Parliament. But he was killed with the president of Rwanda when the plane they were both riding in was shot down over Kigali in April 1994, unleashing genocide in Rwanda. Burundi, amazingly, stayed relatively calm, at least for a while, perhaps in part because of the power of the Tutsi army. The day I met Ntaryamira's successor, Sylvestre Ntibantunganya, also a Hutu, he sounded strong, even bellicose, in an interview with me and a Tutsi journalist. I had the president's private telephone number and called him later in the day, reaching him in his chauffeured presidential car. He agreed to a personal interview. As I climbed the steps of the president's office again, having finally been allowed to enter the outside gate, which was guarded by the military, I was reminded of a harsh reality all three of the Hutu presidents of Burundi had had to face: the Tutsi military still held the real power, and Hutu militants still wanted it. A hard-line Hutu aide de camp was about to follow me into the president's office, but I politely thanked him and closed the door on him. Alone with me, the president, who twenty-four hours earlier had sounded so tough in public, sat down quietly on the same chair President Ndadaye had used when I interviewed him. As we talked, President Ntibantunganya tucked one leg under him, informally. He leaned forward, looking anxious, even desperate. I had no way of knowing that once again I was interviewing a president of Burundi who soon would be taken out of power. He survived a military coup in August 1996 by seeking refuge in the U.S. Embassy.

The man who took his place was former military head of state Buyoya, who claimed he was the only one who could hold the country together. But his return gave the majority Hutu even more reason to suspect the Tutsi. The coup followed shortly after President Ntibantunganya and his Tutsi prime minister had agreed to allow foreign troops to enter the country to help stabilize Burundi. The Tutsi military may have seen this as an intrusion on their own considerable powers. By early 1998, the military, once again under the presidential authority of Buyoya, had undertaken "a massive campaign of military violence against Burundi's civilian population," killing thousands of unarmed people, many of them women and children and elderly who had resisted moving into military-run camps. In the camps themselves "soldiers [had] summarily executed hundreds of people accused of supporting rebel groups and [had] tortured and killed many others alleged to have violated camp rules."[100]

Before the coup that brought Buyoya back to power there had been at least one international initiative to curb the violence. A few blocks from the presidential office, in a downtown hotel, two UN peacekeepers were putting in long hours trying to keep the ethnic pot from boiling over entirely. Both men were Africans: Ould Abdallah, from Mauritania, and Hany Abdelaziz, an Egyptian. The Burundi UN mission "is the world's smallest peacekeeping operation . . . and the most cost effective," Abdallah said when I met him. Both Hutu and Tutsi leaders praised the dedication of the two men but did not point to any particular achievements they had made. One international official in Burundi indicated some of the tensions there were not ethnic. A Mafia-like group of Hutu and Tutsi was anxious to keep things stirred up politically. They did not trust agreements worked out by Hutu and Tutsi politicians, which might bring peace and leave them with less room to do as they pleased. This element made peacekeeping precarious in Burundi. But at least the two UN officials were trying, which was more creative diplomacy than had been practiced in pre-genocide Rwanda.

By mid-1996, killings and revenge killings in Burundi had become frequent. Former Tanzanian president Nyerere was trying to head off a complete collapse of Burundi by bringing political leaders from both sides together for talks. John Shattuck, U.S. assistant secretary of state for democracy, human rights, and labor, was one of several high-level U.S. officials to visit Burundi in 1996. When he returned, he wrote, "Burundi today is standing on the brink of genocide." He described his visit to the King Khaled Hospital in the capital, Bujumbura, which recently had been attacked by Zaire-based Hutu guerrillas trying to overthrow the government. "Windows in the hospital maternity ward had been shattered by rifle butts. On the floor in one room was dried blood where a patient had been shot by the guerrillas. In the courtyard was a charred area where another patient had been set on fire on her mattress." In apparent retaliation for the attack on the patients, a Tutsi militia, armed with machine guns, attacked a camp for displaced Hutu on the outskirts of Bujumbura, killing eight and wounding thirty-two others, according to Shattuck. "I saw bullet-ridden tin shacks where men, women and children were killed or wounded as they slept." At the camp he spoke to some of the survivors. "The women and children at the camp who crowded around me burst into applause when I told them I was there to hear their stories.[101]

Back in the United States, Shattuck called for greater human rights monitoring in Burundi, support for Nyerere's mediation efforts, and said the United States was engaged in "contingency planning with [U.S.] allies to prevent further bloodshed." His concern was genuine; the remedies the United States was pursuing to curb the violence, however, were vague. And the United States was definitely not proposing to send in troops.

A Slender Ray of Hope in Buyenzi, Burundi

In at least one neighborhood in Bujumbura, I found relatively peaceful coexistence between ethnic groups. Buyenzi is one of the oldest parts of the city. Hutu and Tutsi in Buyenzi "work together and talk together; they have grown up together; they pray together," said Michelle Nombe, a local resident. On a side street in the modest neighborhood of mostly mud-walled homes, crowded with displaced relatives from other parts of the country, a tailor told me: "People here aren't into politics. They are into prayers and business."

Iranian teacher Majid Sadat sat on a wooden bench in the one-room library of the Ahlubait Islamic School. Buyenzi, he said, is a mixed neighborhood—both Hutu and Tutsi. Musa Kikwemo, a teenage resident of Buyenzi and student at the school, explained why both groups got along: "We know our neighbors. You can't kill your neighbors." Unfortunately, neighbors did kill neighbors in Rwanda, and it was happening in parts of Burundi, as most of the world looked on.

Military intervention can offer a cooling-off period in potentially explosive nations such as Burundi, but extreme care must be taken to stay—in fact and in appearance—neutral. Creative, preventive diplomacy is needed in such countries long before hatred and fears between ethnic rivals ignite into genocide. Even if places like Buyenzi erupted in violence, the fact that people there got along long after most other parts of Burundi were enmeshed in ethnic killings was a hopeful sign that coexistence might be possible after all. It is that possibility that must be nurtured and developed, with the help of the rest of the world, in Rwanda, Burundi, and anywhere else ethnic tensions flare.

6 ONE FAMILY'S ESCAPE FROM RWANDA

Near Gikongoro, Rwanda, 1994
Rwandans flee to Zaire.
Credit: UNICEF/Betty Press

THE call was from Kigali, Rwanda, from someone named Faustin. How strange, I thought, that in the midst of what was building toward one of the world's worst killing sprees, you could get a phone call from the eye of the capital city, which was already engulfed in mayhem.

On a trip to Rwanda the year before, I had left my journalist business card with a number of people in Kigali. Faustin Hitiyise had seen it and now was calling for help. All across Kigali the Hutu majority was killing the Tutsi minority in what was to become a nationwide case of genocide. Faustin, though a Hutu, was also in grave danger. Any Hutu, especially an educated man like Faustin who was trying to escape Kigali, was suspected of being a Tutsi sympathizer, one unwilling to stand and fight the Tutsi.

Now, in clear and amazingly calm English, Faustin was asking for my help in getting himself and his family out of Rwanda. He needed a paper assuring the UN troops in Kigali that if he and his pregnant wife, Jeannette, and their three-year-old son, Richard, were evacuated, someone would pay for their maintenance abroad until they could return home. The UN troops were evacuating some people who worked for international organizations, as he did; he and his family might be allowed on a flight out of the country if he could obtain a financial sponsor and the proper paper. Could I help? I said I would try. And so I began a nearly round-the-clock effort to help him obtain a financial sponsor. I remember sitting in our big green chair in my "office," a bedroom in our two-bedroom apartment which Betty and I used for our journalistic work. I was so tired. I was very ill and very weak at the time, but people were being killed by the thousands. It all seemed so hopeless, yet suddenly one man's life, and the lives of a young woman and small boy, were within reach of helping.

Nairobi, Kenya, 1994
Faustin Hitiyise, his wife, Jeannette, and their three-year-old
son, Richard, shortly after they arrived safely from Rwanda.

The killing so far was taking place in the suburbs. Faustin had made
it to the downtown office where he worked as an accountant for Family
Health International (FHI), a U.S.-based, nonprofit organization with
contracts with the U.S. Agency for International Development in family planning and AIDS prevention in various African countries. He had
found the office unoccupied but not looted. There he was, sitting by a
fax and a telephone, making international calls, desperately seeking
help to get on one of the last UN evacuation planes.

Very quickly whole neighborhoods had become killing grounds
with Hutu extremists murdering Tutsi and Hutu moderates. The killings had begun within minutes of the shooting down over Kigali of
the airplane carrying Rwandan president Juvénal Habyarimana. Faustin was at home when the plane crashed. "I heard two explosions. We
thought it was grenades, like there are so often in Kigali. I telephoned
a friend, then I went to bed," he said.

As he slept, the killings intensified. "Around 5 A.M. we heard a lot of noise, gunfire. I turned on Radio Rwanda, the state radio; it was classical music. Around 6, Radio Rwanda broadcast a message from the minister of defense, saying the president was dead, assassinated by the enemies of the country. He was not specific. He said people should stay in their homes, that the army would maintain order." But there was no order; militant bands of Hutu had begun roaming the streets, slaying Tutsi and suspected Hutu moderates. The city was beginning to fill up with crude barricades across streets, barricades manned by Hutu killers trying to prevent any Tutsi rebels from entering the city, and blocking Tutsi and Hutu from fleeing.

At first, Faustin stayed home; the word from the government was to stay put, man the barricades, kill the Tutsi. Anyone attempting to leave was considered pro-Tutsi. "I decided to remain home. I was with my family. There was gunfire, everywhere, especially in the neighborhood of Kimihurura, where [government] ministers and many foreigners live. I telephoned two Americans. They said Lando was killed." Lando Ndasingwa, one of the few Tutsi ministers in the Hutu-controlled government of Habyarimana, was minister of labor and social affairs. He was one of the first killed, along with his mother, his wife, and his children.

So Faustin and his family remained at home. But even there they were in danger. And he was nearly forced to join the killing. "Everyone was asked to keep guard, to go to the barricades. If you stayed at home, you risked being labeled as an accomplice" of the Rwandese Patriotic Front (RPF), the Tutsi-led army now entering Rwanda. "We put up stones to stop vehicles from passing, and asked people for documents." Every group was supervised by the *interahamwe* (militia). At the barricades the Hutu demanded to see the government-issued identity cards, which very clearly showed if the bearer was Tutsi, Hutu, or Twa. Tutsi showing their ID cards were usually killed immediately; fleeing Hutu were often killed, too. "I was afraid, because I was not known in the district," Faustin said. He and his family had moved to the neighborhood recently; strangers were suspected as possible spies. The barricades became the killing zones. "I saw long lines of bodies." The *interahamwe* killed one man less than 100 yards from Faustin's house. "They killed him with clubs with nails. Around twenty men came around him and clubbed him to death."

Faustin and his wife, Jeannette, now eight months pregnant, planned to flee the neighborhood before it got caught up in fighting against Tutsi rebels, who were advancing southward from bases in Uganda. What finally convinced the couple to try to escape was the killing by the RPF of four people on the barricade near his home. Faustin had been scheduled to help man the barricade at the time, but he was late arriving, delayed by dinner at home. He feared the *intera-hamwe* would assume he had been plotting with the RPF and blame him for the deaths. "Very early the next morning I made a decision to leave."

Faustin was not a fighter; he was an accountant. Born near Kigali, he attended Christ the King High School in the Rwandan town of Nyanza. After earning a degree in accounting at the National University of Rwanda in 1986, he obtained an advanced degree there in business administration in 1988. He liked to read newspapers and philosophy books. He was a quiet young man, dead serious most of the time. But once in a while he burst into a loud laugh; he was quick to see the irony in a situation. As he told his story, it was as if he were hearing it for the first time himself, and it seemed to amaze him. Had it not resembled the stories of so many others, I might have thought he had exaggerated.

Jeannette finished secondary school in 1989 and wanted to enter any business that allowed her to travel abroad. She married Faustin in 1991. Her first language was Kirwanda, and she knew only a few words in English and spoke French slowly, often searching for the correct word.

His wife needed medical attention, and Faustin knew the fighting could sweep down on them at any moment. So the Hitiyise family stepped bravely out on the street early in the morning, a few days after the killing had started. It was a dangerous moment for them, one of many they would face in their attempt to escape Rwanda. He had been reading in his church textbook about the importance of overcoming fear.[1] Faustin said his prayers helped—"I wasn't at all afraid." During the family's escape from Rwanda, fear might have made him a marked man.

At the first barrier, near their house, he gave his watch to a participant in the *interahamwe* and asked him to accompany them to the main road. "I passed six barricades in 100 to 200 yards. At every barricade there were bodies." Their escort took them to the main road. There he saw Red Cross ambulances passing by. Some ambulances were attacked and the injured pulled out and killed if they were Tutsi. "My escort stopped a private car, and we got in. A kilometer later, at another barricade, they said you should return to the house. I said she [Jeannette] is going to have a baby. I said my first child was born with a caesarean . . . that she had to go to a hospital." He looked around him: there were some fifty bodies lined up along the street. "I asked what happened. They said these are [Hutu] accomplices. The killers also "went into the houses of Tutsi; they took entire families, told them to lie down, and clubbed them to death."

After thirty minutes of discussion and delay at this barricade, a civilian truck carrying government soldiers came along. Faustin and his family were allowed to get aboard with their house servant. "They asked why the servant had to go, and I said to cook for my wife." On the trip toward downtown, they passed grisly scenes. "At each barricade I saw fresh bodies. They were Hutu known to be in the opposition or Tutsi." At another barricade, everyone in the truck, including the military, was questioned. Some soldiers were fleeing the city, and the *interahamwe* wanted to stop them. The militants examined the family's identification cards. And they made them give up the servant, telling Faustin to cook for his wife.

Finally, the family arrived at the center of town. "I was surprised everything was calm." He took his wife and son to a local hospital and went to stay with a friend. But even downtown was not going to be safe very long, since fighting was spreading toward the city center. Nor was it safe to turn back to their home. The day after he left, many of his neighbors fled. Many RPF were passing by and had killed about 100 people along the way. Another 100 or so were killed the next night when the RPF went by again, according to survivors.

I started tracking down his employers in the United States. As night wore on in Nairobi, it was getting closer to closing time for offices on the East Coast. Finally I managed to find the right person in the head office of FHI, who promised to fax me a letter of authorization to support Faustin and his family if they managed to escape from Rwanda. As soon as the fax came through, I relayed it to Faustin. But after all our exchanges of faxes through the evening, he had run out of paper just as the crucial document arrived. For lack of fax paper he and his family might not get out of the killing zone. Faustin said that in the morning he would risk a walk to the hotel nearby where UN guards were protecting Tutsi from Hutu mobs. The hotel had a fax machine, and I could send another fax there in his name. Identifying himself in front of the mob outside the hotel as a person trying to escape could prove fatal, so he found someone in the UN to go into the hotel and inquire quietly if my redirected fax had arrived. It had, but the last plane carrying refugees had just left. So Faustin gathered up his wife and child and, with a permit obtained from the still-in-power Rwandan government, headed south toward Gitarama, a town he hoped would be free of fighting. He traded a small radio for a ride with the military to the town, arriving April 17. There, friends gave the family bus fare to Butare, which they reached the next day.

The Killings Spread

Butare is a classic example of how ethnic tensions can be fanned quickly into violence by politicians. For ten days after the killing began in Kigali, Butare, which had a Tutsi mayor, was calm. Hutu and Tutsi continued to get along. But Faustin's arrival coincided with a turn in events that would prove disastrous for the Tutsi in Butare and nearly cost him his own life. Interim Rwandan president Théodore Sindikubwabo arrived from Kigali and gave a fiery speech, which Hutu extremists took as a signal to start attacking Tutsi. Sindikubwabo later denied the speech was inflammatory, but it triggered an orgy of killing there.

Faustin had temporarily settled his family in Save, a small town a few miles from Butare. The day of the interim president's speech he had gone to Butare to seek permission to travel to neighboring Burundi. In Butare, he found lodging in a home where several Tutsi had sought refuge from the killings in other parts of the country. The morning after the speech, Faustin left the shared lodging and went into the center of town, where he was told the border with Burundi was closed. "I went back [to his lodging] and discovered the horror: The door and windows were smashed. Two Tutsi were lying shot dead on the floor." Had Faustin been in the lodging that morning, instead of getting information downtown, he might easily have been killed, mistaken in the raid for another Tutsi.

It would not be his last brush with death.

Once the killing broke out in Butare, any semblance of order vanished. Faustin's main problem now was that he was a stranger in the area, as in Kigali. He returned to Save. Nearly broke, he wanted to get to Nairobi, Kenya, where he could get money from his employer; FHI had a regional office there. So he went back to Gitarama, hoping to go on to Tanzania via that route. But Gitarama had become as dangerous as Butare. He turned back. Then, walking along the road toward Save, Faustin was grabbed by two men with machetes. "They said they did not know me in the region and said I was a Tutsi rebel."

As Faustin recounted the moment, his voice dropped. "They put their machetes against my neck and were about to kill me." Just then, with timing too supernatural not to be, two other men emerged from a nearby sorghum field. One had a spear; the other, a bayonet. The new arrivals asked if the would-be killers had looked at Faustin's identity card. But even after Faustin produced his ID showing he was a Hutu, just like his intended assailants, the two men with machetes still wanted to kill him. He must be a rebel sympathizer, they said, because he was a stranger. Faustin managed to tell them he was staying with a local priest, a well-known man in the area. The new arrivals knew the priest and accepted Faustin's offer of two dollars to take him there. "It was a miracle," said Faustin. Along the way to the priest's, Faustin saw Hutu armed with machetes, spears, axes, and clubs studded with nails. When he reached home that night Jeannette said, "I thought God made a miracle to save Papa Richard [or Father of Richard, their son, as she affectionately called her husband]."

On May 12, while the family was still in Save, Jeannette gave birth to a baby girl they named Fortunee. On July 1, the advancing Tutsi rebels attacked just three miles from Save. Faustin fled with his family to Gikongoro, which by then was inside the French military's protected "safety zone." I went to the French zone too, to report on events there. Faustin and I missed each other in Gikongoro by only a few days. Faustin had shepherded his family west to Cyangugu, on the border with Zaire. But instead of crossing over to the relative protection of Zaire, Faustin took his family by bus to Gisenyi, in northern Rwanda. Gisenyi was one of the towns still held by the government, and Faustin was hoping to withdraw money from his account with the state bank, at a branch there. The family arrived in Gisenyi just as a human tide of hundreds of thousands of Hutu refugees swept through there to Goma, on the Zaire side. Faustin and his family joined the human flood because the RPF was approaching. A refuge for those fleeing the killing zones of Rwanda, Goma became a dying zone, too, as tens of thousands succumbed to diseases. The refugees crossing the border panicked at one point when the RPF, apparently, lobbed several shells across from Rwanda. A number of people were trampled to death as the Hutu clawed their way into Zaire. "It took four hours [to cross the border] because there were so many people," Jeannette recalled, having just missed the deadly stampede. "I carried a bag with clothing for Fortunee. Faustin's cousin took Richard by the hand."

The family slept in a Pentecostal church. Rwanda and the border area, including Goma, have long been saturated with churches and many foreign missionaries. Some churches welcomed the refugees; others closed their doors, Faustin recalled. Years earlier, Betty and I visited Goma, on Lake Kivu, where I bought some pastries for her birthday; we stayed at Hotel du Lac. Goma had been a tourist town; now it was a disaster. The main streets were packed with refugees, thirsty, starving, afraid, heading out of town to UN camps not yet fully established. The "camps" were little more than open space on a rough lava field. At first there was not enough fresh water to prevent epidemics among the huddled Rwandans, who sat in the open or under scraps of plastic until plastic tarpaulins were delivered.

"I was sick," Faustin said. "During the first and second nights, the military [of Zaire] fired everywhere." Zaire's army, one of the most undisciplined and lowest paid in the world, was unpredictable. At the border, the Zairean soldiers stole at random from arriving refugees. Faustin and his family had managed to get across the border unmolested because they were walking in a group of eighteen, including six men. With easier prey elsewhere, the soldiers let them pass with their goods.

"I cried; Richard cried—because of hunger," said Jeannette of those first days in Zaire. Then Faustin did something most people around him did not: he decided to leave Goma. "There was total insecurity [among the refugees]," he said. Faustin sold another cassette radio he had managed to keep and bought tickets on a boat crossing Lake Kivu south to Bukavu, Zaire, a twelve-hour ride. "It was no problem; it was beautiful," he said. In Bukavu they had no one to stay with; refugees were streaming across the border from Rwanda, and the UN was trying to set up camps. Meanwhile most people were staying in drafty public buildings or under trees, and in any open spot in town. "Papa Richard looked for someone to show us a hotel," Jeannette recalled. Faustin described how he found a place. "I asked a small child where I could stay." The child took him to "a Christian lady" who gave them a small room in her wooden, dirt-floored home. "She was a good Samaritan," he said. Three days later, Richard left for Nairobi, determined to reach the FHI office and get some money to buy passage to Kenya for his wife and two children.

Baby Fortunee was exhausted and crying a lot by the time the family reached Bukavu. On July 22, shortly after Faustin had left for Kenya, Jeannette took her to a hospital. The doctor said there was no medicine at the hospital and that it would cost the equivalent of three dollars at a local pharmacy. "I didn't have any money," she said. On July 23, 1994, Fortunee died. "I was very weak, and sad. I refused to bury the child. I thought she would come back to life." The next day a woman helped her locate a tiny coffin. "I wrote Fortunee's name on the cross; I planted some flowers next to the cross," Jeannette said quietly. Baby Richard was also in anguish at the loss of his sister. Jeannette recalled his words at the time: "Where is the baby? Papa . . . left us and [now] the baby." Young Richard clung to the idea that his mother could somehow "buy another baby."

Faustin, meanwhile, was undergoing new hardships. A doctor he knew had loaned him fifty dollars for the trip to Nairobi. From Bukavu he took a bus south, along the Zaire border, then a train to Dar es Salaam, the Indian Ocean commercial capital of Tanzania. He spent the better part of two days and nights standing in a jammed, third-class car, unable to lie down and sleep, dozing off on his feet. From Dar he continued by bus to Nairobi, crossing the border with no difficulties from Kenyan immigration officials. On August 7, 1994, after a few days in Nairobi, he flew back to Bukavu on a flight carrying relief materials and chartered by Lutheran World Federation. With his wife and surviving child, Faustin took the train, this time by another route, completing the journey to Nairobi by bus, arriving four months after their long escape from Kigali began.

Now, in a clean, comfortable apartment rented by FHI, where the couple told their story, they were finally able to relax and to recover their strength. Throughout their journey they never lost their spirit; they never gave up. Now they were alive, and safe.

"This is paradise," said Faustin of his new surroundings. In the months that followed, Jeannette received word that her parents had survived; she had thought they were dead. She wanted to return to Rwanda, but it was still too dangerous. The Tutsi had won the war and had begun arresting thousands of suspected Hutu collaborators. Anyone could be named. So the family stayed in Kenya where FHI employed Faustin as an accountant for one year. After that the family moved to Mombasa, on the Kenyan coast, where Faustin found more work as an accountant. As the insecurity continued in Rwanda, the family decided it was not safe to go home.

A year after their escape, Jeannette gave birth to a baby boy.

★   ★   ★

The tragic events in Rwanda and Somalia are a crucial part of the history of these nations and should never be forgotten. Moreover, they provide valuable lessons in terms of human rights and international intervention issues. But the violence that wracked Rwanda and Somalia near the end of the century was the exception in Africa; for the most part, the continent was at peace. Rwanda and Somalia represented one end of the human rights and freedom spectrum in Africa in the 1990s. A much more encouraging side of African life was also evident: millions of Africans were achieving greater freedom and dignity in a multitude of individual ways, apart from politics. The inspiring stories of a few individuals follow.

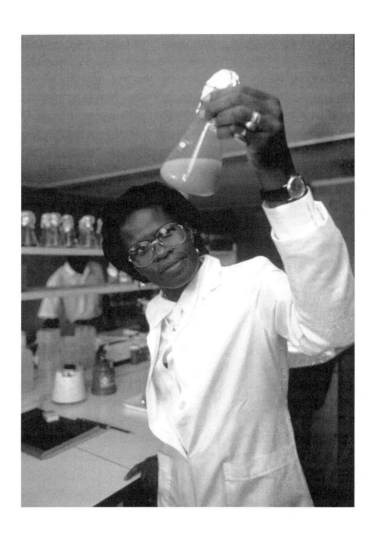

7 PERSONAL FREEDOM

Nairobi, Kenya, 1995
Research scientist Martha Okach

A QUIET revolution is taking place across Africa, one without guns and apart from politics. Africans are seeking more personal freedom and in many cases achieving it. The more dramatic stories of war and political confrontations overshadow what is being accomplished each day by Africans from all walks of life and in almost every part of the continent.

It is a quest for dignity and human rights of all sorts. Many people are attempting to pull themselves ahead economically or educationally. Others are simply trying to stay alive. Women are seeking to break social barriers that would hold them back. All these efforts form a part of the spirit and mental atmosphere of Africa today, an invisible bedrock of hope and expectations upon which future generations can build. Africans are extending personal liberties step by step in almost all fields. The stories that follow are about some of the individuals I have met who took such steps in the 1990s.

A Kenyan shopkeeper tells how a small loan from a private, local organization helped him expand his business; a Kenyan couple living in a dry region show how their careful farming methods reaped results. In West Africa, participants in a women's gardening cooperative in The Gambia, and a baker in Togo, explain how they made small economic gains, and some of the "Mercedes Benz women" of Togo tell how they got rich selling cloth. At the opposite end of the economic scale, Peter, a young homeless man in Kenya, seeks to break away from life on the streets and become a tailor. Students in war zones in Somalia and Sudan strive to get an education against great odds, while a model teacher in Kenya introduces new teaching methods. Women jurists in Mali describe their fight against female genital mutilation; female ex-soldiers in Eritrea seek expanded political and social roles after the war for Eritrean independence. A Nigerian artist tells how she broke free of polygyny and several other local bonds to win greater freedom as a woman.

Such individual efforts may depend on assistance from government, but the desire for greater economic and social freedom does not. Like the Nigerian artist, many Africans are winning more personal freedom, more rights, without any help from government. The stories of such individuals seldom make the news and thus go unnoticed by most Africans and non-Africans alike. Yet they make up an important part of what is happening in Africa today.

Such efforts are often carried out through an association, a private, nongovernment organization (NGO) usually focused on a specific issue, such as women's rights or conservation. This is part of the explosion of activity in what is often called "civil society," as opposed to government activities. One African scholar calls civil society "spaces for communication and discussion over which the state has no control," then narrows it to mean "those groups, organizations, and personalities that pursue freedom, justice, and the rights of citizenship against authoritarian states."[1] Most definitions do not tie civil society to just a political framework. A former U.S. senator called civil society "the place where [people] make their home, sustain their marriages, raise their families, hang out with their friends, meet their neighbors, educate their children, worship their God . . . governed by values such as responsibility, trust, fraternity, solidarity, and love."[2] Experts argue over how effective organized civil society in Africa is in prompting democratic change and under what conditions it thrives best.

There has been a proliferation of private associations in Africa in recent years, especially since the 1980s. Many of these associations, especially development groups, have received some international support as potential key players in Africa's economic advancement. Some experts see them as as a force for achieving further political reform in Africa and as channels for avoiding the "political decay that undermined new African governments a generation ago."[3] At a time when many African governments are not strong enough or wealthy enough to provide all the basic services people need, such groups play a critical role in bringing people together to fill this void.

Civil society has had a political impact. In Zambia, for example, Frederick Chiluba "led the trade union movement into a coalition with business, professional, student, and church groups," and used teachers and civil servants in rural areas to force the government to allow multiparty elections, which Chiluba won in 1991.[4] In Tanzania, women's groups are becoming more politically active.[5] Some farmers in Côte d'Ivoire came together to tackle political and economic problems, to demand more freedom in their lives. These actions, and many others, offer what one researcher calls the promise of a "new politics."[6] But in Kenya, another researcher found that many nongovernment organizations were led by Kikuyus, a group largely in opposition to the government. Any political actions by these groups "may reflect the attempts of displaced elites to regain access to state power," the researcher wrote.[7]

In the quest for freedom, one type of behavior that can be political but is not carried out through any organization is the expression of anger. Apart from actions in a group, many Africans have found ways to express their discontent or anger with politics by channeling these feelings into what amounts to a kind of political resistance. "People get angry when they are systematically oppressed."[8] They express this anger in a variety of ways: political protest music, gestures, "refusal to follow instructions or an irreverent attitude toward the hierarchy in place; . . . [o]fficial bywords, slogans, speeches, leaders' verbal tics—in short the entire vocabulary of domination—is mimicked and mocked with a rare creativity."[9] Additional ways of expressing this anger include "foot dragging, dissimulation, desertion, false compliance, pilfering, feigned ignorance, slander, arson, sabotage, and so on."[10]

I witnessed several expressions of anger over political repression in Kenya. The government organized a celebration of the "Nyayo era," a term which had become the slogan identifying the administration of President Daniel arap Moi or Moi himself.[11] Some Kenyans turned the phrase "Nyayo era" into "Nyayo error." The two phrases are so similar it is practically impossible to tell them apart when they are said quickly. I heard one Kenyan use the latter phrase, which I was able to identify only because his friend laughed after he said it. On another occasion, someone who bravely imitated the gravelly voice of Moi drew raucous laughter from the crowd at a public gathering. Cameroon scholar Célestin Monga contends that this kind of informal protest goes almost unnoticed by most scholars yet plays an important role in the political climate in Africa today, adding, in some cases, to political instability. Channeled anger, which stems from the desire for more political freedom, is not just an urban phenomenon; it has long been part of the rural atmosphere as well, Monga insists. "Peasants in Africa and, more generally, people living in rural areas . . . wanted the quest for dignity to be a top priority on the national agenda."[12]

★   ★   ★

The story of personal freedom is best told by some of the many Africans who have made headway in their own way. One such person is Francis Muthee, who found a way to weaken one of Africa's most persistent foes: poverty.

Borrowing for Progress

Despite economic stagnation in Africa during much of the 1990s, businessmen like Kenyan Francis Muthee, who operates a small, one-room retail shop, have managed to make progress. I drive to his shop in a low-income area of small stores and mostly tin-roofed, one-room homes on the edge of Nairobi. Children are playing in the alleyways and gather curiously around me as I arrive. The roar of buses without mufflers, often belching black smoke, mingles with the metallic noises of old cars and minivans full of paying passengers. Muthee's shop sits just off a main street, on an unpaved alley. He sells through a screened security window, though he often works with the door to his shop partly open to let in air and sunlight. When I enter, he offers me a chair and sits in another one in the unlit, semiobscure interior. We talk as customers continue to step up to his window.

Running a retail business in Kenya is "tough," he says in English, the official language of Kenya, along with Swahili. "You need capital, knowledge, and flexibility in the face of constantly shifting wholesale and retail prices," he explains. Many local shops have closed "because their owners failed to keep abreast of price changes. You study the market; if you can't do that, you're in a mess."

Being a shopkeeper is Muthee's fifth line of work. After graduating from high school in the mid-1960s, Muthee became an assistant export manager in a timber company in Kenya; he was later promoted to export manager. "I was young and ambitious." Later he began farming, but government price controls on the sale of crops made it unprofitable. Next, he became a salesman in a radiator firm, then an insurance salesman. Finally, he turned to retail shopkeeping. After experiencing three major robberies at another location, he moved his business to his present site in 1990.

A customer debates whether to buy a bar of soap costing sixteen Kenya shillings or another at fourteen shillings. She is making "harsh economic decisions," he says. "It's terrible today; it was better ten years ago. Ten years ago, middle-income families had two cars, a telephone, and could educate their children. Now they live in squatter conditions."

Kenya's economy has floundered in part because of massive corruption in the government. Billions of shillings have been lost in various scams involving high officials. Kenya was once the East African economic darling of the West. It was also once a food exporter. As donors blew hot and cold over Kenya, depending on intermittent progress on economic and political reforms, some local development programs showed a reasonable track record. The one that helped Muthee proved successful: it gave him a chance to get a loan so he could expand his business. The Kenya Rural Enterprise Programme (K-REP), funded initially by the U.S. Agency for International Development (USAID), made loans to small business operators. With the loan Muthee received, he was able to make bulk purchases, which translated into lower, more competitive retail prices. The loan enabled him to sell not only more goods but a greater variety, helping him stay competitive while some shops were folding.

Small businesses are one of the mainstays of the African economy. K-REP was established in 1984 by World Education, Inc. and was locally incorporated in 1987. At first the focus was lending to small businesses, usually those involving a number of people, and helping private, nongovernment organizations with technical assistance. But in the late 1980s K-REP began focusing more on lending and less on technical assistance. Its new lending was focused on individuals through a group mechanism known as peer or group pressure, modeled on the Grameen Bank in Bangladesh. Borrowers operating in groups of five agree to pay back their loans or allow the program to collect for nonpayment from their fellow borrowers. Those taking out loans must have a certain amount of money in savings collectable by the agency in case a borrower in their group defaults, which rarely happens.

In its final evaluation of the program, in 1994, USAID concluded that the credit provided "has contributed to business growth, reflected by an increase in employment in most of the businesses assisted through loans."[13] But the program was not without problems. "Nearly 40 percent of the businesses had experienced no employment growth since receiving a loan." Despite plans to make the program self-sustaining, the evaluation report noted that since K-REP's credit programs were part of an organization relying on donor grants, "a sudden decrease in the flow of grants could threaten the survival of the credit programs."[14] The Kenyan heading K-REP, Albert Mutua, in February 1992 noted borrowers had been approved too quickly in some cases, without adequate background checks. This allowed some "proxies for wealthier businessmen, full time employees, or just opportunists" to slip in as borrowers.[15] Repayment rules were not properly explained, leading to defaults on some loans. To make matters worse, some borrowers got three times what they needed; others got less than a fifth of what they required. From 1990 to early 1995, some 22,000 loans were processed.[16] Despite such problems, K-REP's deputy managing director, A. Dondo, told me "we've also learned the people are very vibrant if you trust them. They repay rapidly." K-REP has, in fact, an excellent repayment record. (Most of the relatively low-income clients of K-REP would not have qualifed for bank loans because they could not have met the banks' higher collateral requirements.) Many business owners could do even better except for another major restraint: they don't own the land their business sits on; the government owns it, Dondo pointed out.[17]

★   ★   ★

Muthee stands up and scoops some lard out of a plastic bucket for a customer at the window. He weighs it for the woman. She wants only one tenth of a kilo. Behind him, his shelves are full of toothpaste, flour, cookies, cigarettes, and other items. We talk a while longer, then I get back into my car, which he had advised me to park directly in front of his store to reduce the risk of theft. Car robberies have been on the increase in Kenya in recent years, some even taking place on the open highways, with drivers being forced out of their vehicles.

I had informally tracked K-REP off and on for several years during the time I was a correspondent in Africa (1987–95); it is the only development program I wrote about twice. It has its faults, as does any aid program. And experts warn that such small-loan programs cannot solve the problem of poverty. But it is an example of the kind of aid—narrow in focus and tailored to meet the individual's needs—that can work, that can make a difference.

★   ★   ★

In his book *The Greening of Africa,* Paul Harrison describes many examples of aid programs and local self-help efforts that have paid off. One of the methods he cites as saving farmland in Kenya is terracing. And the place where it is best used, he writes, is the Machakos district between Nairobi and the coast.[18] There I visited a family of farmers who belong to the Kamba tribe, recommended to me by Donald Thomas, a British-born Kenyan expert on soil and water conservation, retired from the University of Nairobi.

Joy and Harvests

Alphonse Muange and his wife, Angela, are no longer young, but they are still working hard on a farm in the dry Machakos area of Kenya. A fresh harvest—just a modest-sized pile of corn—brings such joy that Angela breaks into song and dance. Some of her friends, who are also farmers, join in. These women also sing as they show me how they work together building earth terraces that trap runoff soil. "Singing makes the work easier," Angela says.

Terracing, once required by the colonial British authorities in Kenya, fell out of favor after independence in 1963. It is only since the mid-1970s that it has regained its popularity as a way of increasing food production in an area where topsoil, left untended, washes down the steep slopes when it rains. Putting Kenya's case, and that of the Kamba especially, in context, Harrison writes that "successes in soil conservation are few and far between. Perhaps the most outstanding

Machakos, Kenya, 1995
Farmers Alphonse Muange and his wife, Angela, read the Bible in their home.

Machakos, Kenya, 1995
Two women farmers build terraces to slow erosion.

programme in Africa has been Kenya's."[19] With help from the Swedish government, and much later USAID, an old Kamba terracing method known as *fanya juu* was revived. It involves digging a narrow trench and throwing the dirt uphill to form a ridge. Over time, the terraces level themselves out, providing extra crop planting space and helping to avoid erosion from the occasional and sometimes heavy rains. Various crops can be planted in the ditch and along the upper lip of the new terraces. Machakos, a semiarid area, had been the scene of some of Kenya's worst soil degradation.

Though poor by most standards, Alphonse and Angela display an unmistakable happiness, based on their material progress and spiritual wealth. In their cement-floored, solid-walled home, Angela likes to sit in the living room, furnished with a sofa and two stuffed chairs, and read the family Bible. Both she and her husband are active in their local Catholic parish.

Angela describes their daily routine for me. They get up at 6 A.M. and walk half a mile to the parish for prayers, seven days a week. By 7:45 they are back at home to eat a breakfast of tea, bread, and, when they can afford it, eggs. "Sometimes there is nothing," she says calmly. Then it's off to the fields for hand labor. They own thirteen acres near their house and another plot a fifteen-minute walk away, which they use for grazing and growing trees for firewood. Angela carries the wood home on her back, the way most rural African women do. In Africa women may walk up to several hours in each direction gathering wood. Others walk just as long to haul water home. "It's hard to find wood," she says. And carrying it back, she adds, "you sweat." Women also do the bulk of the farming in most countries. Around 4 P.M., Angela usually takes a short rest before starting the cooking fire for dinner around 6. "Then we pray." The small children go to sleep; the older ones stay up to do their studies until 9 or 9:30. At 6 the next morning, the routine begins afresh.

Angela and her husband are also active in one of the many private, local development groups that function throughout Kamba land. Such cooperative efforts account for much of the building of major terraces and check dams to slow water flow down gullies. Eventually many of the gullies fill up and are then farmed. One product of the cooperative efforts of Kamba women has been sold worldwide: the so-called Kenya bags: purses handwoven from local plants.

★　★　★

On the west coast of Africa, a group of women gardeners are working just as hard on land often just as dry, and they, too, are making some progress.

Women Gardeners of The Gambia

The Gambia is a slender country on the west coast of Africa that looks like a finger pointing into the continent. It is known best to outsiders as the inspiration for the drama *Roots*.[20] The country is so dry that if farms are not irrigated, they turn to dust. Land for farming is becoming scarcer as the population continues to grow. So some of the women of The Gambia have formed cooperatives to grow vegetables in gardens, selling them in local markets. Musu Kegba Drahmmeh is one of them.

Like her fellow cooperative members living near the capital, Banjul, she spends a lot of time hauling water buckets up a well by hand, usually in a brightly colored, loose-fitting, full-length dress. Then she carries the water over to her section of the garden and waters her vegetables. It is a cycle she repeats many times a day as the plants soak up the moisture. Previously when the crop was ready, she would take it to the nearest market for sale, which meant a bus trip and competition with other women gardeners and paying off middlemen. The first middlemen would meet the women at the bus stop and for a fee they would distribute their vegetables to wholesalers. For another fee, the wholesalers would distribute the products to the retailers. Women tried selling their crops at the garden to cut transportation and middlemen costs, but sales were sporadic and the goods often spoiled.

So the Royal Norwegian Society for Rural Development (NRD) stepped in to try to help the women market their vegetables the way they grew them—collectively. The NRD bought two pickup trucks and contracted with one seller to pay cash for the vegetables and absorb any losses from spoilage. "It's a good idea; it's working," says Binta Khan, horticultural coordinator for the cooperative garden where Drahmmeh works. Njuma Cesay is another of the gardeners. She likes the coordinated selling effort, too. "It helps me sell my vegetables. Last year I sold by myself. Now I have more time for domestic work." But at a meeting of the participating women, some questioned the fee that the NRD charges the women. Who benefits from the fees collected? they asked. Claes Elliot, a Swede representing the NRD, countered that "this thing [the program] isn't run without expenses. The project is not profit making." The idea, according to Elliot, is for the project to be self-financing eventually.

But K. E. Nordlie of the NRD estimated in 1994 that the project would end up spending as much as $100,000 on such costs as building coolers and a marketing center, training, and education, plus administrative costs. Self-financing may be a long time coming. But the women gardeners of the cooperative are making some headway meanwhile. So is a woman baker in another West African state.

When Bread Is Money

It is that predawn hour when it is still quiet in Sokodé, Togo, before the city turns up the volume with the high-pitched whine of motorbikes and the deeper growls of taxis and buses.[21] Dunyah Ablavi has already been at work for several hours. The first thing early shoppers look for across Africa is bread, and Ablavi is a baker. She does her baking in the small backyard of her home, using a long-handled, wooden shovel to slide each batch of golden-brown, loaves out of the clay oven. By the end of her workday, she will have baked hundreds of loaves of various sizes. Her efforts are paying off. "I like the work because it helps me feed my family," says Ablavi, whose husband is retired. The year before (1991) she received the equivalent of a $1,000 loan from a Togolese development group to buy greater stocks of flour and other ingredients at wholesale prices, and to repair her oven and cover it with a small roof. The result: she is baking more bread and making more sales and more profits.

The lender, Inter-Professional Artisans Group of Togo, is one of thousands of nongovernment organizations across Africa whose work is aimed at spurring economic development or advancement of various social causes. The organization received funds from both the U.S. Agency for International Development and the U.S.-based Catholic

Sokodé, Togo, 1991
Dunyah Ablavi helps support her family by baking bread to sell. She
enlarged her business with the help of a small loan, which she repaid.

Relief Services (CRS). The average loan under the program is $500,
though a few are as high as $1,500. Borrowers are charged about 2
percent interest, which is lower than Togo's banks charge. The pay-
back record has been good, according to John Corrao, CRS director
in Togo. "I've seen much bigger foreign aid projects that haven't gotten the results we have," he says. Borrowers must maintain a savings
account with the program and can apply for loans up to twice their
amount in savings.

Among the other Sokodé residents who have received such loans is
shoe repair man Tchakpide Traore, who sits cross-legged as he works in
his tiny wooden stall on a main street in Sokodé. The loan of $200
enabled him to buy more leather, shoe glue, and plastic soles to offer his
customers a wider variety of shoes. This attracted more clients, and he
was able to pay back the loan in less than six months, ahead of schedule.

★ ★ ★

Down on the coast of Togo, a group of wealthy businesswomen not only are supporting their families but have acquired a taste for fancy cars.

The "Mercedes Benz" Women of West Africa

On the street outside Boe Allah Lawson Adjua's store in Lomé, the capital of Togo, a crowd of shoppers and ambulant hawkers squeeze by each other, between the shops and temporary stalls full of goods: radios, record players, soap, fruits, and plastic toys.[22] Young women with periscope piles of folded, brightly colored cloth balanced on their heads pass through the sea of people undisturbed. Inside her shop, Lawson is poking at a small adding machine to total up another sale of cloth, the kind of sales that have made her and a group of other women in Lomé wealthy enough to be called the "Nana Benz," or the Mercedes Benz women, after the cars many of them own. Operating out of small shops or even stalls in the central market, these women are highly skilled in business and among the wealthier residents of Lomé.

Lomé, Togo, 1990
Patience Sanvi, a successful businesswoman, with her Mercedes-Benz.

"My mother began this [business] with her mother in a village," says Lawson, pausing between sales, as her mother sits nearby in the shop. Gradually the family built up the business and bought the store in 1975. Fabric sales was one avenue for women of Togo to move up economically. Today, not only are many of these women economically independent, but they provide a regular income for their husbands, using the rest for their children, their parents, and themselves.

One of the best known of these cloth sellers is Patience Sanvi, who lives in a handsome and spacious home in Lomé. Parked in the driveway is her light green Mercedes Benz. I talk with her as she stands next to the car that symbolizes her success, but our conversation is interrupted by a member of Sanvi's house staff, who brings her a cordless telephone. "I have clients from Benin, Nigeria, Ghana, Ivory Coast, and Lomé itself who come to me to buy," she says after taking the call. Then she hollers a command to another member of the staff. Resuming our conversation, she tells me she began selling cloth as a teenager in the Lomé market, gradually building up her business, which she now conducts mostly from her home. Many of the Mercedes Benz women send their children to private schools, "have nice jewels, travel a lot, [and] know Europe better than you or I, probably. They have apartments in Paris and Geneva."[23] Much of the cloth sold is imported from Holland, though some West African countries manufacture their own cloth.

There is no guarantee that yet another generation of cloth sellers is on the way up, but there is little doubt that the children of the Mercedes Benz women of Togo will succeed at something. Perched on a pile of cloth in her mother's stall in the main indoor market building in Lomé, Belmonda Santos tells me she has plans of her own. After selling cloth for four years, she is now looking ahead. "I finished my secretarial training. Life doesn't stop here [in the market]. I have to do what I want to do, and not just follow someone else's goals." She is planning to become a designer of West African dresses. Her mother, Ino Aboi, is not pushing her to keep selling cloth.

★   ★   ★

In sharp contrast to the Mercedes Benz women, many Africans struggle just to have enough to eat to stay alive. Yet the lives of the poor

Nairobi, Kenya, 1993
Peter Chege trained to become a tailor and leave behind a homeless life on the streets of Nairobi.

are often full of dignity and kindness. Peter Chege's life is a good example. He was born in Kenya, but his story, both sad and uplifting—for his courage and dreams, his determination to shake free of poverty—is universal.

From Rags to Stitches: Peter's Plan

One of the color photos in the cheap plastic album showed Peter as I'd never seen him. He was dressed in clean slacks and a long-sleeved shirt, standing jauntily in front of a fake backdrop in some photo studio. He looked more than happy; he looked amused, even cocky, sure of himself—smiling, in a world apart from his other world, the one I had assumed was his only one. A staff member at the YMCA, in Nairobi, Kenya, where Peter had been living, told me Peter had gone to the coastal city of Mombasa. Another photo showed him on the beach there. Peter had never mentioned the trip or the small photo album. Among the few other photos was one of Betty and me which I had given to him soon after we first met in Nairobi on a rainy afternoon. It was a meeting that almost didn't happen.

I was just finishing a long run and saw a young man, perhaps in his twenties, sprawled exhausted on the sidewalk, on a busy corner next to a church. A big bag, partially full of scrap papers, lay beside him. It was about to rain, but no one stopped to help him. I jogged by him on my way home. Sure, I thought, as I veered around him, I should help him. But I was a foreign correspondent, traveling all over a changing continent, ducking in and out of several war zones, and Nairobi was home. Nairobi was sanctuary; when Betty and I were in Nairobi, except for reporting and photographing stories on Kenya, we were in retreat from the world, hiding away from most social obligations, recuperating, rejuvenating ourselves for the next challenging trip to another country. Sometimes we would be on the road for several weeks at a time, so whoever was lying there as I jogged by was definitely not *my* problem. But after a lifetime of hearing the story of the good Samaritan, its message popped into my thoughts. I ignored it and jogged on—until I jogged back.

"It's going to rain," I said to him in English and Swahili, as I knelt down amid the swirl of pedestrian traffic. He was conscious, so I helped him to his feet and together we walked to the nearby doorway of a church. That was enough, I told myself. I had hauled him out of the coming rain, and now I was free to leave. But I knew I wasn't.

"Have you eaten?" I asked him. "*Hapana,*" he answered ("no," in Swahili). I left him there, assuring him I'd be back with food. Then I walked up the hill to a YMCA, where a kind cafeteria employee gave me some *ugi* (porridge) in a tin can. Peter—he'd told me his name—ate it quickly. OK, *now* I was free to go. He was out of the rain; fed. I looked around, planning my escape. But the story of the Samaritan was driving me in another direction; I found myself trying to recall details of the story for a clue as to what to do next. There was something about taking the wounded man to an "inn." The Y staff had told me about a cheaper YMCA in the industrial area, across town. I asked Peter if he had a place to stay.

The question was about as rhetorical as the time I stopped to ask a homeless young man in Washington, D.C., if he had a place to go. He was huddled on top of a heating grate, in a heavy rain, covering himself with some plastic. Then, too, I had been out running. I took him down to the subway and got us both tickets to my stop near the Capitol; I took him to the guest house where Betty and I were staying prior to moving to Africa. The owner graciously accepted the man and gave him a free room on the top floor. He stayed for a couple of weeks, even helping with some of the housework; then he left. Gone. No word. Just gone. I saw him once after that, sitting against an outside wall of a government building, not far from our apartment. He smiled and said something about wanting to be on his own.

Peter's first concern was not a place to stay but getting to a clinic. He was ill and wanted to go to one near a downtown mosque where the poor got cheap help. I jogged home, got my car, and returned, loading him and his dirty bag of wastepaper into the vehicle. (Peter collected the wastepaper to receive a little money at a recycling center, so he did not want to part with it.) Then we set off for the clinic. From his few remarks about his past, I gathered that Peter had grown up poor and had been on his own from a young age, working the streets for a living as many of Africa's children do. (In the 1980s and 1990s the number of African street children was rising due to economic conditions. Many lived full-time on their own; others spent some time at home.) Though Peter rarely talked about his family, he once mentioned having a blind mother on the edge of Nairobi. I was not sure if he was telling the truth or not; he guarded his privacy and avoided answering direct questions about his past.

Now, as an adult, Peter was part of an army of men who squeezed a few coins a day out of their long rounds to the public trash bins. On early morning jogs I would see these unofficial collectors at work in their dirty pants and shirts, carrying their bags over their shoulders. Schoolchildren in clean, pressed uniforms walked briskly by them going to classes with knapsacks full of books. The two groups—the scavengers and the students—passed in the street without a word. It was only after I met Peter that I began paying attention to these trash collectors. Some camped under old sheets of plastic, spread out in vacant lots. There were some youth among them. They started their rounds

early; competition was stiff. They finished late, exhausted, earning perhaps fifty cents a day.

After the clinic staff had checked him out and prescribed some in-
expensive medicine, which I bought, I drove him to the other YMCA,
which had a low-cost hostel. As Peter checked into the Y, I took his trash
bag out of the car, carried it into the dormitory where he would be
staying, and slid it under his bed. He had nearly lost the bag at the
clinic, where an attendant had seen it lying near the door and thrown it
out. I had to retrieve it.

I saw him with that bag only one other time. It was a typically warm
but not hot day in Nairobi. I was running some errands downtown
when I saw Peter, crossing the street, bag over his shoulder. I stopped
and we spoke for a while. He was broke again, out of the pocket money
Betty and I had been supplying him. So he had reverted to collecting
scrap paper, the one way he was sure to make money, even if only a
little. He was also ill again; we stopped by the clinic for more medicine.

The day we met, and on many other occasions, Peter told me he did
not want to go back to street life. His determination to leave the streets
was clear from the moment we arrived at the Y that rainy morning,
Seeing on one of the Y buildings the large letters that spelled out the
name of its training center, Peter got excited. He said he used to do a
little tailoring and asked if the Y offered training in that area. It did. And
so Peter enrolled in a tailoring class and began his effort to learn a
trade. When Betty and I came to visit, he would proudly pull out his
latest patterns from class—shirts and pants, drawn on brown waste
paper. He seemed to know what he was doing.

But the shift from street life to student life is a big one. At first Peter
was often absent from classes, and sometimes he was intoxicated, probably from cheap alcohol, or glue sniffing, a habit from his years on the
streets. Street kids in Nairobi can often be seen sniffing glue from small
plastic bottles, getting a cheap kick, a mental escape from a life of
drudgery, danger, and dirt. The Y staff was incredibly tolerant. Instead
of tossing him out, they would call me and I would talk to him. But they
finally laid down an ultimatum that he had to shape up or leave. We
started looking around for an alternative place, even while I lectured
him in a friendly way about staying sober. Peter finally got the message
when he inquired at a nearby hostel. It had military-like rules, which he

did not like. Nor did he like the fact that the residents were mostly students, much younger than he. The Y started looking better in his eyes; so Peter started staying sober, with only an occasional slip. He became popular at the Y. I remember seeing him one day coming down from his tiny room and greeting some children at the bottom of the stairs. Everyone seemed to like him. He made friends with the cook, the stockroom attendant, the room cleaners. He laughed a lot.

I kept the location of our apartment a secret from him. As much as Betty and I were growing to appreciate Peter, we suspected that if he knew where we lived, he would start hanging around our place. We never invited him over. That was probably not the nicest thing to do, but we valued our privacy. Yet Peter's life and ours gradually became intertwined. One of the links was a slowly growing friendship; another was more concrete: money. Peter was a bargainer. He wasn't afraid to ask for money for his tailoring materials and incidentals, although he never asked for much.

The Y served simple but nutritious meals in a dining room, and he started gaining some weight. His face filled out some, too. At one point he apparently managed to get to the Kenyan coast for that vacation where he had the photos taken of himself. By most Western and Kenyan middle-class standards, Peter's room at the Y—only big enough for a single bed, table, small cabinet, and a chair—was not much. But for Peter, after years of sleeping on the streets and never being sure of food, much less a hot shower, the days at the Y, he told me, were like "heaven."

Peter's trips to the clinic continued; he was never completely well. At first I thought it was a minor problem. The nurses took an interest in him, telling me when I called that he should be sure to take his medicine. His coughing became intense at times but then would subside for weeks. In the meantime, Peter had found, through a friend of the cook at the Y, a single room in a slum at the edge of the city. I was curious to see the place but felt that my presence in his room would mark him for a robbery for having relatively affluent friends, although we did visit some other friends in slums.

Nairobi has an international reputation as a cosmopolitan, modern city, and in many ways it is. It has numerous tall buildings and a skyline that is steadily becoming more crowded. Homes of the wealthy, with trimmed lawns and gardens exploding with flowers, are protected by guards and sometimes dogs as well, day and night. The guards are backed up by their company's roving, radio-equipped, quick-response teams. But in the massive slums around the edges of the city, security is often little more than a cheap padlock securing a bent tin door; a good kick would force it open. Individual and gang robberies in the slums are frequent, but sometimes vigilante gangs of angry neighbors will chase down a suspect and club him to death.

So I stayed away from Peter's new "home." He moved in and purchased a mattress and a small cooker. Except for the Y room, it may have been the only time he had a room by himself as an adult. He continued to prepare for a national examination to obtain a certificate as a tailor.

A few months after his move, I got a phone call from an employee at the Y, who said Peter was sick and needed help. The two sons of Peter's landlady had brought him to the Y, afraid he was going to die in their house. He was very weak, yet he continued to smile and was pleasant, not panicked at all. I paid the two boys some money for their transportation and took Peter with me to the clinic. After that I took Peter back to the Y, where the staff was understanding enough to give him his old room back. The staff expressed concern about his health and a willingness to help him get back on his feet. Once again they demonstrated the compassion that is one of the principles of the YMCA. After a couple of weeks the staff called again saying Peter was in such critical condition he needed to be hospitalized. I took him back to the clinic. That day he finally agreed to take a test for AIDS.

At first AIDS appeared to be concentrated in eastern Africa, but later there was evidence that it had spread across much of the continent. Denial is still the biggest obstacle to curbing AIDS in Africa. Many African governments—Uganda was an early exception—have tried to deny the problem. Kenya's government slowly came to realize it has to do more about the issue. But the AIDS programs are still fairly limited, especially in areas outside the capital. Peter was probably denying the possibility of having AIDS in his earlier refusals to be tested. But now he must have wanted to know why he was doing so poorly. Was it TB? Was it AIDS? A combination of the two, quite common in Africa, was another possibility. So he took the test.

Later that day I got a phone call from the clinic to come get him. Parking at the clinic was always difficult. One time my car was towed away when I was inside the clinic talking to a nurse with Peter. Peter had insisted we go to the police and complain vigorously, but he was too weak to go in when we got to the station. I got my car back with a minimal fine after the taxi driver who took us there pleaded my case, having seen Peter's condition. The driver even loaned me some money so I could pay the fine.

This time at the clinic a staff nurse told me Peter was HIV positive, which meant he had the AIDS virus but not in an active stage. The nurse probably should not have told me, but the staff knew I had been paying his modest clinic bills and I had met them several times. Peter was lying outside on the grass; I helped him into the car. The head nurse came out of the clinic and walked up to the passenger side to tell Peter he had tested HIV positive. Knowing what she was going to say, I stepped out of the car to give him some privacy. When the nurse finished, I got back into the car. I waited for Peter to say something, but he said nothing. We drove to a small hospital about half an hour's drive from Nairobi, in farming country. The head nurse at the clinic had written a note explaining Peter's condition and asking for help admitting him. The hospital staff was quite friendly—at first. Then they started backing off, looking at Peter strangely. The visiting doctor on duty asked me to come into the consulting room with Peter. He asked Peter if he knew what his problem was. Peter answered that he was HIV positive. He had not confirmed this to me in the car, but now it was in the open. The doctor bluntly told Peter there was no cure, but he also said people who are HIV positive sometimes live for years. Peter seemed sad but not grief-stricken. The doctor said the hospital would not admit him because it was not accepting HIV-positive patients. AIDS patients have flooded hospitals in some parts of Africa, cutting services available to others. That problem has made many institutions reluctant to accept an AIDS or HIV-positive person. If admitted, they require much attention yet often lack the money to pay their bills.

As we drove back to the city to look for another hospital, I stopped the car and invited Peter to get out to appreciate the scene. The rolling green fields in front of us extended toward the setting sun. Peter was weak, so we stood outside for only a few minutes, but the view seemed to perk him up. Searching for encouraging words, I told him healthy people never know when they will die; it can happen suddenly. He knew he had the AIDS virus, but death could still be years away. And at least he could live those years with new appreciation for life. It wasn't much, and I don't know if it helped. But I couldn't think of anything else to say. Peter nodded, smiled, and said a few words of agreement. That afternoon I became aware of his inner strength, which enabled him not to be overcome by despair. There were always some problems communicating with Peter because he spoke broken street Swahili in addition to his first language, Kikuyu, and my Swahili was weak. But in his demeanor I saw signs of his grace and dignity, especially in his reaction to the HIV diagnosis.

(In the weeks and months ahead, he sought to regain his health, and renewed his efforts to become a tailor, a dream that seemed so fragile now. Later I tried to enroll him in an HIV/AIDS/TB program operating out of Kenyatta National Hospital. We had to wait a while until the doctors arrived. They took a look at him and said he probably would not qualify, but agreed to give him an AIDS test. The examining Kenyan doctor said that not only did he have the HIV virus, he had a full-blown case of AIDS. Because Peter was not likely to live long enough, the doctor said, he was ineligible for their two-year treatment program. One of the doctors told me privately that Peter was not likely to live more than a few weeks. A Kenyan counselor who talked to Peter told me Peter had been sullen and evasive, especially when asked about his family.)

The general patient section of Kenyatta National Hospital was the logical place to take Peter; AIDS cases were accepted there and comprised a large portion of the patients. But Peter had already taken that route. Once when he was feeling very ill, I stayed with him through an incredible eight-hour check-in process at Kenyatta. After two nights there he managed to walk out of the hospital and return to his rented room, where he lay practically helpless until the landlady's two sons had brought him to the YMCA. Peter later explained that he had not been given a bed at the hospital, just floor space, and patients had to pay for their own medicines. He said he'd rather be at home.

The next hospital we stopped at also refused to admit him, on the grounds of being full, which appeared to be true. The next, also private, refused him for being HIV positive. But the doctor was kind enough to counsel me on how I might get him into some hospital. The paper Peter was still clutching from the clinic clearly stated his condition. The doctor said no hospital was likely to allow him in with that. So he wrote another one without changing the truth, but listing just Peter's symptoms, not the fact that he was HIV positive. It almost worked at the following hospital. But as Peter was about to be signed in, an attendant began questioning why he had had the same symptoms for months. The hospital finally decided against his admission, which was probably for the best. As I looked around, I realized from the appearance of the women patients that we had come to what was mostly a maternity clinic. Finally, we tried the last place on our list: a small, downtown hospital in a tough section of Nairobi. I worried about leaving my car unattended but walked with Peter up to the second-floor admitting area. It was more like a clinic. A doctor on duty took a look at the paper the other doctor had written and agreed to admit Peter. I ran back and parked the car in a safer location. By the time I returned, Peter was being checked in. He sat on a bench waiting until he was shown to a single room, still maintaining his humor and smile; he said he would be all right.

He made progress there and after about ten days was released. I took him back to the Y, where the staff was amazed to see him again. So as not to alarm them, I had coached Peter to walk up the stairs to his old room with as little help from me as possible. He did. For days, Peter was so weak he lay in bed, barely able to lift his head. But after four or five days, though no one else saw a change, I detected signs of progress, not in his movements, but in his expression. The focus was returning to his eyes. He was able to speak more than a few words. Throughout this convalescent period, his most serious so far, he continued to smile frequently and to laugh, though weakly. The Y staff somehow stuck with him, and he slowly regained some strength; he even began walking again and talking about his tailoring plans. Earlier he had taken the national tailoring exam, despite his weakness.

A day I shall always remember from this period was the day Peter saved my life. We were downtown, walking toward the clinic; I was trying to help him keep his balance traversing curbs. At a very busy street, I was not paying attention and started to step out. Peter blocked me with his arm, just as a car I had not seen whizzed by exactly where I would have been after one more step. I thanked him. He laughed and smiled again as we walked on. We both knew I probably owed him my life.

Then for three months I was so ill myself I couldn't help Peter. Betty and a journalist colleague took over my contacts with Peter, meeting with him from time to time to cheer him up and provide pocket money. Peter continued to improve. During the later part of my own recuperation in mid-1994, while I was resting at a ranch in Naivasha, about ninety minutes' drive from Nairobi, Peter was sent back to the same small hospital. I had just returned to Nairobi when a nurse at the hospital called to tell me he had died the night before and would I please pay his bill, including transportation to the city mortuary. When I went to the mortuary later that day to arrange for his burial, the staff there was taken by surprise. He was not in the section where bodies were stored individually. The "street boy," as they called him, had been taken to another section of the building, a common storage area. Now that someone had shown up to inquire about the body, the staff stalled, asking me to go back to the waiting room while they clandestinely rushed him from the common storage area to an individual, pull-out container. When they finally showed me the body, an identification tag had been tied to one of his big toes. The staff tried to convince me there was no need to look closer, but I had to be sure it was him. I recognized the body as Peter's, though it was only a cold shadow of his former self. There seemed little connection between the corpse and the Peter I had known.

He had lost his battle to live and to become a tailor. But he had never lost his sense of humor, nor his dignity and will to keep trying, even after he knew he was dying. What an example he was. He had gained some personal freedom, coming in off the streets, studying a trade, eating and sleeping well for a change. He had, in his own words, lived in "heaven" for a year before he died, which is more than most people can say.

The day he died, I returned briefly to his room at the Y to collect his few personal belongings. As always, it was almost bare except for some of his last medicines—and the photo album. As I flipped slowly through the pages, I stopped at the one of him dressed up and smiling in Mombasa. He must have had a good time.

Freedom from Ignorance

Peter's hunger to break free of a life of ignorance and poverty can be seen in any African country today, even among children in war zones. If there is one force driving African families, it is the desire for education. Most families will cut practically every other expenditure before touching the money they put aside for their children's education. This quest for freedom from ignorance is so strong—among children, teachers, and parents—that even wars cannot completely halt it. In Somalia, during the prolonged civil war of the 1990s, even when the capital, Mogadishu, was still the scene of frequent battles, unpaid teachers such as Mahad Mohamed Moalim would conduct classes for eager children, including many girls. Mahad taught English in a school run by a Muslim organization in a run-down building in which the younger children sat on the floor on plastic sheeting. I asked him why he was teaching, since the school had no money to pay him and there was no

Mogadishu, Somalia, 1992 Mahad Mohamed Moalim worked as an unpaid high school English teacher during the civil war in Somalia.

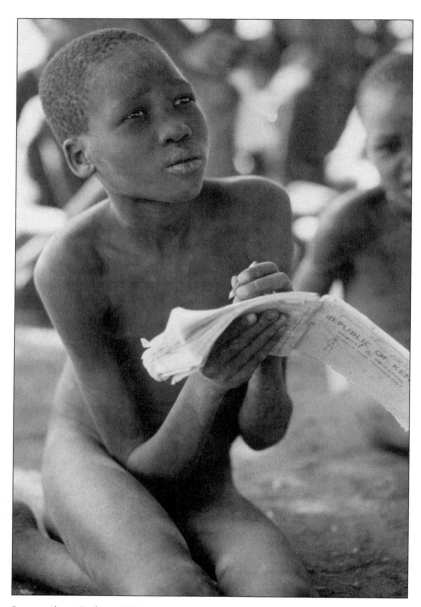

Bor, southern Sudan, 1989
During the years of civil war in southern Sudan,
many children living in extreme poverty continued their basic education. This boy studies under
the shade of a tree.

longer a central government to hire him. "It is my duty [to teach].The country has a lack of education. Instead of sitting at home, it's better to come here and teach them what I know."[24]

In northern Somalia, in the bombed-out city of Hargeisa, one school held classes in a two-room school so badly battered that it had no roof, no windows, and only part of a wall dividing the two classes. Amazingly, the day of our unannounced visit four classes were under way—one on either side of the remnants of the wall (the blackboards had survived in each classroom) and two more outside. The students sat on stones or on the ground. "I'm very happy here," said Abdurahman Ismail, one of the students. He had begun school a week earlier and was studying math, Arabic, and English. Headmaster Hassan Osman Abdi, undeterred by the ruins of the tiny school, looked around at the students and teachers—all four of them graduates of the College of Education at the now-defunct Somali National University in Mogadishu—and said, "We are really proud of this." Parents, he reported, were beginning to contribute small amounts of money for school supplies.

In southern Sudan, which has seen more war than peace since independence in 1956, Betty and I visited a "school" in a rebel-held war zone. It consisted of a class of forty-five young boys and girls sitting in the dirt under a tree in the village of Feriak, near the small town of Bor, deep in rebel territory. The total supplies the teacher, Atiny Makidi Yoao, had were one book, a blackboard (propped up on three sticks), chalk, eraser, and for the pupils—pencil stubs and notebooks from Kenya cut in half to go around.

"This is my name; my name is Afindi. This is my name; my name is Afindi," the children repeated in English after their teacher. Later they counted in English to fifty. The girls wore only a loincloth; the boys were totally naked, not out of custom but out of poverty made worse by the war. As poor as the children were, when they ran up to a relief official or other visitor they would often ask not for money but for a pencil. No sooner did these makeshift schools open—some were in the remnants of the original school buildings—than the classes would fill up. What struck me about the open-air class we visited was the attentiveness of the students. Betty's arrival with two cameras around her neck and a long lens on one of them must have looked as if someone had just landed from Mars. But the children paid her no heed and continued with their lesson. From my vantage point I couldn't even spot children sneaking a sideways glance at her. *The Christian Science Monitor* ran one of Betty's photos of a boy with pencil stub and half a notebook in hand, looking intently at his teacher.

"When there is bombardment, the children are dispersed," said James Mayan Benjaim, who coordinated education in the Bor area for the rebel Sudanese People's Liberation Army (SPLA). "The next day they come and we teach them again. All the teachers and the students are afraid of the bombings." They had a right to be afraid. The Sudan government occasionally sent a Soviet bomber into the area at an altitude high enough to avoid artillery fire from the rebels below. But the height also meant the accuracy was unpredictable. At one point Betty and I were standing outside a UN relief compound in Bor when the plane came overhead and let go with a string of bombs. I lay down in a ditch the UN's local staff had dug in front of our tin-roofed compound, whose roof was clearly marked with the letters *UN*. Betty was determined to get a photo of the plane and ignored my shouts to get down until she got a final shot—showing the bomb bay doors open. The closest bomb missed us by about 800 yards. But one of them did wound a young girl who had just returned from one of the makeshift schools in the area. A bomb fragment dug into one of her legs; the explosion also set fire to the thatched-roof home of her family. She might have ended up a cripple if not for a Sudanese bone specialist living in a nearby village who was able to set the bone properly.

At another school, with grass thatch walls and roof and a dirt floor, scores of children broke into a song when we arrived. A southern Sudanese adult there told me it was a song praising the SPLA, which was at war with the northern-based, Muslim-dominated government to obtain greater autonomy and to block imposition of a Muslim state. When I asked him to repeat his explanation on tape for a radio program, he turned away. SPLA leader John Garang was later accused of luring young boys to SPLA camps with the promise of educating them, only to train them in fighting as well. Many of them eventually joined the SPLA, according to Garang's critics. Garang denied the charges to me in a lengthy interview but admitted the boys got some training with wooden rifles. His onetime assistant, Lam Akol, who later broke with the SPLA, insisted in another interview that Garang had knowingly used education as bait to get thousands of young boys to migrate to SPLA training camps in Ethiopia, where they were trained for the war. Many of the boys died along the way from starvation in treks of up to hundreds of miles on their quest for education and safety.

At the tree-shaded school that day, a student named Garang, unrelated to rebel leader Garang, said through a translator that when he grows up, "I want to continue my education. I want to know what in the world is going on, to know the world, or to be in politics." Was it an accurate translation? Was he coached in his reply, or was he truly as eager to learn about the world as he was to talk to us? Then he said the mosquitoes in the area were so thick at night that some students had returned home for good. "We need mosquito nets and clothes. They are important to us. They are equivalent to exercise books. I don't ask for more."

★ ★ ★

Students' determination to break free of ignorance—and learning in a war zone is an extreme case—calls for equally determined teachers. One such teacher was at work in the next country south of Sudan, Kenya, where some of the boys from the Sudan war later ended up as refugees.

A Teacher Who Listened

Margaret Waigu Githegi taught English in the secondary school in the town of Chuka.[25] The school was constructed of cement blocks with cement floors; the paint was peeling off the doors, and the wooden desks were scarred, but the science lab was well equipped, compared with some other rural schools in Kenya. There was no school librarian, but there was a library, which included many books acquired before Kenya's independence in 1963; among them, a set of Shakespeare's works, which a teacher said the students didn't read much. The English teachers at the school said they had enough books, but in some other classes there were so few books that the teachers spent a lot of time dictating lessons from their book.

Chuka, Kenya, 1992
Margaret Waigu Githegi was an award-winning
English teacher at a rural secondary school.

A Kenyan who speaks five languages (English, Swahili, Kikuyu, Luo, and some Hindi) and loves songs by Dolly Parton, Githegi turned to teaching after graduating from Rajasthan University in India, where she earned a bachelor's degree in English in 1982. "When I came back it was difficult to get a job. [Teaching] was the only job I could get." But she soon discovered she liked the work. She started teaching at Chuka in 1986 and the next year was made head of the nine-teacher English department. She took additional training courses, including one in Cambridge, England, sponsored by the British Council in Kenya. As a result of these courses she started trying different teaching methods. "I think my classes were boring before. I did most of the talking." That changed; she started doing more listening.

Githegi began dividing her class—often numbering forty to forty-five students—into small discussion groups and floating among them like a butterfly, stimulating their talk with questions, letting the students wrestle with questions instead of drawing conclusions for them.

She stopped asking students to memorize material, something many teachers in Kenya and other countries were doing regularly. "I don't like memorization because when they memorize they don't understand exactly what they are doing." She began giving students clippings from the local newspapers and asking them to discuss them. She would ask the group a question such as: "Imagine that you went to your dormitory, and under your bed you found a snake. What would you do?" The first response was silence; then hands started sprouting in the air, as students eagerly vied for a chance to respond. "If there's no stick around, you can even step on it with your feet," one young pupil ventured.

After class, one of her students, Martin Wachira, who said he wants to be an engineer, described his reaction to his teacher. "She uses different methods of teaching, which makes us even understand better. She even encourages us to work hard so we can achieve our goals. She is bright." Richard Arden, an adviser to the Kenya Ministry of Education, described her as one of Kenya's outstanding teachers. "She has a high level of commitment to her work as a teacher," he said. "She has a very positive outlook on adopting new ideas and is a good organizer of in-service teacher training." Not only did she teach well, she was helping others learn to teach better.

★   ★   ★

As Githegi sought to help her pupils break the bonds of ignorance, a group of women jurists in West Africa were trying to help girls break free of a traditional female bond.

Female Freedom: The Fight against Circumcision

A small but growing number of African women are fighting to stop the ancient cultural practice of circumcision, which involves removal of part or all of the clitoris, and often more.[26] Known to its opponents as female genital mutilation, or FGM, this practice is still widely accepted in parts of Africa as a rite of passage to female adulthood, a sign that the female is not promiscuous and will make a good wife. Many mothers and grandmothers insist on its application, and it is often performed without the consent of the female.

Bamako, Mali, 1994
Judge Fatimata Dumbia Dembélé and attorney Bintu Bouare
Sameke sought to use the law to outlaw female circumcision.

Opponents contend that the surgical operation of circumcision or excision is unsanitary and dangerous, leading to infection or even death. Usually the subjects have to be held down forcefully, are given no anesthesia, and in some cases sprain a muscle or dislocate a bone in their efforts to thrash free of the blade.

"Female genital mutilation is the most widespread form of torture in the world," according to an editorial in the newsletter of the National Committee on Traditional Practices of Ethiopia. "It is also one of the most painful," the editorial maintained. "At least 80 million living African girls and women are victims of this trauma. It is inflicted upon millions more every year." The NCTPE was appealing to both Christian and Muslim religious leaders to help educate people about the practice. Cole Dodge, a former director of UNICEF's regional office in Nairobi, Kenya, said FGM is widely practiced in Ethiopia, part of

Eritrea, Sudan, Somalia, and parts of north-central and West Africa, including Mali. Though it predates Islam, in Africa it is most widely practiced in Islamic countries, he said. According to the NCPTE, Muslim scholars disagree over whether the tradition is supported by Islam.

In Mali, which is about 80 percent Muslim, the Association of Malian Court Lawyers, headed by Fatimata Dumbia Dembélé, was dead set against FGM. "We've seen a lot of girls die" as a result of FGM, she said. "It has to stop." But speaking out against FGM had had little effect in Mali, so Dembélé was turning to the law for an answer. She was lobbying for legislation to outlaw the practice. Opening a Malian law book, she turned to a page and found a reference in existing law against abuse, which she claimed already made FGM illegal. But few others interpreted the law the way she did. Even if a law was passed that specifically outlawed the practice, Dembélé admitted the law would probably be ineffective. "Society accepts it. When the society accepts it, the law can't stop it." Another woman, Bintu Bouare Sameke, also a member of the association, added: "It's the grandmothers who insist. They say: 'I did it; you do it'."

Another prominent woman in Mali, Attorney General Manassa Danioko, brushed off the anti-FGM crusade in the country as a "Western idea, not Malian." Certainly a lot has been written in the West about the practice, but the women activists on the issue I spoke with in Mali were not taking their cues from outsiders. H. Assa Diallo Soumare, president of the Action Committee for the Rights of Women and Children, a Malian organization, said her group was sponsoring production of an anti-FGM film. At the back of the crowd watching the filming of one of the scenes, opinions varied about the practice. "It's fine," said one young woman, speaking out of earshot of others. "It's no problem." She added it was not a health risk either. Then she moved away before others could eavesdrop on the conversation.

"I'm in a Muslim family. Excision [a form of FGM] is permitted. But one should not perform it," said a young man in the crowd. A second young man, Kande Drame, a high school student, said: "It is encouraged by old women. They say it purifies the woman." A young woman with a baby wrapped onto her back and balancing a tray of bananas on her head said: "It [FGM] applies to some as part of our custom. The people in the bush [rural areas] accept it, but those of us with education are against it." In the long run, education, not a change of laws, may be the best way to curb the practice of female genital mutilation in Africa.

★   ★   ★

In Eritrea, former women soldiers were fighting after the war for both social and political rights in a male-dominated society.

Female Soldiers Battle for Rights after the War

From 1961 to 1991, Eritrea fought a devastating war against the Ethiopian army to win its independence, which it finally gained when Ethiopian and Eritrean rebels overthrew the government of Ethiopia.[27] The Ethiopian army was backed at various times by the former Soviet Union, the United States, and Israel, and was one of the best equipped in Africa. The Eritrean People's Liberation Front (EPLF) turned to its women to supplement their ranks of fighters, sending them into combat. About 35 percent of the front line soldiers were women. Two years after the war ended, there were still some 20,000 women in the EPLF out of about 100,000, but demobilization had begun. The challenge ahead for the former women fighters was to secure a place in civil society—not as second-class citizens but as full participants in the economic and political life of their newly independent country.

Abrehet Yemane was one of these women. A veteran of fifteen major battles, she had spent eight years in an Ethiopian prison where inmates received only three pieces of bread a day, no blankets, and no clothing. Friends on the outside supplied basic necessities to those they knew inside, she said. Now, in independent Eritrea, she sat behind a wooden desk in the office of the National Union of Eritrean Women (NUEW), in Asmara, the capital. Instead of military fatigues she wore a dress. She said Eritrea's women who fought for their country's freedom have a right to be proud of their record. In addition to fighting, they helped protect villagers and provided many rural families with health and educational services. Through such work, many women soldiers found themselves nudging an ancient, tradition-bound society toward a new appraisal of the worth of women. Not only could they cook, haul water, and have babies, but they could shoot, command men, and help run a country. But adjusting to civilian life would not be easy, partly because of the shift from rural life to city life, Yemane said. "Most are peasants. Their choices in the field were very limited. In the city the choices are so wide."

"We are confident and independent," said Senait Iyob, who spent thirteen years in the military. "You wanted to have your gun, and shoot, and give your life for it [your country]. It's not because you want to kill," she added, explaining why she joined instead of finishing high school. "We sacrificed our youth, our education," she insisted with a soft intensity. Today the ex-women fighters are not about to accept such customs as arranged marriages and male-dominated families, she said. Senait managed to get a job with Eritrean Television and was planning to go to a university to study journalism. But Eritrea was not showing many signs that women had been accepted as equals politically. Only 6 of the 131 members of the EPLF central committee were women, and there were no women on the 19-member political committee, the nation's highest authority.

Some of the adjustment would be social. "To do like city girls, you must know [city life]. It's not a problem of economics, but culture," said Yemane. In a small but crowded café in Asmara, a woman soldier in army jacket and baggy slacks looked up as two Eritrean women in dresses and with stylish haircuts walked in. The fighter's eyes followed them to the counter. Eritrea's former women soldiers would have a lot of adjustments to make. "Everyone presses you to dress like a woman," said Senait, who was still in the military. "The problem is, you are very poor." Fighters earned only the equivalent of ten dollars a month plus one dollar for every year of service. Having survived the war, Eritrea's women veterans were facing new battles for economic survival and a place in their society that would give them the same freedom they had earned as soldiers.

★ ★ ★

Often a woman fighting for her rights does it without the benefit of an organization, calling on her own strength and patience to overcome cultural barriers to her progress. Nike is one of these women.

Nike, a Nigerian artist, established a tuition-free art school in Oshogbo, Nigeria.

A Nigerian Artist Wins Her Freedom

In the front row of a hotel meeting room at an African arts conference in New Orleans sat a Nigerian woman in traditional wraparound dress with a baby secured snugly onto her back with a piece of attractive cloth. For an hour or so, several academicians read their prepared papers about the art of this woman, whom they had not been expecting to show up at the conference. In frustration, I finally interrupted with a question: "Since the artist is here, will she get a chance to speak?" Finally she did, fielding questions from admirers in the audience who recognized her as one of Africa's best-known artists, known by simply one name—Nike (pronounced NEE-kay). It was April 1998, six years after Betty and I had been to her home in Oshogbo, in central Nigeria, and three years after she had stayed overnight in our home in Florida. Between her many greetings to others in the room, and her flashing smiles, she told me quietly that things were still not easy back home; but she had married again, this time to a senior Nigerian police officer—"for security." She invited Betty and me to join her and some other friends for lunch.

During the meal—a fish and pasta buffet on the top floor of the hotel, a meal she appeared to enjoy—she mostly listened as the others talked. Beneath the fancy head wrapper she wore, her eyes seemed to have so much to say; they had seen so much: being passed from one family member to another as a child after the death of her mother; running away from home to join a traveling theater troupe to avoid a marriage her father had arranged; enduring years of physical and mental abuse as one of the sixteen wives of a man who was also a Nigerian artist; and finally breaking free to establish her own life.

Nike broke some of the barriers many African women continue to face, including social pressure on how to dress, and taboos against owning a business and traveling abroad. She had done so her own way, out of necessity. She had pushed back boundaries that denied her certain individual freedoms and human rights.

At the lunch in New Orleans, her baby daughter, Amen (as in "that's my last child—Amen"), now unwrapped, sat quietly on her mother's lap as Nike fed her. All too soon the meal was over. The next day she took a bus to Santa Fe, New Mexico, to visit her son and new grandson. From there she would fly to the United Kingdom to see one of her two former husbands and their two children, then return to Nigeria.

Nike's story is an example of Africans today striving to live fuller lives regardless of the political situation in their country. Nigeria was under military rule during much of the time she was pushing back the limits on her personal freedom.

A Family of Weavers

Nike was born into a family of women weavers and dominant husbands, in the Yoruba culture which favors polygyny (having more than one wife). As in some areas of the United States before the twentieth century, marriage is more a matter of practicality than love. Nike's mother, a weaver, died when Nike was only six. Her mother never wanted to marry Nike's father, a farmer, preferring the greater potential earning power of a taxi driver she had her eye on. Men looked on marriage in a utilitarian way, too. "The men in our village," Nike told author Kim Marie Vaz in her autobiography, "married for business, not for love. They married to make life easier for themselves. They wanted someone to look after them. All they wanted was to sell their daughters in marriage to get the bride price.[28] All men want when they have a daughter is to sell her to a man, who in turn uses her like a slave. I never wanted any man to claim his right to me through a bride price."[29] Her stubbornness would lead her into many adventures.

After her mother died, Nike was sent to live with her grandmother, Oranuiyawo, one of fourteen wives, and a weaver of cloth. She died a year later, and Nike was taken to the home of her great-grandmother, Ibitola, who then took Nike to Jos, in northern Nigeria, where she learned Hausa. Nike took along her total inheritance from her mother and grandmother combined: a single "wrapper," as she called the wraparound cloth used as a skirt. Like her mother, her great-grandmother Ibitola had been forced into a marriage by her family—literally. After her refusal to marry the man, she was taken by her family to the man's house by force. "Her husband's friends helped him to rape her. They held her legs and body tight while he entered her."[30] Ibitola was not above using force on Nike, however, when it came to circumcision. Nike told me she is adamantly opposed to the ritual, which carries with it risk of infection as well as trauma. But her great-grandmother forced her to undergo the ordeal at the age of eight. "I hate it," she said. Women who have to endure it "don't even know the feeling [of sexual intercourse]. I will not let it happen to my children."[31]

In 1959, Nike's family convinced her great-grandmother to move closer to the family. She and Nike moved into the compound of Nike's uncle, where the wives fought among each other. Three years later her father made her move back into his home. She was twelve. Her father woke her up at five to sweep the house and make the four-kilometer round-trip to the nearest well. She was consistently late for her classes, which began at eight. "I did not eat anything until lunchtime. While the other students were eating, I went to the bush to search for palm kernels that had fallen from a tree. I used a stone to open the kernel to get the nuts. [Many lunches] consisted of these palm nuts and water."[32]

Nike finished her primary schooling in 1965. She began making *adire* cloth, something both her mother and great-grandmother had done. But despite selling a few pieces, she remained very poor. At the age of sixteen she took a job as housekeeper with an Indian family. When her father demanded her salary, she refused; she was trying to save what little she was paid to buy more material. He in turn told her he wanted her to marry a certain civil servant.

Having seen the women of her family forced into unwanted marriages, Nike decided to run away and join a theater troupe that was passing through her town. Though lacking experience, she sang and danced and did many of the household chores for the troupe. But her family sent Twins Seven Seven, her future husband, to try to bring her back. As a way to dodge any planned marriage, and to get home, she agreed to go with him, moving into his compound which was home for his numerous wives. Later he moved his wives to Oshogbo, a center for the arts, and began furnishing Nike with supplies for her artwork. Nike continued doing two things she had done with the troupe—wearing trousers, which was unheard of for a woman at that time in central Nigeria, and playing the guitar. She performed in surrounding towns with a band organized by some of the boys staying at Twins's compound.

Twins is featured in a book by Uli Beier, *Contemporary Art in Africa,* about emerging artists; he was described as "clearly foremost among them."[33] Nike, trained by her family in *adire* and design work, soon began designing his paintings and selling his work. She also began selling her own artwork to foreigners who came to visit Twins's gallery. When she could, and sometimes with the help of Victoria Scott, from the United States, she would hide the proceeds from Twins to keep him from spending them. Scott became a close friend of Nike's while living in Nigeria.

Nike soon discovered she had landed in a violent household. Twins fought with his wives—and with Nike, who had fallen into the role of a wife. As Nike recalled, "He jumped on us, beat us, kicked us, stood on our bellies and jumped up and down, and said: 'I want you to die. I want you to die'."[34] Nike and most of the others had no family to whom they could run. She did not want to go home and be forced to marry someone, so she stayed and eventually bore Twins four children, three of whom survived. Twins took on more and more wives until he finally had sixteen, including Nike. "I would never advise my enemy to go into polygyny," she said. "Being in a compound with fifteen other wives, there is a lot of jealousy, fighting, hatred."[35] Sex, especially since she was circumcised, was not an act of pleasure. "In this marriage it was like business, like master and slave or landlord and tenant."[36] There was a great deal of cooperation among the wives, and she became close friends with some of them. Groups of them would scale the family compound walls and sneak into town on various errands. Eventually most of them developed relationships with men outside the family.

Nike finally moved into the home of the man she spent more and more time with, David John Davies, an Englishman whom she later married and by whom she had two more children. Altogether she endured sixteen years in Twins's compound, partly out of fear of what he might do to her if she ran away and caught her, but mostly because of her children. She wanted to wait until they were old enough to decide for themselves whether they wanted to live with her or their father. In the end, they chose her.

Liberating her mind from the limiting concept of a woman's role in Nigeria came slowly. It was not until Nike made a trip to the United States with her husband in 1974 to teach art at a workshop in Maine that she discovered that Twins's behavior was not acceptable every-

Oshogbo, Nigeria, 1992
Kemi Akinwale, a batik artist at Nike's art school, wears a dress made of *adire* cloth.

where. Nike was six months pregnant. Upon arrival at the workshop, she was struggling with a load she was carrying on her head when an American woman told Twins to help her. He refused, saying people would make fun of him back home for helping her, that he didn't want to "spoil" her. The woman insisted, saying things were different in the United States. "I was so impressed that somebody could change this rule of woman carrying everything," Nike recalled.[37]

★   ★   ★

Adire cloth making is an old, traditional art that was in danger of disappearing before Nike began reviving it, starting in the compound she shared with Twins and his other wives. It is an integral part of Yoruba culture. "As profoundly as the talking drum, *adire* cloth expresses the Yoruba culture; it is the art of Yoruba women. It has provided them with economic independence; it is a means of expressing cultural identity, and the iconography of *adire* even provides them a voice on matters of public interest."[38] *Adire* cloth making differs from batik. Batik uses wax to cover portions of the cloth as it is repeatedly dipped in various colored dyes. The *adire* method uses a paste made from cassava, which is applied with a chicken feather. The paste dissolves faster than wax. As the cloth is dipped into pots of indigo, made from local plants, some of the blue seeps under the cassava paste, leaving a lighter blue in the paste-covered areas. Since the cassava paste does not soak through the cloth, like wax used in making batik, the reverse side of *adire* cloth is a solid, dark indigo. The result is a stunning array of different shades of blue. For Nike, *adire* was more than just a traditional fashion. It was "her legacy from her grandmother and all the mothers before her. It had been her means of survival." For Nike, its survival was "a cause."[39]

Unlike Twins, who jealously guarded his designs, Nike shared her knowledge of *adire* and other forms of art, beginning with her co-wives. Soon she was to begin teaching many more people, but only after taking her next big step in her quest for freedom. She decided to break away from Twins. She knew she risked her husband's wrath if he discovered her plans, so she proceeded secretly to set aside money from her art sales to buy land in Oshogbo for a house. A local female magistrate acted as go-between with a doctor who sold the land she bought. She also bought a 1979 Volkswagen Beetle and learned to drive, something few women in Oshogbo did. Her friend Scott had begun to encourage her in 1976 to leave Twins, but it was not until a decade later that she actually did. When she moved into her new house, young women began coming to her for art lessons. It was the start of her art school.

In addition to building a house in the same town as her husband, she acquired land for a center for teaching art. From the start she offered classes free of charge to her young Nigerian students, most of whom came to her from poor families, so they could learn an art form as a way to support themselves. Acutely aware of her childhood poverty, she did not want to turn away potential artists for their lack of tuition fees. By the late 1990s she was teaching up to 150 students a year, an average of 40 or so at any one time. Some of the money Nike was earning from workshops and sales of her own art abroad she plowed back into the school. She applied some of her own hard-won achievements in personal freedom to the running of the school. If a man beat a woman, he was dismissed from the school. Women who fought among each other were suspended. Group meetings were held to give students a chance to air complaints about the school.[40] She was proud of the freedom the school provided her students, especially the women, in terms of a decent living.

"My achievements are my students," she said during her 1998 visit to the United States. "They are free to go out [on the job market] as normal people. They can stand on their feet. I think I have gained a lot of freedom for them so far. A lot of them are independent. With them, power is their money. A lot of them own their own houses." And, she said, her students' new economic freedom gave them another benefit: "the freedom to choose the man they love."[41]

Nike chose to marry Davies but soon discovered that he wanted to "control" her.[42] He told her he had become so African he wanted to take a second wife, she said. Her marriage to Davies, a white man, shocked many residents of traditional Oshogbo. But the marriage was doomed; she had tasted freedom and did not want to give it up again. Yet she felt the need of a man's protection in a society still dominated by men. She was still not free of threats from Twins for having left him. And city authorities seized some of her land in 1994, forcing her into court to win it back. In 1995, she married Reuben Okundaye, a Nigerian police commandant "for security," to help her fend off any further assaults on her land or school, she explained. But she found that she loved him—and that unlike in her previous marriages, they did not fight. Suddenly she had a husband who not only respected her but encouraged her in her art, including her international travels as an artist. Her new husband proved to be a good father, too. "This is the first time I've seen a Nigerian man care for a baby," Nike said.

Nike was planning to open an art school in the commercial capital of Nigeria, Lagos, where children between the ages of five and fifteen could go after school. "There are a lot who have the talent and need to be discovered," she said. "I have to go forward." Many young Nigerians, she said, "are looking up at me" to see if she can continue setting an example of freedom in her life to which they might aspire.[43]

NOTES

1. African Freedom: The Unfinished Journey

1. Sub-Saharan Africa, the portion of Africa below the main part of the Sahara Desert, does not include Morocco, Algeria, Tunisia, Libya, and Egypt. When the term "Africa" is used in this book, it refers to sub-Saharan Africa, not the entire continent.

2. Wiseman, *The New Struggle for Democracy in Africa,* 1. The five were Botswana, The Gambia, Mauritius, Senegal, and Zimbabwe. A military coup in The Gambia ousted the government in July 1994.

3. Ibid., 2. He defines a fully fledged single-party state as one in which "only one political party is allowed, by law, to exist and, where elections take place, participation is confined to members of the party."

4. In modern times, no woman was the head of an African state until September 3, 1996, when Ruth Sando Perry was sworn in as head of the new transitional government in war-shattered Liberia. In both Burundi and Rwanda a woman prime minister briefly filled the role of head of state on an interim basis.

5. Wiseman, 6.

6. Ibid., 174.

7. The phrase is by George B. N. Ayittey, who uses it as the title of his book *Africa in Chaos* (New York: St. Martin's Press, 1998).

8. Wiseman, 4.

9. Mandela, *Long Walk to Freedom*, 367.

10. Ibid., 367.

11. Ibid., 368.

12. Berlin, *The Crooked Timber of Humanity*, 5.

13. Ibid., 7.

14. Ibid., 201.

15. Wiseman, 158.

16. Berlin, 10.

17. Ibid., 11.

18. Ibid.

19. Chiuri Ngugi, interview with the author, DeLand, Florida, September 1995. All quotes by Ngugi are from this interview.

20. Berlin, 13.

21. Ibid., 17.

22. Ibid. Many other authors tackle these broad questions, but few do it as succinctly, yet broadly, as Berlin, which is why this chapter includes numerous citations from his essay "The Pursuit of the Ideal" in his book *The Crooked Timber of Humanity*.

23. Ibid., 19.

24. Mandela, 330.

25. In an extreme case, the Black Panthers showed in court in the 1970s that the federal government's surveillance and harassment of them was due as much to their political views as to their actions. And it remains a harsh fact that blacks in many parts of the United States are stopped by the police not for their political views but because of their race, with many police automatically associating blacks with criminal behavior.

26. "Martin Luther King, Jr.," a video recording of the speeches of Martin Luther King, Jr. (sixty minutes) produced by Darrell Moore, MPI Home Video, c. 1990.

27. Joseph Garba, "Africa: A Time for Hope, Resolve, and Change," *Vital Speeches*, May 15, 1994, 458.

28. Monga, *The Anthropology of Anger*, 11.

29. Ibid.

30. Garba, 463.

31. Ilene R. Prusher, "Inside an African Famine," *The Christian Science Monitor*, October 9, 1998. The war pitted Islamic fundamentalists in the north against mostly non-Muslims in the south. Relief efforts were hampered by government limitations on international relief distributions amid government charges that rebels were diverting some of the aid for their own use.

32. Conrad, *Heart of Darkness*, 29.

33. Ibid.

34. Harden, *Africa*, 26. Harden, who based his book on his travels as a correspondent for the *Washington Post*, has what an Ethiopian friend of his once described as a sharp sense of irony.

35. Reynolds, *Stand the Storm*, 106. A native of Ghana, Reynolds was professor of history at the University of California, San Diego.

36. Ibid., 6.

37. Ibid.

38. Ibid., 7.

39. Ibid., 57. Reynolds cites an estimate by Paul Lovejoy, based on Philip Curtin's earlier research.

40. Ibid., 59.

41. Ibid.

42. Parkenham, *The Scramble for Africa*, 241.

43. Ibid., 241.

44. Ibid.

45. Ibid., 254.

46. Ibid.

47. Sklar, "The Colonial Imprint on African Political Thought," in *African Independence*, 12.

48. Ibid., 12.

49. Ibid., 21.

50. Ibid., 12.

51. Ibid., 19.

52. Ibid., 24.

53. Ibid., 25.

54. Ayittey, 47 and 42.

55. Moffett, *Critical Masses*, 14.

56. Ibid., 12.

57. Suzanne Daley, "In Zambia, the Abandoned Generation," *New York Times*, September 18, 1998.

58. *World Population Data Sheet: Demographic Data and Estimates for the Countries and Regions of the World: 1998* (Washington: Population Reference Bureau, 1998).

59. Callisto Madavo and Jean-Louis Sarbib (vice presidents, Africa Region, World Bank), *International Herald Tribune*, June 21–22, 1997.

60. Donald L. Sparks, "Economic Trends in Africa South of the Sahara 1997," in *Africa South of the Sahara, 1998*, 11.

61. Madavo and Sarbib.

62. Ake, *Democracy and Development in Africa*, 118. Ake died in a plane crash in Nigeria in November 1996.

63. Ibid., 141.

64. Michael Chege, "Can Africa Develop?" (a review of Ake's book *Development and Democracy in Africa*), *Journal of Democracy*, April 1997, 177.

65. Wiseman, 70.

66. Ibid.

67. Mandela, 563. In June 1999, Mandela's African National Congress party won an overwhelming victory in national elections, making his deputy, Thabo Mbeki, the next president.

68. *The Christian Science Monitor* (editorial), May 21, 1997. The editorial noted that foreign debts have "crushed some African nations' growth efforts."

69. Bratton and van de Walle, *Democratic Experiments in Africa,* 271–272. The authors examined the elections from 1990 to 1994 in every sub-Saharan country.

70. Ibid., 272.

71. Wiseman, 63.

72. Video of King's speeches.

73. Ibid.

74. Wiseman, 20–31.

75. *Zambia: Elections and Human Rights in the Third Republic* (New York: Human Rights Watch/Africa, 1996).

76. Bratton and van de Walle, 7–8, 203–4. The authors write that in all twelve flawed elections, "the political survival of the strong man was not meaningfully challenged by international observers funded by foreign donors. Incumbents apparently calculated correctly that the international community was often more interested in political stability than in democracy and sometimes would turn a blind eye to flawed elections" (204).

77. *Chad: Hope Betrayed* (London: Amnesty International, 1997), preface.

78. News release, May 8, 1998, from Amnesty International, London.

79. *Mass Graves of Refugees Uncovered in Congo by Human Rights Watch and International Federation of Human Rights Leagues* (New York: Human Rights Watch/Africa; Paris: International Federation of Human Rights Leagues, 1997).

80. Amnesty International statements announcing release of the report *DRC: A Year of Dashed Hopes,* reported by Reuters, May 15, 1998.

81. *Africa Update: A Summary of Human Rights Concerns in sub-Saharan Africa, September 1997–March 1998* (London: Amnesty International, 1998), 2–4.

82. Howard W. French, "Wave of Strongmen Make West Africa Their Oyster," *New York Times,* October 24, 1996.

83. Bratton and van de Walle, 278.

84. Julius O. Ihonvbere, "Where Is the Third Wave? A Critical Evaluation of Africa's Non-transition to Democracy. (Reassessing Democratic Transitions, 1990–1995)," *Africa Today,* October–December 1996, 347.

85. Ibid., 348.

86. Marina Ottaway, "African Democratization and the Leninist Option," *Journal of Modern African Studies,* 35, no. 1 (1997): 9. The author also notes exceptions in the other direction, such as Saudi Arabia, which is wealthy but shows no signs of democratic transformation. She provides additional "caveats" to the "not ready for democracy" observation.

87. Mamdani, *Citizen and Subject*, 297.

88. Marina Ottaway, "African Democratization: An Update," *CSIS Africa Notes*, April 1995, 6. The total of fifty sub-Saharan African nations, as listed by *Africa South of the Sahara, 1995*, includes Eritrea, which gained independence from Ethiopia in 1993, St. Helena, some 1,200 miles off the southwest coast of Africa, and Réunion, off the east coast of Africa.

89. Ibid., 6.

90. Ibid., 5.

91. *Kenya: Old Habits Die Hard; Rights Abuses Follow Renewed Foreign Aid Commitments* (New York: Human Rights Watch/Africa, 1995), 3–4.

92. Soyinka, *Nigeria's Political Crisis*, 8.

93. Monga, 168.

94. Ibid., 52.

95. Michael Chege, "Democracy's Future: Between Africa's Extremes," *Journal of Democracy*, January 1995, 50.

96. Ake, 132.

97. Monga, 187–88.

98. Bratton and van de Walle, 51.

2. Challenging the Dictators

1. According to Malians I interviewed, the number of people burned to death may have been as high as several dozen.

2. Wiseman, *The New Struggle for Democracy in Africa*, 67.

3. Gray, *Isaiah Berlin*, 19.

4. Wiseman, 46.

5. Bratton and van de Walle, *Democratic Experiments in Africa*, 147–48.

6. Pierre Englebert, "Mali: Recent History," in *Africa South of the Sahara 1995*, 581.

7. Liebenow, "The Military Factor in African Politics," in *African Independence*, 126.

8. Mandela, *Long Walk to Freedom*, 238

9. Antony Goldman, "Ghana's Former Dictator Blazes Unlikely Trail to Democracy," *The Christian Science Monitor*, January 10, 1996.

10. The GNP and life expectancy figures come from the Population Reference Bureau, World Population Data Sheet, 1993. The GNP figure for Mali is for 1991. The World Bank put the GNP for Mali at $310 in 1992. By comparison, the GNP in the United States in 1991 was $22,560, and in France, the former colonial power of Mali, $20,600. Life expectancy in 1991 in the United States was seventy-two years for men and seventy-five years for women; in France it was seventy-three and eighty-one years, respectively.

11. Onyebadi, *How to Be a Nigerian Politician*, 25.

12. Quoted in Owen, *Saga of the Niger*, 133.

13. Quoted in ibid., 129.

14. Liebenow, 153–54.

15. All Africa Press Service, Nairobi, April 21, 1997.

16. Reuters, Bamako, Mali, May 4, 1998.

17. *World Population Data Sheet: 1999.* The census figures for Nigeria have long been a controversial issue.

18. T. C. McCaskie, "Nigeria: Recent History," in *Africa South of the Sahara 1998,* 787.

19. Abiola was arrested in 1994 shortly after proclaiming his right to be president.

20. *Nigeria: Permanent Transition; Current Violations of Human Rights in Nigeria* (New York: Human Rights Watch/Africa, 1996), 29.

21. The trip was organized by the American Center for International Leadership, operating out of the University of Denver. The cost of the trip was underwritten by Kamel Ghribi, a wealthy Tunisian businessman who did business with Nigeria. Neither Ghribi nor the Nigerian government selected the members of the delegation or the people with whom the delegation would meet, according to organizer Stephen Hayes of ACIL. I went on the trip as a private individual and not as a representative of *The Christian Science Monitor* (I was on leave from the *Monitor*). The Nigerian government allowed but tried to minimize our contacts with dissidents, including human rights representatives. Two members of our delegation met with the jailed winner of the annulled 1993 presidential elections, Moshood Abiola, who died in custody in 1998, reportedly of a heart condition, shortly before his anticipated release by a new military regime.

22. *Nigeria: Permanent Transition,* 29–30.

23. Quoted in Olojede and Adinoyi-Ojo, *Born to Run,* 167–68.

24. Quoted in ibid., 167.

25. Ibid., 164.

26. Ibid., 179.

27. Press release, October 23, 1997, announcing release of Human Rights Watch Report *Nigeria: Transition or Travesty* (New York: Human Rights Watch/Africa, 1997).

28. Reuters, Abuja, Nigeria, April 26, 1998.

29. David A. Korn, "Time For Change," *The Christian Science Monitor,* December 5, 1991.

30. Because my way was paid by *The Christian Science Monitor,* and not the UN, I felt free to develop my own stories rather than sit in endless briefings by government officials.

31. Onyebadi, *How to Be a Nigerian Politician,* 20.

32. *Togo: A New Era for Human Rights?* (London: Amnesty International, 1994), 1 and 6.

3. The Politics of Ambiguity

1. Africa Watch, *Kenya: Taking Liberties,* 78–93. The report is consistent with

accounts by other human rights organizations, both international and Kenyan, and with reporting by international journalists based in Kenya. A statement released July 30, 1991, with the Africa Watch report, said, "Torture continues to be used in Kenya's prisons and detention centers."

2. Haugerud, *The Culture of Politics in Modern Kenya*, 83.

3. Waler, "Kenya," in *Africa South of the Sahara 1995*, 487.

4. Alan Rake, "Kenya: Recent History," in *Africa South of the Sahara 1998*, 551. Mwakenya followers "comprised a wide spectrum of opposition to the Moi presidency," according to Rake.

5. Africa Watch, 111–12.

6. Ibid., 83.

7. Ibid., 84–90.

8. Ibid., 84. The report also notes, "Prisoners have described how they are eventually forced to drink the water in the cell, mixed with their own urine and feces, in order to survive. Some have resorted to eating skin peelings from their own limbs" (84).

9. Ibid., 89.

10. Haugerud, 7.

11. Africa Watch, 111.

12. Harden, *Africa*, 254.

13. Ibid., 257.

14. In 1995, donors complained about another of Moi's big projects: the government's plans to build an international airport at Eldoret, a city far from major commercial or population centers, but near Moi's home area.

15. Pheroze Nowrojee, interview with the author, Nairobi, Kenya, July 1995.

16. Ibid.

17. Ibid.

18. Ibid.

19. I witnessed this same defiance in many other countries in Africa in the early 1990s where individuals were angry with authoritarian government.

20. Njeri Kababere, interview with the author, Nairobi, Kenya, July 1995. All quotes by Kababere are from this interview.

21. Ouko's murder prompted an outburst of rage among university students and others in Nairobi, some of whom marched and ran through downtown streets, shouting insults against senior government officials.

22. Nzomo, "Kenya," in *The African State at a Critical Juncture*, 177. Nzomo contends the stripping not only helped win release of the prisoners but gave a boost to women's political clout in Kenya.

23. Ibid., 180–81.

24. *Kenya: Old Habits Die Hard; Rights Abuses Follow Renewed Foreign Aid Commitments* (New York: Human Rights Watch/Africa, 1995) 2.

25. Ibid. In a preface to that report, Human Rights Watch/Africa quotes a pastoral letter issued by the Catholic bishops of Kenya in Nairobi, April 1995: "We

estimates of 5,000 killed and up to 25,000 wounded. Walter Clarke puts the estimated noncombatant deaths at between 30,000 and 50,000 (Clarke, "Failed Visions and Uncertain Mandates," in *Learning from Somalia*).

37. Gilkes, 53.

38. Lyons and Samatar, 22.

39. Somali veterinarian, interview with the author, Nairobi, Kenya, July 1995.

40. Sommer, *Hope Restored?* 2. In a note on page 5, the study, prepared under a contract with the Office of U.S. Foreign Disaster Assistance, of the U.S. Agency for International Development, attributes these estimates to another study, *Excess Mortality and the Impact of Health Interventions in the Somalia Humanitarian Emergency,* by the Refugee Policy Group and the Centers for Disease Control and Prevention, August 12, 1994.

41. Abdi Aziz Mohamed Ali, interview with the author, Nairobi, Kenya, July 1995.

42. Sahnoun, *Somalia,* 16.

43. Based in Nairobi, Kenya, I was assigned to cover East, West, and parts of central Africa, altogether more than thirty countries.

44. Sommer, 22. Bush's denial came in response to a written question by the Refugee Policy Group study team.

45. In the end, the marines guarded only the main shipments from the ports to key distribution centers. There was still a need for a transportation web to get food from urban collection centers to villages, so many relief agencies continued paying guards high sums of money to get food to people.

46. Woods, "U.S. Decisionmaking during Operations in Somalia," in *Learning From Somalia,* 158. Woods served as deputy assistant secretary of defense for African affairs from December 1986 to April 1994.

47. Scott Peterson, "Somalia Relief Agencies Struggle, Await U.S. Troops," *The Christian Science Monitor,* December 8, 1992.

48. George Moffett, "Force in Somalia May Signal More UN Interventions," *The Christian Science Monitor,* December 8, 1992.

49. Pauline Baker, an Africa expert who worked at the Aspen Institute for Humanistic Studies in Washington, D.C., in a telephone interview with the author, ca. December 1992.

50. Robert M. Press, "View in Somalia: U.S. Troops Face Lengthy Stay," *The Christian Science Monitor,* December 3, 1992.

51. Robert M. Press, "U.S. Ignores Key Doubts over Somalia Intervention," *The Christian Science Monitor,* December 3. 1992.

52. Sommer, 34.

53. Human Rights Watch/Africa, *Somalia Faces the Future,* 57.

54. Menkhaus, "Local and National Reconciliation in Somalia," in *Learning from Somalia. Menkhaus* was a special political adviser to the UN in Somalia in 1993 and 1994.

55. In low voices a few residents said they welcomed the Habir Gedir because

the Hawadley had dominated them. The Hawadley had also controlled most key businesses.

56. Richburg, *Out of America,* 81.

57. Ibid.

58. I first drew this analogy in my essay "Somalia: A Flash of Color in the Sunlight," which was published in *The Christian Science Monitor,* March 10, 1993.

59. Berlin, *The Crooked Timber of Humanity,* 38.

60. Richburg, 52.

61. Sommer, 81. The author also writes that UN officials were similarly in the dark regarding Somalia. "Many senior political advisors in UNOSOM II, especially on sensitive political issues, . . . were insensitive to the local culture's requirements."

62. Robert M. Press, "Covey of Critics Raises Doubts about UN Role in Somalia," *The Christian Science Monitor,* September 8, 1994.

63. The international efforts to secure a lasting peace agreement in Somalia involved UN officials from many countries, U.S. military and diplomatic personnel, U.S. and other civilian advisers, Somali employees of the United Nations, and various private organizations.

64. Menkhaus, 57–58.

65. Ahmed Warfa, interviews with the author, Nairobi, Kenya, February and July 1995. I first met Warfa in Mogadishu in 1991 and had periodic contact with him until mid-1995. He is a member of the Hawadley clan. The quotations by him in this section are from the same interviews.

66. Prunier, "Somaliland," in *The Horn of Africa,* 67.

67. Hirsch and Oakley, *Somalia and Operation Restore Hope,* 117–18.

68. Ibid., 118.

69. Ibid. In a footnote, the authors note that "the wording of the resolution and its interpretation by the UN in both New York and Mogadishu were fully supported by the U.S. The Department of Defense and the Joint Chiefs did not express their views at the top levels of this extremely important turning point in policy."

70. Frost, *Frost,* 103.

71. Hirsch and Oakley, footnote on page 118. Hirsch was political adviser to the multinational coalition in Somalia from December 1992 to March 1993.

72. Quoted in Robert M. Press, "Somalia Civil War Is Fueled by Huge Stockpiles of Weapons," *The Christian Science Monitor,* October 14, 1992.

73. Quoted in ibid.

74. Aryeh Neier, "Watching Rights," *Nation,* November 15, 1993, 562. Neier was executive director of Human Rights Watch for nearly fifteen years, until 1993.

75. Ibid.

76. Howe, "Relations between the United States and UN in Somalia," In *Learning from Somalia,* 180, 182.

77. Hirsch and Oakley, 121.

78. Woods, 162.

79. UN officials continued to insist they were working hard to find a political solution, but some Western analysts observed that the focus of the international community in Somalia was more military than political.

80. DeLong and Tuckey, 93. Other details in this section on the Rangers come from the same chapter.

81. Howe, 182.

82. Woods, 165.

83. Ibid.

84. Quoted in Robert M. Press, "Third World Peacekeepers Face Larger Role as U.S. Quits Somalia," *The Christian Science Monitor,* February 3, 1994.

85. Woods, 170.

86. Ibid.

87. Harry Johnston and Ted Dagne, "Congress and the Somalia Crisis," in *Learning from Somalia,* 202.

88. Ibid.

89. African Rights, *Humanitarianism Unbound?* 20.

90. Quoted in Hirsch and Oakley, xv.

91. Quoted in Marcia Kurop, "Why UN Quit as Fireman to the World's Hot Spots," *The Christian Science Monitor,* April 29, 1997.

92. Quoted in ibid.

93. Zartman, 269–70.

94. This idea was recommended by Ken Menkhaus and John Prendergast in an article ("Governance and Economic Survival in Postintervention Somalia") in May 1995, no. 172, of *CSIS Africa Notes,* a publication of the Center for Strategic and International Studies, in Washington, D.C.

95. Lyons and Samatar, 67.

96. Weiss, "Rekindling Hope in UN Humanitarian Intervention," in *Learning from Somalia,* 208.

97. Ibid., 223–24.

98. Robert M. Press, "Retreat from Somalia," *The Christian Science Monitor,* February 27, 1995, an interview with Gilles Stockton, a former UN consultant in Somalia, and former Peace Corps volunteer in Somalia.

99. Menkhaus, 44.

100. Clarke, 16–17. Clarke was deputy chief of mission at the U.S. Embassy in Mogadishu in 1993.

101. Press, "Retreat from Somalia."

102. Menkhaus and Prendergast.

103. Ibid.

104. Ken Menkhaus, "Somalia: Political Order in a Stateless Society," *Current History,* May 1998, 220.

105. Amnesty International, *AI Report 1998: Somalia* (London: Amnesty International, 1998), 2. The report covers the period from January through December 1997.

106. *Courier,* March–April 1997, no. 162, Brussels, inside cover. The *Courier* is a publication of the European Community.

107. Ibid., 46.

5. Genocide Ignored: Rwanda

1. Dawidowicz, *The War against the Jews,* 403. The author puts the number of Jews killed at 5,933,900. Bauer uses the figure of 5,820,960 in *A History of the Holocaust,* 335. Bauer also points out that some 200,000 Gypsies were murdered by the Nazis as part of a deliberate policy aimed at "ridding" Europe of Gypsies and Jews (202).

2. Conquest, *The Harvest of Sorrow,* 306. After citing the United Nations definition of "genocide," Conquest states, "It certainly appears that a charge of genocide lies against the Soviet Union for its actions in the Ukraine" (272).

3. Prunier, *The Rwanda Crisis,* 238.

4. Ibid.

5. Rhode, *End Game,* 295.

6. Ibid., 289.

7. Rubenstein, *The Cunning of History,* 4–5.

8. Ibid., 28.

9. Ibid., 6.

10. Ibid., 42.

11. Ibid., 7.

12. Ibid., 53.

13. Ibid., 53.

14. Ibid., 96.

15. In this book I do not feature my own opinions, though I do express some. Readers should know that I favor international intervention of some sort in the case of mass killings. I later present the U.S. government's rationale for not intervening.

16. Many of those who had tried to flee had been killed.

17. Quoted in African Rights, *Rwanda: Death, Despair, and Defiance,"* 218.

18. Quoted in ibid., 219.

19. *Genocide in Rwanda: April–May 1994,* New York: Human Rights Watch/ Africa, May 1994, 5.

20. Ibid.

21. African Rights, 203. "The killers often wielded their weapons in ways designed to inflict the maximum pain on the victim before death ensued. Victims' limbs were often severed or broken first; they were struck on the neck and head, had their faces and genitals mutilated, and their Achilles' tendons cut. They were often left to die, or were only later despatched. Leonard, an *interahamwe* in Zaire, demonstrated his method to a journalist—on this occasion not for real: First the machete tore a glancing blow at the air that would have caught a man in his midriff. Then it swung back to hit the victim, any victim, across the neck. Finally a blow came down like an executioner's axe on to the skull. Other killing methods were more prolonged and macabrely *[sic]* imaginative."

22. Quoted in African Rights, 268.

23. *Genocide in Rwanda*, 5.

24. Quoted in African Rights, 251.

25. Ibid., 246.

26. James C. McKiney Jr., "Legacy of Rwanda Violence: The Thousands Born of Rape," *New York Times*, September 23, 1996.

27. Ibid.

28. African Rights, 341.

29. Quoted in "It Was Kill or Be Killed, Says Soldier Convicted of War Crimes" (Associated Press), published in the Daytona Beach, Florida, *News-Journal*, June 1, 1996.

30. African Rights, 359–61.

31. Prunier, 368.

32. Ibid., 3.

33. Ibid., 16.

34. "The Genesis of Rwandese Patriotic Front: A Case Study of Roots of Insecurity in an Independent African State," paper submitted at the Africa Leadership Forum in Kampala, Uganda, May 1991, by the Rwandese Patriotic Front Department of Information, 2. The paper states, "The terms Batutsi, Bahutu, and Batwa in their original connotation refer to social stratification which was based on different economic activities and individual fortunes."

35. Destexhe, *Rwanda and Genocide in the Twentieth Century*, 40.

36. Prunier, xii–xiii.

37. Ibid., 7.

38. Destexhe, 41.

39. Prunier, 9.

40. Ibid., 39.

41. Lemarchand, *Burundi*, 9, 22. Regarding the economic and social relations between Tutsi (a minority in both Rwanda and Burundi) and Hutu, Lemarchand writes: "Even though most cows were indeed the property of Tutsi elements, it was by entrusting their cattle to the Hutu that the Tutsi were able to establish clientage ties with Hutu elements, thus bringing Hutu and Tutsi together into a complex web of reciprocal rights and obligations. Far from driving a wedge between Hutu and Tutsi, their different occupational statuses provided the basis for a closer union" (9).

42. Prunier, 49.

43. Ibid., 63.

44. Reyntjens, "Rwanda: Recent History," in *Africa South of the Sahara 1995*, 740.

45. *Genocide in Rwanda*, 2.

46. Africa Watch, *Beyond the Rhetoric: Continuing Human Rights Abuses in Rwanda* (New York: Africa Watch, 1993), 4.

47. Ibid., 13.

48. Africa Watch, *Rwanda: Talking Peace and Waging War: Human Rights since the October 1990 Invasion* (New York: Africa Watch, 1992), 8.

49. Ibid., 11.

50. Ibid., 15–16.

51. R. Degni-Ségui, *Report on the Situation of Human Rights in Rwanda* (a United Nations document), 1994, 7. Degni-Ségui was the United Nation's special rapporteur on Rwanda.

52. Ibid., 7–8.

53. The United Nation's special rapporteur on Rwanda makes clear in his report (page 12) that the "main enemy" of the Hutu killers was the Tutsi population and that Hutu moderates were killed as supporters of the main enemy.

54. *Beyond the Rhetoric*, 16. An international commission was formed by several human rights organizations to investigate atrocities in Rwanda following the start of the war in 1990. Africa Watch, the International Federation of Human Rights (Paris), the Inter-African Union of Human Rights (Ouagadougou, Burkina Faso), and the International Center for Human Rights and Democratic Development (Montreal) named ten experts to the commission. Coordination was carried out by Africa Watch and the International Federation of Human Rights.

55. Ibid., 16.

56. Ibid., 45.

57. World Bank, *African Development Indicators, 1994–95*, 346.

58. Degni-Ségui, 15.

59. Ibid., 44.

60. René Lemarchand, "Managing Transition Anarchies: Rwanda, Burundi, and South Africa in Comparative Perspective," *Journal of Modern African Studies* 32, no. 4 (1994): 603. Lemarchand adds that "no amount of retrospective guilt can diminish its [France's] place in history as the principal villain in the Rwanda apocalypse."

61. François-Xavier Verschave, "Autopsy of a Planned Genocide," *Le Monde Diplomatique,* March 1995, 10.

62. *Genocide in Rwanda*, 3.

63. Burundi has approximately the same ethnic proportions as Rwanda, but in Burundi, the Tutsi minority controlled the military even after the election of a Hutu President.

64. Degni-Ségui, 6.

65. Ibid.

66. *Genocide in Rwanda* states, "After extensive investigation among reliable sources, both Rwandan and foreign, representing clergy, staff of nongovernmental organizations, and journalists, Human Rights Watch/Africa has concluded that there is at present no credible evidence that the RPF has engaged in any widespread slaughter of civilian populations, although there are reports of less systematic abuses" (7).

67. Amnesty International, *Rwanda: Reports of Killings and Abductions by the*

Rwandese Patriotic Army, April–August 1994 (London: Amnesty International, 1994), 3.

68. Verschave, 10.

69. Quoted in Joyce Hackel, "Burundi's Peace May Hinge on One Man," *The Christian Science Monitor*, June 19, 1996.

70. Quoted in Lara Santoro, "Rwanda Massacres Were Avoidable, General Says," *The Christian Science Monitor*, February 27, 1998.

71. Destexhe, 48.

72. The author of the *New Yorker* article, Philip Gourevitch, wrote a book from which the quotes by UN official Iqbal Riza are taken. The book is *We Wish to Inform You That Tomorrow We Will Be Killed with Our Families* (New York: Farrar Straus and Giroux, 1998), 105–6.

73. Quoted by Bernard Edinger, Reuters, May 19, 1998.

74. Quoted by UPI, May 7, 1998, from Kigali, Rwanda.

75. Quoted by UPI, May 4, 1998, from Nairobi, Kenya.

76. Quoted in John F. Harris, "Clinton Tells Rwandans: World Too Slow to Act," *Washington Post*, March 26, 1998.

77. Ibid.

78. Quoted in Elaine Sciolino, "New U.S. Peacekeeping Policy De-emphasizes Role of the U.N.," *New York Times*, May 6, 1994. Clinton kept the U.S. troops in Somalia under U.S., not United Nations, command.

79. Jason DeParle, "The Man Inside Bill Clinton's Foreign Policy," *New York Times Magazine*, August 20, 1995, 38.

80. Sciolino, "New U.S. Peacekeeping Policy."

81. Hirsch and Oakley, *Somalia and Operation Restore Hope*, 171.

82. Quoted in "The Clinton Administration's Policy on Reforming Multilateral Peace Operations," *U.S. Department of State Dispatch* 5, no. 20 (1994): 314.

83. Destexhe, 49. The author adds, "The PDD trapped the UN in a vicious circle: the United States would refuse any new deployment of UN blue helmets unless all the necessary conditions (logistical, financial, troop deployments, etc.) were fulfilled—yet they could never be fulfilled *without* the active support of the superpower" (50).

84. Barbara Crossette, "The Rwandans: Why Washington and the World Largely Failed to Act to Head Off the Blood Bath," *New York Times*, March 25, 1998.

85. Herman J. Cohen, telephone interview with the author, March 1996.

86. The troops were there as part of a regional West African force apart from the small number of United Nations troops sent to monitor peace agreements. The bulk of the African troops came from Nigeria and Ghana.

87. Lara Santoro, "One for the Law Books: In Africa, a UN Court Prosecutes Genocide," *New York Times*, September 27, 1996.

88. Minh T. Vo, "Women Activists See Victory in Verdict's Inclusion of Rape," *The Christian Science Monitor*, September 11, 1998.

89. Lara Santoro, "For Rwandans, Justice Done Only for Others," *The Christian Science Monitor,* September 11, 1998.

90. Amnesty International, *Rwanda: No One Is Talking about It Anymore* (London: Amnesty International, 1997), 1.

91. Ibid., 3.

92. This estimate of the number of accused Hutu is the highest I have heard from a Rwandan official. By the time the Rwandan government began its own genocide trials in 1997, however, at least 100,000 persons had been detained in extremely overcrowded prisons in Rwanda, awaiting trials on charges related to the genocide.

93. Various international human rights organizations contend that many Hutu were coerced to join the killing, while many others apparently joined in more freely.

94. "The Rough Road to Peace in Rwanda," All Africa News Agency, February 23, 1998. The unnamed reporter ends the article by suggesting his own solution: hand over the planners and principal executioners to the international tribunal and allow the others to "repent" before a South Africa–style truth commission.

95. African Rights, "An Open Letter to His Holiness, Pope John Paul II," May 13, 1998, 3. The letter is signed by Rakiya Omaar, director. It includes the statement by the Pope responding to allegations of involvement of some Catholic clergy in the genocide.

96. Published in East Sussex, England, by Highland Books, 1991.

97. *Life after Death: Suspicion and Reintegration in Post-Genocide Rwanda* (Washington: U.S. Committee for Refugees, 1998), 17.

98. Kathi Austin, "World Withdrawal Portends Disaster in Burundi," *The Christian Science Monitor,* January 12, 1996.

99. According to the results of the June 1, 1993, election, Ndadaye had 65 percent of the vote and Buyoya 33 percent. Since the Hutu represent approximately 85 percent of the population, Buyoya was correct in assuming he had some Hutu support, but not enough. When I asked him in an interview after the election why he had allowed a competitive election against a Hutu, he said, "I thought I would win."

The interview took place in the presidential residence, even though he had lost the election. He said he was going to move out soon but apparently felt in no rush. Around this time I met some Hutu who said Buyoya was popular with them; that some Tutsi had photos of Buyoya in their homes but hid them to avoid making Hutu militants angry.

During his first period as dictator of the country, many Hutu were killed by the Tutsi army.

100. "Human Rights Watch Condemns Targeting of Civilians in Burundi Civil War," press release distributed with its report *Proxy Targets: Civilians in the War in Burundi,* April 8, 1998.

101. John Shattuck, "More Than Words Are Needed to Stop Terror in Burundi," *The Christian Science Monitor,* June 24, 1996.

6.One Family's Escape from Rwanda

1. The textbook *is Science and Health with Key to the Scriptures,* by Mary Baker Eddy (Boston: First Church of Christ Scientist, 1875).

7. Personal Freedom

1. Monga, *The Anthropology of Anger,* 4.

2. Bill Bradley, "Democracy's Third Leg," *The Christian Science Monitor,* February 27, 1995.

3. John W. Harbeson, "Civil Society and Political Renaissance in Africa," in *Civil Society and the State in Africa,* 1–2.

4. Bratton and van de Walle, *Democratic Experiments in Africa,* 199.

5. Ali Mari Tripp, "Civil Society in Tanzania," in *Civil Society and the State in Africa,* 166.

6. Jennifer A. Widner, "Civic Association in Côte d' Ivoire," in *Civil Society and the State in Africa,* 209.

7. Ndegwa, *The Two Faces of Civil Society,* 116. The book focuses on two NGOs in Kenya, the Undugu Society of Kenya and the Green Belt Movement, headed by internationally known conservationist Wangari Maathai.

8. Monga, 5.

9. Ibid., 116.

10. James Scott in ibid., 6.

11. *Nyayo* is Swahili for "footsteps."

12. Monga, 7.

13. *The Kenya Rural Enterprise Program under Cooperative Agreement No. AID–615–0238–A–00–7026–00: A Final Evaluation,* September 1994, vii.

14. Ibid., ix. The report also noted that some businesses may have grown in ways that cannot be captured with employment data.

15. Albert Mutua, "The Change from a Traditional Integrated Method to a Financial System Approach: K-REP Occasional Paper No. 19," Nairobi, February 1992.

16. *Programme Report for the Period of 1st October 1994 to 31st March, 1995, K-REP,* 22.

17. A. Dondo, interview with the author, Nairobi, Kenya, July 1995.

18. Harrison, *The Greening of Africa.*

19. Ibid., 118.

20. This section draws on Robert M. Press, "Gambian Women Dig for Pay Dirt," *The Christian Science Monitor,* March 29, 1994, which is based on the author's visit to The Gambia.

21. This section draws on Robert M. Press, "Big Payoff for Small Loans," *The Christian Science Monitor,* January 2, 1992, which is based on the author's visit to Sokodé, Togo.

22. This section draws on Robert M. Press, "Togo's 'Mercedes-Benz Girls'," *Christian Science Monitor,* October 30, 1990, which is based on the author's visit to Lomé, Togo.

23. The remark was made by a non-Togolese official of an international organization in Lome, who requested anonymity.

24. Robert M. Press, "Even Amid Anarchy, Somalis Hunger to Learn and to Teach," *The Christian Science Monitor,* December 24, 1992.

25. This section draws on Robert M. Press, "Adopting New Ideas—with Zest: Kenya's Margaret Waigu Githegi Teaches Pupils for Whom English Is a Third Language," *The Christian Science Monitor,* March 30, 1992.

26. This section draws on Robert M. Press, "An Ancient Africa Custom Comes under Fire," *The Christian Science Monitor,* December 30, 1994.

27. This section draws on Robert M. Press, "Eritrea Women Fighters Face Difficult Transition," *The Christian Science Monitor,* May 24, 1993, which is based on the author's visit to Eritrea. The statement that 35 percent of front line soldiers were women was made by Roy Patemen, a professor of political science at the University of California at Los Angeles. In 1999 Eritrea and Ethiopia engaged in major border disputes and battles.

28. Vaz, *The Woman with the Artistic Brush,* 25. The book is in Nike's words, as told to the author. Many of the details in this section about her childhood come from this book.

29. Ibid., 26.

30. Ibid., 5.

31. Nike, interview with the author, DeLand, Florida, November 1995, during Nike's visit to the United States.

32. Vaz, 13.

33. Victoria Scott, "Nike's Story," paper presented in April 1998 at the Arts Council of the African Studies Association in New Orleans.

34. Vaz, 39.

35. Nike, interview with the author, November 1995.

36. Vaz, 42.

37. Nike, interview with the author, November 1995.

38. Scott, 5. Scott adds, "In the early 1970s the *adire* sellers' stalls in Lagos stretched far along the length of the market shed. By the end of the decade, they numbered only a few. The last of the women to use the traditional dye pots in Oshogbo, died only recently."

39. Ibid.

40. Vaz, 83.

41. Nike, telephone interview with the author, April 1998.

42. Vaz, 74.

43. Nike, telephone interview with the author, April 1998.

SELECT BIBLIOGRAPHY

The following lists only the books and chapters cited in the note section. All other sources, including journal articles, newspaper articles, reports, and interviews, are listed in detail in that section.

Adam, Hussein M. "Somalia: A Terrible Beauty Being Born?" In *Collapsed States: The Disintegration and Restoration of Legitimate Authority*, ed. I. William Zartman. Boulder, Col.: Lynne Rienner, 1995.

African Rights. *Humanitarianism Unbound? Current Dilemmas Facing Multimandate Relief Operations in Political Emergencies*. London: African Rights, 1994.

―――. *Rwanda: Death, Despair, and Defiance*. London: African Rights, 1994.

Africa South of the Sahara, 1995. London: Europa, 1994.

Africa South of the Sahara, 1998. London: Europa, 1997.

Africa Watch. *Kenya: Taking Liberties*. New York: Africa Watch, 1991.

Ake, Claude. *Democracy and Development in Africa*. Washington: Brookings Institute, 1996.

Ayittey, George. *Africa in Chaos*. New York: St. Martin's Press, 1998.

Bauer, Yehuda. *A History of the Holocaust*. New York: Franklin Watts, c. 1982.

Berlin, Isaiah. *The Crooked Timber of Humanity: Chapters in the History of Ideas.* Ed. Henry Hardy. New York: Knopf, 1991.

Bratton, Michael, and Nicolas van de Walle. *Democratic Experiments in Africa: Regime Transitions in Comparative Perspective.* Cambridge: Cambridge University Press, 1997.

Carter, Gwendolen, and Patrick O'Meara, eds. *African Independence: The First Twenty-five Years.* Bloomington: Indiana University Press, 1985.

Cassanelli, Lee V. "Somali Land Resource Issues in Historic Perspective." In *Learning from Somalia: The Lessons of Armed Humanitarian Intervention,* ed. Walter Clarke and Jeffrey Herbst. Boulder, Col.: Westview Press, 1997.

Clarke, Walter. "Failed Visions and Uncertain Mandates in Somalia." In *Learning from Somalia: The Lessons of Armed Humanitarian Intervention,* ed. Walter Clarke and Jeffrey Herbst. Boulder, Col.: Westview Press, 1997.

Clarke, Walter, and Jeffrey Herbst, eds. *Learning from Somalia: The Lessons of Armed Humanitarian Intervention.* Boulder, Col.: Westview Press, 1997.

Conquest, Robert. *The Harvest of Sorrow: Soviet Collectivization and the Terror-Famine.* New York: Oxford University Press, 1986.

Dagne, Ted. "Congress and the Somali Crisis." In *Learning from Somalia: The Lessons of Armed Humanitarian Intervention,* ed. Walter Clarke and Jeffrey Herbst. Boulder, Col.: Westview Press, 1997.

Dawidowicz, Lucy. *The War against the Jews, 1933–1945.* New York: Holt, Rinehart and Winston, 1975.

DeLong, Kent, and Steven Tuckey. *Mogadishu: Heroism and Tragedy.* Westport, Conn.: Praeger, 1994.

Destexhe, Alain. *Rwanda and Genocide in the Twentieth Century.* New York: New York University Press, 1995.

Englebert, Pierre. "Mali: Recent History." In *Africa South of the Sahara 1995.* London: Europa, 1994.

Esman, Milton J. *Ethnic Politics.* Ithaca, N.Y.: Cornell University Press, 1994.

Frost, Robert. *Frost: Collected Poems, Prose, and Plays.* New York: Library of America, 1995.

Gilkes, Patrick. "Descent into Chaos: Somalia, January 1991–December 1992." In *The Horn of Africa,* ed. Charles Gurdon. London: University College of London Press, 1994.

———. "Somalia: Recent History." In *Africa South of the Sahara 1995.* London: Europa, 1994.

Gray, John. *Isaiah Berlin.* Princeton, N.J.: Princeton University Press, 1996.

Harbeson, John W., Donald Rothchild, and Naomi Chazan, eds. *Civil Society and the State in Africa.* Boulder, Col.: Lynne Rienner, 1994.

Harden, Blaine. *Africa: Dispatches from a Fragile Continent.* New York: Norton, 1990.

Harrison, Paul. *The Greening of Africa: Breaking Through in the Battle for Land and Food.* New York: Viking Penguin, 1987.

Haugerud, Angelique. *The Culture of Politics in Modern Kenya.* New York: Cambridge University Press, 1995.

Hirsch, John L., and Robert B. Oakley. *Somalia and Operation Restore Hope: Reflections on Peacemaking and Peacekeeping.* Washington: United States Institute of Peace Press, 1995.

Howe, Jonathan T. "Relations between the United States and the UN in Somalia." In *Learning from Somalia: The Lessons of Armed Humanitarian Intervention,* ed. Walter Clarke and Jeffrey Herbst. Boulder, Col.: Westview Press, 1997.

Human Rights Watch. *Somalia: A Government at War with Its Own People: Testimonies about the Killings and the Conflict in the North.* New York: Africa Watch, 1990.

———. *Somalia Faces the Future: Human Rights in a Fragmented Society.* New York: Human Rights Watch/Africa, 1995.

Lemarchand, René. *Burundi: Ethnocide as Discourse and Practice.* Cambridge: Woodrow Wilson Center Press and Cambridge University Press, 1994.

Lewis, I. M. *Understanding Somalia: Guide to Culture, History, and Social Institutions.* London: HAAN Associates, 1981.

Liebenow, Gus J. "The Military Factor in African Politics: A Twenty-five Year Perspective." In *African Independence: The First Twenty-five Years,* ed. Gwendolen M. Carter and Patrick O'Meara. Bloomington: Indiana University Press, 1985.

Lyons, Terrence, and Ahmed I. Samatar. *Somalia: State Collapse, Multilateral Intervention, and Strategies for Political Reconstruction.* Washington: Brookings Institution, 1995.

Mamdani, Mahmood. *Citizen and Subject: Contemporary Africa and the Legacy of Late Colonialism.* Princeton, N.J.: Princeton University Press, 1996.

Mandela, Nelson. *Long Walk to Freedom: The Autobiography of Nelson Mandela.* Boston: Little, Brown, 1995.

Menkhaus, Ken. "Local and National Reconciliation in Somalia." In *Learning from Somalia: The Lessons of Armed Humanitarian Intervention,* ed. Walter Clarke and Jeffrey Herbst. Boulder, Col.: Westview Press, 1997.

Moffett, George. *Critical Masses: The Global Population Challenge.* New York: Viking Penguin, 1994.

Monga, Célestin. *The Anthropology of Anger: Civil Society and Democracy in Africa.* Boulder, Col.: Lynne Rienner, 1996.

Ndegwa, Stephen N. *The Two Faces of Civil Society: NGOs and Politics in Africa.* West Hartford, Conn.: Kumarian Press, 1996.

Nzomo, Maria. "Kenya: The Women's Movement and Democratic Change." In *The African State at a Critical Juncture: Between Disintegration and Reconfiguration,* ed. Leonardo A. Villalón and Phillip A. Huxtable. Boulder, Col.: Lynne Rienner, 1998.

Olojede, Dele, and Onukaba Adinoyi-Ojo. *Born to Run: The Story of Dele Giwa.* Ibadan, Nigeria: Spectrum Books, 1987.

Onyebadi, Uche. *How to Be a Nigerian Politician.* Lagos, Nigeria: Stallion Communications, 1990.

Osborn, H. H. *Fire in the Hills: The Revival Which Spread from Rwanda.* East Sussex, Eng.: Highland Books, 1991.

Owen, Richard. *Saga of the Niger.* London: Robert Hale, 1961.

Parkenham, Thomas. *The Scramble for Africa, 1876–1912.* New York: Random House, 1991.

Prunier, Gérard. *The Rwanda Crisis, 1959–1994: History of a Genocide.* London: Hurst, 1995.

————. "Somaliland: Birth of a New Country?" In *The Horn of Africa,* ed. Charles Gurdon. London: University of London College Press, 1994.

Reynolds, Edward. *Stand the Storm: A History of the Atlantic Slave Trade.* Chicago: Ivan R. Dee, 1990.

Reyntjens, Filip. "Rwanda: Recent History." In *Africa South of the Sahara 1995.* London: Europa, 1994.

Rhode, David. *End Game: The Betrayal and Fall of Srebrenica: Europe's Worst Massacre since World War II.* New York: Farrar, Straus and Giroux, 1997.

Richburg, Keith B. *Out of America: A Black Man Confronts Africa.* New York: HarperCollins, 1997.

Rubenstein, Richard L. *The Cunning of History: The Holocaust and the American Future.* New York: Harper and Row, 1975.

Sahnoun, Mohamed. *Somalia: The Missed Opportunities.* Washington: United States Institute for Peace Press, 1994.

Samatar, Ahmed I., ed. *The Somali Challenge: From Catastrophe to Renewal?* Boulder, Col.: Lynne Rienner, 1994.

Sklar, Richard L. "The Colonial Imprint on African Political Thought." In *African Independence: The First Twenty-five Years,* ed. Gwendolen M. Carter and Patrick O'Meara. Bloomington: University of Indiana Press, 1985.

Sommer, John G. *Hope Restored? Humanitarian Aid in Somalia, 1990–1994.* Washington: Refugee Policy Group, 1994

Soyinka, Wole. *Nigeria's Political Crisis: Which Way Forward?* Washington: National Endowment for Democracy, 1995.

Tripp, Ali Mari. "Civil Society in Tanzania." In *Civil Society and the State in Africa,* ed. John W. Harbeson, Donald Rothchild, and Naomi Chazan. Boulder, Col.: Lynne Rienner, 1994.

Vaz, Kim Marie. *The Woman with the Artistic Brush: A Life History of Yoruba Batik Artist Nike Davies.* Armonk, N.Y.: M. E. Sharple, 1995.

Villalón, Leonardo A., and Phillip Huxtable. *The African State at a Critical Juncture: Between Disintegration and Reconfiguration.* Boulder, Col.: Lynne Rienner, 1998.

Waler, Richard. "Kenya." In *Africa South of the Sahara 1995.* London: Europa, 1994.

Weiss, Thomas G. "Rekindling Hope in UN Humanitarian Intervention." In *Learning from Somalia: The Lessons of Armed Humanitarian Intervention,* ed. Walter Clarke and Jeffrey Herbst. Boulder, Col.: Westview Press, 1997.

Wiseman, John A. *The New Struggle for Democracy in Africa.* Aldershot, Eng.: Avebury, 1996.

Woods, James L. "U.S. Decisionmaking during Operations in Somalia." In *Learning from Somalia: The Lessons of Armed Humanitarian Intervention,* ed. Walter Clarke and Jeffrey Herbst. Boulder, Col.: Westview Press, 1997.

World Bank. *African Development Indicators, 1994–95.* Washington: World Bank, 1995

Zartman, I. William. "Posing the Problem of State Collapse." In *Collapsed States: The Disintegration and Restoration of Legitimate Authority,* ed. I. William Zartman; Boulder, Col.: Lynne Rienner, 1995.

———. "Putting Things Back Together." In *Collapsed States: The Disintegration and Restoration of Legitimate Authority,"* ed. I. William Zartman; Boulder, Col.: Lynne Rienner, 1995.

Zartman, I. William, ed. *Collapsed States: The Disintegration and Restoration of Legitimate Authority.* Boulder, Col.: Lynne Rienner, 1995.

INDEX

Note: References to illustrations are in italics.

About the Author and the Photographer

For eight years, from 1987 to 1995, Robert Press was a correspondent for *The Christian Science Monitor*, based in Nairobi, Kenya, and traveling widely in East, West, and central Africa. From 1995 to 1997 he was a visiting scholar at Stetson University in DeLand, Florida, where he was also an adjunct professor of journalism. In 1998 he was a visiting professor at Principia College in Elsah, Illinois, where he taught both African history and African politics.

Betty Press worked in Africa as a photojournalist from 1987 to 1995. Her photographs have appeared in *The Christian Science Monitor*, the *New York Times*, *Newsweek*, *Time*, United Nations publications, and elsewhere. She is represented by Panos Pictures in London and Woodfin Camp and Associates in New York. She is an adjunct professor of photography at Stetson University.

Robert and Betty Press live in DeLand, Florida.